LYRIC RELIGION

The Romance of Immortal Hymns

LYRIC RELIGION

THE ROMANCE OF IMMORTAL HYMNS

BY

H. AUGUSTINE SMITH

PROFESSOR OF FINE ARTS IN RELIGION
BOSTON UNIVERSITY SCHOOL OF RELIGIOUS EDUCATION
AND SOCIAL SERVICE

THE CENTURY CO.

NEW YORK LONDON

PRINTED IN U. S. A.

FOREWORD

Hymn singing is vital to Protestant worship. Luther wrote hymns for his people, that God might speak directly to them in his Word and that they might directly answer him through their hymns.

Hymn singing has again and again risen to high tide: at Edessa in Asia Minor during the third century; in Milan, Italy, during the fourth century, under the guidance of Bishop Ambrose; during the Crusades and after the Crusades in various sections of Europe, carried thither by flagellants, troubadours, and court musicians; throughout the Reformation and the Thirty Years' War in Germany; during the Watts and Wesley days in Great Britain; and in America, led by Lowell Mason and the singing school masters, and quickened by missionary propaganda, lay evangelism, and the social-mindedness of Protestant religion.

Congregational singing is showing signs of weakening to-day because of the sophistication of church people and their easily acquired habit of listening-in rather than participating, their futile attempts at emotional expression, and their consequent suffocation in the midst of organ and choir, priestly monologues and symbolism.

New organs and effective playing of them, attractive and catholic hymn books, efficiency in lighting and acoustics, choral and orchestral leadership—all may help toward a hymn-singing Renaissance, but these alone cannot bring in the new day of universal song.

The hymn itself must be elevated to a high place in worship through reverent and thoughtful singing at all times. It should be lifted off the floor, where conventions, conferences, and social gatherings, Sunday night popular services and evangelistic song-leader tricks have all but tossed it through their singing anything, any time, anywhere, amidst confusion, jollification, the inauspicious entrance of late comers, and last-minute errands—making it something of a sporting mania.

Those who sing from hymn books to-day are fast becoming students of lyric religion, searchers after its hidden treasures, its factual history, its romance and biography, its geographic and international implications, its interest to the foreign traveler, its brilliant metaphors and pictures and drama, its processions, coronations, and reformations, its call to battle and to peace after victory, its shrines of worship—in short, the spiritual experience of the human race through all ages. Ample time is needed, fifteen, thirty, forty-five minutes, behind closed doors, free from interruption, to build these immortal lyrics into life-size stature. The Sunday morning service, with all of its fixity and liturgic poise, is increasingly emphasizing one hymn with two more as satellites, and giving time, position, facts, and interpretation to make the major hymn glow with light and warmth.

Lyric Religion presents 150 hymns as studies, interpretations, syntheses, bases actual worship procedure, pictorial life of the past and present, to arouse lethargic congregations, ministers, song leaders, and organists to a discovery and appreciation of, and enthusiasm for, hymns. Every legitimate device has been used to stir the imagination, strengthen the will to sing, and so live out the teachings of Jesus and follow his torch-bearers who in all ages have sung the faith that was in them.

The author is grateful to his editorial associates:

Jeremiah Bascom Reeves
Earl Marlatt
Charles Arthur Boyd

and to many ministers, professors, students, and laymen who have made both major and minor contributions to *Lyric Religion.*

The Bible text used in *Lyric Religion* is taken from the American Standard Edition of the Revised Bible, copyright 1929 by the International Council of Religious Education, and used by permission.

The author reserves his last paragraph for the dedication of *Lyric Religion:*

TO
THE MEMORY OF HIS MOTHER
AND TO
THE HONOR OF HIS FATHER'S NINETY-THREE YEARS

H. AUGUSTINE SMITH.

Boston University,
September 1, 1931.

CONTENTS

ILLUSTRATIONS

LYRIC RELIGION

The Romance of Immortal Hymns

LYRIC RELIGION

The Romance of Immortal Hymns

A MIGHTY FORTRESS IS OUR GOD

1. A mighty fortress is our God,
A bulwark never failing;
Our helper he, amid the flood
Of mortal ills prevailing.
For still our ancient foe
Doth seek to work us woe;
His craft and power are great;
And armed with cruel hate,
On earth is not his equal.

2. Did we in our own strength confide,
Our striving would be losing;
Were not the right man on our side,
The man of God's own choosing.
Dost ask who that may be?
Christ Jesus, it is he,
Lord Sabaoth his name,
From age to age the same,
And he must win the battle.

3. And though this world, with devils filled,
Should threaten to undo us;
We will not fear, for God hath willed
His truth to triumph through us.
The prince of darkness grim,
We tremble not for him;
His rage we can endure,
For lo, his doom is sure,
One little word shall fell him.

4. That word above all earthly powers,
No thanks to them, abideth;
The Spirit and the gifts are ours
Through him who with us sideth;
Let goods and kindred go,
This mortal life also;
The body they may kill;
God's truth abideth still,
His kingdom is forever.

Martin Luther, 1529.
Translated by Frederick H. Hedge, 1853.

Biblical Text.

God is our refuge and strength,
A very present help in trouble.
Therefore will we not fear, though the earth do change,
And though the mountains be shaken into the heart of the seas;
Though the waters thereof roar and be troubled,
Though the mountains tremble with the swelling thereof.
The Lord of hosts is with us,
The God of Jacob is our refuge.

Psalm 46: 1, 2, 3, 11.

LIGHTING THE PROTESTANT FIRES AROUND THE WORLD

"The greatest hymn of the greatest man in the greatest period in German history."[1] With its magnificent tune, also by Luther, it quickly spread over all Germany and overnight became the unrivaled hymn of national days, church anniversaries, and world crises. Carlyle said of it: "There is something in it like the sound of Alpine avalanches or the first murmur of earthquakes: in the very vastness of which dissonance a higher unison is revealed to us." Many a Huguenot died joyfully as a martyr with this hymn on his lips. Gustavus Adolphus's entire army sang it just before the battle of Leipzig.

Four hundred years of constant and ever-widening use have served to enhance rather than to dull this Luther hymn.

Martin Luther (1483–1546) is known as "the Apostle of the Reformation." He was also the father of congregational singing, for with him began the chorus of congregational praise which has resulted in the publication, during four centuries, of one hundred thousand German hymns.

His first hymn book, 1524, contained only eight hymns, four of which were by Luther himself. This was only seven years after his famous "Ninety-five Theses" were nailed to the church door at Wittenberg, and only three years after the Diet of Worms.

The occasion which led Luther to write hymns was the burning at the stake of two youths of Brussels in 1523. Their crime was their profession of the reformed faith. In honor of these two martyrs he wrote his first hymn. Soon all Germany was singing, and hymns became one of the most effective agencies for the advancement of the Reformation. This particular hymn, "A Mighty Fortress Is Our God," is a paraphrase of the Forty-sixth Psalm, which both reflects it and goes beyond it.

[1] *Handbook to the Church Hymnary* (1927), by James Moffatt, copyright by Oxford University Press.

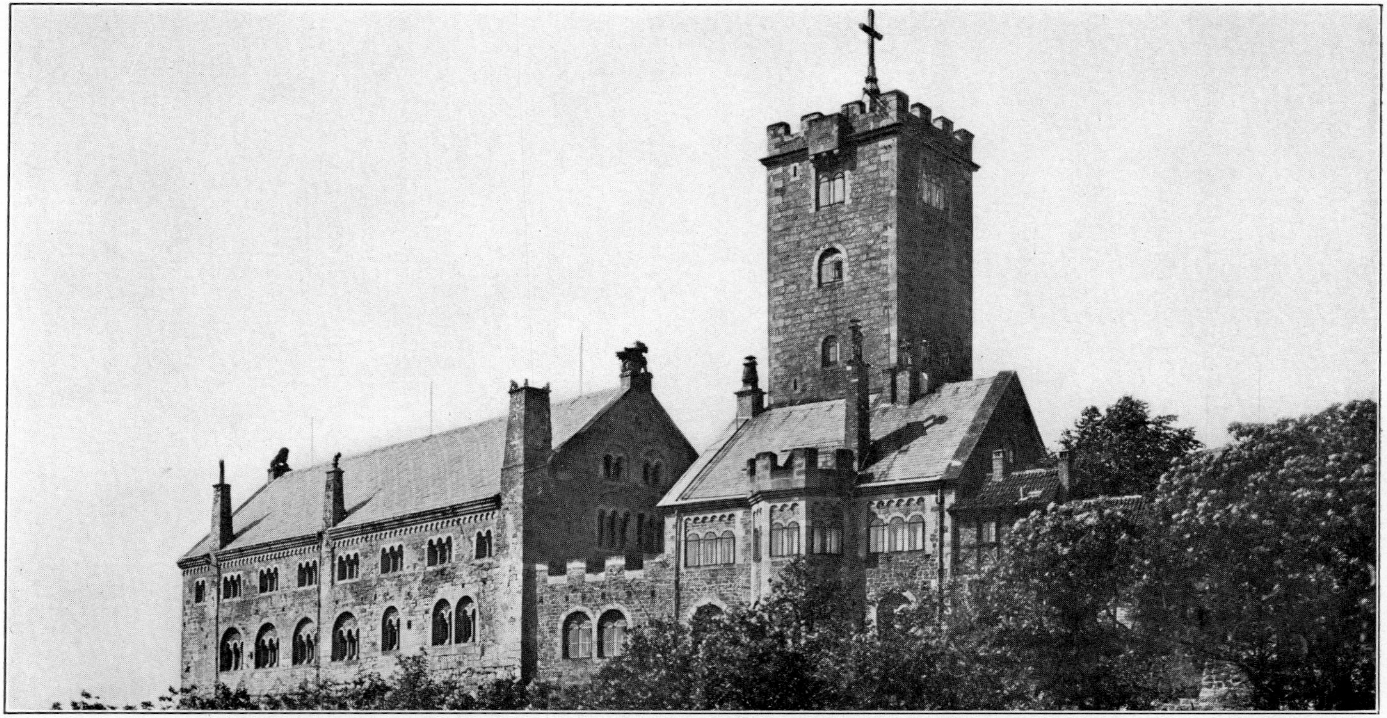

Verlag der Neuen Photogr. Gesellschaft G. m. b. H., Berlin.

THE WARTBURG, NEAR EISENACH, GERMANY

Here Luther wrote his translations of the Bible and his EIN FESTE BURG.

It is a spiritual tonic for the discouraged and distressed. Conflict with "the prince of darkness grim," difficulties like a "flood of mortal ills," "the world with devils filled," "threatening to undo us"—all of these are reminders of Luther's heroic words on entering the city of Worms in 1521: "Though there be as many devils in Worms as tiles on the housetops, I must go"; and of the equally heroic declaration before the great Council there: "I am bound by the Scripture; my conscience is submissive to the will of God. I can recant nothing and will recant nothing." Triumphantly rings out his confidence in "the man of God's own choosing," "from age to age the same," who surely "must win the battle."

Every line of each of the four stanzas is important; none should be omitted, one or two may be sung, the remainder read in concert. The fourth stanza is meaningless unless following the third because "that word" refers directly to the last line of the third stanza, "one little word shall fell him."

The text is majestic and powerful, inspiring a conviction of the invincibility of Christ's followers and the inevitability of his Cause.

In England, the translation by Thomas Carlyle takes precedence:

> "A safe stronghold our God is still,
> A trusty shield and weapon."

In America the favored translation is by Rev. Frederick Henry Hedge (1805–1890), who was born at Cambridge and who, while still a child, traveled in Germany with the historian George Bancroft. Subsequently he was pastor of churches in Maine, Massachusetts, and Rhode Island. More than thirty years of his life were spent as Professor of Ecclesiastical History in the Harvard Divinity School.

✣

THE HYMN TUNE. Luther was an accomplished amateur musician and is credited with a number of chorales, either original or arranged by him from Latin chants, vernacular sacred songs, and secular folk-songs. As a boy he was an excellent singer, and he became increasingly skilful as a flute and lute player. He passionately loved the art.

This tune forms the central theme in Meyerbeer's opera *The Huguenots*. Mendelssohn used it in his "Reformation Symphony," Wagner in his "Kaiser March," and Bach in one of his sacred cantatas.

ABIDE WITH ME: FAST FALLS THE EVENTIDE

1. Abide with me: fast falls the eventide;
The darkness deepens; Lord, with me abide:
When other helpers fail, and comforts flee;
Help of the helpless, O abide with me.

2. Swift to its close ebbs out life's little day;
Earth's joys grow dim, its glories pass away;
Change and decay in all around I see;
O, thou who changest not, abide with me.

3. I need thy presence every passing hour;
What but thy grace can foil the tempter's power?
Who like thyself my guide and stay can be?
Through cloud and sunshine, O abide with me.

4. I fear no foe, with thee at hand to bless;
Ills have no weight, and tears no bitterness:
Where is death's sting? Where, grave, thy victory?
I triumph still, if thou abide with me.

5. Hold thou thy cross before my closing eyes;
Shine through the gloom, and point me to the skies;
Heaven's morning breaks, and earth's vain shadows flee;
In life, in death, O Lord, abide with me.

HENRY F. LYTE, 1847.

BIBLICAL TEXT.

And they constrained him, saying,

Abide with us; for it is toward evening, and the day is now far spent. And he went in to abide with them.

LUKE 24:29.

Even as the Father hath loved me, I also have loved you: abide ye in my love.

JOHN 15:9.

AT EVENING TIME THERE SHALL BE LIGHT

The afterglow of a radiant Sabbath drenched Brixham with quiet splendor, but under the graying glory there was gloom instead of peace. That morning the village pastor, weak and ill, had preached his farewell sermon. On the following day he was to start for Italy in the hope of recovering his health. Loving eyes were turned to the rectory, where, in the lowering darkness, a light shone from the study window. That afternoon some of the villagers had seen their pastor walking in the garden, among the flowers he loved. Many prayers were said for him that evening.

In his study, the pastor, the Reverend Henry F. Lyte, was busy at his desk. He was not writing next Sunday's sermon. He realized that he would probably never preach again. He was writing a hymn, the words and first music of which he handed to a relative when he came out of his study that evening.

Not an academic literary production, but a song of the heart, "Abide with Me" came out of the experiences of that day and of the days of weakness and illness which had preceded it—out of the grief of farewell which had made the morning service so difficult for the sick man that at times he had wondered if he could go through with it—out of the peace and quiet beauty of the afternoon in the garden in sight of the sea he loved—out of the soothing glow of the sunset, came this great hymn.

Earlier in life he had written, in one of his poems, a prayer which was happily fulfilled in his last song:

> "O Thou, whose touch can lend
> Life to the dead, thy quickening grace supply,
> And grant me, swanlike, my last breath to spend
> In song that may not die."

Henry Francis Lyte (1793–1847) was a native of Ednam, Scotland. He graduated from Trinity College, Dublin, and after being jostled from one parish to another, he went to the village of Brixham, England, as a curate. There he gave his life in ministry to a parish of villagers, fisher-folk, a few soldiers from a neighboring garrison, and occasional visitors. There Lyte entered into the spirit of his own hymn, "Jesus, I my cross have taken." He relinquished society, culture and everything to follow Jesus. He took up the cross of his hard labor and carried it successfully until his death. It was there, too, he wrote his swan-song, "Abide with Me."

The day after that Sunday he started for Italy, but went no farther than Nice, France, where he died, pointing upward and saying, "Peace, joy!" He was buried in the English Cemetery at Nice.

✣

THE HYMN TUNE. The tune EVENTIDE, by William Henry Monk (1823–1889), is almost a perfect hymn tune. It has adaptation to the text, singable melody and parts, sound musical writing, and a haunting, unforgettable quality.

It has the downward slant of an evening tune, also a low and limited range, as contrasted with the upward and extended tone flights in such tunes as NICÆA and LAUDES DOMINI, where morning is the keynote.

Eventide has much elasticity, bending to the softest and slowest breathings of "Hold thou thy cross before my closing eyes"; stretching and square-timbering to such challenges as "I fear no foe with thee at hand to bless"; and "Where is death's sting, where, grave, thy victory!" It is all accomplished within the range of six tones and through a total of forty black and white notes.

Dr. Monk wrote this tune at a time of great sorrow, a fact which further explains its appropriate wedding to Dr. Lyte's words. Mrs. Monk writes of it, "Together we watched the glories of the setting sun. As the last golden ray faded, he took some paper and penciled that tune which has gone over all the earth."

Dr. Monk was a man of deep religious conviction and devotional feeling. He always sought worship values in his church music. "The organ was to him an instrument, not for the display of skill, but for touching the souls of men." He was a champion of congregational song and saw to it that the church in which he directed the music for nearly forty years, St. Matthias, Stoke Newington, was a hymn-loving church. He was the musical editor of *Hymns Ancient and Modern.* His word was so authoritative that it was often called "Monk's Book." Henry Francis Lyte composed a tune for this hymn the same night that he wrote the words, and gave both into the keeping of a relative. The original Lyte tune follows:

Henry Francis Lyte's Own Music for "Abide with Me"

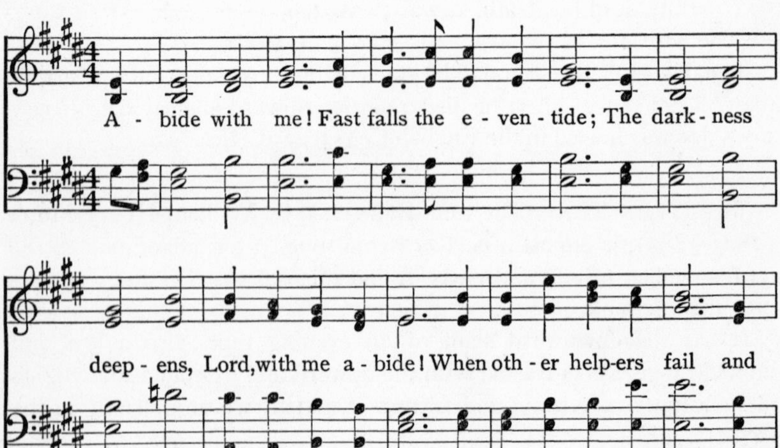

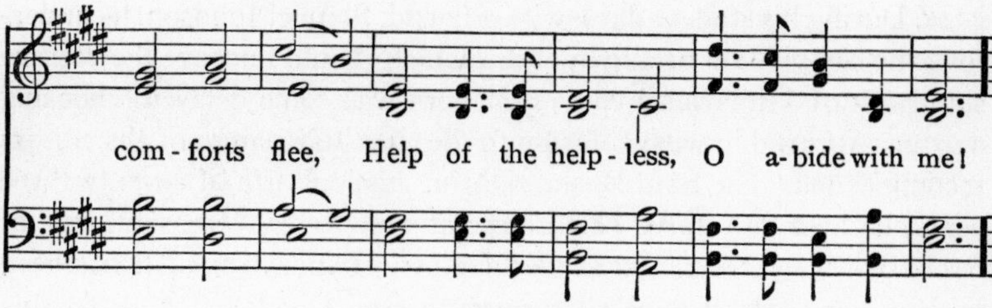
com - forts flee, Help of the help - less, O a-bide with me!

AGAIN, AS EVENING'S SHADOW FALLS

1. Again, as evening's shadow falls,
We gather in these hallowed walls;
And vesper hymn and vesper prayer
Rise mingling on the holy air.

2. May struggling hearts that seek release
Here find the rest of God's own peace;
And, strengthened here by hymn and prayer,
Lay down the burden and the care.

3. O God, our Light, to thee we bow;
Within all shadows standest thou;
Give deeper calm than night can bring;
Give sweeter songs than lips can sing.

4. Life's tumult we must meet again,
We cannot at the shrine remain;
But, in the spirit's secret cell,
May hymn and prayer forever dwell.

Samuel Longfellow, 1860.

Biblical Text.

Let my prayer be set forth as incense before thee;
The lifting up of my hands as the evening sacrifice.

Psalm 141 : 2.

SUNDAY VESPERS IN BROOKLYN

The Sunday evening service was evidently not a problem in a certain church in Brooklyn in 1860, for the pastor developed a series of "Vesper Services" which met and filled a living need. Not only did these Services minister to that particular congregation, but, through them, its minister made a lasting contribution to American worship services. For these Vespers he wrote "Again, as evening's shadow falls."

That pastor was the Reverend Samuel Longfellow, brother of the famous New England poet, Henry Wadsworth Longfellow. He was born in Portland, Maine, in 1819, graduated from Harvard College at the age of twenty, and from Cambridge Divinity School seven years later. During his student days, with a friend, Samuel Johnson, he undertook the compilation of a hymn book which should improve the literary standards of Unitarian hymnody. There was some delay in choosing a name. A friend in witty allusion to the Christian names of the editors recommended "The Sam Book." During his long life of seventy-three years, he held only three pastorates: at Fall River, Massachusetts, at Brooklyn, New York, and at Germantown, Pennsylvania. It has been said of him, "He was in all respects a man worth knowing for his own sake: a sympathetic pastor, a sunny-hearted gentleman, a man of deep, earnest, consecrated will."

ANALYSIS. First Stanza: Time, place, and program: "Evening's shadow," "hallowed walls," "vesper hymn and vesper prayer."

Second Stanza: Participants: "Struggling hearts"—worshippers who are consciously striving for release from the prison-house of circumstances.

Third Stanza: The upreach: "our Light"—definite prayer. Twilight outside has deepened into darkness, but "within all shadows" He stands Who is the Light. Note that the prayer asks only two things: calm and song.

Fourth Stanza: The Outreach: here, in this "Vesper Service," in the "hallowed walls" of God's house, peace, calm, release from "burden and care." Tomorrow, Monday's toil and trouble, noise and hurry. How fine it would be to stay here always! But "we cannot at the shrine remain." Out in the busy rush of daily toil, there can, there should be, a "secret cell," and there, even in noise and hurry and worry, "hymn and prayer" may "dwell." One is reminded of John Oxenham's words:

"'Mid all the traffic of the ways,
Turmoils without, within,
Make in my heart a quiet place,
And come and dwell within.

"A little shrine of quietness,
All sacred to Thyself,
Where Thou shalt all my soul possess,
And I may find myself." [1]

A Day's Prayers in Hymns

Matins—5 A. M.—"Still, still with thee."
Prime—6 A. M.—"O Master, let me walk with thee."
Tierce—9 A. M.—"I would be true."
Sext—12 M.—"I thank thee, Lord, for strength of arm."
Nones—3 P. M.—"In the hour of trial."

[1] From *The Vision Splendid,* by John Oxenham, copyright, 1917, by Doubleday, Doran and Company, and used by permission.

Vespers—Sunset—"Again, as evening's shadow falls."
Compline—9 P. M.—"Peacefully round us the shadows are falling."

✣

THE HYMN TUNE. This tune, ABENDS, was composed by Sir Herbert Stanley Oakeley (1830–1903), English organist and composer. He studied in Dresden and Leipzig, and was Professor of Music in the University of Edinburgh for many years. In that capacity he worked ardently for the development of choral and orchestral music throughout Scotland and for the reintroduction of the organ into Scottish churches. In 1876 he was knighted; in 1881 he was made Composer of Music to Her Majesty in Scotland.

Sir Herbert is said to have had a remarkable gift for improvisation and to have been an organ player of exceptional ability. He composed songs and anthems, a jubilee cantata, a motette, and a few instrumental works.

ALL BEAUTIFUL THE MARCH OF DAYS

1. All beautiful the march of days,
As seasons come and go;
The hand that shaped the rose hath wrought
The crystal of the snow;
Hath sent the hoary frost of heaven,
The flowing waters sealed,
And laid a silent loveliness
On hill and wood and field.

2. O'er white expanses sparkling pure
The radiant morns unfold;
The solemn splendors of the night
Burn brighter through the cold;
Life mounts in every throbbing vein,
Love deepens round the hearth,
And clearer sounds the angel-hymn,
"Good-will to men on earth."

(Stanza usually omitted)

Oh, glory of the winter land!
The peace of nature's rest,
And sweet the dream of coming spring
That stirs within her breast.
On move the resurrection hours,
The Easter heralds throng,—
Till sudden bursts the miracle
Of blossom and of song.

3. O, Thou, from whose unfathomed law
The year in beauty flows,

Thyself the vision passing by
In crystal and in rose;
Day unto day doth utter speech,
And night to night proclaim,
In ever-changing words of light,
The wonder of thy Name.

FRANCES WHITMARSH WILE, 1912.

BIBLICAL TEXT.

He giveth snow like wool,
He scattereth the hoar-frost like ashes.
He casteth forth his ice like morsels;
Who can stand before his cold?

PSALM 147:16, 17.

Hast thou entered the treasuries of the snow,
Or hast thou seen the treasuries of the hail?
Out of whose womb came the ice?
And the hoary frost of heaven, who hath gendered it?

JOB 38:22, 29.

Day unto day uttereth speech,
And night unto night showeth knowledge.

PSALM 19:2.

THE GLORY OF THE WINTER LAND

"There is no hymn about the beauty of winter." This was strangely true when Dr. W. C. Gannett and Dr. F. L. Hosmer were compiling the hymn book, "Unity Hymns and Carols." In it they were planning a section for the hymns of the seasons. Spring songs were available, many summertime songs, a number of autumn and harvest-home songs, but nothing for winter!

So Dr. Gannett wrote to his friend Mrs. Frances Whitmarsh Wile, asking if she would not like to write a hymn for winter. "All Beautiful the March of Days" was the result. Not that it came all at once, full-grown in all its present beauty. Far from it! At intervals throughout a whole year's "March of Days" the editor and the author worked at it, revising, changing, eliminating, substituting, until finally "The Winter Hymn" was complete.

Mrs. Frances Whitmarsh Wile was born in Bristol Valley, New York, in 1878. In her childhood this beautiful valley was secluded and quiet, especially in winter, when the mails came only once a week. The first stanza of the hymn, with its reference to "A silent loveliness on hill and wood and field" was inspired directly by winter scenes in Bristol Valley.

The author's later years have been spent in Rochester, N. Y., where

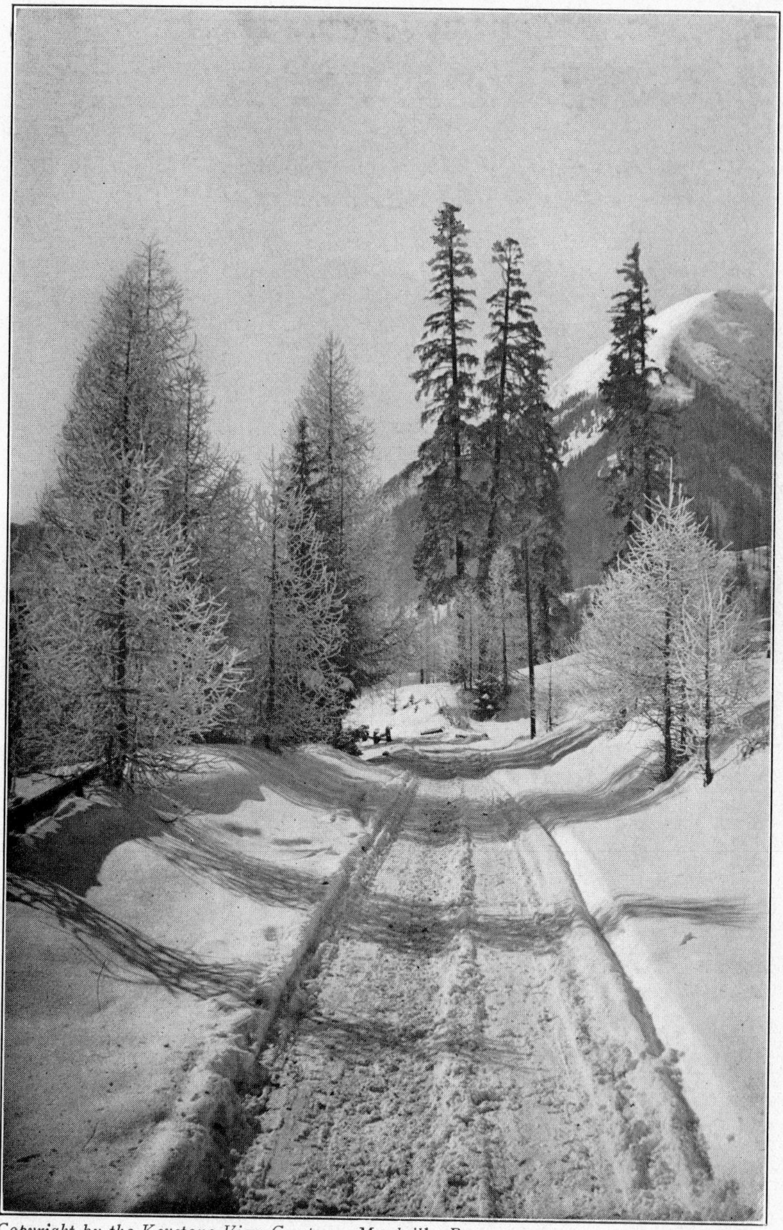

Copyright by the Keystone View Company, Meadville, Pa.

"All beautiful the march of days,
As seasons come and go;
The hand that shaped the rose hath wrought
The crystal of the snow;
Hath sent the hoary frost of heaven,
The flowing waters sealed,
And laid a silent loveliness
On hill and wood and field."

she has been one of the founders of the Women's City Club and where she has taken an active part in the movement for the larger place of woman in civic affairs.

ANALYSIS. First Stanza: "All beautiful"—not merely summer and its roses, but also winter, with its wonder-crystals of the snow.

"Silent loveliness"—frost and ice, the Creator's handiwork, are not jailers or thieves, robbing us of beauty; but rather, makers of "loveliness."

Second Stanza: "Radiant morns"—and "Solemn splendors of the night" tell of winter sunrise and star-spangled skies.

"Love deepens round the hearth"—Whittier, in his "Snow Bound" sings of the intimate joys of family life on winter evenings around the hearth:

"Shut in from all the world without,
We sat the clean-winged hearth about,
Content to let the north-wind roar
In baffled rage at pane and door. . . .
What matter how the night behaved?
What matter how the north-wind raved?
Blow high, blow low, not all its snow
Could quench our hearth-fire's ruddy glow.
. . . grateful sense of happiness
For food and shelter, warmth and health,
And love's contentment more than wealth.
. . . Life is ever Lord of Death,
And Love can never lose its own!" [1]

Third Stanza: "Thyself—in crystal and in rose." Wise and happy he who finds his Creator's hand in the beauty of every season, to whom the myriad voices of day and night, in winter as well as in summer, tell "the wonder of His Name."

Twenty Women Hymn Writers and Their Hymns

Mary, Mother of Christ—The *Magnificat*
A Benedictine Abbess—"Jesus, the very thought of thee"
Cecil Frances Alexander—"Jesus calls us o'er the tumult"
Sarah Flower Adams—"Nearer, my God, to thee"
Katharine Lee Bates—"O, beautiful for spacious skies"
Anna L. Coghill—"Work, for the night is coming"
Elizabeth Clephane—"Beneath the cross of Jesus"
Charlotte Elliott—"Just as I am, without one plea"
Emily Elliott—"Thou didst leave thy throne"
Katherine Hankey—"I love to tell the story"

[1] From *Snow Bound,* by John Greenleaf Whittier, copyright by Houghton Mifflin Company.

Annie Sherwood Hawks—"I need thee every hour"
Frances Ridley Havergal—"Take my life and let it be"
Julia Ward Howe—"Mine eyes have seen the glory"
Mary A. Lathbury—"Day is dying in the west"
Jemima Luke—"I think when I read that sweet story"
Adelaide Anne Procter—"My God, I thank thee who hast made"
Harriet Beecher Stowe—"Still, still with thee"
Mary Ann Thompson—"O, Zion, haste, thy mission high fulfilling"
Dorothy Ann Thrupp—"Saviour, like a Shepherd lead us"
Anna L. Waring—"In heavenly love abiding"

✣

THE HYMN TUNE. SHACKELFORD, by Frederick Henry Cheeswright, composed in 1889, is rich in color, whether with words or as a "song without words." No hymn should be sung straight through without expression. Interpretation gives reality, vitality, and power to a hymn. First stanzas will invariably be sung full-voiced and straightforward, thus overcoming any inertia in a congregation. Toward the end of the first stanza of this hymn the singing may be softer, closing very subdued "On hill and wood and field." The second stanza should increase in tone, reaching a climax on "And clearer sounds the angel-hymn," then suddenly soft on "Good-will to men on earth." The third stanza may begin mezzo voice, picking up strength toward the close and ending in superb climax on "the wonder of Thy Name."

ALL GLORY, LAUD AND HONOR

1. All glory, laud and honor
To thee, Redeemer, King,
To whom the lips of children
Made sweet hosannas ring.
The people of the Hebrews
With palms before thee went;
Our praise and prayer and anthems
Before thee we present.

2. Thou art the King of Israel,
Thou David's royal Son,
Who in the Lord's name cometh
The King and blessed One!
To thee, before thy passion,
They sang their hymns of praise;
To thee, now high exalted
Our melody we raise.

3. Thou didst accept their praises;
Accept the prayers we bring,
Who in all good delightest,
Thou good and gracious king.
All glory, laud and honor

To thee, Redeemer, King;
To whom the lips of children
Made sweet hosannas ring!

THEODULPH OF ORLEANS, 820 A. D.

BIBLICAL TEXT.

Lift up your heads, O ye gates;
And be ye lifted up, ye everlasting doors:
And the King of glory will come in.
Who is the King of glory?
The Lord strong and mighty,
The Lord mighty in battle.
Lift up your heads, O ye gates;
Yea, lift them up, ye everlasting doors:
And the King of glory will come in.
Who is this King of glory?
The Lord of hosts,
He is the King of glory.

PSALM 24:7–10.

And when he was come into Jerusalem, all the city was stirred, saying Who is this? And the multitudes said, This is the prophet, Jesus, from Nazareth of Galilee.

But when the chief priests and the scribes saw the wonderful things that he did, and the children that were crying in the temple and saying Hosanna to the son of David; they were moved with indignation, and said unto him, Hearest thou what these are saying? And Jesus saith unto them. Yea: did ye never read, Out of the mouth of babes and sucklings thou hast perfected praise?

MATTHEW 21:10, 11, 15, 16.

A PALM SUNDAY PROCESSIONAL OF THE NINTH CENTURY

A prominent clergyman in prison, with a spirit that refused to be confined; a group of choir boys in the prison yard learning a new song; a pious king in a Palm Sunday procession to the Cathedral; a sudden burst of surprising song from the prison as the procession passes; a highly pleased king; and a clergyman free for his church duties once more—these are some of the "highlights" with which tradition and legend have illumined this medieval hymn.

Naturally, eleven centuries of use would gather a halo of legend around a hymn, especially when composed by a Bishop and enjoyed by a King. But the legends and traditions give vividness and life to the hymn. Add the glamour of the legends to the real worth of the words and one does not wonder that this hymn has shown imperishable vitality.

Theodulph of Orleans (760–821), a native of Italy, Abbot of a Florentine monastery, was brought to France by Charlemagne and made Bishop of Orleans. After the death of the illustrious Empire builder, Theodulph was suspected of disloyalty to Louis the Pious and of favoring the cause of Barnard of Italy. He was thrust into prison at Angiers. It was probably during this imprisonment that he wrote this hymn "Gloria, Laus et Honor." The hymn has seventy-eight lines, twenty-four of which are ordinarily used. The following quatrain will be regarded as a fortunate omission, hardly conducive to a spirit of worship:

"Be thou, O Lord, the rider
And we the little ass,
That to God's holy city
Together we may pass."

The use of this hymn as a Palm Sunday processional dramatizes the story of its imprisoned author. At Hereford, Tours and Rouen, it was sung at the gate of the city. The gates were closed and the choir boys mounted to the wall above the gate and there sang the hymn, suggesting both the imprisoned condition of the author and also the approach of Christ in his Triumphal Procession to the gates of Jerusalem on the first Palm Sunday.

The English translation was made by Dr. John Mason Neale, to whom the English-speaking world owes so great a debt of gratitude for his research among the Greek and Latin manuscripts of the early centuries.

While distinctly an "occasional hymn" written for a special day and used on Palm Sunday, this hymn is deserving of a wider use than a mere once-a-year singing. For Children's Day and for many Sundays as a Children's Processional it is timely and picturesque.

THE HYMN TUNE. ST. THEODULPH was composed early in the seventeenth century by Melchior Teschner (1584–1635), an Austrian clergyman, choir-master, and composer of church music. This chorale is used by Bach in his "St. John's Passion." An older setting is the PLAIN SONG melody from the SARUM GRADUAL.

ALL HAIL THE POWER OF JESUS' NAME

1. All hail the power of Jesus' name,
Let angels prostrate fall;
Bring forth the royal diadem,
And crown him Lord of all.

2. Crown him, ye martyrs of your God
Who from his altar call;
Extol the stem of Jesse's rod,
And crown him Lord of all.

3. Ye seed of Israel's chosen race,
Ye ransomed of the fall,
Hail him who saves you by his grace,
And crown him Lord of all.

4. Let every kindred, every tribe,
On this terrestrial ball,
To him all majesty ascribe,
And crown him Lord of all.

5. O that with yonder sacred throng,
We at his feet may fall;
Join in the everlasting song,
And crown him Lord of all.

EDWARD PERRONET, 1779.

BIBLICAL TEXT.

Thou shalt also be a crown of beauty in the hand of Jehovah, and a royal diadem in the hand of thy God.

ISAIAH 62:3.

And I heard a voice of many angels and the living creatures and the elders, and the number of them was ten thousand times ten thousand, and thousand of thousands; saying, "Worthy is the Lamb that hath been slain to receive the power, and riches, and wisdom, and might, and honor, and glory, and blessing."

And every created thing heard I saying, "Unto him that sitteth on the throne, and unto the Lamb, be the blessing, and the honor, and the glory, and the dominion, for ever and ever."

REVELATION 5:11–13.

And he hath a name written,
King of Kings and Lord of Lords.

REVELATION 19:16.

A SONG OF TRIUMPH IN TIMES OF TROUBLE AND PERSECUTION

Published anonymously in 1779 in *The Gospel Magazine,* this hymn appeared again six years later in a little book with this caption: "Occasional Verses, Moral and Sacred, published for the instruction and amusement of the candidly serious and religious."

Again, no name appeared with the hymn. However, an acrostic poem, the initial letters of which spell the name "Edward Perronet," is an incontestable proof that Perronet was the author of both the book and the hymn.

Edward Perronet (1726–1792) was a man of courage. He was moreover a person of means, the son of an Anglican priest. Converted at the age of twenty-one, he became an intimate friend of the Wesleys and threw himself heart and soul into their evangelical revivals. John Wesley's diary mentions his sufferings for the Cause: "We were in perils of robbers, who were abroad, and had robbed many the night before. We commended ourselves to God, and rode over the heath singing." He further adds: "Edward Perronet was thrown down and rolled in the mud and mire. He got a deal of abuse thereby, and not a little dirt, both of which he took very patiently."

After some years of association with the Wesleys, Perronet became convinced that they all ought to separate from the Anglican Church and found a new ecclesiastical organization. This the Wesleys were not ready to do, so Perronet, obeying his convictions, withdrew from them, and founded an independent church in Canterbury, which church he served until his death. It was here, in all probability, that he wrote at the age of fifty-eight, the hymn by which he is remembered, "All Hail the Power of Jesus' Name."

PICTURE SYNTHESIS. Fra Angelico's "Crucifixion" has been called a literal picturization of the TE DEUM. Since the TE DEUM and CORONATION have much in common the following bits of the former may be used advantageously with "All Hail the Power of Jesus' Name."

Before first stanza:

"We praise thee, O God:
We acknowledge thee to be the Lord.
All the earth doth worship thee, the Father everlasting,
To thee all angels cry aloud;
The heavens, and all the powers therein;
To thee cherubim and seraphim continually do cry."

Before second stanza:

The glorious company of the apostles,
The goodly fellowship of the prophets,
The noble army of martyrs praise thee."

Before fourth stanza:

The holy church throughout all the world doth acknowledge thee;
The Father of an infinite majesty;
Thine adorable, true, and only Son:
Also the Holy Ghost, the Comforter.

Before fifth stanza:

"Thou art the King of Glory, O Christ:
Thou art the everlasting Son of the Father."

❖

THE HYMN TUNES. CORONATION was composed by Oliver Holden (1765–1844), a native of Shirley, Massachusetts, and a resident, for most of his life, of Charlestown across the river from Boston. By trade a carpenter, he was active in rebuilding his home city after its burning by the British. He became a prosperous real-estate dealer, a pillar of the church, the organizer and conductor of many singing schools. He was among the first to use music type in Boston. Such was his reputation that when George Washington visited Boston in 1789, the city authorized young Holden to write the music and words and train the male choir that was to sing the triumphal ode as Washington reached the Old State House. Holden wrote CORONATION just after the birth of his firstborn, a daughter, which accounts for the unalloyed joy running through his pattern of notes. The little organ on which it was played into being is in the Old State House, Boston. It is an instrument of four and a half octaves. Holden was a member of the First Baptist Church, and later of the Second Baptist Church, Charlestown. His last words were, "I have some beautiful airs running through my head, if I only had strength to note them down."

The English tune, MILES LANE, long a favorite in England, is now coming into wider use in America. It is more difficult than CORONATION, because of wider range, sustained notes, and interrupted pace. But it has a majestic, stately rhythm and a rare dignity, befitting the splendid words of the poem. It marches on to a magnificent climax in the four-fold repetition of "Crown Him." It was composed in the organ gallery at Canterbury Cathedral, 1779, by William Shrubsole (1760–1806), shipwright, bank clerk, secretary, organist for two years at Miles Lane and Shrubsole, London. Next he went to Bangor Cathedral and here his troubles began, for he was too sympathetic with the dissenters, and even attended some of their conventicles. "If the William Shrubsole shall be found to frequent any conventicle or religious assembly, where anything is taught which is contrary to the Doctrine or Discipline of the Church of England, the Dean shall be impowered to discharge him from his place of organist." Two months later he was discharged. He returned to London where he became teacher of music and organist in Lady Huntingdon Chapel.

In his early days while a chorister in Canterbury Cathedral he became acquainted with Edward Perronet, then in charge of a Congregational chapel there.

Such close friends did they become that Perronet appointed him an executor of his will, with this appreciation of his friend Shrubsole: "A fine disinterested affection he has ever shown me from my first acquaintance, even when a proverb of reproach, cast off by all my relatives, disinherited unjustly, and left to sink or swim as afflictions and God's providence should appoint." The memory of this friendship lives in the words of Perronet and the tune of Shrubsole, so indissolubly wedded.

Henry Smart once played MILES LANE in astounding fashion. He refused to play interludes between stanzas. A grumbler in the congregation resented the omission of this musical interstice. Smart said nothing but awaited his opportunity. It came when MILES LANE was given out as the tune. "All went well at the first stanza and everybody seemed prepared to make a joyful noise. But in the interlude between verses one and two, the organist modulated ever so cleverly and imperceptibly, into the key of B; between stanzas two and three into the key of C; and between stanzas three and four into the key of D flat, and so on until the high notes on 'Crown Him' must have joined the company of the 'Lost Chord.' The organist silenced his critics."

An English Variation of "Miles Lane," named "Scarborough"

The Scotch or "Hiccough" Version

The Florid Irish Version

ALL PEOPLE THAT ON EARTH DO DWELL

1. All people that on earth do dwell,
   Sing to the Lord with cheerful voice;
   Him serve with fear, his praise forth tell,
   Come ye before him and rejoice.

2. The Lord ye know is God indeed;
   Without our aid he did us make;
   We are his folk, he doth us feed;
   And for his sheep he doth us take.

3. O enter then his gates with praise,
Approach with joy his courts unto;
Praise, laud, and bless his name always,
For it is seemly so to do.

4. For why? The Lord our God is good,
His mercy is forever sure;
His truth at all times firmly stood,
And shall from age to age endure.

WILLIAM KETHE, 1561.

BIBLICAL TEXT.

Make a joyful noise unto the Lord, all ye lands.

PSALM 100: 1.

THE GRAND OLD PURITAN ANTHEM

Three and a half centuries of constant use is the record of this quaint old hymn, the oldest of the English Psalm-versions now commonly sung. It was first published in Day's Psalter in 1561, and subsequently in almost every Psalter and hymn book from that time until now, gathering around it a host of traditions and memories.

The Hundredth Psalm and this paraphrase have always had a peculiar hold on the Reformed Church of Christ. "The Psalm contains a promise of Christianity, as winter at its close contains a promise of spring. The trees are ready to bud, the flowers are just hidden by the light soil, the clouds are heavy with rain, the sun shines in his strength; only a genial wind from the south is wanted to give new life to all things."[1] When new life came through Jesus Christ, this Psalm was felt to express the Church's gratitude, and, in the metrical version, her official Hymn of Thanksgiving.

This is one of the few Psalms to which Shakespeare definitely refers, *Merry Wives of Windsor,* Act II, Scene I, "They do no more adhere and keep place together than the Hundredth Psalm to the tune of GREEN SLEEVES."

William Kethe (–1594) was a Scotch minister who was an exile for his faith in Frankfort and Geneva during the stormy period when freedom of thought was struggling for existence. Almost the first definite record of Kethe is that he was sent on a mission with letters to fellow-exiles in Basel, Strassburg, and other cities. Twenty-five of his Psalm-versions are included in the famous old *Anglo-Genevan Psalter.* He was one of the translators of the famous *Geneva Bible.*

A vivid picture of the life of the exiles in Geneva is given by one of them: "A most interesting sight is offered in the City on week-days,

[1] From *Annotations upon Popular Hymns,* by Charles S. Robinson.

when the hour for service approaches. As soon as the first sound of the bell is heard, all shops are closed, conversation ceases, business is put on one side, and from all parts the people hasten to the nearest church. Arrived there, each one draws from his pocket a small book which contains some psalms with notes, and thus the congregation sings before and after the sermon, while everyone testifies how great consolation is derived from this custom."

In such fashion did the Genevan congregation in the time of William Kethe sing "Al Peopull yt" to the tune of OLD HUNDREDTH.

✣

THE HYMN TUNE. OLD HUNDREDTH, even older than the Kethe Psalm from which it gets its name, was composed by Louis Bourgeois in 1551. He followed Calvin to Geneva in 1541, became master of the choristers there and musical editor of the Genevan Psalter. He was exempted from guard duty and other work that he might spend all of his time teaching adults and children to sing, and in writing and rearranging music. He was once thrown into prison for making unauthorized alterations in certain well-known tunes. "Historians," says Robert Bridges, "who wish to give a true philosophical account of Calvin's influence at Geneva ought probably to refer a great part of it to the enthusiasm attendant on the singing of Bourgeois 'melodies.'" This tune was first associated with Psalm 134, and might therefore be called OLD HUNDRED AND THIRTY-FOURTH.

Hymn Tune Names

1. Hymn tunes are named from the words of the first line: THE FIRST NOEL,
2. From the first line of the Latin: DOMINUM REGIT ME (The Lord Is My Shepherd),
3. From the author of the hymn long associated with tune: ST. THEODULPH (All glory, laud, and honor),
4. From the composer of the tune itself: MENDELSSOHN (Hark, the herald angels sing. Dykes named a tune from his own name, spelled backwards—SEKYD),
5. From names of famous people: KING EDWARD,
6. From names of saints and famous churches: ST. CHRYSOSTOM,
7. From towns or cities in which the composers resided: CHAUTAUQUA,
8. From streets or squares on which lived the composers: FEDERAL STREET, Salem, Massachusetts, where lived General Oliver,

9. From countries or nations: AUSTRIA and AMERICA,
10. From events in history: ARMAGEDDON and NICÆA.

The First Form of "Al Peopull y^{t}" and "Old Hundredth"

Day's Psalter, 1561 — LOUIS BOURGEOIS, 1551

MELODY IN THE TENOR

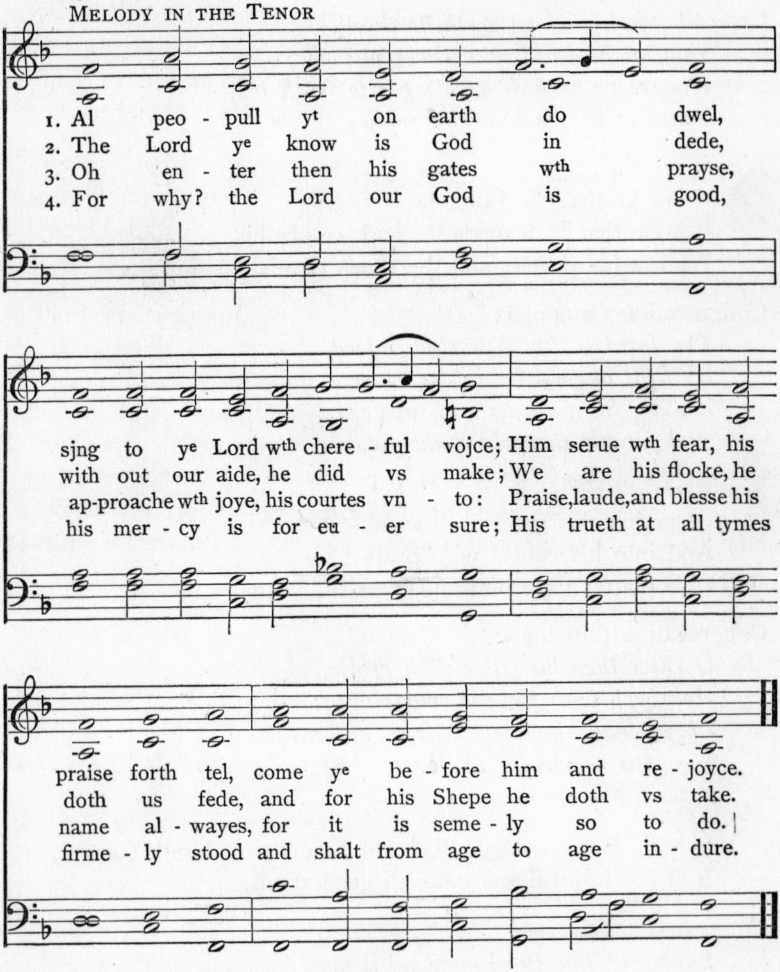

1. Al peo - pull y^{t} on earth do dwel,
2. The Lord y^{e} know is God in dede,
3. Oh en - ter then his gates wth prayse,
4. For why? the Lord our God is good,
sjng to y^{e} Lord wth chere - ful vojce; Him serue wth fear, his
with out our aide, he did vs make; We are his flocke, he
ap-proache wth joye, his courtes vn - to: Praise, laude, and blesse his
his mer - cy is for eu - er sure; His trueth at all tymes
praise forth tel, come y^{e} be - fore him and re - joyce.
doth us fede, and for his Shepe he doth vs take.
name al - wayes, for it is seme - ly so to do.
firme - ly stood and shalt from age to age in - dure.

RESPONSIVE SERVICE

(Based on this Psalm version)

(The minister will read from this page, the congregation turning to the hymnal and singing the hymn, with pauses between stanzas for Scripture.)

Minister:

Make a joyful noise unto the Lord, all ye lands.
Serve the Lord with gladness:
Come before his presence with singing.

Congregation (singing):

All people that on earth do dwell,
Sing to the Lord with cheerful voice;
Him serve with fear, his praise forth tell,
Come ye before him and rejoice.

Minister:

Know ye that the Lord, he is God:
It is he that hath made us, and we are his;
We are his people, and the sheep of his pasture.

Congregation (singing):

The Lord ye know is God indeed,
Without our aid he did us make;
We are his folk, he doth us feed,
And for his sheep he doth us take.

Minister:

Enter into his gates with thanksgiving,
And into his courts with praise;
Give thanks unto him and bless his name.

Congregation (singing):

O enter then his gates with praise,
Approach with joy his courts unto;
Praise, laud, and bless his name always,
For it is seemly so to do.

Minister:

For the Lord is good; his lovingkindness endureth forever,
And his faithfulness unto all generations.

Congregation (singing):

For why? The Lord our God is good,
His mercy is forever sure;
His truth at all times firmly stood,
And shall from age to age endure.

Amen.

ANCIENT OF DAYS

1. Ancient of Days, who sittest throned in glory,
To thee all knees are bent, all voices pray;
Thy love has blessed the wide world's wondrous story
With light and life since Eden's dawning day.

2. O Holy Father, who hast led thy children
In all the ages, with the fire and cloud,
Through seas dry-shod, through weary wastes bewildering;
To thee, in reverent love, our hearts are bowed.

3. O Holy Jesus, Prince of Peace and Saviour,
To thee we owe the peace that still prevails,
Stilling the rude wills of men's wild behavior,
And calming passion's fierce and stormy gales.

4. O Holy Ghost, the Lord and the Life-giver,
Thine is the quickening power that gives increase;
From thee have flowed, as from a pleasant river,
Our plenty, wealth, prosperity and peace.

5. O Triune God, with heart and voice adoring,
Praise we the goodness that doth crown our days;
Pray we that thou wilt hear us, still imploring
Thy love and favor kept to us always.

William C. Doane, 1886.

Biblical Text.

Thrones were placed, and one that was Ancient of Days did sit . . . thousands of thousand ministered unto him, and ten thousand times ten thousand stood before him.

Daniel 7:9, 10.

A CITY EXALTED IN SONG

The Bicentennial of the city of Albany, N. Y., in 1886, was of special interest because Albany was the first chartered city in America. For this celebration one of the noble hymns of the Church was written. The sponsors of the celebration were evidently men of faith in God, men who recognized the importance of the religious note in a civic celebration.

Bishop William Croswell Doane (1832–1913), author of the words, came naturally by his hymn-writing ability, for his father, Bishop George Washington Doane, is remembered as the author of "Softly Now the Light of Day," "Fling Out the Banner," and other hymns.

William Doane was ordained in 1856, and for a time assisted his father in the church at Burlington, N. J. He became Bishop of the Protestant Episcopal Diocese of Albany in 1869. He received the

Honorary Degrees of D.D. from Oxford, and LL.D. from Cambridge. He writes of this hymn: "Of course it was not exactly in its present shape then (at the celebration of the Bicentennial), but was somewhat changed in form when the committee decided to put it into our church hymnal."

ANALYSIS: The hymn is an apostrophe to the Triune God. Its descriptions are directly on the attributes and work of each Person of the Trinity:

First Stanza: "Ancient of Days" is an unusual title for God. It is found only in *Daniel,* repeated three times in one chapter (7:9, 13, 22). It is significant as an opening phrase for a "Bicentennial Ode."

Second Stanza: "Holy Father," the leader "in all the ages."

Third Stanza: "Holy Jesus, Prince of Peace and Saviour," an application to mental and spiritual realms of the incident recorded in Mark 4:35–41.

Fourth Stanza: "Holy Ghost . . . Life-giver." Note the reference to the city's prosperity and peace, and the acknowledgment of the source of these blessings.

Fifth Stanza: Praise for the past, and prayer for the future.

An illuminating hymnic service may be arranged by interpolating appropriate Scripture readings with the singing of the stanzas. As for example:

First stanza: *Daniel* 7:9, 10, 13, 14, 21, 22.
Second stanza: *Psalm* 105:39, 42, 43.
Third stanza: *Isaiah* 9:6; *Matthew* 8:23–27.
Fourth stanza: *John* 14:16, 17; *Acts* 2:4, 17, 18.
Fifth stanza: *Psalm* 127:1.

Names of Deity in Hymns

This hymn suggests that an interesting list of names and titles of God may be compiled from hymns. A few of the more familiar ones follow: Ancient of Everlasting Days, Almighty King, Holy Father, Eternal Lord, Everlasting Light, God of the Earnest Heart, Father of All, Lord of Love, Lord of All Being, Lord God of Hosts, Life of Ages, Grace Divine, Maker, Monarch, Source Divine, Sun of Righteousness, Rock of Ages, Love that Fillest All, Potentate of Time.

✣

THE HYMN TUNE. ANCIENT OF DAYS (the tune so named from the opening phrase of the hymn) was composed for these words, and was used at the Bicentennial Celebration of the city of Albany. J.

Albert Jeffrey (1851–   ), the composer, was at that time the organist of the Protestant Episcopal Cathedral there. He was an English musician. Later he was an organist and teacher of music in Boston.

ANGEL VOICES, EVER SINGING

1. Angel voices, ever singing
Round thy throne of light,
Angel harps, forever ringing,
Rest not day nor night;
Thousands only live to bless thee,
And confess thee,
Lord of might.

(Omitted Stanza)

Thou who art beyond the farthest
Mortal eye can scan,
Can it be that thou regardest
Songs of sinful man?
Can we feel that thou art near us,
And wilt hear us?
Yea, we can.

2. Yea, we know thy love rejoices
O'er each work of thine;
Thou didst ears and hands and voices
For thy praise combine;
Craftsman's art, and music's measure
For thy pleasure
Didst design.

3. Here, Great God, today we offer
Of thine own to thee;
And for thine acceptance proffer,
All unworthily,
Hearts and minds and hands and voices,
In our choicest
Melody.

4. Honor, glory, might and merit,
Thine shall ever be,
Father, Son and Holy Spirit,
Blessed Trinity;
Of the best that thou hast given
Earth and heaven
Render thee.

Francis Pott, 1861.

Biblical Text.

Through him then let us offer up a sacrifice of praise to God continually, that is, the fruit of lips which make confession to his name.

Hebrews 13:15.

Praise him for his mighty acts;
Praise him according to his excellent greatness.
Praise him with trumpet sound:
Praise him with psaltery and harp.
Praise him with stringed instruments and pipe.
Let everything that hath breath praise the Lord.

PSALM 150:2, 3, 4, 6.

List! the cherubic host, in thousand choirs,
Touch their immortal harps of golden wires,
With those just spirits that wear victorious palms,
Singing everlastingly devout and holy psalms.

JOHN MILTON.

PROCESSIONAL HYMNS FOR ENGLISH CATHEDRALS

This hymn, written for "the dedication of an organ and the meeting of choirs," was first sung February 10, 1861, at the opening of the new organ in the Church of St. John the Evangelist at Wingate. The most effective singing during the day was that of a special hymn, "Angel Voices, Ever Singing," to which Dr. Monk had written a spirited tune. Dr. Pott objected to the tune by Sullivan, which he thought was written "with the first stanza alone in mind; and the rest of the hymn in contrast therewith."

The appropriateness of these stanzas for organ dedication is obvious: "Craftsman's art" may easily be taken to refer to the intricate art of organ building, while "music's measure" has an equal reference to the organ and to the choir. "Hearts and minds and hands and voices" is another indication that the author was extolling more than the ordinary music of a church service.

Francis Pott (1832–1909) was an Oxford graduate, and a clergyman of the Church of England. He served as Rector of Northill, his last charge, twenty-five years, until he was compelled to retire by increasing deafness. He was a member of the original committee which edited *Hymns Ancient and Modern.*

Mr. Pott is remembered as the translator of a number of Latin and Syriac hymns, among them "Alleluia, the Strife is O'er."

Other hymns written for organ dedication and choir festivals are:

"Rejoice, ye Pure in heart," for the Peterborough Choral Festival;

"Forward be our Watchword," for the Canterbury Festival;

"Saviour, Again to thy Dear Name we Raise," for the Malpas, Middlewich, and Nantwich Festivals;

"Onward Christian Soldiers," for the Horbury Bridge Festival.

Vocal and Instrumental Music in Hymns

Far, far away, like *bells* at evening pealing,
The voice of Jesus sounds o'er land and sea.
From "Hark, hark my soul"

For not with sword's loud clashing,
Nor roll of stirring *drums.*
From "Lead on, O King eternal"

To holy convocations
The *silver trumpet* calls.
From "O day of rest and gladness"

From angels bending near the earth
To touch their *harps of gold.*
From "It came upon the midnight clear"

He has sounded forth the *trumpet* that shall never call retreat.
From "Mine eyes have seen the glory"

With all the *angel choirs,*
With all the saints on earth,
Pour out the strains of joy and bliss,
True rapture, noblest mirth!
From "Rejoice, ye pure in heart"

Let *music* swell the breeze,
And ring from all the trees
Sweet freedom's *song.*
From "My country, 'tis of thee"

Responsive Service for Organ Dedication

Leader:
For the praise of Almighty God with the voice of melody, and the jubilant anthem:

Congregation:
We dedicate this organ.

Leader:
For the leading and inspiring of the service of song, that all the people may praise the Lord:

Congregation:

We dedicate this organ.

Leader:

For the culture of the finer and deeper emotions, for the broadening and elevation of character:

Congregation:

We dedicate this organ.

Leader:

For the resolving of the soul's discords in peaceful harmonies; for the uplifting of the depressed and the comforting of the sorrowful by its tones of sympathy and cheer; for the stirring of the hearts of men to purposes of duty and to deeds of heroic service in the name of Christ our Lord:

Congregation:

We dedicate this organ.

Leader:

Praise ye the Lord,
Praise God in his sanctuary:
Praise him in the firmament of his power.

Congregation:

Praise him for his mighty acts:
Praise him according to his excellent greatness.

Leader:

Praise him with trumpet sound:
Praise him with psaltery and harp.

Congregation:

Praise him with timbrel and dance:
Praise him with stringed instruments and pipe.

Leader:

Praise him with loud cymbals:
Praise him with high-sounding cymbals:

Congregation:

Let everything that hath breath praise the Lord.
Praise ye the Lord.

PSALM 150.

✣

THE HYMN TUNE. ANGEL VOICES, by Arthur Sullivan, was written in 1872.

Sir Arthur Seymour Sullivan (1842–1900) was one of England's most noted musicians. Born in London, he received his musical education at the Royal Academy of Music there and at the Leipzig Conservatory. His first song was published when he was a lad of thirteen. He served as organist of a number of London churches, as principal of the National Training School for Music, conductor of the Glasgow Choral Union, the Leeds Festival, and of the Philharmonic Society. He received the decoration of the Legion of Honor in 1878 and was knighted in 1883. He wrote several oratorios, many songs, a Festival Te Deum, a large number of hymn tunes, and the music for Sir W. S. Gilbert's light operas.

ART THOU WEARY, ART THOU LANGUID

1. Art thou weary, art thou languid,
Art thou sore distressed?
"Come to Me," saith One, "and coming
Be at rest."

2. Hath He marks to lead me to Him,
If He be my guide?
"In His feet and hands are wound-prints,
And His side."

3. Is there diadem, as Monarch,
That His brow adorns?
"Yea, a crown, in very surety;
But of thorns."

4. If I find Him, if I follow,
What His guerdon here?
"Many a sorrow, many a labor,
Many a tear."

5. If I still hold closely to Him,
What hath He at last?
"Sorrow vanquished, labor ended,
Jordan passed."

6. If I ask Him to receive me,
Will He say me nay?
"Not till earth, and not till heaven
Pass away."

7. Finding, following, keeping, struggling,
Is He sure to bless?

"Saints, apostles, prophets, martyrs,
Answer, Yes."

St. Stephen, the Sabaite, Eighth Century,
Translated by John M. Neale, 1862.

Biblical Text.

Come unto me, all ye that labor and are heavy laden, and I will give you rest.

Matthew 11:28.

THE WILDERNESS SHALL BREAK FORTH INTO SINGING

It was a most unusual chain of circumstances which led to the writing of "Art Thou Weary, Art Thou Languid." The first link was forged in the city of Damascus, about the end of the seventh century, when a prosperous citizen of that city was attracted to a fair-haired youth on sale in the slave market. He bought him, and later made him tutor for his son John. Years afterward this tutor-slave was given his freedom and retired to the Monastery of Mar Saba, in Palestine.

The second link is the romantic career of John. He became a high officer of state in Damascus, but was dissatisfied with the honors which came to him. After the former slave and foster-brother, Cosmas, had retired to Mar Saba, John followed him there and spent the last years of his life in the solitudes of the Kedron Valley. Here it was that he and Cosmas sang those songs which have made Mar Saba famous, among them, "The Day of Resurrection," and "Come, Ye Faithful, Raise the Strain." The former, by John of Damascus, is still sung every Easter in Greek Orthodox Churches.

The third link in the chain of circumstances concerns a ten-year-old lad, Stephen, a nephew of John. When John retired to Mar Saba, he took with him this little lad. There, in the quiet and seclusion of the monastery, Stephen grew up. There he heard the songs his uncle and Cosmas composed. There he fasted, did penance, spent hours in lonely vigils, and pondered deeply on the things of Christ. And there, in his old age, after uncle and friend had been taken away, he wrote this hymn.

The Monastery of Mar Saba is in the Wilderness of Judea, only about ten miles from Jerusalem, but far removed from the busy life of that city. Situated on a lofty cliff, one looks down from its walls five hundred feet to the silvery thread of the Kedron straight below. The rocks on either side of the gorge are almost perpendicular, and of a weird reddish hue; one is compelled to wonder how the monastery is able to cling, like an eagle's nest, to the very face of the cliff. The chapel is hewn out of the solid rock, and there, for more than a thousand years, the monks have held their daily and nightly services.

For the fourth link in this chain we must go to England, to an almshouse at East Grinstead called "Sackville College," to the study of the Warden of that "college." There we shall find the Reverend John M. Neale, working for the munificent salary of twenty-seven pounds a year, and spending his leisure hours delving into the treasure store of the ancient Greek and Latin hymns. One day Dr. Neale found, in the course of his researches, the words of Stephen's song, sung in old Mar Saba, more than eleven hundred years before. From these words in a dust-covered, ponderous, old Greek quarto, Dr. Neale has given to the Christian Church this hymn. It can hardly be called a translation, but rather a re-creation, for it has in it not only the experiences of Stephen the Sabaite, but also those of Dr. Neale. Combined, these make a text so simple, so dramatic, that it is one of the greatest English hymns.

An antiphonal hymn, it will be made more effective if used thus, by choir and congregation, or by minister and congregation, as a Responsive Service.

A Responsive Service

Minister (*reading*):

Come unto me, all ye that labor and are heavy laden, and I will give you rest. Take my yoke upon you and learn of me; for I am meek and lowly in heart; and ye shall find rest unto your souls. For my yoke is easy, and my burden is light.

MATTHEW 11:28–30.

Choir (singing):

Art thou weary, art thou languid,
Art thou sore distressed?

Congregation (singing):

"Come to me," saith One, "and coming
Be at rest."

Minister (*reading*):

Thomas said, Except I shall see in his hands the print of the nails, and put my hand into his side, I will not believe. And after eight days again his disciples were within, and Thomas with them. Jesus cometh, the doors being shut, and said, "Peace be unto you." Then saith he to Thomas, "Reach hither thy finger, and see my hands; and reach hither thy hand, and put it into my side: and be not faithless but believing." Thomas answered and said unto him, "My Lord and my God."

JOHN 20:25–28.

Choir (singing):

Hath He marks to lead me to Him,
If He be my guide?

Congregation (singing):

"In His feet and hands are wound-prints
And His side."

Minister (reading):

And the soldiers platted a crown of thorns, and put it on his head, and arrayed him in a purple garment; and they came unto him and said, "Hail, King of the Jews!"

JOHN 19:2, 3.

Congregation (singing):

Is there diadem, as Monarch,
That His brow adorns?
"Yea, a crown, in very surety,
But of thorns."

Minister (reading):

And Jesus said unto him, The foxes have holes, and the birds of the heaven have nests; but the Son of man hath not where to lay his head.

LUKE 9:58.

Ye shall weep and lament, but the world shall rejoice: ye shall be sorrowful, but your sorrow shall be turned into joy. In the world ye have tribulation: but be of good cheer; I have overcome the world.

JOHN 16:20, 33.

Choir or Solo Voice (singing):

If I find Him, if I follow,
What His guerdon here?
"Many a sorrow, many a labor,
Many a tear."

Minister (reading):

Let not your heart be troubled: . . . in my Father's house are many mansions; if it were not so I would have told you; for I go to prepare a place for you. And if I go and prepare a place for you, I will come again, and will receive you unto myself; that where I am, there ye may be also . . . I am the way, and the truth, and the life.

JOHN 14: 1–3, 6.

Choir (singing):

If I still hold closely to Him,
What hath He at last?

Congregation (singing):

"Sorrow vanquished, labor ended,
Jordan passed."

Minister (*reading*):

Him that cometh to me I will in no wise cast out.

JOHN 6: 37

Heaven and earth shall pass away, but my words shall not pass away.

MARK 13: 31

Choir (singing):

If I ask Him to receive me,
Will He say me Nay?

Congregation (singing):

"Not till earth, and not till heaven
Pass away."

Minister (*reading*):

These are they that come out of the great tribulation. . . . They shall hunger no more, neither thirst any more, . . . for the Lamb that is in the midst of the throne shall be their shepherd, and shall guide them unto fountains of waters of life: and God shall wipe away every tear from their eyes.

REVELATION 7: 14, 16, 17.

Therefore let us also, seeing we are compassed about with so great a cloud of witnesses, lay aside every weight, and the sin which doth so easily beset us, and let us run with patience the race that is set before us, looking unto Jesus, the author and perfecter of our faith, who for the joy that was set before him endured the cross, despising shame, and hath sat down at the right hand of the throne of God.

HEBREWS 12: 1, 2.

Choir and Congregation (singing):

Finding, following, keeping, struggling,
Is he sure to bless?
"Saints, apostles, prophets, martyrs,
Answer, 'Yes.'"

✣

The Hymn Tune. The tune Stephanos, named after St. Stephen of Mar Saba, was the work of Sir Henry Williams Baker (1821–1877), distinguished editor-in-chief of *Hymns Ancient and Modern* which, in its sale of over fifty million copies, attests to the accurate diagnosis of the needs of the English church during the nineteenth century and the determination and skill to provide for them. Editor supreme, captain of men under him, ruthless hymn mender and adjuster, a man of tremendous power, yet in his hymn, "The King of Love My Shepherd Is" and in this tune Stephanos how tender the man!

The tune structure is antiphonal, thus voicing the question and answer of the text. The tune fails however to mount into shouts of triumph and irresistible climax:

Finding, following, keeping, struggling,
Is he sure to bless?
"Saints, apostles, prophets, martyrs,
Answer, 'Yes.'"

Here an anthem setting is needed like Chadwick's in G minor and G major, a quartet or chorus supplying the brilliant music beginning with "Finding, following, keeping, struggling."

AS WITH GLADNESS MEN OF OLD

1. As with gladness men of old
Did the guiding star behold;
As with joy they hailed its light,
Leading onward, beaming bright;
So, most gracious Lord, may we
Evermore be led to thee.

2. As with joyful steps they sped
To that lowly manger-bed,
There to bend the knee before
Him whom heaven and earth adore;
So may we with willing feet
Ever seek thy mercy seat.

3. As they offered gifts most rare,
At that manger rude and bare,
So may we with holy joy,

Pure and free from sin's alloy,
All our costliest treasures bring,
Christ, to thee, our heavenly King.

4. Holy Jesus, every day
Keep us in the narrow way;
And, when earthly things are past,
Bring our ransomed souls at last
Where they need no star to guide,
Where no clouds thy glory hide.

WILLIAM C. DIX, 1861.

BIBLICAL TEXT.

Now when Jesus was born in Bethlehem of Judea in the days of Herod the King, behold, Wise-men from the east came to Jerusalem, saying, Where is he that is born King of the Jews? for we saw his star in the east, and are come to worship him.

MATTHEW 2:1, 2.

FOLLOWING THE STAR THROUGH THE HYMN BOOK

Since this is a layman's hymn, there is peculiar appropriateness in its beautiful tribute to the journey of those "laymen" of old, the Wise Men of the East, written, as it was, by a young layman of the West. The author was only twenty-three years of age when he wrote this hymn during his recovery from a serious illness. It is, therefore, a song in the night, a longing for more light and joy and power.

William Chatterton Dix (1837–1898) was born at Bristol, England, the son of a surgeon. He was trained for mercantile life, and held for many years the position of manager of a marine insurance company in Glasgow. Among the forty or more hymns he wrote, four will be found in many modern hymnals: "As with Gladness," "Alleluia, Sing to Jesus," "Joy Fills our Inmost Hearts Today," and "Come Unto Me, Ye Weary."

Laymen as Hymn Writers

Laymen have achieved distinction as hymn writers.

Prudentius (Lawyer and Judge)—"Now with creation's morning song."

Fortunatus (Troubadour)—"Welcome, happy morning."

John Byrom (Inventor of Shorthand)—"Christians, awake."

James Montgomery (Editor of a newspaper for thirty years)—"Hail to the Lord's anointed."

Robert Grant (Governor of Bombay—"O worship the King."

John Hay (Secretary of State)—"Not in dumb resignation."

Edward Osler (Surgeon)—"Praise the Lord, ye heavens, adore him."

James Edmeston (Architect and Surveyor)—"Saviour, breathe an evening blessing."

Rossiter Raymond (Mining Engineer)—"There's a beautiful star."

Harriet Beecher Stowe (Novelist)—"Still, still with thee."

Woodrow Wilson (A President of the United States)—hymn book editor.

Miss Caroline Bird Parker, writing from The Century Co. offices in New York City, says: "The history of the late President Wilson's share of work in the "In Excelsis" is brief but interesting. Both Mr. Wilson, who was then Professor of English at Princeton, and Reverend Maltbie D. Babcock, who was then pastor of the Brick Church here, were greatly interested in the scheme of the book. They went over the manuscript, made suggestions, and helped materially all through the editorial work. Toward the end of President Wilson's administration we made *The Army and Navy Hymnal,* and I had a beautiful letter from him stating that he had the greatest appreciation for the work we were doing."

Responsive Service

1. APOSTROPHE TO THE STAR

Leader (*reading*):

Brightest and best of the sons of the morning,
Dawn on our darkness and lend us thine aid;
Star of the East, the horizon adorning,
Guide where our infant Redeemer is laid.

REGINALD HEBER.

2. THE MAGI FOLLOW THE STAR

Solo:

We three kings of Orient are,
Bearing gifts, we traverse afar
Field and fountain, moor and mountain,
Following yonder star.

Congregation (singing):

O star of wonder, star of light,
Star with royal beauty bright,
Westward leading, still proceeding,
Guide us to thy perfect light.

JOHN HOPKINS.

3. THE STAR DRAWS NIGH TO BETHLEHEM

Congregation (singing):

This star drew nigh to the northwest,
O'er Bethlehem it took its rest,
And there it did both stop and stay,
Right over the place where Jesus lay.
Noel, Noel, Noel, Noel,
Born is the King of Israel.

TRADITIONAL.

4. THE STAR AT THE BIRTHDAY OF A KING

Congregation (singing):

There's a song in the air,
There's a star in the sky,
There's a mother's deep prayer,
And a baby's low cry.
And the star reigns its fire while the beautiful sing,
For the manger of Bethlehem cradles a King.

JOSIAH HOLLAND.

5. HAIL THE STAR! WORSHIP THE BABE!

Unison reading:

Come, then, let us hasten yonder,
Here let all, great and small,
Kneel in awe and wonder;
Love him who with love is yearning,
Hail the star, that from far
Bright with hope is burning.

PAUL GERHARDT.

6. FOLLOWING THE STAR AND BRINGING GIFTS.

Unison reading or Solo Voice:

We would see Jesus, lo! his star is shining
Above the stable while the angels sing;
There in a manger on the hay reclining,
Haste, let us lay our gifts before the King.

J. EDGAR PARK.

7. THE STAR IN ALL AGES AND IN ALL LANDS.

Congregation (singing):

In the light of that star
Lie the ages impearled;
And that song from afar

Has swept over the world:
Every hearth is aflame, and the beautiful sing
In the homes of the nations that Jesus is King![1]

JOSIAH HOLLAND.

✣

THE HYMN TUNE. A German Chorale, written about 1838, DIX is effective with these words. Although Mr. Dix protested against its being named after him, saying, "I dislike it, I did not christen it," the tune which bears his name has survived nearly seventy years of intimate association with his words, and seems likely to continue to live in this happy "married state." See page 101 for Conrad Kocher, arranger of the tune.

It has brightness, movement, and an attractive rhythm, which seems to express the thought of gladness and joy welling up through the words. It also gives opportunity for thoughtful prayer in the quieting music of the last bar.

The Original Melody: Treuer Heiland — wir sind hier

AT LENGTH THERE DAWNS THE GLORIOUS DAY

1. At length there dawns the glorious day
By prophets long foretold;
At length the chorus clearer grows
That shepherds heard of old.
The day of dawning brotherhood
Breaks on our eager eyes,
And human hatreds flee before
The radiant eastern skies.

2. For what are sundering strains of blood,
Or ancient caste and creed?
One claim unites all men in Christ
To serve each human need.
Then here together, brother men,
We pledge the Lord anew
Our loyal love, our stalwart faith,
Our service strong and true.

3. One common faith unites us all,
We seek one common goal;
One tender comfort broods upon
The struggling human soul.
To this clear call of brotherhood
Our hearts responsive ring;
We join the glorious new crusade
Of our great Lord and King.

OZORA STEARNS DAVIS, 1909.

BIBLICAL TEXT.

For ye are all sons of God, through faith, in Christ Jesus.

GALATIANS 3:26.

Ye are no more strangers and sojourners, but ye are fellow-citizens with the saints, and of the household of God.

EPHESIANS 2:19.

SINGING THE NEW CRUSADE OF BROTHERHOOD

Ozora Stearns Davis (1866–1931) was born in Wheelock, Vermont, and spent his boyhood in White River Junction, a railroad town, where he mastered telegraphy, and at fifteen was an expert operator. He attended St. Johnsbury Academy and Dartmouth College, graduating in 1889. A Hartford Theological Seminary fellowship enabled him to study at the University of Leipzig. After holding pastorates in Springfield, Vermont, in Newtonville, Massachusetts, and New Britain, Connecticut, he was called in 1909 to the presidency of the Chicago Theological Seminary, a position which he held through twenty years. In 1927 he was elected Moderator of the National Council of Congregational Churches.

Dr. Davis (PH.D. Leipzig, D.D. Dartmouth, LL.D. Colorado College and Washburn College) was the author of about fifteen books, including, *John Robinson, the Pilgrim Pastor; International Aspects of Christianity; Comrades in the Great Cause,* and *Preaching the Social Gospel.*

In the summer of 1909, Dr. Davis was walking in the woods near his summer home, on the shore of Lake Sunapee, New Hampshire, and thinking of the coming meeting of the National Congregational Brotherhood at Minneapolis. His great desire "to express the inner meaning of Christian brotherhood as the unifying force in humanity," finally shaped itself into this hymn. First printed in a small pamphlet with other hymns for use at the Convention, it has found its way, in twenty years, into most hymnals.

The Hymn Tune. All Saints was composed for "The Son of God Goes Forth to War" by Henry Stephen Cutler (1824–1902), an American organist and choir director. He was organist at St. Paul's Cathedral, Boston, and later at Trinity Church, New York. While at the Church of the Advent, Boston, in 1856, Dr. Cutler was the first American choirmaster to introduce a vested boys' choir. In 1860 in Trinity Church, New York, on the occasion of the visit of the Prince of Wales, he was the first to introduce the robing of the choir in cassock and cotta and to seat them in the chancel. Heretofore the boys and men had sung outside of the chancel and in citizen's dress. Dr. Cutler had made a special study of the use of vestments in the English cathedrals. His bold action turned the tide of opinion in favor of a more churchly tradition.

BEFORE JEHOVAH'S AWFUL THRONE

1. Before Jehovah's awful throne,
Ye nations, bow with sacred joy;
Know that the Lord is God alone;
He can create, and he destroy.

2. His sovereign power, without our aid,
Made us of clay, and formed us men;
And when like wandering sheep we strayed,
He brought us to his fold again.

3. We are his people, we his care,
Our souls, and all our mortal frame;
What lasting honors shall we rear,
Almighty Maker, to thy name?

4. We'll crowd thy gates with thankful songs,
High as the heavens our voices raise;
And earth, with her ten thousand tongues,
Shall fill thy courts with sounding praise.

5. Wide as the world is thy command,
Vast as eternity thy love;
Firm as a rock thy truth must stand,
When rolling years shall cease to move.

Isaac Watts, 1719.

Biblical Text.

Make a joyful noise unto the Lord, all ye lands.
Serve the Lord with gladness:
Come before his presence with singing,
Know ye, that the Lord, he is God;
It is he that hath made us, and we are his;
We are his people, and the sheep of his pasture.
Enter into his gates with thanksgiving,

And into his courts with praise:
Give thanks unto him, and bless his name.
For the Lord is good; his lovingkindness endureth forever,
And his faithfulness unto all generations.

PSALM 100.

SOUNDING PRAISE IN THE COURTS OF OUR LORD

An invitation from a former Lord Mayor of London for a week's visit at his country home, which lengthened into thirty-seven years, gave to an invalid minister, obliged to resign his pastorate, the chance to become an eminent writer, the Father of English Hymnody.

Isaac Watts (1674–1748) was the son of a Dissenting Deacon of Southampton in the days when dissent was a crime. His own and his parents' staunch adherence to principle is revealed in their refusal of a generous offer from a friend to finance his education, provided he would become a priest of the Church of England. At the age of twenty-four he was ordained assistant pastor of the Independent Chapel, Mark Lane, London, and soon became its pastor. But he was obliged to resign on account of ill-health.

The forlorn bachelor was invited to the palatial home of Sir Thomas and Lady Abney. Isaac Watts himself says: "This day thirty years I came hither to the home of my good friend, Sir Thomas Abney, intending to spend but one single week under his friendly roof, and I have extended my visit to the length of exactly thirty years."

"Watts measured only about five feet in height, and was of a slender form. His complexion was pale and fair, his eyes small and gray, but when animated, became piercing and expressive; his forehead was low, his cheek bones rather prominent; but his countenance was, on the whole, by no means disagreeable. His voice was pleasant, but weak. A stranger would, probably, have been most attracted by his piercing eye, whose very glance was able to command attention and awe."

It was in the quiet refinement and beauty of Abney Park that Isaac Watts did his life work as an author. His learned dissertations on Logic, Philosophy and Science are largely forgotten, though they were masterful treatises for the time. It is as a hymn-writer that Watts is remembered. Even now, nearly two centuries after his death, more of Isaac Watts' hymns are to be found in our modern hymnals than those of any other author.

Montgomery, himself a hymnist of wide reputation, calls Watts "the greatest name among hymn writers." Dr. Johnson says, "He has provided instruction for all ages—from those who are lisping their first lessons, to the enlightened readers of Malebranche and Locke; he has left neither corporeal nor spiritual nature unexamined; he has taught us the art of reasoning and the science of the stars."

Remembering that metrical versions of the Psalms formed the only material for congregational singing in the time of Watts, we marvel at the courage of this frail man in attempting to bring "the royal author, David, into the common affairs of the Christian life," and even more, to substitute hymns of his own composition for the *Psalms of David.*

Analysis: It has been said that a characteristic feature of the hymns of Watts is his overwhelming sense of God's holiness. This is particularly evident in this hymn.

First Stanza: We are indebted to John Wesley for the thought-compelling opening lines, a real improvement over Watts' words,

"Nations attend before his throne,
With solemn fear, with sacred joy."

And also the omission of this entire stanza:

Sing to the Lord with joyful voice,
Let every land his name adore;
The British isles shall send the noise
Across the ocean to the shore.

Second Stanza: "His sovereign power"—another emphasis on Watts' conception of the greatness and grandeur of God, his majesty and sublimity. Yet the stanza closes with tenderness, for this same Majestic God is now a Seeking Shepherd, bringing the straying sheep back to the fold.

Third Stanza: Because "we are his people" it is but natural that we, with Watts, should ask how we may worthily praise his name.

Fourth Stanza: "Earth, with her ten thousand tongues," is a peculiarly appropriate phrase from a man who could write a treatise on the stars, and who dwelt in the beauty of an English country estate.

Fifth Stanza: The hymn mounts to a majestic climax in this final stanza. The splendid dignity of each opening phrase should be noted and fully appreciated and full values be given to the words "wide," "vast," "firm."

Compare this paraphrase of the "One Hundredth Psalm" with the Psalm itself and also with the older work by William Kethe, "All people that on earth do dwell."

The Hymn Tune. The tune Park Street, by F. M. A. Venua (1788–1872), is a favorite of long standing in America, though little known in England. Frederick Marco Antonia Venua was one of the oldest members of the Royal Society of Musicians. In 1858 he retired to Exeter after an active musical life.

BENEATH THE CROSS OF JESUS

1. Beneath the cross of Jesus
I fain would take my stand,
The shadow of a mighty rock
Within a weary land;
A home within the wilderness,
A rest upon the way,
From the burning of the noon-tide heat,
And the burden of the day.

2. Upon that cross of Jesus
Mine eye at times can see
The very dying form of One
Who suffered there for me;
And from my smitten heart with tears
Two wonders I confess,—
The wonders of his glorious love,
And my unworthiness.

3. I take, O cross, thy shadow
For my abiding place;
I ask no other sunshine than
The sunshine of his face;
Content to let the world go by,
To know no gain nor loss,
My sinful self my only shame,
My glory all the cross.

Elizabeth C. Clephane, 1868.

Biblical Text.
And they sat and watched him there.

Matthew 27:36.

"BREATHING ON THE BORDER"

Elizabeth Cecilia Douglas Clephane (1830–1869) was as a child fond of poetry. With a younger sister she held "literary séances." Blessed with a vivid imagination she improvised thrilling stories with hairbreadth escapes. Gentle and generous, she was known among the poor and suffering in Melrose, Scotland, as "The Sunbeam." She spent all her income, beyond her meager needs, on charity. She is remembered for two significant hymns. "The Ninety and Nine" was made famous by Ira D. Sankey, through his use of it in the Moody-Sankey meetings in Scotland in 1873 and '74. The other, "Beneath the Cross of

Jesus," appeared only a year before Miss Clephane's death at the age of thirty-nine. Written, doubtless, in the midst of pain and suffering, it breathes a spirit of confident trust and definite assurance which has made it live.

All of Miss Clephane's hymns were published by William Arnot, under the title, "Breathing On the Border." An introduction explains the caption: "Written on the very edge of this life, with the better land fully in view of faith, they seem to us footsteps printed on the sands of time, where these sands touch the ocean of eternity. These footsteps of one whom the Good Shepherd led through the wilderness into rest, may contribute to comfort and direct succeeding pilgrims."

This hymn is a commentary on Isaiah's prophecy of a "Man" who should be "as the shade of a great rock in a weary land," coupled with the story of Calvary.

Analysis. First Stanza: "The mighty rock," affording a cooling shade and welcome shelter from "the burning heat," is illustrated in the last picture painted by William L. Taylor, "The Shadow of a Mighty Rock." It should be studied in connection with this stanza.

Dr. George Adam Smith suggests that the "great rock in a weary land" is of value not only as a shade from the "burning heat," but also in that it "stops the drift" of the ever-shifting sands. It was Christ alone among the great men of the ages who successfully withstood all the "drifts" of the smothering sands of sin, and in the shelter of whose life other lives are given the chance to grow.

Second Stanza: "Two wonders"—striking and startling contrast, "His glorious love," "my unworthiness." The white light of the Cross is starkly revealing!

Third Stanza: "My abiding place." Quiet and content, trusting not in the merits of self, nor the accomplishments of one's own life, but wholly and solely in the sacrificial life and death of the Saviour—this is Miss Clephane's "swan-song."

Hymns in the Night

From Persecution—"Ye Servants of God."
From Prison—"All Glory, Laud and Honor."
From War—"I Heard the Bells on Christmas Day."
From Invalidism—"Lord, Speak to Me that I May Speak."
From Blindness—"Pass Me Not, O Gentle Saviour."
From Shipwreck—"Brightly Beams Our Father's Mercy."

THE HYMN TUNE. ST. CHRISTOPHER, by Frederick Charles Maker (1844–1927), was written for these words by an organist who spent all of his life, eighty-three years, in one city, Bristol, England, and seventy-five of these years as a singer and organist.

BLEST BE THE TIE THAT BINDS

1. Blest be the tie that binds
Our hearts in Christian love;
The fellowship of kindred minds
Is like to that above.

2. Before our Father's throne
We pour our ardent prayers;
Our fears, our hopes, our aims are one,
Our comforts and our cares.

3. We share our mutual woes,
Our mutual burdens bear,
And often for each other flows
The sympathizing tear.

4. When we asunder part,
It gives us inward pain;
But we shall still be joined in heart,
And hope to meet again.

JOHN FAWCETT, 1782.

BIBLICAL TEXT.

If we walk in the light . . . we have fellowship one with another.

I JOHN 1:7.

A new commandment I give unto you, that ye love one another; even as I have loved you, that ye also love one another. By this shall all men know that ye are my disciples, if ye have love one to another.

JOHN 13:34, 35.

A TIE THAT BOUND FOR FIFTY YEARS

Wainsgate, a Yorkshire village, was mourning because the minister was moving. A call had come to a much larger church in London; he was to be the successor of the noted expositor, Dr. Gill. The salary paid by the village church, two hundred dollars a year, was altogether too small for the needs of his growing family, so the move seemed to be the natural, in fact, the only thing to do. The men were loading the wagons with the minister's furniture and books; they had come to the last load. All around the wagons the men and women and children of Wainsgate were weeping over the loss of their beloved pastor. Seated on one of the packing cases, the pastor and his wife could not restrain their tears. At last the wife said, "John, I cannot bear this! I know not how to go!" And the pastor replied, "Nor I either. Nor will we go; unload the wagons, and put everything in the place where it was before."

And so, out of a genuine Christian love for their people, they stayed at the little Baptist church to which Fawcett's conversion at the age of sixteen through a sermon of George Whitefield's had indirectly led him.

Out of this experience John Fawcett (1740–1817) wrote from his heart the hymn which has made him known wherever Christians meet and sing—"Blest be the tie that binds."

Although like Chaucer's and Goldsmith's poor parsons, he preferred to remain the pastor of an obscure country parish in England, Fawcett was honored with the degree of Doctor of Divinity by Brown University in 1811.

This gentle and neighborly hymn, sung year in and year out, over the English-speaking world, has had great power in making for charity, harmony and happiness of life.

✣

THE HYMN TUNE. Hans G. Naegali (1768–1836), the composer of DENNIS, was born at Wetezikon, near Zurich. He was a music publisher there and President of the Swiss Association for the Cultivation of Music. He published much of Beethoven's music, including three of his piano sonatas. It is rumored that he actually succeeded in interpolating four measures into one of the sonata movements. Pardoned for his crime, he continued on most affectionate terms with the great Master.

DENNIS and NAOMI were two tunes purchased by Lowell Mason while in Europe in 1837, and brought back with him to enrich his hymn books.

BOYLSTON, by Lowell Mason (1792–1872), was named after the town of Boylston, Massachusetts. Mason was the father of American church music. Largely self-educated, he owed his unquestioned success to perseverance, energy, and enthusiasm. He introduced the Pestalozzian system into his public-school music teaching. His teacher's conventions drew musicians from all over the nation. His hymn tunes, while lacking in originality and power, are straightforward and easy to sing.

BREAK THOU THE BREAD OF LIFE

1. Break thou the bread of life,
Dear Lord, to me,
As thou didst break the loaves
Beside the sea;
Beyond the sacred page
I seek thee, Lord;
My spirit pants for thee,
O living Word!

2. Bless thou the truth, dear Lord,
To me, to me,
As thou didst bless the bread
By Galilee;
Then shall all bondage cease,
All fetters fall;
And I shall find my peace,
My All-in-All.[1]

MARY A. LATHBURY, 1877.

BIBLICAL TEXT.

And he took the five loaves and the two fishes, and looking up to heaven, he blessed and brake, and gave the loaves to the disciples, and the disciples to the multitudes.

MATTHEW 14:19.

And ye shall know the truth, and the truth shall make you free.

JOHN 8:32.

I am the bread of life: he that cometh to me shall not hunger.

JOHN 6:35.

Blessed are they that hunger and thirst after righteousness for they shall be filled.

MATTHEW 5:6.

THE POET LAUREATE OF CHAUTAUQUA

Mary A. Lathbury spent the summer of 1877 at the then new religious resort and summer school, Chautauqua, on Chautauqua Lake, New York. It had been started by Bishop John H. Vincent and his friend, Mr. Lewis H. Miller, three years before.

This seemingly trivial fact has had significance not for Chautauqua alone, but for the whole Christian church; for it was during that summer that Dr. Vincent asked Miss Lathbury to write two hymns for Chautauqua. This she did: the first was a "Vesper Hymn" for use in the unique Sunday Vesper Service on the shore of the lake, "Day is Dying in the West." The other was a "Study Hymn," "Break Thou the Bread of Life," for the rapidly extending "Chautauqua Literary and Scientific Circle." The "C. L. S. C." with its wide-awake courses

[1] Copyright by the Chautauqua Press.

of study still continues its advance throughout the world, numbering among its graduates each year men and women of distinction. The class of 1930 graduated Mr. and Mrs. Thomas A. Edison.

Miss Mary Artemisia Lathbury (1841–1913) was the daughter of a Methodist minister. She studied art at Worcester, Massachusetts, and taught drawing, painting and French in Newbury Academy, Vermont, and in New York. She was a frequent contributor to *St. Nicholas, Harper's Young People* and *Wide Awake*. Frances E. Willard said of her: "A high courageous faith, a loyalty to the best ideals, and a devotion to the truth that gave inspiration to all with whom she came in contact, characterized 'our Mary.' "

ANALYSIS. "Break Thou the Bread of Life" is a true lyric. It has the brevity, balance, fervor, poise and clear integrity of an abiding work of art.

First Stanza: A picture of that late afternoon scene on the grassy hillside sloping up from Galilee, when the Master of men broke the five loaves and the two tiny fishes and gave food to his disciples to distribute to the multitude. And "five thousand men, beside women and children" were fed from the lad's meager lunch! But that is not enough for the eagerly seeking soul. Not satisfied with a mere historic Christ recorded on "the sacred page," the eager inquirer for truth seeks a "living Word," as truly present now as by Galilee of old.

Second Stanza: C. L. S. C. students were usually busy, often handicapped folks who had missed many opportunities. So for them the singer prays, "Bless thou the truth." Bless this new truth which comes with all the force of a new relevation, which comes to set men free from the bondage of superstition, to break all the fetters of ignorance. And the blessed result of such reverent search for the fullness of the truth will be calm and rest and peace; for in that truth will be found him who is "The Way and the Truth and the Life" and therefore, "All-in-All."

This hymn has become the common property of all Christians. It is frequently used as an introduction to the sermon by ministers, and quite commonly as a prelude to the distribution of the bread in the service of the Lord's Supper.

✣

THE HYMN TUNE. This is one of William Fiske Sherwin's (1826–1888) tunes, written at Chautauqua. He was all that was lovable and witty and devout. Such a genial personality won for him a great host of warm friends. In his own family there was nothing but the most whole-hearted and unquestioning adoration for husband and father. There is a Sherwin memorial window in the little church at Buckland, Massachusetts, where he was born; it is also the birthplace of Mary Lyon.

He was at one time musical editor for Bigelow and Main. As director of music at Chautauqua, New York, he conducted large choirs, led the mighty amphitheater audiences, and wrote his best hymn tunes for the Lathbury poems. For the Recognition Day Service which has been used through fifty-five consecutive years, Sherwin wrote:

"Sing pæans over the past" (sung as the C. L. S. C. classes pass through the Golden Gate and under the arches),

C. L. S. C. Anniversary Ode—"Bright gleams again Chautauqua's wave,"

Night Song—"All the earth is wrapped in shadow,"

Alumni Song—"Join, O friends, in a Memory Song,"

And the two Vesper Hour tunes—CHAUTAUQUA for "Day is dying in the West," and BREAD OF LIFE, for "Break thou the Bread of Life."

INTERPRETATION. This hymn is one of the shortest in the English language, seventy-one words. At moderate pace it takes just seventy-five seconds to sing it entire. It is intense, full of varied colors, contrasts of tone and time. The white notes should be held full length with increase of tone throughout each one. Toward the close of each stanza both mounting music and triumphant words override the meditation for the moment—first in "I seek thee, Lord," and second in "Then shall all bondage cease, all fetters fall."

BREATHE ON ME, BREATH OF GOD

1. Breathe on me, Breath of God,
Fill me with life anew,
That I may love what thou dost love,
And do what thou wouldst do.

2. Breathe on me, Breath of God,
Until my heart is pure,
Until with thee I will one will,
To do or to endure.

3. Breathe on me, Breath of God,
Till I am wholly thine,
Till all this earthly part of me
Glows with thy fire divine.

4. Breathe on me, Breath of God,
So shall I never die,
But live with thee the perfect life
Of thine eternity.

EDWIN HATCH, 1886.

BIBLICAL TEXT.

The Spirit of God hath made me,
And the breath of the Almighty giveth me life.

JOB 33:4.

And when he had said this, he breathed on them
and saith unto them, Receive ye the Holy Spirit.

JOHN 20:22

EASTER EVENING IN THE UPPER ROOM

That scene in some "Upper Room" in old Jerusalem on that first Easter evening is made to live again in the lines of Dr. Hatch's hymn. Through this quiet prayer of the heart one can almost feel the tenseness of that moment of awe, wonder and deepest joy, when the eleven beheld their Risen Lord and heard his uttered benediction, "Peace be unto you."

Edwin Hatch (1835–1889) was an Anglican clergyman and professor of the classics in English and Canadian Universities. He was one of the few English clergyman to win a European reputation for original research. He was master in historical investigations. Harnack translated his Bampton lectures into German and said of him: "In his learning that of England's great old theologians, Ussher and Pearson, lived to me again. He was a glorious man, whose loss I shall never cease to mourn." For three years he was professor of the classics in Trinity College, Toronto. Returning to England, he became Vice-Principal of St. Mary's Hall, Oxford. He was a man of deep piety, of virile faith, and of broad sympathies, as the following lines of his on heaven indicate:

"Some seek a heaven for rest,
And some an ample shore
For doing work they cannot do
While they are prisoned here.

Some seek a heaven of song,
And others fain would rise
From an articulate utterance
To silent ecstasies.

Some seek a home in heaven,
And some would pray to be

Alone with God, beyond the reach
Of other company.

But in God's perfect heaven
All aspirations meet,
Each separate longing is fulfilled
Each separate soul complete."

ANALYSIS. A definite, direct prayer, this hymn should always be sung thoughtfully and quietly as a real prayer in sincere devotion and genuine aspiration.

First Stanza: "Life anew," "love," "do," the doing must be preceded by the loving and that in turn by the "filling."

Second Stanza: The union of the human will with the divine is a natural result of the "breathing of the Breath of God."

Third Stanza: Compare with *Psalm* 34: 5—"they looked unto him and were radiant." It is interesting in this connection to read again the story of Pentecost. (*Acts* 2.)

Fourth Stanza: Immortality is assured through union of the individual soul with the "perfect life" of the "Breath of God."

In connection with this hymn, read the creation of life in Genesis and compare with Michelangelo's "Creation of Man" on the ceiling of the Sistine Chapel.

"These are the generations of the heavens and of the earth when they were created, in the day that the Lord God made the earth and the heavens. And every plant of the field before it was in the earth, and every herb of the field before it grew: for the Lord God had not caused it to rain upon the earth, and there was not a man to till the ground. But there went up a mist from the earth, and watered the whole face of the ground. And the Lord God formed man out of the dust of the ground, and *breathed* into his nostrils the breath of life; and man became a *living* soul." (King James Version.)

The Life of Christ in Hymns and Carols

The life of the Master has captivated the poet and hymn-writer through the years, the miracle of his personality, the incidents in his life, the dramatic climaxes. Following is a brief outline story of Jesus told in hymns and carols:

Prophecy—"Hail to the Lord's anointed."
Nativity—"Hark, the herald angels sing."
Epiphany—"Brightest and best of the sons."
Boyhood—"O, Master workman of the race."
The Call of the Disciples—"Jesus calls us o'er the tumult."
The Ministry of Healing—"Thine arm, O Lord, in days of old."
The Ministry of Teaching—"Thou didst teach the thronging people."

The Ministry of Comfort—"When the Lord of love was here."
Master and Disciples—"In the hour of trial."
The Parables—"Love for all and can it be."
Going up to Jerusalem—"Ride on, ride on, in majesty."
The Last Supper—"Break thou the bread of life."
Gethsemane—" 'Tis midnight and on Olive's brow."
Tragedy and Triumph—"When I survey the wondrous cross."
Easter Morning—"Christ the Lord is risen today."
Easter Evening—"Breathe on me, breath of God."
The Ascension—"Look, ye saints, the sight is glorious."
The Missionary Christ—"Christ for the world we sing."

✣

THE HYMN TUNE. TRENTHAM was composed by Robert Jackson (1842–1914) of Oldham, England. St. Peter's Church of Oldham has the very unique distinction of having had father and son in charge of its music as organist and choir director for over ninety years! Robert Jackson, in addition to the instruction of his father, studied at the Royal Academy of Music. He was a member for some time of the famous Halle Symphony Orchestra at Birmingham.

CHRIST FOR THE WORLD WE SING

1. Christ for the world we sing;
The world to Christ we bring,
With loving zeal;
The poor and them that mourn,
The faint and over-borne;
Sin-sick and sorrow-worn,
Whom Christ doth heal.

2. Christ for the world we sing;
The world to Christ we bring,
With fervent prayer;
The wayward and the lost,
By restless passion tossed,
Redeemed at countless cost,
From dark despair.

3. Christ for the world we sing;
The world to Christ we bring,
With one accord;
With us the work to share,
With us reproach to dare,
With us the cross to bear,
For Christ, our Lord.

4. Christ for the world we sing,
The world to Christ we bring,
With joyful song;
The new-born souls, whose days,
Reclaimed from error's ways,
Inspired with hope and praise,
To Christ belong.

SAMUEL WOLCOTT, 1869.

BIBLICAL TEXT.

Also the foreigners, that join themselves to the Lord, to minister unto him, and to love the name of the Lord, to be his servants, every one that . . . holdeth fast my covenant; even them will I bring to my holy mountain, and make them joyful in my house of prayer; . . . for my house shall be called a house of prayer for all peoples.

ISAIAH 56:6, 7.

And other sheep I have, which are not of this fold; them also I must bring, and they shall hear my voice; and they shall become one flock, one shepherd.

JOHN 10:16.

AN EVERGREEN MOTTO

An evergreen motto over the platform of the church in Cleveland, Ohio, where the State Y. M. C. A. Convention of 1869 was held, inspired this missionary hymn. That motto read: "Christ for the world, and the world for Christ." As a delegate to the convention, a pastor's heart was mightily stirred by this slogan. Later, walking home through the streets of Cleveland, he put the motto into hymnic form.

Reverend Samuel Wolcott (1813–1886), after graduating from Andover Theological Seminary in 1837, sailed for Syria as a missionary; but ill health forced him to return to the United States after two years' service. He held pastorates in Belchertown, Massachusetts, in Providence, Rhode Island, and Cleveland, Ohio.

The hymn's description of those who are to be brought to Christ makes touching and soul-stirring poetry for the church to sing and to ponder: "The poor and them that mourn; the faint and over-borne; sin-sick and sorrow-worn." Perhaps Mr. Wolcott was thinking of those needy souls whom he had known in his service in Syria; perhaps of the needs of his own congregation in Cleveland; perhaps of some specific needs of the young men of Ohio, referred to in the convention he had just attended. Who knows? But the words fit every land and every time. And it is quite remarkable that, in a day when the line of demarcation between Home and Foreign Missions was clear and emphatic, there should be produced a missionary hymn so completely universal in its character.

The hymn moves steadily forward from the conception of the "sin-sick, the wayward and the lost," "redeemed, at countless cost, from dark despair," till these who are thus brought to Christ are eagerly "sharing the work," "daring reproach" and "bearing the cross," recognizing that their days "inspired with hope and praise" "to Christ belong."

✣

THE HYMN TUNE. The ITALIAN HYMN to which this hymn is frequently sung, was composed by Felice de Giardini (1716–1796), an eminent Italian violinist, director and composer. He spent many years in London, part of the time as leader of the Italian Opera there. Although he received large sums of money for his services, he was always poor. He once replied to a question as to the reason for this: "My dear sir, I candidly confess to you that I never in my life had five guineas in my pocket, but I was in a fever till they were gone." It is said that it was partly these spendthrift habits which gave this tune to the world. A hymn book was being compiled; Giardini was in great distress financially; so he wrote tunes for the new hymnal and was paid handsomely for his work. The general capricious character and splenetic disposition of Giardini were his undoing through life. He spoke well of few, and quarreled with many of his most valued friends. Nothing but his very superior musical talents could have upheld him during the time he was in favor with the public. Careless of his own interest, and inattentive to all those means which would have promoted his success in the world, he at length sank under misfortunes of his own creating, and died in Moscow, 1796, weighed down by penury and distress.

The three-four count of the ITALIAN HYMN suggests the perfect time of medieval chorus singing, symbolic of the three persons of the Trinity.

See musical interpretation under "Come Thou Almighty King."

CHRIST IN HIS WORD DRAWS NEAR

1. Christ in his word draws near;
Hush, moaning voice of fear,
He bids thee cease;
With songs sincere and sweet
Let us arise, and meet
Him who comes forth to greet
Our souls with peace.

2. Rising above thy care,
Meet him as in the air,
O weary heart;
Put on joy's sacred dress;
Lo, as he comes to bless,
Quite from thy weariness
Set free thou art.

3. For works of love and praise
He brings thee summer days,
Warm days and bright;
Winter is past and gone,
Now he, salvation's Sun,
Shineth on every one
With mercy's light.

4. From the bright sky above,
Clad in his robes of love,
'Tis he, our Lord!
Dim earth itself grows clear
As his light draweth near;
O let us hush and hear
His holy Word.

THOMAS TOKE LYNCH, 1855.

BIBLICAL TEXT.

The opening of thy words giveth light;
It giveth understanding unto the simple.

PSALM 119:130.

Every scripture inspired of God is also profitable for teaching, for reproof, for correction, for instruction which is in righteousness, that the man of God may be complete, furnished completely unto every good work.

II TIMOTHY 3: 16, 17.

CHRIST COMES FORTH FROM HIS HOLY WORD

Thomas Toke Lynch (1818–1871) was a Nonconformist English minister. Throughout his entire life he labored under the handicap of ill-health. For many years he had only sufficient strength to preach one sermon on Sunday, but he always wrote another for the evening service, and had it read to the congregation by a friend. His was the type so vividly described by Henry Ward Beecher as "a sharp and glittering sword which cuts through the scabbard of the poor flesh holding him." Something of that bodily condition is, perhaps, reflected in the second line of this hymn.

He ministered to several small churches in London in succession. He was never a popular preacher, yet "he gathered round him by the individuality, freshness and spirituality of his pulpit work a congregation of thoughtful and devoted people."

In 1855 Lynch published a little volume of hymns of his own composition under the title, *The Rivulet; a Contribution to Sacred Song.* "Christian poetry is indeed a river of the water of life, and to this river my rivulet brings its contribution."

Lynch wrote:

"See him in the street,
Serve him in the shop,
Sow with him thy wheat,
House for him thy crop.
Sail with him at sea,
Work with him on land;
Tell him faithfully
All that thou hast planned."

Spurgeon denounced Lynch and his hymns. The poet met the attack with sweetness of spirit. "The air will be all the clearer for this storm," he said. "We must conquer our foes, by suffering them to crucify us, rather than by threatening them with crucifixion." A musician as well as a poet, he composed tunes for his hymns and at his death was heard humming one of them to "Guide me, O thou great Jehovah." His last words were, "Now I am going to begin to live."

If the average Sunday morning congregation in the average church could somehow sense the real and deep significance of this hymn, what a different attitude the congregation would have toward the Scripture Lesson; what an opportunity to gain freedom from "weariness," "the moaning voice of fear," the coldness of spiritual "winter." Lynch closes his hymn with an exclamation and appeal, "O let us hush and hear his holy Word."

THE HYMN TUNE. Edward Bunnett (1834–1923), who wrote the tune KIRBY BEDON, was trained in Norfolk Cathedral under Dr. Zechariah Buck. For many years he was conductor of the Norwich Musical Union, organist of the Norwich Musical Festival and borough organist. In 1849 he sang at the Norwich Musical Festival in the trio, "Lift up Thine Eyes," with Jenny Lind and Miss Dolby. His musical "jubilee" was celebrated in Norwich in 1896 by a testimonial from his fellow-citizens and an address from the Mayor. His musical publications include cantatas, anthems, carols, organ selections and "Twenty-four Original Tunes to Favorite Hymns."

This tune is also used with "Shepherd of Tender Youth."

CHRIST THE LORD IS RISEN TODAY

1. "Christ the Lord is risen today,"
Sons of men and angels say;
Raise your joys and triumphs high,
Sing, ye heavens, and earth reply.
Alleluia!

2. Lives again our glorious King:
Where, O death, is now thy sting?
Dying once, he all doth save:
Where thy victory, O grave?
Alleluia!

3. Love's redeeming work is done,
Fought the fight, the battle won;
Death in vain forbids him rise;
Christ has opened Paradise.
Alleluia!

4. Soar we now, where Christ has led,
Following our exalted Head;
Made like him, like him we rise,
Ours the cross, the grave, the skies.
Alleluia![1]

CHARLES WESLEY, 1739.

BIBLICAL TEXT.

O death, where is thy sting? O grave, where is thy victory? The sting of death is sin; and the power of sin is the law; but thanks be to God, who giveth us the victory through our Lord Jesus Christ.

I CORINTHIANS 15: 55, 56, 57.

A HALLELUJAH HYMN FOR EIGHTEENTH-CENTURY METHODISTS

Charles Wesley's contribution through his hymns to the progress of the Evangelical Revival of the eighteenth century was a close to the organizing and preaching ability of his more famous brother, John. He wrote the surprising total of over six thousand hymns! For every hundred hymns written by Isaac Watts, Charles Wesley wrote a thousand. In this lengthy list there is hardly a text of the Bible which has not a hymn to fit it. Fifty-six hymn books and hymn tracts were published by the Wesleys through a period of fifty-three years.

The youngest of eighteen Wesley or Wellesley children born in a country rectory, Charles Wesley knew what poverty was. Moreover, the experiences of persecution and difficulty in his later life were by no means easy. With this somewhat somber background, the well-nigh universal note of joy and gladness, of confident trust and assurance of victory running through his hymns, seems all the more remarkable.

[1] From the poem "The Easter Children" in the book by Elsa Barker, *The Frozen Grail,* copyright by Duffield and Green. Used by permission.

Dr. Benson says of the Wesley hymns and hymn books: "The hymns were a part of John Wesley's scheme of education. Behind the long succession of books was the single purpose of elevating the humble minds of his followers by the inspirations of poetry, and the unfailing conviction that in his brother's verse he had found the medium." [2]

From the preface of John Wesley's *Methodist Hymn Book of 1780* come these lines: "When poetry thus keeps its place, as the handmaid of piety, it shall attain not a poor perishable wreath, but a crown that fadeth not away."

Charles Wesley's Christmas hymn, "Hark, the Herald Angels Sing," is a worthy companion to this one for Easter. Another of Wesley's hymns, "Jesus, Lover of My Soul," is termed "the best-loved hymn in the language; the favorite of learned and illiterate, high and humble."

✣

The Hymn Tune. Easter Hymn or Worgan from the fourteenth century caught, in particular, the Methodists who desired something more than the slow-moving Psalm-tunes. So they cultivated this along with other strongly rhythmic tunes, with embellishments, fugues, and alleluias.

Alleluias. This ascription of praise from the two Hebrew words, is the shortest of all hymns, if such it may be called. It is sometimes translated, "Praise ye the Lord; the Lord's name be praised." Jerome wrote: "Christian ploughmen shouted 'Alleluia' while at their work." Apollinaris said: "Sailors used it as the shout of encouragement while plying their oars." St. Germanus' victory over the Picts and Scots in the fifth century was known as the "Alleluia Victory" because the Britons shouted the word as their battle cry.

Most appropriately is it used at Easter, since from earliest times Christians saluted each other on Easter morning with "Alleluia, the Lord is risen. He is risen indeed."

"Alleluias" were very common in Methodist singing. If the original hymn did not feature the word, new tune settings and the desirability of dialogue singing would call into being endless alleluias.

Easter Hymn or Worgan was used by the Methodists with other texts, notably with Charles Wesley's "Hark, the herald angels sing."

[2] From *The Hymnody of the Christian Church,* by Louis F. Benson, copyright by Doubleday, Doran and Co.

MENDELSSOHN was not written and rearranged as a hymn tune until 1850. Therefore, during one hundred and eleven years Wesley's Christmas Hymn was without fitting music. It will prove a worthwhile experiment to sing "Hark, the Herald Angels Sing" to the EASTER HYMN, or WORGAN. This tune comes from *Lyra Davidica,* 1708.

In time the EASTER HYMN fell into disrepute. Other music was sought for "Christ the Lord is risen today," such as: "SEE THE CONQUERING HERO COMES," from "Judas Maccabæus," and A MUSICAL DIALOGUE between Beethoven's "Romance in G," and Handel's "Hallelujah Chorus."

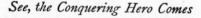

See, the Conquering Hero Comes

From "Judas Maccabaeus"

Beethoven's Romance for Violin and Handel's Hallelujah Chorus

Je - sus Christ is ris'n to - day, Hal - le - lu - jah,
Hal - le - lu - jah. Our tri - umph - ant ho - ly day,
Hal - le - lu - jah, Hal - le - lu - jah. Who so late - ly
on the cross, Hal - le - lu - jah, Hal - le - lu - jah.
Suf - fered to re - deem our loss, Hal - le - lu - jah,
Hal - le - lu - jah, Hal - le - lu - jah, Hal - le - lu - jah!

CHRISTIAN, DOST THOU SEE THEM?

1. Christian, dost thou see them
On the holy ground,
How the powers of darkness
Compass thee around?
Christian, up and smite them,
Counting gain but loss,
In the strength that cometh
By the holy cross.

2. Christian, dost thou feel them,
How they work within,
Striving, tempting, luring,
Goading into sin?
Christian, never tremble,
Never be downcast;
Gird thee for the battle,
Watch and pray and fast.

3. Christian, dost thou hear them,
How they speak thee fair,
"Always fast and vigil,
Always watch and prayer?"
Christian, answer boldly,
"While I breathe I pray!"
Peace shall follow battle,
Night shall end in day.

4. "Well I know thy trouble,
O my servant true;
Thou art very weary,
I was weary, too;
But that toil shall make thee
Some day all mine own,
And the end of sorrow
Shall be near my throne."

Andrew of Crete, 660–732,
Translated by John M. Neale, 1862.

Biblical Text.

Be strong in the Lord, and in the strength of his might. For our wrestling is not against flesh and blood, but against the principalities, against the powers, against the world-rulers of this darkness, against the spiritual hosts of wickedness in the heavenly places. Wherefore take up the whole armor of God, that ye may be able to withstand in the evil day, and, having done all, to stand.

Ephesians 6: 10, 12, 13.

THE AUTOBIOGRAPHY OF A HERETIC

A prisoner in Rome, but always mindful of the welfare of the churches, Paul wrote a letter to Titus his "true child after a common faith," whom he had left in Crete that he might set in order the things that were wanting. His conclusion was that "denying ungodliness and worldly lusts, we should live soberly and righteously and godly in this present world."

About six hundred and fifty years later Andrew was made Bishop of Crete. Naturally interested in Titus and his work on that island, Andrew wrote a homily on "Titus, the First Bishop of Crete." Andrew's homily is forgotten, but the hymns he wrote while Bishop of Crete are still sung by the Greek Church, especially his "Great Canon" of two hundred and fifty stanzas, sung on Thursday in Mid-Lent.

Evidently Andrew of Crete (660–732) made diligent study of Paul's letter to Titus, for Paul's exhortation to "sober and righteous living and zeal of good works" is reflected in the hymn by which Andrew is best known, "Christian, Dost thou see Them?"

A hymn with searching question and stirring answer in every stanza, it brings a real challenge to modern life far removed from the monkish vigils, fasts and prayers, and theological hair-splitting of the eighth century.

It reflects the personal experience of Andrew himself, when for a time he fell into accord with the Monothelite heresy, and the words "striving, tempting, luring, goading into sin" make a vivid picture of the torture of a soul torn by doubts. We would like to believe that the hymn was aimed against the invading Mohammedans who just about this time were defeated by Charles Martel at Tours, 732 A. D.

Far different as are the situations of modern Christians from these old monastic days of the Early Church, this hymn has a genuinely human element which makes it live, an appropriate expression for Christians of every land and age.

The forces of evil are varied in their manifestations: "see them," "feel them," "hear them," both without, "on the holy ground," and "within." However clever and subtle they may be, the Christian has really no cause for fear; he has strength sufficient to smite them, "the strength that cometh by the holy cross."

Strongest of lines is "Christian, answer boldly, 'While I breathe I pray!' "

The devotion of the entire fourth stanza to an expression of the

Master's appreciation and commendation is a bit of real artistry, which lifts the hymn to a glowing climax.

It is to Dr. John Mason Neale that the modern church is indebted for the rescue of this old Greek hymn from oblivion and its availability in this beautiful translation.

✣

THE HYMN TUNE. Dr. John B. Dykes, the composer of many hymn tunes, shows his real genius in ST. ANDREW OF CRETE, where the opportunity for the dramatic in music is great. The tune is powerfully expressive of the thought and feeling of the poem.

The first four music lines are in C minor. The melody creeps along with hesitant steps and small intervals, never going higher than C, and emphasizing the fifth note in such a way as to denote uncertainty and fear.

The beginning of the fifth line marks the time for action, the movement is quicker and much more spirited. The harmony changes to C Major. The melody is militant and bounds forward triumphantly like a valiant soldier about to smite the foe. The inner parts likewise move quickly onward and upward.

CHRISTIANS, LO, THE STAR

1. Christians, lo, the star appeareth;
Lo, 'tis yet Messiah's day;
Still with tribute treasure laden
Come the wise men on their way.

2. Where a life is spent in service
Walking where the Master trod,
There is scattered myrrh most fragrant
For the blessed Christ of God.

3. Whoso bears his brother's burden,
Whoso shares another's woe,
Brings his frankincense to Jesus
With the men of long ago.

4. When we soothe earth's weary children
Tending best the least of them,
'Tis the Lord himself we worship,
Bringing gold to Bethlehem.

5. Christians, lo, the star appeareth
Leading still the ancient way;

Christians, onward with your treasure;
It is still Messiah's day.

JAMES A. BLAISDELL, 1900.

BIBLICAL TEXT.

Is not this the fast that I have chosen: to loose the bonds of wickedness, to undo the bands of the yoke, and to let the oppressed go free, and that ye break every yoke? Is it not to deal thy bread to the hungry, and that thou bring the poor that are cast out to thy house?

When thou seest the naked, that thou cover him; and that thou hide not thyself from thine own flesh?

Then shall thy light break forth as the morning, and thy healing shall spring forth speedily; and thy righteousness shall go before thee; the glory of the Lord shall be thy reward.

Then shalt thou call, and the Lord will answer; thou shalt cry, and he will say, Here I am.

ISAIAH 58:6-9.

THE MODERN MAGI

This is a hymn of the present tense. Not, "the star appeared" long ago, in a dim and distant past, to three "Kings of the Orient," but "lo, the star appeareth"—here and now, in the present day, to modern Christians.

The author comments: "This hymn has grown through a considerable period of time, inspired by the feeling that the church days and forms must be interpreted in terms of present-day life if they are to get hold upon the men and women of this generation."

He has succeeded in putting the thought of the Magi's gifts of gold, frankincense and myrrh, into the terminology of modern thought and life, and in linking up the story of the wise men, in Matthew 2, with the story of these on the King's right hand, greeted with his "Inasmuch," in Matthew 25.

James A. Blaisdell (1867-) was born at Beloit, Wisconsin, graduated from Beloit College in 1889, and Hartford Theological Seminary in 1892. His pastorates were at Waukesha, Wisconsin, and Olivet, Michigan. In 1903 he returned to Beloit as professor of Biblical Literature and Ancient Oriental History. He was called to the presidency of Pomona College, Claremont, California, in 1910. Since 1927 he has been president of the Claremont Colleges.

Hymns by College Presidents

The hymnal has gathered its poetic treasures from many sources. Laymen and ministers, professors and poets, men and women of many walks in life have made their contributions. Here is a hymn by a living college president. Other educational leaders have made their contributions to hymnody:

Timothy Dwight, President of Yale, 1795–1817—"I Love Thy Kingdom, Lord."

Jeremiah E. Rankin, President of Howard University—"God be with you till we meet again."

William DeWitt Hyde, President of Bowdoin College—"Creation's Lord, we give thee thanks."

Melancthon Woolsey Stryker, of Hamilton College, 1892–1917—"Almighty Lord, with one accord."

Ozora Stearns Davis, President of Chicago Theological Seminary, 1909–1929—"At length there dawns the glorious day."

THE HYMN TUNE. SARDIS is from the Romance for Violin, Opus 40, No. 1, by Ludwig van Beethoven (1770–1827).

It has been said of Beethoven that "the moment he takes his pen in hand he becomes the most cautious and hesitating of men. . . . There is hardly a bar in his music of which it may not be said with confidence that it had been rewritten a dozen times. . . . Mendelssohn used to show a correction of a passage by Beethoven in which the latter had pasted alteration after alteration up to thirteen in number. Mendelssohn had separated them, and in the thirteenth, Beethoven had returned to the original version."

Before Beethoven died he received the sacrament (he was a Catholic). As the priest left the apartment he said, *Plaudite, amici; comedia finita est* ("Applaud, friends; the farce is finished"). The musician used to say there were two closed chapters—religion and thorough bass. Was he not a religious man?

To his brothers he wrote: "God looks into my heart. He searches it and knows that love for man and feelings of benevolence have their abode there."

"What are all human efforts compared with the works of the great Master above the clouds? We are all dwarfs, even the greatest upon the earth, beside the Omnipotent."

Human independence is the motive of the Fifth Symphony, love of nature of the Sixth, love of life of the Seventh, and the omnipotence of the Creator and nobility of humanity of the Ninth.

COME, THOU ALMIGHTY KING

1. Come, thou almighty King,
Help us thy name to sing,
Help us to praise:
Father, all-glorious,
O'er all victorious,
Come, and reign over us,
Ancient of Days.

2. Come, thou incarnate Word,
Gird on thy mighty sword,
Our prayer attend:
Come, and thy people bless,
And give thy word success;
Spirit of holiness,
On us descend.

3. Come, holy Comforter,
Thy sacred witness bear
In this glad hour:
Thou who almighty art,
Now rule in every heart,
And ne'er from us depart,
Spirit of power.

4. To the great one in three,
Eternal praises be
Hence evermore.
His sovereign majesty
May we in glory see,
And to eternity
Love and adore.

GEORGE WHITEFIELD'S *Hymn Book,* 1757.

BIBLICAL TEXT.

O Lord, open thou my lips;
And my mouth shall show forth thy praise.

PSALM 51:15.

A LITERARY WAIF

One of the most popular of all church hymns is a literary waif, "Come, Thou Almighty King." This anonymous composition, often attributed to Charles Wesley, made its first appearance in a tract of hymns, published by George Whitefield in 1757.

The hymn appeared again in 1763 in a collection compiled by Reverend Spencer Madan and was set to the tune "God Save the King." It is quite possible that the words were written in imitation of this national hymn.

During the Revolutionary War, a company of British soldiers attended a church on Long Island filled with American patriots. They demanded, with the insolence of superior force, that the congregation sing "God Save the King." The congregation, in apparent obedience, sang the tune, but the words they used were "Come, Thou Almighty King!" Theirs was a heart-felt prayer, "Help us thy name to sing."

Its Universal Use. This hymn has found a place in the hymnals of all branches of the Christian Church, has been translated into many languages and has been altered to suit the needs of differing beliefs. This "Hymn to the Trinity" is sung by Unitarians, with the omission of the last stanza and a change in the second to read:

"Come, thou all-gracious Lord
By heaven and earth adored!
Our prayer attend.
Come, and thy children bless;
Give thy good word success;
Make thine own holiness
On us descend."

Analysis. Although distinctively a prayer hymn, these words are often sung as a hymn of praise and more frequently classified under "Praise" than under "Prayer."

It is a definite appeal to each Person of the Triune God to "Come" to assist the worshipper in rendering acceptable praise. The closing words of the "Sunrise Hymn," Psalm 19, have a similar thought:

"Let the words of my mouth, and the meditation of my heart
Be acceptable in thy sight,
O Lord, my rock and my redeemer."

Psalm 19: 14.

Note the variety of the titles of the Deity in these four stanzas: Almighty King, Incarnate God, Almighty, Father all-glorious, Spirit of Holiness, Great One in Three, Ancient of Days, Holy Comforter, Sovereign Majesty.

Significant are the petitions which this hymn includes: "Help us to praise," "Give thy word success," "Ne'er depart," "Reign over us," "Witness bear," "Thy people bless," "Rule in every heart."

And in strict accord with the prevalent custom of the eighteenth-century hymn-writers, the petitions of the last stanza are entirely concerned with the future life. The worshipper who has enjoyed the privilege of prayer and praise here looks forward to the joy of ceaseless praise hereafter.

Companion Trinitarian Doxologies are found in the following hymns, a few of the many:

"Ancient of Days."
"Angel Voices, ever singing" (Last Stanza).
"Come ye faithful, raise the strain" (Last Stanza).
"Eternal Father, strong to save."
"Gloria Patri."
"Holy, Holy, Holy, Lord God Almighty."
"May the grace of Christ, our Saviour."
"O Day of rest and gladness" (First and Last Stanzas).
"Praise God from whom all blessings flow."

Correlated Scripture

After stanza one:

Behold, the virgin shall be with child, and shall bring forth a son, and they shall call his name Immanuel, which is being interpreted, God with us.

MATTHEW 1:23.

After stanza two:

In the beginning was the Word, and the Word was with God, and the Word was God. . . . All things were made through him; . . . In him was life; and the life was the light of men.

JOHN 1:1, 3, 4.

After stanza three:

Jesus said: And I will pray the Father, and he shall give you another Comforter, that he may be with you forever: even the Spirit of truth . . . ye know him, for he abideth with you; and shall be in you.

JOHN 14:16 and 17.

✣

THE HYMN TUNE. The ITALIAN HYMN or MOSCOW, as it is known in England, was composed by a native of Italy, Felice Giardini, in 1769. Giardini began his musical career as a choir boy in the Cathedral of Milan. He studied singing, composition and the harpsichord with the famous Paladini, and later the violin with Semis. In 1750 he made his first appearance in London as a concert violinist and was enthusiastically received. After thirty-four years in England, he returned to Italy. The closing years of his life were spent in Russia, where he died at the age of eighty. This tune has a hint of Russian vigor, ruggedness and openness of chords. In its original form it is even more square-timbered than in the present Italianized form.

Musical Interpretation. Care should be taken to set a proper tempo for such hymns as "Come, Thou Almighty King," "Joyful, Joyful, we adore Thee" and "From all that dwell below the skies." There is danger of singing them too rapidly.

The natural expression of awe and sublimity, of adoration and praise of the Supreme Being, is subdued and slow, quite different from the expression of joy and pleasure which arises from the things about us or the experiences of daily life. To sing this type of hymn too fast is to rob it of its dignity.

Of more than usual importance is that first word, "Come." It should be sung by every one, promptly and vigorously.

CROWN HIM WITH MANY CROWNS

1. Crown him with many crowns,
The Lamb upon his throne;
Hark! how the heavenly anthem drowns
All music but its own!
Awake, my soul, and sing
Of him who died for thee,
And hail him as thy matchless King
Through all eternity.

2. Crown him the Lord of love:
Behold his hands and side,
Rich wounds, yet visible above,
In beauty glorified.
No angel in the sky
Can fully bear that sight,
But downward bends his burning eye
At mysteries so bright.

3. Crown him the Lord of peace,
Whose power a sceptre sways
From pole to pole, that wars may cease,
And all be prayer and praise!
His reign shall know no end,
And round his pierced feet
Fair flowers of Paradise extend
Their fragrance ever sweet.

4. Crown him the Lord of years,
The Potentate of time,
Creator of the rolling spheres,
Ineffably sublime.
All hail, Redeemer, hail!
For thou hast died for me:
Thy praise shall never, never fail
Throughout eternity.

Matthew Bridges, 1851.

Biblical Text.

And his eyes are a flame of fire, and upon his head are many diadems; and he hath a name written which no one knoweth but he himself.

Revelation 19:12.

THE SONG OF THE SERAPHS

Matthew Bridges (1800–1894) was one of that small group of scholars who, during the Oxford Movement, left the Church of England and embraced Roman Catholicism. Among them were Cardinal Newman, author of "Lead, Kindly Light"; Frederick William Faber, who wrote "Faith of Our Fathers"; Edward Caswell and Thomas Potter. Bridges was only twenty-five years of age when he published his first book of poetry. Five years after he became a Catholic he published a volume of poems on "The Passion of Jesus" (1852). Included in this collection was "The Song of the Seraphs," the author's original title for "Crown Him with Many Crowns."

Canticles of Praise

Read:

Sing, O heavens, and be joyful, O earth!
For, lo, the winter is past and gone!
The flowers appear upon the earth:
The time of the singing of birds is come:
The voice of their music is heard in the land:

Sing:

(To "Diademata")

This is my Father's world
And to my listening ears,
All nature sings, and round me rings
The music of the spheres:
This is my Father's world,
I rest me in the thought
Of rocks and trees, of skies and seas:
His hand the wonders wrought.

Read:

Worthy is the Lamb that was slain,
And hath redeemed us to God by his blood;
To receive power, and riches, and wisdom, and strength,
And honor, and glory and blessing.

Sing:

(To "Diademata")

Crown him with many crowns,
The Lamb upon the throne.
Hark! how the heavenly music drowns
All music but its own!
Awake, my soul, and sing
Of him who died for thee,
And hail him as thy matchless King
Through all eternity.

Read:

Blessed are they that mourn, for they shall be comforted.
God shall wipe away all tears from their eyes;
There shall be no more death, neither sorrow nor crying.
O death, where is thy sting? O grave, where is thy victory?

Sing:

(To "Pilgrims")

Hark, hark my soul! angelic songs are swelling
O'er earth's green field and ocean's wave-beat shore;
How sweet the truth those blessed strains are telling
Of that new life when sin shall be no more.

Angels of Jesus, angels of light,
Singing to welcome the pilgrims of the night. Amen.

✣

THE HYMN TUNE. The tune DIADEMATA (Crowns) was composed by George Job Elvey (1816–1893). He was born at Canterbury, baptized in the Presbyterian Chapel there, educated in the school of Canterbury Cathedral and took his Music Degree at Oxford.

For almost a full half century he served as organist in St. George's Chapel, Windsor. For the services of this church and for special anniversary occasions in the Royal House he wrote many hymn tunes and anthems. To one of them he gave the name of the church, "ST. GEORGE'S, WINDSOR." "No one could be long in his presence without being struck by his devout, religious spirit, and it was this spirit that went into all his work." George Elvey believed that mighty cathedrals and profound music should go together; that the music should suggest worship just as much as soaring nave, springing arch and beautiful window. He desired to make his compositions so genuinely worshipful that a stranger, listening at a distance and unable to catch the words, would be compelled to say, "That is sacred music!" "In mystery of arch and aisle, in splendor of massive towers and tall spires—in the towers of York and the spire of Salisbury, in Bach's Mass in B Minor—there is the Kingdom and the Power and the Glory." [1]

DAY IS DYING IN THE WEST

1. Day is dying in the west;
Heaven is touching earth with rest;
Wait and worship while the night
Sets her evening lamps alight
Through all the sky.

Refrain

Holy, holy, holy, Lord God of Hosts!
Heaven and earth are full of thee,
Heaven and earth are praising thee,
O Lord most high!

2. Lord of life, beneath the dome
Of the universe, thy home,
Gather us who seek thy face
To the fold of thy embrace,
For thou art nigh.

Refrain

3. While the deepening shadows fall,
Heart of love, enfolding all,
Through the glory and the grace
Of the stars that veil thy face,
Our hearts ascend.

Refrain

4. When forever from our sight
Pass the stars, the day, the night,
Lord of angels, on our eyes,
Let eternal morning rise
And shadows end.

Refrain [2]

MARY A. LATHBURY, 1877.

BIBLICAL TEXT.

Holy, holy, holy is the Lord of hosts: the whole earth is full of his glory.

ISAIAH 6:3.

In peace will I both lay me down and sleep; for thou, Lord, alone makest me dwell in safety.

PSALM 4:8.

Abide with us, for it is toward evening, and the day is now far spent.

LUKE 24:29.

[1] G. A. Studdert-Kennedy.
[2] Copyright by the Chautauqua Press.

THE VESPER HYMN OF A NATION

"Day is Dying in the West" holds the record of having been used as the opening hymn of the Sunday evening service at Chautauqua Assembly (Chautauqua Lake, New York) for over fifty-five years. It is one of the two hymns written by Miss Mary A. Lathbury at Bishop Vincent's request as special Chautauqua hymns. The other was "Break Thou the Bread of Life."

In the amphitheater and beside Lake Chautauqua, at many campsites, assembly grounds, on mountain top and beside the sea shore, this hymn is preëminently the Vesper hymn of a nation. It voices the exquisite beauty of the evening—the awe, the wonder and the reverence which instinctively belong to such hours.

Some hymns "arrive" dramatically. Others lie dormant, or practically so, for a thousand years as in the case of "Christian, dost thou see them?" and "Art thou weary, art thou languid?" Other hymns strike fire at once through some master book that carries them to a reading world, as "Lord of all being," from "The Professor at the Breakfast Table" (Holmes), "Immortal love, forever full," from "The Eternal Goodness" (Whittier), "Sun of my Soul," from "The Christian Year" (Keble), "Ring out, wild bells," from "In Memoriam" (Tennyson).

Other hymns come to immediate popularity through conventions, revival campaigns, and anniversaries, like "The Battle Hymn of the Republic" (Peace Jubilee, Boston, 1869), "The Son of God Goes Forth to War" (reborn at the Student Volunteer Convention, Nashville, Tenn.), "Lead on, O King eternal" (Methodist Centenary, Columbus, 1920), "True-hearted, whole-hearted" (Christian Endeavor Conventions), and "Day is Dying in the West" (through the Chautauqua Literary and Scientific Circle and Summer Camps).

✣

THE HYMN TUNE. William Fisk Sherwin (1826–1888) was a native of Massachusetts. He began his study of music under Lowell Mason in Boston at the age of fifteen. He became a teacher of vocal music at the New England Conservatory of Music and elsewhere.

Intimately associated with Professor Sherwin at Chautauqua was George C. Stebbins. The first use of the hymn was on Saturday, August 5, 1876, in an outdoor service of worship:

"On Saturday evening about two thousand people gathered on the shores of Lake Chautauqua. On the water near the shore was a boat in which were Professor Sherwin, who conducted the service, and the Stebbins brothers with their cornets. About this central boat were thirty other little boats, filled with men, women and children, each with a copy of the ritual in hand. Professor Sherwin led the singing, and as leader of the service, read alternately with the congregation. It was a beautiful scene and very impressive."

Musical Interpretation. The refrain should begin softly, becoming more and more intense in tone until the culmination is reached in the words, "Lord God of Hosts," a glad shout of praise.

Careful attention should be paid to the words of the different stanzas, for example, in the second stanza "Lord of Life (*sung full-voiced*)," in the third stanza "While the deep'ning shadows (*sung quietly*)."

The entire tune is suggestive of the quietness of sunset time beside the lake, with the evening breeze just fluttering the leaves of the trees.

DEAR GOD, OUR FATHER, AT THY KNEE CONFESSING

1. Dear God, our Father, at thy knee confessing
Our sins and follies, close in thine embrace,
Children forgiven, happy in thy blessing,
Deepen our spirits to receive thy grace.

2. Not for more beauty would our eyes entreat thee,
Flooded with beauty, beauty everywhere;
Only for keener vision that may greet thee
In all thy vestures of the earth and air.

3. The stars and rainbows are thy wondrous wearing,
Sunlight and shadow moving on the hills;
Holy the meadow where thy feet are faring,
Holy the brooklet that thy laughter fills.

4. Not for more love our craving hearts implore thee,
But for more power to love until they glow
Like hearths of comfort, eager to restore thee,
Hidden in human wretchedness and woe.

5. In souls most sullen thou art softly dreaming
Of saints and heroes wrought from thy divine
Pity and patience, still the lost redeeming;
Deepen our spirits for a love like thine.[1]

Katharine Lee Bates, 1926.

Biblical Text.
Worship the Lord in the beauty of holiness.

Psalm 96:9.

[1] Copyright by Houghton Mifflin Company.

Beloved, let us love one another: for love is of God; and every one that loveth is begotten of God, and knoweth God.

I JOHN 4:7.

A PRESENT-DAY PRAYER FOR DEEPENED SPIRITS

So new that it is not at all familiar, so much of the present that it cannot be called a "heritage," so completely modern that at first glimpse it seems hardly like a hymn, this late message from the pen of the author of "America the Beautiful" is worthy of careful study and of wide use.

To get acquainted with this new hymn, it is necessary, first of all, to read it. And this reading must not be done casually or carelessly, but with thoughtfulness and concentrated attention.

Beginning with a confession of sins and follies, relieved by a confidence of the forgiveness assured through the revelation of God's word and of personal experience, the prayer proceeds to petition. But the petitions of this prayer-hymn are different from the ordinary requests for daily bread, for guidance, and for specific blessings. They are worthy of careful study.

"Not for beauty . . . only for keener vision." As might be expected from a poet who saw so deeply as to envisage "America the Beautiful," we find here in concentrated essence the joy and the glory of "beauty everywhere." These references to the presence of the God of Beauty in stars and rainbows, in sunlight and shadow, in meadow and stream, would have stirred the heart of another psalmist who sang,

"O Lord, how manifold are thy works!
In wisdom hast thou made them all:
The earth is full of thy riches."

PSALM 104:24.

"Not for more love (receiving) . . . but for more power to love (giving)." Beautiful beyond most of our hymn pictures is this one in the fourth stanza—"Like hearths of comfort"—intimately linked with the Saviour's own thought in his matchless "Inasmuch."

Breathing through all the stanzas is the deep-lying consciousness of the intimate nearness of God to human life in all its beauty and joy, in all its wretchedness and woe. Only an immanent, ever-present Redeemer could have dreamed of "saints and heroes," wrought from "souls most sullen" by the transfiguring power of "pity and patience."

In "Hail and Farewell," a Memorial Address, delivered in the Wellesley College Chapel, May 12, 1929, Dr. Earl Marlatt recounted the circumstances connected with the composition of this hymn.

"Not so long ago," he said, "I called at 'The Scarab,' Miss Bates' home in Wellesley. I wanted her to write a hymn-text for 'The American Student Hymnal,' on which Professor H. Augustine Smith and I were then working.

" 'But what,' she asked, 'shall I write about?'

" 'The immanence of God,' I said.

"Miss Bates looked appalled at the prospect of writing a poem about that. She demurred, insisting that she had no notion of what that meant. I assured her that it was very simple, merely the idea that God is causally present in, without being substantially identified with, everything in nature, and that his attributes are most perfectly manifested in personality.

" 'Was there anything else you'd like to have me put into that hymn?' Miss Bates inquired, as the avalanche receded.

"Seeing the sparkle in her eye and understanding, I replied, 'I'd like you to say some way that God has a sense of humor.'

"That was Saturday afternoon. On Monday morning I received the text for the hymn. It was called 'For Deeper Life' and was written to the music of Mendelssohn's CONSOLATION or FELIX. In a very real sense it illustrates Miss Bates' supreme art, the same ability which she showed in "America the Beautiful," a genius for taking profound, but as others express them, ponderously theological or political truths, and making them quietly luminous . . . redeeming."

Katharine Lee Bates (1859–1929) was born at Falmouth, Massachusetts, the daughter of a clergyman. After her college course at Wellesley, she taught in the Natick High School and at Dana Hall, and in 1885 returned to Wellesley as Instructor in English Literature. Becoming full professor in 1891, she remained in that position until 1925, when she retired as Professor Emeritus. She died at her Wellesley home, March 28, 1929.

Miss Bates' first book was a book of poems, published in 1887, only seven years after her graduation from college. She is credited with seventeen books, including poetry, lectures, children's stories and travel records. In addition, she was the editor of a large number of editions of various classics in English and American Literature.

She received the honorary degree of LL.D. from Wellesley, and LITT.D. from Middlebury and Oberlin.

✣

THE HYMN TUNE. This hymn may best be sung to the music of FELIX arranged from one of Mendelssohn's "Songs without Words."

Mendelssohn was once importuned to write a new long meter tune. He declined in his usual courteous way, enclosing an organ piece and saying: "I was sorry I could not write exactly what you desired me to do, but I do not know what a "long measure psalm-tune" means, and there is nobody to whom I could apply for an explanation. Excuse me, therefore, if you receive something else than what you wished." Mendelssohn did write one hymn tune—LEIPZIG, but it is not universally used.

DEAR LORD AND FATHER OF MANKIND

1. Dear Lord and Father of mankind,
Forgive our feverish ways;
Reclothe us in our rightful mind;
In purer lives thy service find,
In deeper reverence, praise.

2. In simple trust like theirs who heard,
Beside the Syrian sea,
The gracious calling of the Lord,
Let us, like them, without a word,
Rise up, and follow thee.

3. O Sabbath rest by Galilee!
O calm of hills above,
Where Jesus knelt to share with thee
The silence of eternity,
Interpreted by love.

4. Drop thy still dews of quietness,
Till all our strivings cease;
Take from our souls the strain and stress,
And let our ordered lives confess
The beauty of thy peace.

5. Breathe through the heats of our desire
Thy coolness and thy balm;
Let sense be dumb, let flesh retire,
Speak through the earthquake, wind, and fire,
O still small voice of calm.

JOHN GREENLEAF WHITTIER, 1872.

BIBLICAL TEXT.

For thus said the Lord God, the Holy One of Israel, in returning and rest shall ye be saved; in quietness and in confidence shall be your strength.

ISAIAH 30: 15.

And, behold, the Lord passed by, and a great and strong wind rent the mountains, and brake in pieces the rocks . . . and after the wind an earthquake, . . . and after the earthquake a fire: . . . and after the fire, a still small voice.

I KINGS 19: 11, 12.

FROM A POETIC TEMPEST INTO LYRIC SUNSHINE

No one can fully appreciate the rare beauty and depth of this great hymn unless he sees it in its setting in the poem "The Brewing of Soma." This poem has been well described as a "poetical thunder-storm."

In vivid language the poet describes the brewing of "the drink of gods," the "Soma," prepared by the priests in old Vedic days in "the morning twilight of the race." Intoxicated by this drink, the worshippers went into strange transports of joy, "soared upward, with strange joy elate," then, "sobered, sank to earth." Then, true to his Quaker upbringing and instinct, Whittier accuses "each after-age" of striving, "by music, incense, vigils drear, and trance, to bring the skies more near, or lift men up to heaven."

Having portrayed in graphic, "thunder-storm" style, the folly and horror of all such attempts, whether in the "morning twilight of the race," or in "each after-age," the poet brings his accusation down to his own day and time with the stanza:

"And yet the past comes round again,
And new doth old fulfill;
In sensual transports wild as vain
We brew in many a Christian fane
The heathen Soma still!"

With this line, the poetic tempest ceases, and now begins one of the world's most reverent and quietly beautiful prayer hymns, "Dear Lord and Father of Mankind."

John Greenleaf Whittier (1807–1892) is one of the best-loved of American poets. Many of his poems reflect the Quaker teachings of his New England farm home, and the principles of deep personal religion which governed his entire life. A strong abolitionist, he became through his writing a mighty factor in developing the public sentiment which created the emancipation movement. He was editor, successively, of the *American Manufacturer,* the *New England Review* and the *Pennsylvania Freeman,* and corresponding editor of the *National Era.*

Most of his adult life was spent at Amesbury, Massachusetts, but his closing years were at Oak Knoll, Danvers, Massachusetts. In contrast to his urban contemporaries, Emerson, Longfellow, Holmes, and Lowell, Whittier's boyhood was spent in hard manual labor on a New England farm, with very little formal schooling. Read his "Snow Bound" for word pictures of this farm life.

With characteristic modesty, Whittier once said, "I am not really a hymn-writer, for the good reason that I know nothing of music. Only a very few of my pieces were written for singing." Dr. Julian (Dictionary of Hymnology) lists no less than sixty-four of Whittier's hymns in common use; and Dr. Moffatt in his "Handbook to the Church Hymnary" mentions "over fifty hymns by him found in modern hymn books." This is a remarkable testimony to the truth of Whittier's remark about hymns: "A good hymn is the best use to which poetry can be devoted."

This hymn shows Whittier's intimate acquaintance with the Bible.

Hymn and Scripture Responsive Service

Dear Lord and Father . . .
In deeper reverence, praise.

The hour . . . now is, when the true worshippers shall worship the Father in spirit and truth; for such doth the Father seek to be his worshippers.

JOHN 4:23.

In simple trust . . .
Let us, like them . . .
Rise up, and follow thee.

Jesus said unto them, Come ye after me . . . and straightway they left the nets, and followed him.

MARK 1:17, 18.

O Sabbath rest . . .
Where Jesus knelt . . .

In the morning, a great while before day, he rose up and went out and departed into a desert place, and there prayed.

MARK 1:35.

And let our ordered lives . . .
The beauty of thy peace.

And the peace of God, which passeth all understanding, shall guard your hearts and your thoughts in Christ Jesus.

PHILIPPIANS 4:7.

Speak through the earthquake, wind, and fire,
O still small voice of calm!

And after the fire, a still small voice . . . When Elijah heard it, he wrapped his face in his mantle.

I KINGS 19:12, 13.

Hymn and Pictorial Illustrations

"Dear Lord and Father"—"Come Unto Me," Bloch

"In simple trust"—"Christ and the Fishermen," Zimmermann

"O Sabbath rest by Galilee"—"Jesus Walking by the Sea," Gruenwald

"Drop thy still dews"—"Christ the Remunerator," Ary Scheffer

"Breathe through the heats"—"God Speaks Through the Whirlwind," Russell

❖

THE HYMN TUNE. The tune, WHITTIER, by Frederick C. Maker (1844–1927), expresses the depth of religious feeling which lies in this hymn. It reflects the quiet, gentle character and intense religious nature of the poet himself. Its quiet reverence and earnest tone make it especially fitting for a prayer.

It should be sung thoughtfully, slowly enough for good expression, but not "drag-ily." Careful attention should be given to the vowel sounds in such words as "calm," "balm," "cease," "strain," "peace." In the last stanza there is a unique opportunity for the expression of contrast between the two phrases "earthquake, wind, and fire (*loud and dramatic*)" and "O still small voice of calm (*subdued*)."

There are times when transposition of keys will add to congregational singing pace, zest, and resolve, or the opposite, meditation, thoughtfulness and worship. This tune is often too low, too dark, and too supine. Try it in D flat or in D, particularly for the drama of earthquake, wind and fire with which it closes.

Fairest Lord Jesus

(CRUSADER'S HYMN. Irregular)

Silesian Folk Song,
in Schleischen Volkslieder, Leipzig, 1842

17th Century German Hymn — Descant by CHARLES REPPER, 1929

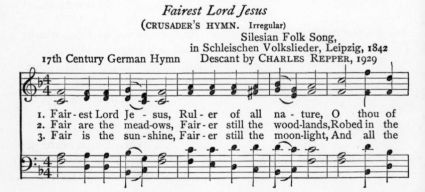

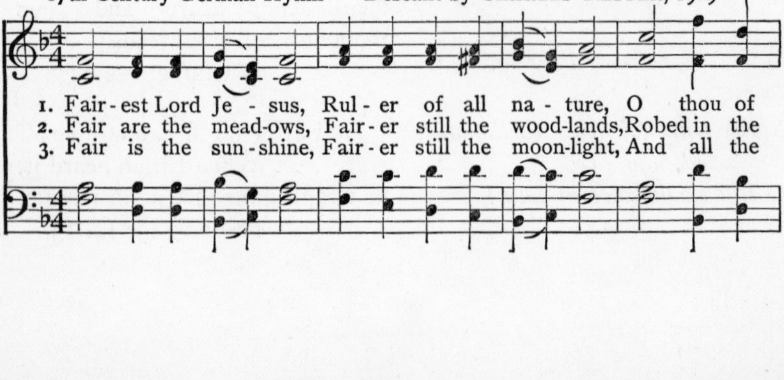

1. Fair-est Lord Je - sus, Rul - er of all na - ture, O thou of
2. Fair are the mead-ows, Fair - er still the wood-lands, Robed in the
3. Fair is the sun - shine, Fair - er still the moon-light, And all the

Descant with 2nd and 3rd stanzas
2. Je - sus is fair - er, Je - sus . .
3. Je - sus shines brighter, Je - sus . .
God and man the son! Thee will I cher - ish, Thee will I
bloom-ing garb of spring; Je - sus is fair - er, Je - sus is
twink-ling star - ry host; Je - sus shines bright-er, Je - sus shines
. . is pur - er, He who makes the heart to sing.
. . shines pur - er, Than the an - gels heaven can boast. A-MEN.
hon - or Thou, my soul's glo - ry, joy and crown.
pur - er, Who makes the woe - ful heart to sing.
pur - er Than all the an - gels heaven can boast. A-MEN.

Descant from *Twice 55 Community Songs* (Brown Book). Copyright by C. C. Birchard & Company. Used by permission.

Optional Stanzas

4 All fairest beauty,
Heavenly and earthly,
Wondrously, Jesus, is found in thee:
None can be nearer,
Fairer or dearer
Than thou, my Saviour, art to me.

5 Beautiful Saviour;
Lord of the nations;
Son of God and Son of man.
Glory and honor,
Praise, adoration,
Now and evermore be thine.

BIBLICAL TEXT.

One thing I asked of the Lord, that will I seek after:
That I may . . . behold the beauty of the Lord.

PSALM 27:4.

He is altogether lovely.

SONG OF SOLOMON 5:16.

The Lord will arise upon thee, and his glory shall be seen upon thee. And nations shall come to thy light, and kings to the brightness of thy rising.

ISAIAH 60:2, 3.

A MARCHING SONG OF THE OUT-OF-DOORS

In spite of all the proofs that the Crusaders never sang this hymn, it still is, and probably will continue to be called, "The Crusaders'

Hymn." The Crusaders unquestionably sang *"Jesu, Dulcis Memoria"* (Jesus the very thought of thee) or *"Vexilla regis Prodeunt"* (The royal banners forward go) as they moved toward the Holy City.

Written in 1677 the air and the hymn were undoubtedly sung by the German pilgrims on their way to Jerusalem. The hymn was published in America by Richard Storrs Willis in 1850.

Correlation with Scripture and Other Literature

As an introduction to the singing of this first stanza, the minister may read:

> In the beginning was the Word, and the Word was with God, and the Word was God. All things were made through him, and without him was not anything made that hath been made. In him was life, and the life was the light of men.
>
> JOHN 1:1–4.

Introducing the second stanza, Emerson's poem "Music" should be read:

> It is not only in the rose,
> It is not only in the bird,
> Not only where the rainbow glows,
> Nor in the song of women heard,
> But in the darkest, meanest things
> There alway, alway something sings.[1]

As an introduction to the third stanza, the "Midnight Hymn" of the Psalmist (Psalm 8) may profitably be read:

> When I consider thy heavens, the work of thy fingers,
> The moon and the stars, which thou hast ordained;
> What is man, that thou art mindful of him,
> And the son of man, that thou visitest him?
> For thou hast made him but little lower than God,
> And crownest him with glory and honor.
>
> PSALM 8:3–5.

Vivid are the concluding phrases of each stanza: Jesus is the "soul's glory, joy and crown"; it is He who "makes the woeful heart to sing"; and more beautiful than any of Nature's wonders on earth or in the skies, He is brighter, fairer, purer, "than all the angels heaven can boast."

The English translation closely follows the German original:

> *Schönster Herr Jesu,*
> *Herrscher aller Erden*
> *Gott und Marias Sohn;*
> *Dich will ich lieben,*

[1] Ralph Waldo Emerson, copyright by Houghton Mifflin Company.

Dich will ich ehren,
Du meiner Seelen Freund und Kron.

Schön sind die Felder,
Noch schöner sind die Wälder
In der schönen Frühlingszeit;
Jesu ist schöner
Jesu ist reiner
Der unser traurig Herz erfreut.

Schön leucht't die Sonne,
Noch schöner leucht't der Mond
Und die Sternlein allzumal;
Jesu leucht't schöner
Jesu leucht't reiner
Als all die Engel in Himmelsall.

The picture most frequently used with this hymn is Hofmann's "Christ at twelve years." Here we see a truly fair Jesus with all of the ideal beauty which we like to attribute to him as a boy. It reminds us too of Luke: "And Jesus increased in wisdom and stature and in favor with God and man." Before this is set up as the type of Jesus, consider well that Jesus was an oriental, and if reality is sought, this picture will not do. With some such thought as this in mind, study Holman Hunt's "The Finding of Christ in the Temple."

THE HYMN TUNE. The tune, CRUSADER'S HYMN, was arranged in 1850 by Professor Richard Storrs Willis (1819–1900) from a Silesian folk-song which appeared in 1842 in a collection of Folk Songs. In the preface one of the editors, Dr. Hofmann, says: "In the summer of 1836 I visited a friend in Westphalia. Towards evening I heard the haymakers singing: I made inquiries: they sang folk-songs which seemed to me worthy of being collected. For this purpose I associated myself with my friend, Richter, and we divided the work between us. He had charge of the musical portion, and I took the rest. How far back this melody goes cannot be determined. It is sung by all classes and all ages, from the shepherd on the hillside to the lisping urchin in the nursery." Franz Liszt makes large use of this tune in his oratorio "St. Elizabeth."

FAITH OF OUR FATHERS

1. Faith of our fathers, living still
In spite of dungeon, fire and sword,

O how our hearts beat high with joy
Whene'er we hear that glorious word!

Refrain

Faith of our fathers, holy faith,
We will be true to thee till death.

2. Our fathers, chained in prisons dark,
Were still in heart and conscience free,
And blest would be their children's fate,
If they, like them, should die for thee.

Refrain

3. Faith of our fathers, we will strive
To win all nations unto thee;
And through the truth that comes from God
Mankind shall then indeed be free.

Refrain

4. Faith of our fathers, we will love
Both friend and foe in all our strife,
And preach thee, too, as love knows how,
By kindly words and virtuous life.

Refrain

FREDERICK W. FABER, 1849.

BIBLICAL TEXT.

Now faith is assurance of things hoped for, a conviction of things not seen.

These all died in faith, not having received the promises, but having seen them and greeted them from afar . . . wherefore God is not ashamed of them, to be called their God.

HEBREWS 11:1, 13, 16.

Fight the good fight of the faith, lay hold on the life eternal.

I TIMOTHY 6:12.

CHURCH UNION IN THE HYMN BOOK

"The Last Prayer" is the title of one of Gérôme's paintings. It shows a company of Christian martyrs kneeling in the arena, praying in the single moment before the hungry lions rush upon them. For their faith in their new-found Master and Lord they are willing to die.

That same ideal of supreme devotion is suggested in Faber's "Faith of Our Fathers." Perhaps the author, as he wrote, may have had a vision of his Huguenot ancestors in France, on terrible St. Bartholomew's Day (1572) when seventy thousand Huguenots perished in a few hours for their loyalty to their faith.

This hymn is deservedly one of the most popular of all the modern hymns of the Church. It is a most vigorous hymn, a challenging call to fidelity, loyalty and devotion.

Strong confidence in the "Faith of Our Fathers" is evident in that first line. It is "living still,"—still no matter how fierce and fanatical have been the storms of cruelty, oppression and imperial edict by which men have endeavored to stamp it out. Truly, every heart may, nay must, "beat high with joy" as it contemplates this glorious fact.

All great hymns must have both timely and timeless elements. The third stanza and its significant changes illustrate this truth. Faber wrote this hymn after he had passed through the mental and spiritual struggle which resulted in his following his intimate friend and ideal, John Henry Newman, into the fold of the Roman Catholic Church. He wrote it as a hymn "For singing and reading" by loyal Catholics.

"Faith of our Fathers! Mary's prayers
Shall win our country back to thee:
And through the truth that comes from God
England shall then indeed be free."

Altered for Protestant use, it reads:

"Faith of our fathers, we will strive
To win all nations unto thee;
And through the truth that comes from God
Mankind shall then indeed be free."

A real climax is reached in the fourth stanza. "Strife" against the forces of evil must go on, but even in this strife the truest loyalty to the "faith of our fathers" is to follow the Saviour's new teaching: "Love your enemies, and pray for them that persecute you." The truest, most effective preaching is not in Roman Cathedral, Anglican Abbey, or Non-Conformist Chapel, but in everyday living by millions of nameless, humble Christians, who express their faith "in kindly words and virtuous life."

An Interpretative Service

(For minister, choir, and congregation)

Congregation (singing):

Faith of our fathers, living still,
In spite of dungeon, fire and sword,
O how our hearts beat high with joy,
Whene'er we hear that glorious word!
Faith of our fathers, holy faith,
We will be true to thee till death.

Minister:

And what shall I more say? For the time will fail me if I tell of Gideon, Barak, Samson, Jephthah; of David and Samuel and the prophets, who through faith subdued kingdoms, wrought righteousness, obtained promises, stopped the mouths of lions, quenched the power of fire, escaped the edge of the sword, from weakness were made strong, waxed mighty in war, turned to flight armies of aliens. HEBREWS 11:32, 33, 34.

Congregation (singing to the "Portuguese Hymn"):

When through fiery trials thy pathway shall lie,
My grace all sufficient shall be thy supply;
The flame shall not hurt thee; I only design
Thy dross to consume, and thy gold to refine.

Minister:

They were stoned, they were sawn asunder, they were tempted, they were slain with the sword; they went about in sheepskins, in goatskins; being destitute, afflicted, ill-treated, wandering in deserts and mountains and caves and the holes of the earth.
HEBREWS 11:37, 38.

Choir (singing to the "Portuguese Hymn"):

Fear not, I am with thee, O be not dismayed;
For I am thy God, I will still give thee aid;
I'll strengthen thee, help thee, and cause thee to stand,
Upheld by my righteous, omnipotent hand.

Minister:

These all having had witness borne to them through their faith, received not the promise, God having provided some better thing concerning us, that apart from us they should not be made perfect. HEBREWS 11:39, 40.

All (singing):

Faith of our fathers, we will love
Both friend and foe in all our strife,
And preach thee, too, as love knows how,
By kindly words and virtuous life.
Faith of our fathers, holy faith,
We will be true to thee till death.

✣

THE HYMN TUNE. The tune ST. CATHERINE bears the names of two composers, Henri Frederic Hemy (1818–1888), and James

George Walton (1821–1905). The reason for this unusual combination is the fact that Mr. Walton's arrangement of this melody is found in Mr. Hemy's book, *Crown of Jesus Music,* published in 1864.

Mr. Hemy was an English organist and compiler of music. He edited a pianoforte-tutor, which bears his name. He was born at Newcastle-on-Tyne.

FATHER IN HEAVEN, WHO LOVEST ALL

Land of our birth, we pledge to thee
Our love and toil in years to be,
When we are grown and take our place
As men and women with our race.

1. Father in heaven, who lovest all,
O help thy children when they call,
That they may build from age to age
An undefiled heritage.

2. Teach us to bear the yoke in youth,
With steadfastness and careful truth,
That, in our time, thy grace may give
The truth whereby the nations live.

3. Teach us to rule ourselves alway,
Controlled and cleanly night and day,
That we may bring, if need arise,
No maimed or worthless sacrifice.

4. Teach us to look in all our ends
On thee for Judge, and not our friends,
That we, with thee, may walk uncowed
By fear or favor of the crowd.

5. Teach us the strength that cannot seek,
By deed or thought, to hurt the weak,
That, under thee, we may possess
Man's strength to comfort man's distress.

6. Teach us delight in simple things,
And mirth that has no bitter springs,
Forgiveness free of evil done,
And love to all men 'neath the sun.[1]

Land of our birth, our faith, our pride,
For whose dear sake our fathers died;
O Motherland, we pledge to thee
Head, heart, and hand through the years to be.

RUDYARD KIPLING, 1906.

[1] Rudyard Kipling in *Puck of Pook's Hill,* 1906. Reprinted by permission of the author and Messrs. A. P. Watt and Sons, Agents, and Doubleday, Doran & Co., Publishers.

BIBLICAL TEXT.

He hath showed thee, O man, what is good; and what doth the Lord require of thee, but to do justly, and to love kindness, and to walk humbly with thy God?

MICAH 6:8.

Cease to do evil; learn to do well; seek justice, relieve the oppressed, judge the fatherless, plead for the widow.

ISAIAH 1:16, 17.

If ye be willing and obedient, ye shall eat the good of the land.

ISAIAH 1:19.

THE VIRTUES OF AN UPRIGHT LIFE

Rudyard Kipling (1865–) is one of the best-known authors and poets of the present day. A genuine Englishman, his opportunities for world-observation have been exceptional. Born in Bombay, India, he was educated at the United Services College, Westward Ho, Devon; later he was, for a time, a journalist in India, a resident of the United States (at Brattleboro, Vermont), and for many years a sympathetic but critical observer of English life from his home in Sussex.

Dr. James Moffatt calls him "the unofficial Poet Laureate of the Empire, a passionate patriot, an extoller of the virile virtues of clean living and manly duty and cheerfulness and stoic endurance, and, in his highest moments, as in 'Recessional' and 'The Children's Song,' a singer of the faith that has made Britain great." [2]

Both of Kipling's grandfathers were Wesleyan preachers. His mother came from a family of four sisters, one of whom was the wife of Sir Edward Burne-Jones; another was the mother of Stanley Baldwin, Prime Minister of England from 1924 to 1929.

The hymn suggests admirable prayer items for thoughtful young people: "that they may build . . . an undefiled heritage"; "to bear the yoke in youth"; "to rule ourselves alway, controlled and cleanly night and day"; "no maimed or worthless sacrifice" (note the reference to the Old Testament law of sacrifice, Leviticus 22:22); "walk uncowed by fear or favor of the crowd"; "man's strength to succor man's distress"; and, the climax of all, "love to all men 'neath the sun."

✣

THE HYMN TUNE. A number of different tunes are used with these words: SAXBY, by Timothy Matthews (1826–1910); PENTECOST, by William Boyd, (1847–). Other tunes in use include TRURO, LEST WE FORGET, MAINZER, GALILEE, RIVAULX, and LONG MILFORD.

[2] From the *Handbook to the Church Hymnery,* by James Moffatt, 1927, copyright by Oxford University Press.

Much is said about the wedding of hymn and tune, as though the gods had decreed that such unions must continue inviolate. Many a tune, latterly wedded, was never meant for its mate; for example, AURELIA (Golden) belongs to "Jerusalem the golden" and not to "The Church's one foundation"; MATERNA (Mother) was first made for "O, Mother dear, Jerusalem," and not for "O beautiful for spacious skies"; PENTECOST was composed for a tender Holy Spirit Hymn and not for "Fight the good fight"; LANCASHIRE was intended for "From Greenland's icy mountains," and not for "Lead on, O King eternal."

Misfits are to be met with throughout the hymn book, and sentiment, not judgment, keeps them mated. Many of our finest hymns are handicapped by weak, colorless, sugary tunes. Thus the singing drags along into final droning and flatting of stanzas, when by right these last strophes should pulse with resolves and heartburnings.

Our hymn books are full of second and third rate tunes. Our newer English and American hymnals are courageously breaking ground by introducing magnificent new tunes such as SINE NOMINE, PIONEERS, JERUSALEM, THORNBURY, JUBILATE, PHŒNIX, QUEENSWOOD, EBENEZER, TOWN OF BETHLEHEM, WOODLANDS, FOREST GREEN, GOSTERWOOD, and MARCHING.

FIGHT THE GOOD FIGHT

1. Fight the good fight with all thy might!
Christ is thy strength, and Christ thy right;
Lay hold on life, and it shall be
Thy joy and crown eternally.

2. Run the straight race through God's good grace,
Lift up thine eyes, and seek his face;
Life with its way before us lies.
Christ is the path, and Christ the prize.

3. Cast care aside, upon thy Guide
Lean, and his mercy will provide;
Trust, and the trusting soul shall prove
Christ is its life, and Christ its love.

4. Faint not nor fear, his arms are near,
He changeth not and thou art dear;
Only believe, and thou shalt see
That Christ is all in all to thee.

JOHN S. B. MONSELL, 1863.

Biblical Text.

Fight the good fight of the faith, lay hold on the life eternal, whereunto thou wast called.

I Timothy 6:12.

Every man that striveth in the games exerciseth self-control in all things. Now they do it to receive a corruptible crown; but we an incorruptible. I therefore so run, as not uncertainly; so fight I, as not beating the air.

I Corinthians 9:25, 26.

A CHALLENGE TO ACTIVITY

There is a story of a celebrated physician, Ursinus, who was condemned to death for his faith in Christ. He trembled at the thought of death, wavered, and seemed about to retract his faith. An old friend named Vitalis came close to him, and said: "What! have you been so industrious heretofore to preserve men's bodies and will you now shrink at the saving of your own soul? Be courageous!" These words strengthened Ursinus, but caused the condemnation of his friend. The two men died together for their faith.

This hymn has the brevity, color, feeling and devotion of the greatest hymns. Notice the prominence given to verbs, "fight," "lay hold," "run," "lift up," "seek," "cast," "lean," "faint not nor fear," "believe." This hymn may rightly be called a "Challenge to Activity."

A meaningful passage is that of the latter half of the first stanza,

"Lay hold on life, and it shall be,
Thy joy and crown eternally."

Does it refer to the "good fight of faith"? Is it that which is to be "thy joy and crown eternally"? Or, is it that "life" which is to be "laid hold on" which forms the eternal joy and crown? Apparently the latter, meaning that the days of this earthly life rightly spent shall be a "joy and crown" in the stretches of eternity, when years shall be no more.

The figures of speech change rapidly; life is a fight, a race-course, a progress of one weary or wounded. The references to Christ are splendidly inclusive and rich in meaning. Christ is the fighter's strength, the runner's path and prize, the care-worn traveler's guide, the trusting soul's life and love. In all the changing figures of speech, suggesting so eloquently the changing scenes of life, Christ is the unchanging "the same yesterday, today and forever"; the soul's "all in all."

The last stanza, for simplicity, tenderness and rockbound faith is unexcelled.

A Service of Challenge to Youth

The following service, with this hymn as a climax, will have a special appeal to young people at times of decision such as New Year's or Easter:

Processional: "Awake, My Soul, Stretch Every Nerve."
Hymn: "Father, Hear the prayer we offer,
Not for ease that prayer shall be."
Responsive Reading: Ephesians 6: 10–18.
Prayer.
Hymn: "Once to every man and nation."
Antiphonal singing by choirs: "Christian, dost thou see them?"
Address: Theme "More Than Conquerors." (Romans 8: 37).
Reading: "A Prayer."

1. We know the paths wherein our feet should press
Across our hearts are written thy decrees;
Yet now, O Lord, be merciful to bless
With more than these.

2. Grant us the will to fashion as we feel,
Grant us the strength to labor as we know,
Grant us the purpose, ribbed and edged with steel,
To strike the blow.

3. Knowledge we ask not, knowledge thou hast lent,
But, Lord, the will,—there lies our bitter need,
Give us to build above the deep intent,
The deed, the deed.[1]

Hymn: "Fight the Good Fight."
Recessional: "Lead On, O King Eternal."

✣

THE HYMN TUNE. Concerning the tune PENTECOST, the *Musical Times,* December 1, 1908, says: "Reverend William Boyd tells how he wrote PENTECOST for 'Come, Holy Ghost, Our Souls Inspire,' at the request of Reverend Sabine Baring-Gould, his former tutor, for use at a Whitsuntide gathering of colliers at Harbury in Yorkshire; and that it was first printed in *Thirty-two Hymn Tunes,* composed by members of the University of Oxford, 1868."

[1] By John Drinkwater. Copyright by Houghton Mifflin Company.

"He continues: 'One day as I was walking along Regent Street, I felt a slap on my back, and turning around saw my dear old friend, Arthur Sullivan. "My dear Billy," he said, "I've seen a tune of yours which I must have." (He was then editing *Church Hymns.*) "All right," I said, "send me a check and I agree."

" 'No copy of the book, much less proof, was sent to me, and when I saw the tune I was horrified to find that Sullivan had assigned it to "Fight the Good Fight." We had a regular fisticuff about it, but judging from the favor with which the tune has been received, I feel that Sullivan was right in so mating music and words.'

"Later, Reverend Boyd made a stipulation that PENTECOST should be set to this hymn."

Reverend William Boyd (1847–1927) was born at Montego Bay, Jamaica, of Scotch ancestry. He began his musical career by composing at the early age of ten. At Oxford he was organ scholar of his college. He was ordained priest of the Anglican Church in 1882 and served as vicar of All Saints, Norfolk Square, London, for twenty-five years, until his retirement in 1918.

FLING OUT THE BANNER

1. Fling out the banner! let it float
Skyward and seaward, high and wide;
The sun that lights its shining folds,
The cross on which the Saviour died.

2. Fling out the banner! angels bend
In anxious silence o'er the sign,
And vainly seek to comprehend
The wonder of the love divine.

3. Fling out the banner! heathen lands
Shall see from far the glorious sight,
And nations, crowding to be born,
Baptize their spirits in its light.

4. Fling out the banner! Sin-sick souls
That sink and perish in the strife,
Shall touch in faith its radiant hem,
And spring immortal into life.

5. Fling out the banner! wide and high,
Skyward and seaward, let it shine:
Nor skill, nor might, nor merit ours;
We conquer only in that sign.

GEORGE WASHINGTON DOANE, 1848.

Biblical Text.

Thou hast given a banner to them that fear thee,
That it may be displayed because of the truth.

Psalm 60:4.

I am not ashamed of the gospel: for it is the power of God unto Salvation to everyone that believeth.

Romans 1:16.

THE HYMN OF THE CHRISTIAN FLAG

Although Bishop George Washington Doane (1799–1859) died long before the Christian flag was thought of, yet the hymn he wrote is preëminently "the hymn of the Christian flag." Whenever one stands before that flag of white, with its field of blue, and its crimson cross, and repeats the pledge: "I pledge allegiance to the flag of the Church, and to the Saviour for whose kingdom it stands, one brotherhood, uniting all mankind in service and in love," the stirring strains of this hymn of world-brotherhood come to mind.

There were two major ideals in the life of Bishop Doane: the promotion of Christian education, and the extension of the Gospel around the world. These two ideals are united in this hymnic legacy which he gave the world.

St. Mary's School at Burlington, New Jersey, was to have a flag raising. Since a distinctive hymn for the occasion was desired, Bishop Doane, then Protestant Episcopal Bishop of the Diocese of New Jersey, was asked to write a special song.

"Fling out the Banner" was the Bishop's response to this request. Although written for one school and for one special occasion, there is a majestic sweep and a world-embracing thought in this hymn too mighty to be confined to one school, or to one communion. It expresses in golden poetry what every Christian in his heart knows that Christianity can and should do. Breed says: "What can be more stirring, more ringing, than these triumphant notes? How original and how striking is the reference in the fourth verse to the hem of the Saviour's garment, and the use of '*In hoc signo*' in the last verse. What a fine use is made of the scriptural truth, of the angels' interest in the work of redemption, in the second verse. How unusual the conception of the spiritual birth of nations, in 'crowding to be born.'"[1]

George Washington Doane was born in Trenton, New Jersey, in the year in which George Washington died, and was named for the "Father of his country." His first church work was as assistant min-

[1] From *The History and Use of Hymns and Hymn Tunes,* by David R. Breed, copyright by Fleming Revell Co.

ister at Trinity Church, New York. From 1828 to 1832 he served as Rector of Trinity Church, Boston, where Phillips Brooks was one of his most famous successors. From 1832 to his death he was the Bishop of New Jersey. Known as the "missionary Bishop," because of his intense interest in missionary work, his energy, learning and force of character made him one of the outstanding leaders of church life in America.

Another hymn by Bishop Doane commonly used, is "Softly now the light of day," sung every Wednesday evening in his memory at St. Mary's Hall, which he founded.

Dramatic Correlations

Two correlations, one simple, the other more elaborate, may help to make this hymn more vivid and impressive. Both are based on the use of the Christian Flag.

I. The Illuminated Flag

In a darkened auditorium a large Christian flag is held by a young woman draped in white, with blue scarf and girdle, to suggest loyalty to the church. While the organ plays the tune, as a prelude to the singing, a spot of light is thrown on the flag:

First stanza: Stereopticon slide of the crucifixion, or of the Cross alone.

Second stanza: A picture of angels.

Third stanza: Group of native Christians in Africa, China, India, or other mission field.

Fourth stanza: A slide of Armitage's picture "Faith," showing the woman touching the hem of Jesus' garment.

Fifth stanza: As the words "seaward and skyward" are sung, let the flag-bearer move to the center in front of the screen, with flag fully unfurled, full light of the stereopticon on the flag. Care should be taken to have the cross on the flag clearly visible.

II. Christianity, The Basis for Internationalism

For this more elaborate correlation, the stereopticon screen should be placed at the side, while a small elevated platform in the exact center of the large one, gives a place for the Bearer of the Christian Flag.

Hymn (*words on screen*): "These things shall be" (J. A. Symonds). As the third stanza is sung, the Bearer of the Christian Flag enters and takes her place.

Hymn (*illustrated set*): "America the Beautiful." At the first "America, America," the Bearer of the American Flag (*young man in uniform*) enters, taking his stand at left front. At end of hymn he takes his place near center, slightly to the rear.

Hymn (*by Choir*) "God of our Fathers, Known of Old" (Kipling). Bearer of British flag enters, front, stands with flag unfurled; at end of hymn, steps to rear with flag grounded, partially furled.

National Hymns, or typical songs, of as many nations as practicable, while representatives, in national costumes and with national flags enter, stand at front for a time, then step to rear, forming a semi-circle around the Christian Flag.

Climax: "Fling out the Banner," sung from screen by entire congregation. At the last line of the first stanza all flag bearers kneel, lowering their flags, pointing them toward the Christian flag, which Flag Bearer raises high at that moment.

Recessional: (*to organ music of* WALTHAM *without singing*): The Flag-Bearer of the Christian flag leading, the others following two by two.

Conclusion: "The Lord's Prayer" with special emphasis on the words, "Thy Kingdom Come, thy will be done on earth."

✣

THE HYMN TUNE. The tune, WALTHAM, is invariably associated with these words. John Baptiste Calkin (1827–1905) was born in London, studied under his father, and was organist, precentor and choirmaster at St. Columba's College, Ireland, and afterward at several churches in London. He was professor at the Guildhall School of Music and Croydon Conservatory up to his death. No hymn tunes, even by Dykes and Barnby, surpass NOX PRAECESSIT and WALTHAM. The latter will prove more rhythmic and forceful if sung a tone higher than usual (Key of F) and the last word of each stanza is held firmly and long.

FOR THE BEAUTY OF THE EARTH

1. For the beauty of the earth,
For the glory of the skies,
For the love which from our birth
Over and around us lies:

Refrain

Lord of all, to thee we raise
This, our hymn of grateful praise.

2. For the wonder of each hour,
Of the day and of the night,
Hill and vale, and tree and flower,
Sun and moon, and stars of light:

Refrain

3. For the joy of ear and eye,
For the heart and mind's delight,
For the mystic harmony
Linking sense to sound and sight:

Refrain

4. For the joy of human love,
Brother, sister, parent, child,
Friends on earth, and friends above,
For all gentle thoughts and mild:

Refrain

5. For thy church that evermore
Lifteth holy hands above,
Offering up on every shore
Her pure sacrifice of love:

Refrain

FOLLIOTT S. PIERPOINT, 1864.

BIBLICAL TEXT.

O Lord, how manifold are thy works!
In wisdom hast thou made them all:
The earth is full of thy riches.

PSALM 104:24.

Oh that men would praise the Lord for his lovingkindness,
And for his wonderful works to the children of men!

PSALM 107:21.

NATURE, ART, HOME, CHURCH

In many hymnals this hymn will be found in the "Nature" section, because of the significance of the first and second stanzas. It is a "universal" hymn of praise, singularly all-inclusive in its reasons for gratitude to God.

This hymn was written for Holy Communion, or for Flower Services, with the following stanza of special significance:

6. For thyself, best Gift Divine,
To our race so freely given,
For that great, great love of thine,
Peace on earth, and joy in heaven;
Christ our God, to thee we raise,
This our hymn of grateful praise.

Folliott Sandford Pierpoint was born at Bath, England, in 1835. He studied at Queens' College, Cambridge, where he distinguished himself in the classics. He was classical master at Somersetshire College for a time, and then moved to Babbicombe, where he did occasional classical teaching. Although he published a book of poems, he is remembered chiefly for this one note of lyrical praise. In its original form the hymn had eight stanzas.

A Responsive Service

A synthesis of Scripture and song to bring out the deeper significance of this hymn is suggested:

Minister:

The heavens declare the glory of God;
And the firmament showeth his handiwork.

PSALM 19:1.

The earth is the Lord's, and the fulness thereof;
The world, and they that dwell therein.
For he hath founded it upon the seas,
And established it upon the floods.

PSALM 24:1, 2.

Congregation: (sings Stanza One)

Minister:

When the morning stars sang together,
And all the sons of God shouted for joy.

JOB 38:7.

Consider the lilies of the field, how they grow; they toil not, neither do they spin: yet I say unto you, that even Solomon in all his glory was not arrayed like one of these.

MATTHEW 6:28, 29.

Congregation: (sings Stanza Two)

Minister:

Open thou mine eyes, that I may behold
Wondrous things out of thy law.

PSALM 119:18.

I, the Lord, have called thee in righteousness, and will hold thy hand, and will keep thee, and give thee for a covenant of the people, for a light of the Gentiles; to open the blind eyes.

ISAIAH 42:6, 7.

The heart of the prudent getteth knowledge;
And the ear of the wise seeketh knowledge.

PROVERBS 18: 15.

Congregation: (sings Stanza Three)

Minister:

The soul of Jonathan was knit with the soul of David, and Jonathan loved him as his own soul.

I SAMUEL 18: 1.

A friend loveth at all times;
And a brother is born for adversity.

PROVERBS 17: 17.

Love suffereth long, and is kind;
Love envieth not; love vaunteth not itself;
Love beareth all things, believeth all things, hopeth all things, endureth all things.

I CORINTHIANS 13: 4, 7.

Congregation: (sings Stanza Four)

Minister:

The holy Church throughout all the world doth acknowledge thee;
The Father of an infinite majesty; thine adorable, true and only Son;
Also the Holy Ghost, the Comforter.

From the "Te Deum Laudamus."

As Christ also loved the church, and gave himself up for it; that he might sanctify it . . . that he might present the church to himself a glorious church, not having spot or wrinkle or any such thing; but that it should be holy and without blemish. EPHESIANS 5: 25–27.

Congregation: (sings Stanza Five)

Minister:

For God so loved the world, that he gave his only begotten Son, that whosoever believeth on him should not perish, but have eternal life.

JOHN 3: 16.

The good shepherd layeth down his life for the sheep.

JOHN 10: 11.

There is therefore now no condemnation to them that are in Christ Jesus.

ROMANS 8:1.

Behold what manner of love the Father hath bestowed upon us, that we should be called children of God; and such we are.

I JOHN 3:1.

Congregation: (sings Stanza Six)

A Unison Prayer:

Almighty God, our heavenly Father, from whom cometh every good and perfect gift; we call to remembrance thy loving-kindness and thy tender mercies which have been ever of old, and with grateful hearts we lift up to thee the voice of our thanksgiving. For all the comforts and gladness of life; for our homes and all our home-blessings; for the love, sympathy, and good-will of men: we praise thee, O God. For the gift of thy Son, Jesus Christ, and all the helps and hopes which are ours as his disciples; for the presence and inspiration of thy Holy Spirit, we praise thee, O God.

And now, O Lord, having praised thee with our lips; grant that we may also praise thee in consecrated and faithful lives; through Jesus Christ, our Lord, Amen.[1]

✣

THE HYMN TUNE. Conrad Kocher (1786–1872), a native of Würtemberg, went to St. Petersburg at the age of seventeen as a tutor. Later on he went to Rome to master *Palestrina* and *a capella* singing. Out of this grew his attempt to reform church music in Germany. Beginning in his home city, Stuttgart, he founded a school of church music and popularized four-part singing, besides acting as organist and director in the Stiftskirche. He spent much time revising hymn books and composing new tunes.

The name DIX comes from the association of this music with William Dix's hymn, "As with Gladness Men of Old."

MUSICAL INTERPRETATION. The music of this tune permits full expression of the separate, yet intimately connected phrases of the hymn. It should be noted that there is no rest after the half-note at the end of the second bar, but that the refrain comes immedi-

[1] By D. T. Mc Gill.

ately, and logically, after the slightest pause of the comma at the end of the stanza.

The accented beats permit, almost compel, the proper emphasis on the important words, "human love," "brother, sister, parent, child," in the fourth stanza, and "thy church" in the fifth stanza.

Careful attention to the phrasing, accented and sustained notes, will be a real help in making this hymn an act of united praise to God.

This hymn tune is antiphonal in structure. It has answering phrases, first score versus the second, with all voices uniting in the refrain.

FORWARD, BE OUR WATCHWORD

1. Forward, be our watchword,
Steps and voices joined;
Seek the things before us,
Not a look behind:
Burns the fiery pillar
At our army's head;
Who shall dream of shrinking,
By our Captain led?
    Forward through the desert,
    Through the toil and fight;
    Jordan flows before us;
    Zion beams with light.

2. Glories upon glories
Hath our God prepared,
By the souls that love him,
One day to be shared;
Eye hath not beheld them,
Ear hath never heard;
Nor of these hath uttered
Thought or speech a word.
    Forward, marching eastward
    Where the heaven is bright,
    Till the veil be lifted,
    Till our faith be sight.

3. Far o'er yon horizon
Rise the city towers,
Where our God abideth;
That fair home is ours.
Flash the streets with jasper,
Shine the gates with gold;
Flows the gladdening river
Shedding joys untold.
    Thither, onward thither,
    In the Spirit's might,

Pilgrims, to your country;
Forward into light.

HENRY ALFORD, 1871.

BIBLICAL TEXT.

Speak unto the children of Israel, that they go forward.

EXODUS 14:15.

And he brought forth his people with joy,
And his chosen with singing.

PSALM 105:43.

A NOTABLE CHOIR FESTIVAL IN CANTERBURY CATHEDRAL

On June 6th, 1871, convened at Canterbury Cathedral, England, the Tenth Festival of the Parochial Choirs of the Canterbury Diocesan Union. Outstanding was the singing of a new Processional Hymn by the combined choirs of nine hundred singers. It is said that the effect was almost overwhelming and quite baffled description. It took a full half hour for the entire procession to pass within the Choir Screen. Each pair of choristers started singing when they reached a specified spot, and ceased singing when they set foot on the last step of the ascent to the choir, so that there was a continuous and harmonious volume of praise.

This new Processional Hymn had been written for the occasion by Henry Alford, Dean of the Cathedral, at the request of Reverend J. G. Wood, the eminent naturalist. His first hymn was not a good processional. Dr. Wood wrote back: "Would the Dean kindly go into his cathedral, walk slowly along the course which the procession would take, and compose another hymn as he did so?" "Forward, Be Our Watchword" was the result. Along with this hymn went a humorous note to the effect that the Dean had just put his hymn into its hat and boots (soprano and bass); but that someone else might add the coat and trousers (alto and tenor). Unfortunately, the Dean was not present to hear the overpowering effect of his hymn. He had been called to join "the choir invisible" before the Festival transpired.

Henry Alford (1810–1871) was born and bred in London. When sixteen he wrote on the fly-leaf of his Bible: "I do this day in the presence of God and my own soul renew my covenant with God and solemnly determine henceforth to become his and to do his work as far as in me lies."

He was an author of note, including among his writings such diversified material as *An Edition of Homer,* a volume on *The*

Queen's English, a volume of *Descriptive English Poetry*, and, his greatest work, *The Greek Testament*. He wrote many hymns, but is remembered as a hymn-writer by this one outstanding hymn.

There is a significant connection between the purpose of the sixteen-year-old boy, written on the fly-leaf of his Bible, the last hymn he wrote, based on God's guidance of the Children of Israel through the wilderness, and the inscription which he wrote for his tombstone, "The inn of a pilgrim travelling to Jerusalem."

Omitted Stanzas

The hymn originally had eight double stanzas, each followed by a brilliant chorus of four lines. Here are three which have obvious relationship to the Processional in Canterbury Cathedral:

Forward, when in childhood
Buds the infant mind;
All through youth and manhood,
Not a thought behind;
Speed through realms of nature,
Climb the steps of grace;
Faint not, till in glory
Gleams our Father's face.
    Forward! all the life time,
    Climb from height to height;
    Till the head be hoary,
    Till the eve be light.

Into God's high temple,
Onward as we press,
Beauty spreads around us,
Born of Holiness;
Arch and vault and carving,
Lights of varied tone,
Softened words and holy,
Prayer and praise alone;
    Every thought upraising,
    To our city bright,
    Where the tribes assemble,
    Round the throne of light.

Naught that city needeth
Of these aisles of stone;
Where the Godhead dwelleth,
Temple there is none:
All the saints that ever
In these courts have stood,
Are but babes, and feeding
On the children's food.
    On through sign and tokens,
    Stars amidst the night;

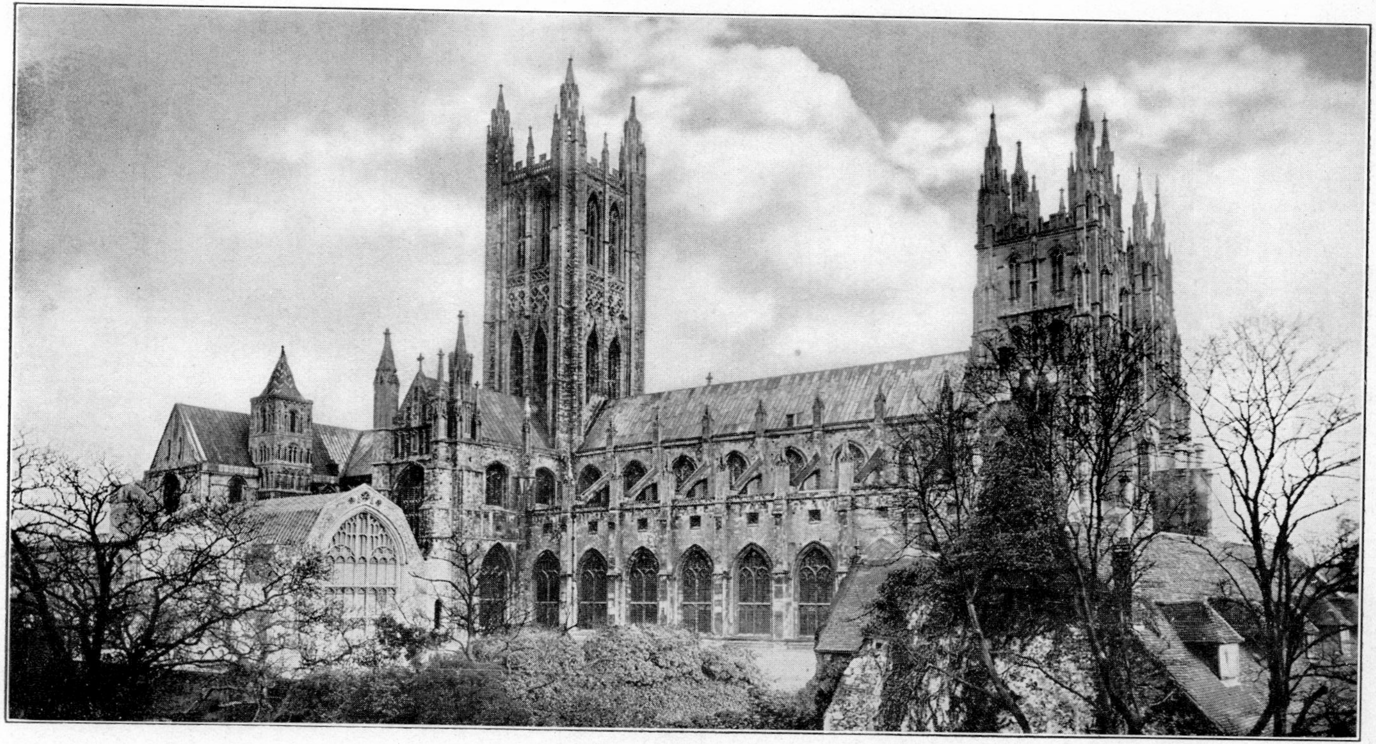

CANTERBURY CATHEDRAL

Forward through the darkness,
Forward into light.

✣

THE HYMN TUNE. WATCHWORD was composed for these words after the Canterbury event, by Henry Smart (1813–1879). Smart was born in London, declined the offer of a commission in the Indian Army, made a four-year trial of the profession of law, and gave it up to devote himself to music.

He became one of the most proficient organists in England, and was an expert also in planning and erecting organs. In 1865 his eyesight, which had always been poor, failed altogether. Although blind for the last fourteen years of his life, he continued to play and to compose music. He was the composer of a large number of anthems and hymn tunes, some cantatas and one oratorio. This tune which fits so admirably the "Forward" challenge of the hymn, was composed after the musician had become totally blind.

Blind poets and musicians in the Immortal Song of the church number in their ranks, George Matheson, Fanny Crosby, Henry Smart, Timothy Dwight and John Milton whose poem follows:

I am old and blind!
Men point at me as smitten by God's frown:
Afflicted and deserted of my kind,
Yet am I not cast down.

I am weak, yet strong;
I murmur not that I no longer see;
Poor, old, and helpless, I the more belong,
Father supreme, to thee!

All-merciful One!
When men are furthest, then art thou most near;
When friends pass by, my weaknesses to shun,
Thy chariot I hear.

Thy glorious face
Is leaning toward me; and its holy light
Shines in upon my lonely dwelling place,
And there is no more night.

I have naught to fear;
This darkness is the shadow of thy wing;
Beneath it I am almost sacred; here
Can come no evil thing.

Oh, I seem to stand
Trembling, where foot of mortal ne'er hath been,

Wrapt in that radiance from the sinless land,
Which eye hath never seen!

Visions come and go:
Shapes of resplendent beauty around me throng;
From angel lips I seem to hear the flow
Of soft and holy song.

Give me now my lyre!
I feel the stirrings of a gift divine:
Within my bosom glows unearthly fire,
Lit by no skill of mine.

FORWARD THROUGH THE AGES

1. Forward through the ages,
In unbroken line,
Move the faithful spirits,
At the call divine;
Gifts in differing measure,
Hearts of one accord,
Manifold the service,
One the sure reward.

Refrain

Forward through the ages,
In unbroken line,
Move the faithful spirits,
At the call divine.

2. Wider grows the kingdom,
Reign of love and light;
For it we must labor,
Till our faith is sight:
Prophets have proclaimed it,
Martyrs testified,
Poets sung its glory,
Heroes for it died.

Refrain

3. Not alone we conquer,
Not alone we fall;
In each loss or triumph
Lose or triumph all.
Bound by God's far purpose
In one living whole,
Move we on together,
To the shining goal.

Refrain

FREDERICK L. HOSMER, 1908.

BIBLICAL TEXT.

Now there are diversities of gifts, but the same Spirit. And there are diversities of workings, but the same God, who worketh all things in all.

I CORINTHIANS 12:4, 6.

Therefore let us also, seeing we are compassed about with so great a cloud of witnesses, lay aside every weight, and the sin which doth so easily beset us, and let us run with patience the race that is set before us, looking unto Jesus, the author and perfector of our faith.

HEBREWS 12:1, 2.

THE UNBROKEN LINE

Formed for a battle in the shelter of a little clump of woods, a company of the Fourteenth New Hampshire Regiment in the Civil War, could see nothing of the rest of the regiment. But when the command to "Advance" was given, and they marched out of the woods, they found themselves on a hill-top; suddenly they caught a glimpse of a long line of blue—the rest of their regiment and other regiments of their brigade, stretching out in both directions as far as eye could see. The late Reverend F. H. Buffum, telling this incident in his history of the Fourteenth Regiment, noted the startling change in the feelings of the men. Feeling that they were "not alone to conquer, not alone to fall," but a part of a mighty army marching resistlessly forward, they advanced with new courage and determination to win the day.

Something of that same feeling is needed by the scattered "companies" of Christians, who sometimes wonder about their essential unity. Dr. Hosmer must have sensed such questionings and written this hymn as his answer.

Frederick L. Hosmer, (1840–1929) was born in Framingham, Massachusetts. After graduating from Harvard University and Harvard Divinity School, he held pastorates in Unitarian churches at Northboro, Massachusetts; Quincy, Illinois; St. Louis, Missouri, and Berkeley, California.

With W. C. Gannett and J. V. Blake in 1880 he edited *Unity Hymns and Carols,* and with Dr. Gannett, in 1911, a revised and enlarged edition of this hymnal. In 1908, the year in which this hymn was written, Dr. Hosmer was the Lecturer on Hymnody at Harvard. He was the author of a number of hymns which have found their way into the more modern hymnals. They are hymns of challenge, courage, and faith in the fitness of the Gospel message for modern life. Among them may be noted, "O Thou in All Thy Might So Far," "Thy Kingdom Come, O Lord, Wide Circling as the Sun"; "O Beautiful, my Country," and "From Age to Age They Gather."

The author here has given a poetic commentary on Paul's message to the Corinthians concerning the diversity, yet unity, of "spiritual gifts" (I Corinthians 12). Notice how closely he follows Paul's thought, "Gifts in differing measure," "Manifold the service," and "Prophets," "Martyrs," "Poets" and "Heroes." These words are worthy of careful study; the author has condensed volumes into single phrases.

Compare with this hymn of the twentieth century, the "Te Deum Laudamus" of the fourth century:

"The glorious company of the apostles
The goodly fellowship of the prophets } Praise thee;"
The noble army of martyrs

also the eighth century monastic hymn, "Art Thou Weary, Art Thou Languid?" which reads:

"Finding, following, keeping, struggling,
Is he sure to bless?
Saints, apostles, prophets, martyrs,
Answer 'Yes!'

✣

THE HYMN TUNE. ONWARD, by J. W. Barrington, was written in 1893 for other words. Latterly this text and this tune have been mated with the evident consent of all who use hymns. The tune has good stride, a quick pace, large and daring intervals, with a folk-song repetition that makes it singable, remembered, convincing.

FROM THE EASTERN MOUNTAINS

1. From the eastern mountains,
Pressing on, they come,
Wise men in their wisdom,
To his humble home;
Stirred by deep devotion,
Hasting from afar,
Ever journeying onward,
Guided by a star.

Refrain

Light of life that shineth,
Ere the worlds began,
Draw thou near, and lighten
Every heart of man.

2. Thou who in a manger
Once hast lowly lain,
Who dost now in glory
O'er all kingdoms reign,
Gather in the people,
Who in lands afar,

Ne'er have seen the brightness
Of thy guiding star.

Refrain

3. Gather in the outcasts,
All who've gone astray;
Throw thy radiance o'er them,
Guide them on their way;
Those who never knew thee,
Those who've wandered far,
Guide them by the brightness
Of thy guiding star.

Refrain

4. Until every nation,
Whether bond or free,
'Neath thy starlit banner,
Jesus, follows thee
O'er the distant mountains
To that heavenly home,
Where nor sin nor sorrow
Evermore shall come.

Refrain

GODFREY THRING, 1873.

BIBLICAL TEXT.

We saw his star in the east and are come to worship him.

MATTHEW 2:2.

The root and the offspring of David, the bright, the morning star.

REVELATION 22:16.

And nations shall come to thy light, and kings to the brightness of thy rising.

ISAIAH 60:3.

Come unto me, all ye that labor and are heavy laden, and I will give you rest.

MATTHEW 11:28.

A PROCESSIONAL OF ALL PEOPLES

Because of the very common tendency to limit our use of certain hymns to particular seasons, and the difficulty of "cross-indexing" the hymnal, our services are robbed of much inspirational material which might otherwise brighten and energize them. This hymn, listed under "Nativity," is an admirable missionary and evangelistic hymn and is as appropriate for June or September as for December.

Because of its use only at Christmas time, "From the Eastern Mountains" is sung very seldom in American churches, which is unfortunate, because the hymn is one of those rare ones which has a rightful and equally appropriate place in two or three sections of the hymnal.

Godfrey Thring (1823–1903) was the son of a Church of England rector, born at Alford, Somersetshire. After his training at Shrewsbury School and Balliol College, Oxford, and in several curacies, at the age of thirty-five he succeeded his father in the rectory of Alford, which he held for many years. Mr. Thring was not only a writer of hymns, but also a hymnologist of note. He was the editor of the *Church of England Hymn Book*. He also published three volumes of his own hymns. His hymns are more familiar to English congregations than to American, but one of them, "The Radiant Morn Hath Passed Away," set in anthem form, is frequently used by American church choirs.

Dr. Thring's brother Edward, who was famous as a schoolmaster in Uppingham, wrote concerning Godfrey's hymns: "Be sure that no painting, no art work you could have done, by any possibility could have been so powerful for good, or given you the niche you now occupy. As long as the English language lasts, sundry of your hymns will be read and sung, yea, even to the last day, and many a soul thrill with your words. What more can a man want? Very likely if you had had all that old heathendom rammed into you, as I had, and all the literary slicing and pruning, and been scissored like me, you would just have lost the freshness and simple touch which makes you what you are. No, my boy, I make a tidy schoolmaster and pass into the lives of many a pupil, and you live on the lips of the Church. So be satisfied. And what does it matter, if we do the Master's will?"

✣

THE HYMN TUNE. ROSMORE by Henry Gough Trembath (1844–1908), written for the Presbyterian Hymnal, 1895, by this English organist, has an infectious march rhythm which makes both hymn and tune effective as a pageant-processional, with the wise men, the people of all nations, the poor and the outcast, all gathering about the manger of the King of kings.

GLORY BE TO THE FATHER

(Gloria Patri)

Glory be to the Father, and to the Son,
and to the Holy Ghost;
As it was in the beginning, is now, and
ever shall be, world without end.
Amen.

ANONYMOUS, Second Century.

BIBLICAL TEXT.

To the only God our Saviour, through Jesus Christ our Lord, be glory, majesty, dominion and power, before all time, and now, and for evermore. Amen.

JUDE 1:25.

A SECOND CENTURY HYMN OF PRAISE

The *"Gloria Patri"* is called the "Lesser Doxology" to distinguish it from "The Greater Doxology," the *"Gloria in Excelsis Deo."* It is one of the very oldest bits of Christian praise. The first half of it goes back, possibly, to the time of the Apostles themselves. At any rate, it is certainly as early as the second century when Christians sang, rapturously, as Philo, the learned Jew of Alexandria, records: "Hymns composed to the praise of God, in many metres, and to various melodies; in one, singing together and in unison, and in another, with antiphonal harmonies, being transported with divine enthusiasm. . . . Perfectly beautiful are their motions, perfectly beautiful their discourse, and the final aim of their motions and their discourse is piety."

The second half of the "Gloria Patri" was added later, just when is not known, but certainly before 529 A. D. In that year the Second Council of Vaison "enjoined the use of the second half in France, as being already in general use throughout the whole East, Africa and Italy, and as directed against heretics who denied the eternity of the Son of God."

As sung by martyrs in the Coliseum and in the Circus Maximus in the days of Roman supremacy, it ran in this wise:

"Gloria patri et Filio et Spiritui Sancto;
Sicut erat in principio, et nunc, et semper,
et in saecula saeculorum. Amen."

An old Scotch edition of the Psalter, dated 1595, found in Edinburgh, has this version of the "Gloria":

Gloire to the Father and to the Sone
And to the Halie Gaist,
As it was in the beginning,
Now, and ay shall last.

It was commonly sung after the Psalms, prayers, or sermons as the individual church dictated.

The *"Gloria Patri"* has been a favorite in Christian churches of every name and nation for centuries and has a place in the service which nothing else can fill. Through it millions of Christians unite, every Lord's Day, in reaffirming their belief in the Triune God of the past, the present, and ageless eternity.

This ascription of praise has also been a help and comfort to millions of individual Christians. Polycarp, among the earliest of the Church Fathers, is said to have sung it as the flames mounted around the cruciform stake, to which he was bound. When the Venerable Bede, the foremost scholar of his age, lay dying on May 26, 735, he asked his friends to carry him to that part of the room where he always prayed. There he sang the "Gloria Patri," and when he had sung, *"in saecula saeculorum, Amen,"* his spirit went to join the Triune God of whom he sang.

✣

THE HYMN TUNE. Several tunes are in general use with the *"Gloria Patri,"* one by Christopher Meinecke (1782–1850). He was a native of Germany, but came to America at the age of eighteen, landed in Baltimore, and made his home there for the rest of his life. He was an accomplished pianist and organist, and served St. Paul's Episcopal Church of Baltimore for many years. In 1844, John Cole of that city published a book entitled *Music for the Church,* "composed for the choir of St. Paul's Church, Baltimore, by C. Meinecke, organist." Near the end of this small book of one hundred pages appears the music of the "Gloria Patri."

The other tune to which these words are commonly sung is by Henry Wellington Greatorex (1811–1858), the son of Thomas Greatorex, who, during the reign of George IV, was for twelve years the organist at Westminster Abbey. There is a story current that while talking with the king one day, he claimed higher power than his sovereign, explaining it thus: "You are only a king; I am a Greater-Rex." In 1838, the son, Henry Wellington Greatorex, migrated to the United States, to become organist at the Center Congregational Church, Hartford, Connecticut, "for whose services the organ silently waited for weeks." Later he served St. John's Church, also St. Paul's Church and Calvary Episcopal in New York City. He was a remarkable player for the time and was extremely popular. The last five years of his life were spent as organist in Charleston, South Carolina, where he fell a victim to yellow fever. In 1851 he published *A Collection of Sacred Music* which contained thirty-seven pieces of his own composition, among them his GLORIA PATRI.

GLORIOUS THINGS OF THEE ARE SPOKEN

1. Glorious things of thee are spoken,
Zion, city of our God;
He, whose word cannot be broken
Formed thee for his own abode:
On the Rock of Ages founded,
What can shake thy sure repose?
With salvation's walls surrounded,
Thou mayest smile at all thy foes.

2. See, the streams of living waters,
Springing from eternal love,
Well supply thy sons and daughters,
And all fear of want remove:
Who can faint, while such a river
Ever flows their thirst to assuage?
Grace, which, like the Lord the Giver,
Never fails from age to age.

3. Round each habitation hovering,
See the cloud and fire appear
For a glory and a covering,
Showing that the Lord is near:
Glorious things of thee are spoken,
Zion, city of our God;
He, whose word cannot be broken,
Formed thee for his own abode.

John Newton, 1779.

Biblical Text.

Glorious things are spoken of thee,
O city of God.

Psalm 87:3.

There is a river, the streams whereof make glad the city of God,
The holy place of the tabernacles of the Most High.

Psalm 46:4.

And I saw the holy city, new Jerusalem, coming down out of heaven from God, made ready as a bride adorned for her husband.

Revelation 21:2.

THE CAPTAIN OF A SLAVE SHIP TURNS HYMN-WRITER

A man who had been engaged in the slave trade for many years could hardly be expected to qualify as a hymn-writer. Yet this ex-seaman, adventurer, and one-time slave-trader, is represented in the hymn book of all faiths, one hymnal containing no less than thirteen of his compositions. "The child of many prayers, the profligate youth, the wicked sailor boy, the contrite penitent, the happy Christian, the consecrated minister, the eminent divine, the sweet-singer,"—this is Newton as Nutter and Tillett picture him.[1]

As a child at his mother's knee, John Newton (1725–1807) learned many a Bible text. But, unfortunately, this deeply religious mother died when the lad was only seven. After two years of schooling he went to sea with his father. A thoroughly wild youth, profligate and blasphemous, he sailed the "seven seas" for eighteen years, six of them as the captain of a slave ship, which landed at least one cargo of its human freight in Charleston, South Carolina. At the age of twenty-three, while steering a ship through a gale that threatened at every moment to overwhelm it, he began to pray, and turned from infidelity to God. Subsequently he settled down in Liverpool for nine years of office work and study for the ministry. He was ordained as Curate of the Church in Olney, in 1764, remaining there for sixteen years. From 1780 to 1807 he served as rector of St. Mary Woolnoth, London. When the infirmities of eighty years had made him unable to read his text, he was urged to give up preaching. He replied, "What! Shall the old African blasphemer stop while he can speak!"

During the years at Olney, Newton formed that intimate friendship with the poet Cowper which bore such rich fruition in *The Olney Hymns.* This was one of the outstanding contributions of the eighteenth century to the development of English hymnody. Of the three hundred and forty-eight hymns in this collection, Cowper wrote sixty-eight and Newton two hundred eighty. Among them are the following, in more or less common use today: "Amazing Grace, How Sweet the Sound," "How Sweet the Name of Jesus Sounds," "Safely through Another Week." His epitaph, composed by himself, reads:

John Newton, Clerk,
Once an Infidel and Libertine,
A servant of Slaves in Africa,
Was, by the rich mercy of our Lord and Saviour
JESUS CHRIST
Preserved, restored and pardoned,
And appointed to preach the Faith
He had long labored to destroy,
Near 16 years at Olney in Bucks
And . . . years in this church.

[1] From *The Hymns and Hymn Writers of the Church,* copyright by the Methodist Book Concern.

The hymn "Glorious things of thee are spoken," originally had five stanzas. One of the omitted stanzas has peculiar significance when the facts of Newton's life are recalled:

Saviour, if of Zion's city,
I through grace a member am;
Let the world deride or pity,
I will glory in thy name:
Fading is the worldling's pleasure;
All his boasted pomp and show;
Solid joys and lasting treasure,
None but Zion's children know.

This captain of a slave ship took his Bible to sea with him and studied it in his cabin. He even had prayers with the ship's company, for as yet his moral sense was nil. The wretched negroes chained together down in the hold did not move him to compassion. He, the rough sailor, looked upon them as so many cattle. Newton reminds us of another captain described by Stephen Vincent Benét in his *John Brown's Body:*

PRELUDE—THE SLAVER

He closed the Bible carefully, putting it down
As if his fingers loved it.
Then he turned.
"Mr. Mate."
"Yes, sir."
The captain's eyes held a shadow.
"I think, while this weather lasts," he said, after a pause,
"We'd better get them on deck as much as we can.
They keep better that way. Besides," he added, unsmiling,
"She's begun to stink already. You've noticed it?"
The mate nodded, a boyish nod of half-apology,
"And only a week out, too, sir."
. . . .
"Well, you'd better take another look-see, Mr. Mate."
The mate felt his lips go dry. "Aye, aye, sir," he said,
Wetting his lips with his tongue. As he left the cabin
He heard the Bible being opened again.
Lantern in hand, he went down to the hold.
. . . .
This was black, here,
This was black to see and feel and smell and taste,
The blackness of black, with one weak lamp to light it
As ineffectually as a firefly in Hell,
And, being so, should be silent.
But the hold
Was never silent.

There was always that breathing,
Always that thick breathing, always those shivering cries.

A few of the slaves
Knew English—at least the English for water and Jesus.
"I'm dying." "Sick." "My name Cæsar."
Those who knew
These things, said these things now when they saw the lantern
Mechanically, as tamed beasts answer the whipcrack.
Their voices beat at the light like heavy moths.
But most made merely liquid or guttural sounds
Meaningless to the mate, but horribly like
The sounds of palateless men or animals trying
To talk through a human throat.
The mate was used
To the confusion of limbs and bodies by now.
At first it had made him think of the perturbed
Blind coil of blacksnakes thawing on a rock
In the bleak sun of spring, or Judgment Day
Just after the first sounding of the trump
When all earth seethes and crumbles with the slow
Vast, moldy resurrection of the dead.
But he had passed such fancies.
He must see
As much as he could. He couldn't see very much.
They were too tightly packed but—no plague yet,
And all the chains were fast. Then he saw something.
The woman was asleep but her baby was dead.
He wondered whether to take it from her now.
No, it would only rouse the others. Tomorrow!
He turned away with a shiver! [2]

HYMN TUNE. There is a sonorous note in the tune AUSTRIA which fits particularly well with the triumphant words of Newton's hymn. This tune, by Franz Joseph Haydn (1732–1809), is one of those national songs which have been taken over by the church for its own use.

Haydn, most distinguished of the Austrian composers, was a devoutly religious man who regarded his musical talent as a treasure lent to him by God. In recognition of this every one of his scores is prefaced by the words, *"In nomine Domini,"* and concludes with the words, *"Laus Deo."* His religious nature, in striking contrast to that of John Newton, was joyous in the extreme. "When I think of God," he said, "my heart dances within me, and my music has to dance, too."

The music was composed at the suggestion of the Prime Minister

[2] From *John Brown's Body* published by Doubleday, Doran & Co. Copyright, 1927, 1928, by Stephen Vincent Benét.

of Austria for the "Hymn to the Emperor" and was first performed on the Emperor's birthday, February 12, 1797. The words by Hauschka, *"Gott erhalte Franz den Kaiser,"* translated into English, read:

God preserve our noble Emperor,
Franz, our Emperor, good and great.
Mighty ruler, high in wisdom,
We his glory celebrate.
Love shall twine him laurel garlands,
They become his regal state.
God preserve our noble Emperor,
Franz, our Emperor, good and great.

This tune was a great favorite of Haydn's. The story is told that when the French were bombarding Vienna in the closing year of his life, he asked to be led to the piano. Sitting down at the instrument, he played "The Hymn to the Emperor." This was his last musical performance. His death occurred five days later.

The writer of these hymn sketches heard the "Austrian Hymn" sung at the Schubert Centennial in Vienna in 1928 by thirty thousand Germans and Austrians in one mighty chorus supported by band and orchestra. To breathe into this music something of the majesty, the profound depths, the rich vibrant tone that shook the very foundations of Vienna during those days, should be a challenge to American congregations today. The last score should always be repeated, the second time sung broader and fuller, building into superb climax.

Repeat this score
With sal - va -tion's walls sur-rounded, Thou may'st smile at all thy foes.

GOD OF OUR FATHERS, KNOWN OF OLD

1. God of our fathers, known of old,
Lord of our far-flung battle line,
Beneath whose awful hand we hold
Dominion over palm and pine:

Lord God of hosts, be with us yet,
Lest we forget, lest we forget.

2. The tumult and the shouting dies;
The captains and the kings depart;
Still stands thine ancient sacrifice,
An humble and a contrite heart:
Lord God of hosts, be with us yet,
Lest we forget, lest we forget.

3. Far-called our navies melt away,
On dune and headland sinks the fire;
Lo, all the pomp of yesterday
Is one with Nineveh and Tyre!
Judge of the nations, spare us yet,
Lest we forget, lest we forget.

4. If drunk with sight of power we loose
Wild tongues that have not thee in awe,
Such boasting as the Gentiles use
Or lesser breeds without the law:
Lord God of hosts, be with us yet,
Lest we forget, lest we forget.

5. For heathen heart that puts her trust
In reeking tube and iron shard;
All valiant dust that builds on dust,
And, guarding, calls not thee to guard;
For frantic boast and foolish word,
Thy mercy on thy people, Lord! [1]

RUDYARD KIPLING, 1897.

BIBLICAL TEXT.

Blessed is the nation whose God is the Lord,
The people whom he hath chosen for his own inheritance.
The Lord looketh from heaven;
He beholdeth all the sons of men; . . .
He that fashioneth the hearts of them all,
That considereth all their works,
There is no king saved by the multitude of a host:
A mighty man is not delivered by great strength. . . .
Behold, the eye of the Lord is upon them that fear him,
Upon them that hope in his lovingkindness:
To deliver their soul from death,
And to keep them alive in famine.

PSALM 33: 12–13, 15, 16, 18, 19.

LEST WE FORGET

There was great drumming and marching throughout England; "the captains and the kings" had come from all over the British

[1] From *The Five Nations*, by Rudyard Kipling. Reprinted by permission of the author and that of Messrs. A. P. Watt and Son, Agents, and Doubleday, Doran and Co., publishers.

Empire's "far-flung battle line," to do honor to their beloved Queen. It was the occasion of the Diamond Jubilee of Victoria's reign, a reign longer than that of any other English sovereign. In the processions and displays of "pomp and power" were Mounted Rifles from Victoria and New South Wales, from the Cape and Natal, from the Dominion of Canada. There were Hausers from the Niger and the Gold Coast, colored men from West India, Zaptieths from Cyprus, Chinamen from Hong Kong, and Dyaks from British North Borneo. On the hill-tops from Ben Nevis in Scotland to the South Downs were kindled bonfires, two thousand five hundred of them "on dune and headland."

Quite naturally, so great an occasion called for great poetry. So the London *Times* asked the "uncrowned poet-laureate," Kipling, for a poem suitable for so august a day. Kipling has said of it: "That poem gave me more trouble than anything I ever wrote. When it came due I had nothing that satisfied me. The *Times* began to want the poem badly, and sent letter after letter asking for it. I made many more attempts, but no further progress. Sitting down with all my previous attempts before me, I searched through those dozens of sketches till at last I found just one line I liked. That was 'Lest we forget.' Round these words 'The Recessional' was written."

Perhaps nothing Kipling ever wrote caused so much discussion and called down upon his head so many anathemas as this poem. It appeared in the London *Times* of July 17, 1897. Less than three weeks before there had been the magnificent Jubilee Procession which had taken four hours to pass in review before the Queen; there had been, also, the equally impressive Naval Review. When, as "captains and kings," troops and navies, had begun to "melt away" on their return to their homes or stations, the influential London *Times* dared to print on its front page such words as these, there were condemnations in plenty for both paper and poet, but it went straight to the heart of the English-speaking peoples, and the anthologies and song books and hymn books accept it as one of the major songs of the race.

"Although written in the language of modern life, it is full of Biblical solemnities of diction and luxuriance of figure. Its combination of military and Biblical tone is not accidental. The poet's life, one remembers, is saturated with the spirit of the British army and navy; and on the other hand, both of his grandfathers were Methodist preachers. It is a touchstone of great hymnody; it moves off with a grand sweeping first line; its phrases have a sounding smoothness that gratifies the ear, fills the voice, and reëchoes in the memory; its images are vivid, clear cut, readily apparent; its thought moves swiftly and straight forward; and it is alive with the spirit of true religion." [2]

"Still stands thine ancient sacrifice,
An humble and a contrite heart."

The sacrifices of God are a broken spirit: a broken and a contrite heart, O God, thou wilt not despise."

PSALM 51:17.

"On dune and headland sinks the fire;
Lo, all the pomp of yesterday
Is one with Nineveh and Tyre!"

And he will make Nineveh a desolation, and dry like the wilderness.

ZEPHANIAH 2:13.

(Nineveh—so complete a desolation that the investigations of expert archæologists are needed to determine its very location!)

I will make thee (Tyre) a bare rock; . . . thou shalt be built no more, for I the Lord have spoken it.

EZEKIEL 26:13, 14.

"All valiant dust that builds on dust,
And, guarding, calls not thee to guard."

Except the Lord keep the City,
The watchman waketh but in vain.

PSALM 127:1.

Not England alone, but America as well, and all the nations of the modern world, so engrossed in the mad race for prosperity, (pomp, pleasure, and power), need to sing often, and to heed earnestly these revealing words:

"Judge of the nations, spare us yet,
Lest we forget, lest we forget."

✣

THE HYMN TUNE. This hymn has had many musical settings, among them RECESSIONAL, by John H. Gower (1855–1922).

John Stanier's MAGDALEN was written for these words, so also, G. F. Blanchard's LEST WE FORGET.

Less than a year after the publication of the words, Kipling wrote

[2] From *The Hymn in History and Literature,* by Jeremiah B. Reeves, published by The Century Co.

to Sir Arthur Sullivan, in reply to an inquiry from him: "Many thanks for your note. If a layman may speak in the presence of a master, I quite recognize the difficulty you find about 'Recessional.' The thing is a hymn in spirit and method, and it seems to me, should be dealt with on hymn lines. . . . I generally find that as soon as I have formally picked up the notion of a story or rhyme, the idea I have been hunting arrives. It may be—and I shall be lucky if this is so—that some day you will see your way to one inevitable setting that must be floating around somewhere. It is far better that it should go unset than be badly done, and I have seen nothing in the scores of vamps sent to me 'for approval and immediate authorization' that makes me change my mind. Please accept the thing as yours if you care to use it, and when you care to use it. There will be no other setting authorized by me."

Evidently Sir Arthur's death, which occurred two years after these words were written, came too suddenly for him to find that "inevitable setting" which was "floating around somewhere."

GOD OF OUR FATHERS, WHOSE ALMIGHTY HAND

1. God of our fathers, whose almighty hand
Leads forth in beauty all the starry band
Of shining worlds in splendor through the skies,
Our grateful songs before thy throne arise.

2. Thy love divine hath led us in the past,
In this free land by thee our lot is cast;
Be thou our ruler, guardian, guide and stay,
Thy word our law, thy paths our chosen way.

3. From war's alarms, from deadly pestilence,
Be thy strong arm our ever sure defence;
Thy true religion in our hearts increase,
Thy bounteous goodness nourish us in peace.

4. Refresh thy people on their toilsome way,
Lead us from night to never-ending day;
Fill all our lives with love and grace divine,
And glory, laud and praise be ever thine.

Daniel C. Roberts, 1876.

Biblical Text.

We have heard with our ears, O God,
Our fathers have told us,
What work thou didst in their days,
In the days of old.
Thou didst drive out the nations with thy hand;
But them thou didst plant:

Thou didst afflict the peoples;
But them thou didst spread abroad.
For they gat not the land in possession by their own sword,
Neither did their own arm save them;
But thy right hand, and thine arm, and the light of thy countenance,
Because thou wast favorable unto them. . . .
In God have we made our boast all the day long,
And we will give thanks unto thy name forever.

PSALM 44: 1–3, 8.

A SONG CENTENNIAL HONORING THE DECLARATION OF INDEPENDENCE

On July 4th, 1876, the town of Brandon, Vermont, in common with thousands of other towns all over the United States, held a Centennial Celebration in honor of the one hundredth anniversary of the signing of the Declaration of Independence. But there was one feature of the Brandon Celebration which other communities did not have—a "Centennial Hymn," which has lived to pass its own semi-centennial in ever-increasing popularity and use.

Reverend Daniel C. Roberts (1841–1901), who wrote the hymn, was an Episcopal clergyman, born in Bridgehampton, Long Island. He was ordained in 1866 and held pastorates in Montpelier and Brandon, Vermont; Lowell, Massachusetts, and Concord, New Hampshire. He was a famous Civil War veteran, having enlisted with the Eighty-fourth Regiment of Ohio Volunteers. He writes of a soldier's day thus:

"Now silence broods with shadowy wings,
The watchful sentry's footfall rings,
The soldier sleeps beneath the sky,
While night winds murmur lullaby."

This hymn found its way into the hymnal purely on the merits of its poetry, without any undue influence of the author's name or a "catchy" tune to carry it. (It was first sung to the RUSSIAN HYMN.) Dr. Roberts' own story of its publication, as told in a personal letter to Dr. Benson, is as follows:

"The hymn was written in 1876 for a celebration of the Centennial Fourth of July, and sung at Brandon, Vermont, to the tune called RUSSIAN HYMN! When our General Convention appointed a Commission to revise the Hymnal, I sent it, without my name, promising to send the name if the hymn were accepted. It was accepted and printed anonymously in the report of the Commission. Before the Hymnal was printed, the Reverend Dr. Tucker, late of Troy, editor of our best musical Hymnal, and Mr. George William

Warren, organist of St. Thomas' Church, New York, were appointed a committee to choose a hymn for the centennial celebration of the adoption of the Constitution. They selected this hymn, then anonymous, and, wanting a tune, Mr. Warren composed a tune to which it has since been set in the *Tucker Hymnal*."

These words have a peculiar appropriateness for national anniversaries such as the Fourth of July. The first stanza is a remarkably beautiful pæan of praise to God with an intimation of the majesty of his power. In the second there is both gratitude for the past, thanksgiving for the privileges of the present, and confidence in, and prayer for, the future. The four terms applied to God in the third line are significant: Ruler, Guardian, Guide, and Star. The third stanza is a prayer for peace, which places due importance on religion in the national life, and emphasizes trust in God as the surest national defense. The fourth looks forward to a "never-ending day," to lives that shall be filled with "love and grace divine," all the praise for which shall be given to God. Altogether, it is a hymn worthy of the important occasion for which it was written, and of the larger usefulness to which it has grown in its more than fifty years of circulation.

A Message from the Bells of Hingham (Massachusetts)— A Responsive Reading

First Bell:
I recall forgotten days before the settlers came.
Second Bell:
I ring the memory of the founders of this free Plantation.
Third Bell:
I ring their courage.
Fourth Bell:
I ring their toil.
Fifth Bell:
I ring their perseverance.
Sixth Bell:
I ring their love of freedom.
Seventh Bell:
I ring their love of truth.
Eighth Bell:
I ring their faith in God.

Ninth Bell:

I say unto you that many prophets and righteous men have desired to see the things that ye see, and have not seen them; and to hear the things that ye hear, and have not heard them.

Tenth Bell:

I charge you: remember your heritage.

Eleventh Bell: (*the tenor bell—the "Prophet"*):

I prophesy the time when the earth shall be full of the knowledge of God as the waters cover the sea.

(*Carillon or bells may be played during the reading.*)

✣

THE HYMN TUNE. As indicated above, in the words of the author of the hymn, the tune NATIONAL HYMN was composed by George William Warren (1828–1902), expressly for these words, as the hymn for use at the Centennial of the Constitution in New York. It was published in Tucker's edition of the *Hymnal for the Episcopal Church,* in 1894, and in the *Presbyterian Hymnal,* in 1895. Since then it has become popular and is now found in all good hymnals.

George William Warren was born in Albany, New York, and began his musical career as organist of St. Peter's Church when he was only eighteen years of age. He served that church for twelve years, going from there to the Church of the Holy Trinity in Brooklyn, and later, to St. Thomas' Church, New York. In 1888 he published a volume of *Hymns and Tunes as Sung in St. Thomas' Church.* His thirty years at St. Thomas' Church were his greatest. The music became a popular feature of New York life, thousands crowding into the church at all times. At his death not a note of music sounded through the church, the import being that no longer was there any one worthy to lead the music of St. Thomas'.

The trumpets in this tune make effective interludes and help to promote the feeling of patriotism which emanates from the words. With such a setting the hymn becomes rightfully majestic.

GOD OF THE EARTH, THE SKY, THE SEA!

1. God of the earth, the sky, the sea!
Maker of all above, below!
Creation lives and moves in thee,
Thy present life through all doth flow.

Refrain

We give thee thanks, thy name we sing,
Almighty Father, heavenly King.

2. Thy love is in the sunshine's glow,
Thy life is in the quickening air;
When lightnings flash and storm-winds blow,
There is thy power; thy law is there.

Refrain

3. We feel thy calm at evening's hour,
Thy grandeur in the march of night;
And, when thy morning breaks in power,
We hear thy word, "Let There be Light."

Refrain

SAMUEL LONGFELLOW, 1864.

BIBLICAL TEXT.

In him we live, and move, and have our being.

ACTS. 17:28.

One God and Father of all, who is over all, and through all, and in all.

EPHESIANS 4:6.

In whose hand is the soul of every living thing,
And the breath of all mankind?
With *God* is wisdom and might;
He hath counsel and understanding. . . .
He uncovereth deep things out of darkness,
And bringeth out to light the shadow of death.

JOB 12:10, 13, 22.

GOD OF THE SINGING PATHWAYS

Edward Everett Hale has described the world of nature as a place of "A thousand sounds, and each a joyful sound," the dragon flies, the humming birds, the clethra "all alive with buzzing bees," the "separate whisper" of each leaf—all the "thousand sounds of joy and love," and then he rebukes man for his dullness in not knowing that "He was there who all this love displayed," and concludes with the reason for this dullness: "And all because I did not hear the word, 'It is the Lord.' "[1]

Very similar to Doctor Hale's appreciation of the immanence of God in his world is Samuel Longfellow's Nature hymn, "God of the Earth, the Sky, the Sea!" It was published, with several others, by Longfellow in his *Hymns of the Spirit,* prepared for use in his new *Vesper Services* in Brooklyn.

Samuel Longfellow's fame as a poet was eclipsed by that of his greater brother, Henry Wadsworth Longfellow. He was very fond of the seashore and compiled a little volume which he planned should contain "all the charming bits of poetry in the language about the sea and the seashore." It was called *Thalatta.*

The abiding faith of Samuel Longfellow in the omnipresence and the immanence of God are shown in two significant quotations from

[1] Copyright by Houghton Mifflin Company.

his writings. In 1882 his intimate friend and associate in hymn-book editing, Samuel Johnson, died, and shortly afterwards Longfellow's own brother, Henry. In the introduction of his sermon on the Sunday following his brother's funeral, with the double bereavement fresh in his mind, he said: "I bring to you a message from the chamber of death and from the gateway of the tomb. And that message is Life, Life immortal, uninterrupted, unarrested, not cut off." The other is from one of the most popular of his hymns:

"I look to thee in every need,
And never look in vain;
I feel thy strong and tender love,
And all is well again;
The thought of thee is mightier far
Than sin and pain and sorrow are.

"Thy calmness bends serene above,
My restlessness to still;
Around me flows thy quickening life,
To nerve my faltering will:
Thy presence fills my solitude;
Thy providence turns all to good."

ANALYSIS. First Stanza: The last lines of this stanza are significant expression in poetry of the truth enunciated by Jesus when he answered the complaint of the Jews by saying, "My Father worketh even until now, and I work" (John 5:17). Not something happening in some far-distant past, a world set in motion and then left by an absentee God to run itself; no, Creation "lives and moves (*present tense*) in thee," and it is "thy present life" which "through all doth flow."

Second Stanza: The author finds God in every aspect of Nature, the majesty of the storm, and the quiet beauty of the sun. In this respect he is like the Psalmist of old, who expressed in the great "Thunder-storm Hymn" (Psalm 29) his conviction of the presence of God in both storm and calm:

The voice of the Lord is upon the waters,
The God of glory thundereth.
The voice of the Lord cleaveth the flames of fire.
The voice of the Lord shaketh the wilderness.

. . . .

The Lord will give strength unto his people;
The Lord will bless his people with peace.

PSALM 29: 3, 7, 8, 11.

Third Stanza: Sung to the tune ST. CATHERINE, it is natural to bring out the important words of this stanza, "calm," "evening," "grandeur," "morning," "power." And a proper emphasis vivifies the climactic words, "Let there be light."

Fourth Stanza: This "omitted stanza" is an interesting completion of the poet's thought, and is intimately linked up with Paul's oration on Mars Hill:

But higher far, and far more clear,
These in man's spirit we behold;
Thine image and thyself are there,—
The indwelling God, proclaimed of old.
In him we live, and move, and have our being, and
The man whom he hath ordained.

ACTS 17:28, 31.

Scripture to Be Read before the Singing of Each Stanza

Scripture:

O come, let us worship and bow down: let us kneel before the Lord our Maker. In his hand are the deep places of the earth; the strength of the hills is his also. The sea is his, and he made it; and his hands formed the dry land.

The God that made the world and all things therein, giveth to all life, and breath, and all things; for in him we live, and move, and have our being.

First Stanza (singing):

Scripture:

God is love; for he maketh his sun to rise on the evil and on the good, and sendeth rain on the just and on the unjust.

Behold, God doeth loftily in his power; he causeth his wind to blow, and the waters flow.

By the breath of God frost is given; and the breadth of the waters is straitened. Yea, he ladeth the thick cloud with moisture; he spreadeth abroad the cloud of his lightning.

O Lord, how great are thy works! and thy thoughts are very deep.

Second Stanza (singing):

Scripture:

Yea, the darkness hideth not from thee; but the night shineth as the day; the darkness and the light are both alike to thee. The day is thine, the night is also thine; thou hast prepared the light and the sun. O Lord, our Lord, how excellent is thy name in all the earth! who hast set thy glory above the heavens.

Third Stanza (singing):

❖

THE HYMN TUNE. ST. CATHERINE. (See hymn, "Faith of Our Fathers.")

GOD OF THE NATIONS, WHO FROM DAWN OF DAYS

1. God of the nations, who from dawn of days,
Hast led thy people in their widening ways,
Through whose deep purpose stranger thousands stand
Here in the borders of our promised land.

2. Thine ancient might rebuked the Pharaoh's boast,
Thou wast the shield for Israel's marching host,
And, all the ages through, past crumbling throne
And broken fetter, thou hast brought thine own.

3. Thy hand has led across the hungry sea
The eager peoples flocking to be free,
And, from the breeds of earth, thy silent sway
Fashions the nation of the broadening day.

4. Then, for thy grace to grow in brotherhood,
For hearts aflame to serve thy destined good,
For faith, and will to win what faith shall see,
God of thy people, hear us cry to thee.[1]

W. RUSSELL BOWIE, 1913.

BIBLICAL TEXT.

Lord, thou hast been our dwelling-place
In all generations.

PSALM 90:1.

Save us, O Lord our God,
And gather us from among the nations,
To give thanks unto thy holy name,
And to triumph in thy praise.

PSALM 106:47.

THE NATION OF THE BROADENING DAY

This hymn, by Reverend W. Russell Bowie (1882–), is a vivid and exultant expression of faith in the progress of God's purpose for the human race, and the progress of human freedom and justice impelled by love. It expresses a high ideal and prayer for the destiny of America which is at the same time good hymnody and good politics.

Dr. Bowie's reference to America as "The nation of the broadening day" is an apostrophe worthy to stand with Miss Bates' "O, beautiful for patriot dream that sees beyond the years"; Reverend

[1] Copyright by W. Russell Bowie.

Cross' "The temple of the love of man, the house of brotherhood"; and Dr. Hosmer's "Be righteousness thy scepter, justice thy diadem."

W. Russell Bowie is a native of Richmond, Virginia, and a graduate of Harvard. He went to Grace Episcopal Church, New York City, in 1923, after a twelve-year pastorate at St. Paul's Church, Richmond. He recently declined the office of Bishop, feeling that he had not yet finished his work in New York. He is a member of the Commission for the World Conference on Faith and Order and the Commission of his Church on Social Service; he also served during the World War as Chaplain of Base Hospital 45. He is the author of several books, among them *The Inescapable Christ.*

✣

THE HYMN TUNE. The two dates in connection with this hymn are of interest: 1913 for the words, 1543 for the tune. There is romance in this wedding of twentieth-century words to a sixteenth-century tune. There may be also just a hint that Dr. Bowie in this prayer of "the broadening day" may be a poet-prophet of the twentieth century, beckoning on the church of today, even as Louis Bourgeois was a music-prophet of the sixteenth century, beckoning on the church of his day to a much wider use of the Psalms through more singable tunes.

Louis Bourgeois (1500–1561) is remembered for his association with Calvin, John Knox and others in the *Genevan* and *Anglo-Genevan Psalters* of 1556 and 1558. Robert Bridges, late Poet-Laureate of England, says of him: "Bourgeois turned out to be an extraordinary genius in melody. Of his eighty-five tunes in the *Genevan Psalter* almost all are of great merit and many of the highest excellence. Bourgeois' tunes are masterpieces, which have remained popular on the continent from the first, and the best that can be imagined for solemn congregational singing of the kind we might expect in England."

Dr. Benson adds, "It was their beauty that made the Genevan Psalmody and gave it wings."

This tune TOULON was originally set to Psalm 124 and called "Old 124th." The eighth verse as printed in this old Psalm and appearing in *The Bay Psalm Book* (the first book printed in America) reads:

> "The succor which weedoe in joye, is in Jehovah's Name:
> Who is the maker of the earth, and of the heaven's frame."

It also was included in the *Ainsworth Psalter* and sung by the Pilgrims at Plymouth in such fashion:

"Toulon" or "Old 124th" in the Ainsworth Psalter

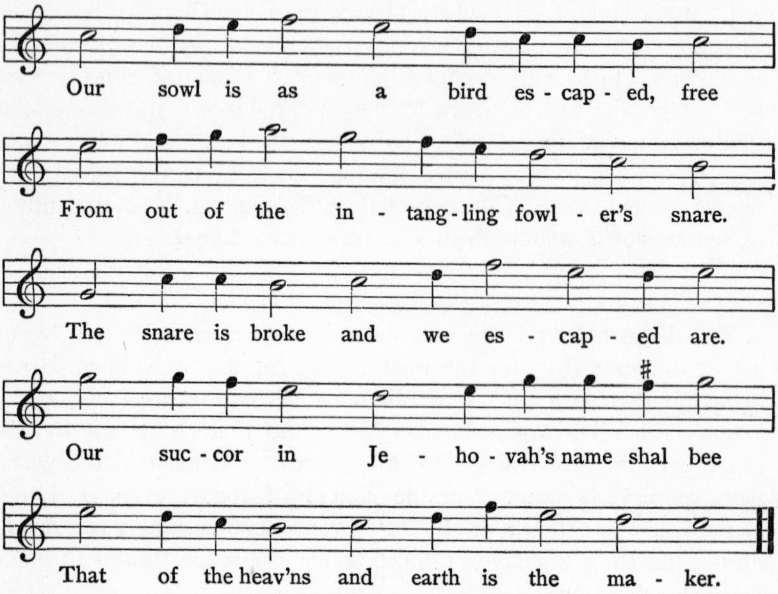
Our sowl is as a bird es - cap - ed, free
From out of the in - tang - ling fowl - er's snare.
The snare is broke and we es - cap - ed are.
Our suc - cor in Je - ho - vah's name shal bee
That of the heav'ns and earth is the ma - ker.

GOD, THE OMNIPOTENT!

1. God, the omnipotent! King, who ordainest
Great winds thy clarions, lightnings thy sword;
Show forth thy pity on high where thou reignest,
Give to us peace in our time, O Lord.

2. God the All-merciful! earth hath forsaken
Thy ways of blessedness, slighted thy word;
Bid not thy wrath in its terrors awaken;
Give to us peace in our time, O Lord.

3. God the All-righteous One! man hath defied thee;
Yet to eternity standeth thy word,
Falsehood and wrong shall not tarry beside thee;
Give to us peace in our time, O Lord.

4. God the All-wise! by the fire of thy chastening,
Earth shall to freedom and truth be restored;
Through the thick darkness thy kingdom is hastening;
Thou wilt give peace in thy time, O Lord.

5. So shall thy children, with thankful devotion,
Praise him who saved them from peril and sword,
Singing in chorus from ocean to ocean,
Peace to the nations, and praise to the Lord.

HENRY F. CHORLEY, 1842.
JOHN ELLERTON, 1870.

BIBLICAL TEXT.

He will judge between the nations, and will decide concerning many peoples; and they shall beat their swords into plowshares, and their spears into pruning-hooks; nation shall not lift up sword against nation, neither shall they learn war any more.

ISAIAH 2:4.

For as the rain cometh down and the snow from heaven, and returneth not thither, but watereth the earth, and maketh it bring forth and bud, and giveth seed to the sower and bread to the eater; so shall my word be that goeth forth out of my mouth; it shall not return unto me void, but it shall accomplish that which I please, and it shall prosper in the thing whereto I sent it. For ye shall go out with joy, and be led forth with peace.

ISAIAH 55:10, 11, 12.

THE FRANCO-PRUSSIAN WAR AND A PRAYER FOR PEACE

This hymn is a composite. It is not a matter of collaboration, for a glance at the date lines will reveal the fact that twenty-eight years elapsed between the writings.

In 1842 Henry F. Chorley (1808–1872), then the musical critic of the London Athenæum, wrote a hymn with the title, "In Time of War." Just what war he referred to in the title is not known, as England was not at that time engaged in active war with any nation. There were four four-line stanzas in Chorley's hymn, the first stanza of which is identical with the hymn as printed above.

Chorley was intended for a commercial life, but early showed a taste for literature, which led to his employment on the staff of the *Athenæum* in 1833. This connection he retained through the rest of his life. He wrote several books on music, among them *Thirty Years' Musical Recollections* and *The National Music of the World*.

Twenty-eight years later, on August 28, 1870, John Ellerton, then Vicar of Crew Green, wrote an "imitation" of Chorley's hymn. The fact that this was written during the Franco-Prussian War adds significance to Ellerton's "Prayer for Peace." Just how these two hymns came to be dovetailed into each other is not explained, even by Dr. Julian. But the hymn as we have it today is a composite, the first and third stanzas coming from Chorley, and the others from Ellerton.

John Ellerton (1826–1893) was a graduate of Trinity College,

Cambridge. He spent most of his life as a country clergyman, but is best known as a hymn-writer and hymnologist. Dr. Moffatt says that "his word as a hymnologist was of first importance." He was chief compiler and editor of two important hymn books, *Church Hymns* and *The Children's Hymn Book,* and joint compiler of the last edition of that great hymnal which, above all others, is dearest to the heart of the English Church, *Hymns Ancient and Modern.* In fact, it is no exaggeration to say that his hand may be traced and his voice heard in every hymn book of importance during the last thirty years before his death; "while no less than eighty-six hymns, original or translated, proceeded from his own pen."

Among his best known hymns are:

"Behold us, Lord, a Little Space, from daily tasks set free" ("Mid-day; for a City Church"—his own title explains it).

"Our day of Praise is done" (A hymn for Sunday evening).

"Saviour, again to thy Dear Name" (A hymn for the close of worship).

"This is the Day of Light" (A Lord's Day hymn).

"Welcome, Happy Morning" (An Easter hymn).

"Now the Laborer's Task is O'er" (A burial hymn of confident trust in the Resurrection).

Although John Ellerton lived most of his life in the comparative obscurity of country parishes, and although a half-century or more has gone since he wrote most of his hymns, it is a genuine testimony to their real value to find invariably in most of the modern hymnals at least five of Ellerton's hymns.

✣

THE HYMN TUNE. The RUSSIAN HYMN was composed as the National Anthem of the old Russia, by Alexis Lwoff (1799–1870) (sometimes spelled "Lvov"). He was trained for the army and rose to be Adjutant to Czar Nicholas I. In 1836 he left the army to become the successor of his father as head of the Imperial Choir. He composed this National Anthem in 1833. His other compositions included three operas, some violin pieces, a Stabat Mater, six Psalms and other church music. Tschaikowsky in his *1812 Overture,* pictures Napoleon's Invasion of Russia, the burning of Moscow, the final and fatal thrust at the French by pitting the "Marseillaise" against

By permission of Curtis and Cameron, owners of the copyright.

"THE SONG OF AGES," BY ETHEL WRIGHT

"On earth, peace, good will toward men."

the "Russian Hymn" and in the fury of drums, high mounting flutes and piccolos and rushing violins, staging a duel between these tunes, with the "Russian Hymn" sweeping all before it in the Finale.

HAIL THE GLORIOUS GOLDEN CITY

1. Hail the glorious golden city,
Pictured by the seers of old!
Everlasting light shines o'er it,
Wondrous tales of it are told:
Only righteous men and women
Dwell within its gleaming wall;
Wrong is banished from its borders,
Justice reigns supreme o'er all.

2. We are builders of that city,
All our joys and all our groans
Help to rear its shining ramparts;
All our lives are building stones:
Whether humble or exalted,
All are called to task divine;
All must aid alike to carry
Forward one sublime design.

3. And the work that we have builded,
Oft with bleeding hands and tears,
Oft in error, oft in anguish,
Will not perish with our years:
It will live and shine transfigured,
In the final reign of right;
It will pass into the splendors
Of the city of the light.

Felix Adler, 1878.

Biblical Text.

And I saw the holy city, new Jerusalem, coming down out of heaven from God . . . and I heard a great voice out of the throne, saying, Behold, the tabernacle of God is with men, and he shall dwell with them, and they shall be his peoples.

And showed me the holy city . . . having the glory of God, her light was like unto a stone most precious, as it were a jasper stone, clear as crystal.

And I saw no temple therein: for the Lord God the Almighty, and the Lamb, are the temple thereof. And the city hath no need of the sun, neither of the moon, to shine upon it; for the glory of God did lighten it, and the lamp thereof is the Lamb. And the nations shall walk amidst the light thereof.

Revelation 21: 2, 3, 10, 11, 22–24.

A MODERN HYMN OF THE NEW JERUSALEM

It is significant to find this Hebrew Professor of Social Ethics, the son of a Hebrew Rabbi, writing a hymn so singularly in line with modern interpretations of the New Testament teachings concerning the "Holy City, new Jerusalem." It is a hymn of remarkable social and religious harmony; a hymn in which Christians of many names and forms of creed may unite with sincere enthusiasm. Notable is the third stanza for its sublime faith in the permanence of individual contributions to the building of the Golden City. Well may church workers sing for their own encouragement:

And the work that we have builded,
Oft with bleeding hands and tears,
Oft in error, oft in anguish,
WILL NOT PERISH WITH OUR YEARS.

Its first publication was in the Pilgrim Hymnal, 1904, under this first line, "Sing we of the Golden City."

Typically modern in tone, in its pictures and in its message, is this new "Jerusalem the Golden." Compare this hymn of the nineteenth century with the hymns of the Middle Ages on the same theme; *e. g.*, "Jerusalem, My Happy Home," "O Mother, dear, Jerusalem," "Jerusalem the Golden," "For Thee, O Dear, Dear Country."

✣

THE HYMN TUNE. The tune SANCTUARY is most often used with Professor Adler's hymn. SANCTUARY was composed by John B. Dykes in 1871.

More familiar to the average congregation, and equally appropriate for the words, is the tune BEECHER by John Zundel, which is regularly used with the words "Love Divine, all Love Excelling." (See account under "Love Divine.")

The title suggests, appropriately enough, Henry Ward Beecher's characterization of "true tunes": "They are never forgotten. They cling to us through our whole life. Such tunes give new harmony and sweetness even to the hymns which float upon their current. And when some celestial hymn of Wesley, or of the scarcely less inspired Watts, is wafted upon such music, the soul is lifted up above all its ailments, and rises into the very presence of God, with joys no longer unspeakable, though full of glory."

HARK, HARK, MY SOUL!

1. Hark, hark, my soul! angelic songs are swelling
O'er earth's green fields and ocean's wave-beat shore;
How sweet the truth those blessed strains are telling
Of that new life when sin shall be no more.

Refrain

Angels of Jesus, angels of light,
Singing to welcome the pilgrims of the night.

2. Onward we go, for still we hear them singing,
"Come, weary souls, for Jesus bids you come";
And through the dark, its echoes sweetly ringing,
The music of the gospel leads us home.

Refrain

3. Far, far away, like bells at evening pealing,
The voice of Jesus sounds o'er land and sea;
And laden souls by thousands meekly stealing,
Kind Shepherd, turn their weary steps to thee.

Refrain

4. Angels, sing on, your faithful watches keeping;
Sing us sweet fragments of the songs above;
Till morning's joy shall end the night of weeping,
And life's long shadows break in cloudless love.

Refrain

FREDERICK W. FABER, 1854.

BIBLICAL TEXT.

Weeping may tarry for the night,
But joy cometh in the morning.

PSALM 30:5.

The angel of the Lord encampeth round about them that fear him,
And delivereth them.

PSALM 34:7.

For he will give his angels charge over thee,
To keep thee in all thy ways.

PSALM 91:11.

And I heard a voice of many angels round about the throne . . . saying, Worthy is the Lamb that hath been slain to receive the power, and riches, and wisdom, and might, and honor, and glory, and blessing.

REVELATION 5:11, 12.

THE HOME-BECKONING MUSIC OF THE GOSPEL

The lure of music, the charm of true poetry and the beauty of the Gospel of Christ, the Good Shepherd—all these are here, in these four brief stanzas of Faber's hymn. Too often relegated to the last pages of a hymnal this hymn received scant attention. Perhaps its seeming "other-worldliness" sets it aside, along with "Jerusalem the Golden," and "O Paradise, O Paradise," as a hymn of "Heaven." Whatever the reason, it is unfortunate that the average congregation does not fully know and appreciate this rarely beautiful hymn.

Frederick William Faber (1814–1863), son of an English clergyman of Huguenot descent, was born at Calverley, Yorkshire, went to Harrow, and then to Balliol College, Oxford. He entered the Anglican ministry, serving the church at Elton nine years. He was a gifted minor poet, a devout man, and a leader in social reform. He was strongly influenced by Cardinal Newman; this coupled with his travels on the continent where he came under strong Catholic influence, led him to say to his people at a Sunday evening service, that he could no longer remain in the Church of England, and bidding them farewell, he entered the Roman Catholic Church.

In 1849 he established the London Oratorians, or the "Priests of the Congregation of St. Philip Neri," on the Strand. Later at Brompton he served as head of this mission, writing his hymns and testing them out there. He wished to do for the English Catholicism what Luther's, Wesley's, Cowper's, Newton's and later, the Oxford writers' hymns had done for Protestantism.

Faber says of his own hymn-writing: "It seemed in every way desirable that Catholics should have a hymn book for reading which should contain the mysteries of the faith in easy verse, for different states of heart and conscience, depicted with the same unadorned simplicity, as for example, 'O for a closer walk with God' of the Olney hymns." These hymns in spirit and (with certain omissions and slight changes) in the letter, are good hymns of praise, catholic in the broader sense of the word, a spiritual heritage for the whole church. Some of his verses are over-fervent; some contain material and physical specifications very strange to English ears.

The Brompton Oratory early instituted popular evening services, at which the eighty-four Faber hymns were featured. "On Sunday nights," writes Curwen, "the place is full, and with a procession of some ninety men and twenty priests each with a candle and hymn book, the congregation caught the infection of the vigorous singing of the choir. I have not heard anything more hearty or thrilling in the way of congregational sound. The refrain or chorus which many of the hymns have is also a secret of their power. As the couplet returns, verse after verse, the most listless can join." [1]

[1] From *Studies in Worship Music,* by John Curwen, copyright by J. Curwen and Sons.

Dr. Gillman says of Faber, "He was a born poet, as no less a judge than Wordsworth has testified. As a hymnist, he did for Roman Catholicism what Watts did for Nonconformity and Heber for Anglicanism."

This hymn as published in *Oratory Hymns* (1854) contained seven four-line stanzas. A stanza usually omitted is:

> Darker than night life's shadows fall around us,
> And, like benighted men, we miss our mark;
> God hides himself, and grace hath scarcely found us,
> Ere death finds out his victim in the dark.

Among Faber's hymns, which are as popular with Protestants as with Roman Catholics, may be mentioned: "Faith of our Fathers," "There's a Wideness in God's Mercy," "My God, how Wonderful thou Art," "O Paradise, O Paradise," and "Workman of God, O Lose not Heart."

✣

THE HYMN TUNE. The popularity of this hymn is due largely to the musical settings which accompany the words. True beauty is its own excuse for being, and the following tunes alone would justify retaining the text in our hymn books: VOX ANGELICA by John Bacchus Dykes (1823–1876), and PILGRIMS, or, as it is sometimes called, PILGRIMS OF THE NIGHT, by Henry Smart (1813–1879). The latter, better adapted for congregational singing, contains a plaintive wistfulness which expresses the longing for "that new life when sin shall be no more."

HARK! THE HERALD ANGELS SING

1. Hark! the herald angels sing,
'Glory to the new-born King;
Peace on earth, and mercy mild,
God and sinners reconciled!'
Joyful all ye nations, rise,
Join the triumph of the skies;
With th' angelic host proclaim,
'Christ is born in Bethlehem!'
Hark! the herald angels sing,
'Glory to the new-born King!'

2. Christ, by highest heaven adored,
Christ, the everlasting Lord!
Come, Desire of Nations, come,
Fix in us thy humble home.

Veiled in flesh the Godhead see;
Hail th' Incarnate Deity,
Pleased as man with men to dwell;
Jesus, our Emmanuel;
Hark! the herald angels sing,
'Glory to the new-born King!'

3. Hail, the heaven-born Prince of Peace!
Hail, the Sun of Righteousness!
Light and life to all he brings,
Risen with healing in his wings;
Mild he lays his glory by,
Born that man no more may die,
Born to raise the sons of earth,
Born to give them second birth;
Hark! the herald angels sing,
'Glory to the new-born King!'

CHARLES WESLEY, 1739.

BIBLICAL TEXT.

For unto us a child is born, unto us a son is given; and the government shall be upon his shoulder; and his name shall be called Wonderful, Counsellor, Mighty God, Everlasting Father, Prince of Peace.

ISAIAH 9:6.

And suddenly there was with the angel a multitude of the heavenly host praising God, and saying:
Glory to God in the highest,
And on earth peace among men in whom he is well pleased.

LUKE 2:13, 14.

CAROL BROADCASTING AROUND THE WORLD

It would be an intriguing bit of mental exercise to imagine just how many millions of people the world around listened to or joined in the singing of this popular carol last Christmas time. Was there a radio broadcasting station in Europe or America which did not send out over the air at least once the strains of this hymn? Was there a Community Christmas tree anywhere, around which the carollers gathered to sing, where this carol was not sung? Everywhere, in stately Cathedral, in humble Chapel, or in way-side Meeting-house, Wesley's hymn was there!

In 1739, it began:

Hark, how all the welkin rings
Glory to the King of Kings.

Martin Madan in 1760, changed the lines to:

Universal nature say
Christ the Lord is born today.

Whitefield published the opening lines as they stand today, obviating the obsolete word "welkin" and giving the whole a touch of higher poetic distinction.

Mr. Kelley, the book steward at Wesleyan conference office, in going through the cellars on Castle Street, London, discovered a small underground room, boarded up. He found fourteen volumes of manuscript hymns in the handwriting of Charles, John, and Samuel Wesley. Four thousand were published in the life time of the Wesleys, about twenty-five hundred were left in manuscript. Both Charles and John were promoters of good music. For several years they held subscription concerts at their father's home, No. 1 Chesterfield Street. The subscribers included many distinguished people. The house must have been large, for it contained two organs and other instruments, and is said to have held fifty people. Charles was organist for many years at St. George's, Hanover Square. Both John and Charles Wesley sought everywhere for musical compositions for their hymns. They met Lampe who became a Christian under their influence and who wrote many tunes for the forthcoming hymns.

John Wesley's singing rules for Methodists everywhere were:

"1. Learn the tune.
2. Sing them as they are printed.
3. Sing all. 'If it is a cross to you, take it up and you will find a blessing.'
4. Sing lustily and with a good courage.
5. Sing modestly. Do not bawl.
6. Sing in time. Do not run before or stay behind.
7. Above all, sing spiritually. Have an eye to God in every word you sing. Aim at pleasing him more than yourself, or any other Creature. In order to do this, attend strictly to the sense of what you sing, and see that your heart is not carried away with the sound, but offered to God continually."

Mr. Moore gives the following description of Charles Wesley's absorption in his work, even when nearly eighty years of age: "He rode every day (clothed for winter even in summer) a little horse, gray with age. When he mounted, if a subject struck him, he proceeded to expand and put it in order. He would write a hymn thus given him, on a card kept for that purpose, with his pencil, in shorthand. Not infrequently he has come to the house in the City Road, and having left the pony in the garden in front, he would enter, crying out, 'Pen and ink! pen and ink!' These being supplied, he wrote the hymn he had been composing. When this was done, he would look round on those present and salute them with much kindness, and thus put all in mind of eternity."

✣

THE HYMN TUNE. This hymn was in use for one hundred and twenty years before it became associated with any fixed tune. In 1855 Dr. Cummings, principal of the Guild Hall School of Music, found this tune while hunting through Mendelssohn's *"Festgesang,"* which had been written in 1840 to celebrate the anniversary of printing. It is the second chorus in the book, *"Gott ist Licht."*

In view of its present widespread use, always with Mendelssohn's music, the following words of the composer about this tune are of special interest: "I am sure this piece will be liked by singers and hearers, but it will never do for sacred words. There must be a national and merry subject found out, something to which the soldier-like and buxom motion of the piece has some relation, and the words must express something gay and popular as the music tries to do."

Jacob Ludwig Felix Mendelssohn-Bartholdy (1809–1847) will always be remembered as the sixteen-year-old marvel, since he was, at that early age, a finished player on the piano, organ and viola, and an expert composer. He had already written the "Overture to the Midsummer Night's Dream." Many honors came to him, outstanding among them, the directorship of the Gewandhaus Orchestra at Leipzig. His tours to England were invariable triumphs. The last one, the Birmingham Festival of 1846, was made memorable by the first presentation of his oratorio, "Elijah." He has greatly enriched the church through his cantatas and oratorios such as "Elijah," "St. Paul," "Hymn of Praise," "Christus," "Lauda Zion," "Hear My Prayer," and eight settings of the Psalms.

One of the approved eighteenth century combinations was the singing of "Hark, the Herald Angels Sing" to WORGAN or the EASTER HYMN. Try these words to this music.

Interpretation in Art

Stanza One: "The Announcement to the Shepherds," Plockhorst
"The Nativity," Hofmann
Stanza Two: "Holy Night," Correggio
"Detail from Holy Night," Correggio
Stanza Three: "Sistine Madonna," Raphael
"Mother and Child," Bodenhausen

HE LEADETH ME

1. He leadeth me; O blessed thought!
O words with heavenly comfort fraught!

Whate'er I do, where'er I be,
Still 'tis God's hand that leadeth me.

Refrain

He leadeth me, he leadeth me,
By his own hand he leadeth me;
His faithful follower I would be,
For by his hand he leadeth me.

2. Sometimes 'mid scenes of deepest gloom,
Sometimes where Eden's bowers bloom,
By waters calm, o'er troubled sea,
Still 'tis his hand that leadeth me.

Refrain

3. Lord, I would clasp thy hand in mine,
Nor ever murmur nor repine;
Content, whatever lot I see,
Since 'tis my God that leadeth me.

Refrain

4. And when my task on earth is done,
When, by thy grace, the victory's won,
E'en death's cold wave I will not flee,
Since God through Jordan leadeth me.

Refrain

JOSEPH H. GILMORE, 1862.

BIBLICAL TEXT.

The Lord is my shepherd; I shall not want.
He leadeth me beside still waters,
He guideth me in the paths of righteousness for his name's sake.

PSALM 23: 1, 2, 3.

The Lamb that is in the midst of the throne shall be their shepherd, and shall guide them unto fountains of waters of life.

REVELATION 7: 17.

REINTERPRETING THE SHEPHERD PSALM

It is somewhat unusual to have a Gas Company pay tribute to a hymn and its writer by the erection and formal dedication of a beautiful bronze tablet on its building. The tablet reads: "'He Leadeth Me,' sung throughout the world, was written by the Reverend Dr. Joseph H. Gilmore, a son of a Governor of New Hampshire, in the home of Deacon Wattson, immediately after preaching in the First Baptist Church, Northwest Corner Broad and Arch Streets (Philadelphia, Pennsylvania), on the 26th day of March, 1862. The Church and Deacon Wattson's home stood on the ground upon which this building is erected. The United Gas Improvement Company, in recognition of the beauty and fame of the Hymn, and in remembrance of its distinguished author, makes this permanent record on the first day of June, 1926."

Following is Doctor Gilmore's own story of the origin of the hymn: "As a young man who recently had been graduated from Brown University and Newton Theological Institution, I was supplying for a couple of Sundays the pulpit of the First Baptist Church in Philadelphia. At the mid-week service, on the 26th of March, 1862, I set out to give the people an exposition of the Twenty-third Psalm, which I had given before on three or four occasions, but this time I did not get further than the words 'He Leadeth Me.' Those words took hold of me as they had never done before, and I saw in them a significance and wondrous beauty of which I had never dreamed.

"It was the darkest hour of the Civil War. I did not refer to that fact,—that is, I don't think I did—but it may subconsciously have led me to realize that God's leadership is the one significant fact in human experience, that it makes no difference how we are led, or whither we are led, so long as we are sure God is leading us.

"At the close of the meeting a few of us in the parlor of my host, good Deacon Wattson, kept on talking about the thought which I had emphasized; and then and there, on a blank page of the brief from which I had intended to speak, I penciled the hymn, talking and writing at the same time, then handed it to my wife and thought no more about it. She sent it to *The Watchman and Reflector,* a paper published in Boston, where it was first printed. I did not know until 1865 that my hymn had been set to music by William B. Bradbury. I went to Rochester to preach as a candidate before the Second Baptist Church. Going into their chapel on arrival in the city, I picked up a hymnal to see what they were singing, and opened it at my own hymn, 'He Leadeth Me.'"

Joseph Henry Gilmore's (1834–1919) great life work was in connection with The University of Rochester, where he occupied the Chair of English Literature for about forty years, and remained as Professor Emeritus until his death in 1919.

✣

THE HYMN TUNE. William B. Bradbury (1816–1868) was well known as an American composer of church and Sunday school music, and compiler of hymn books. Finding Dr. Gilmore's poem in *The Watchman and Reflector,* he composed for it the tune with which it has ever since been associated. His "Juvenile Musical Festivals" in the Baptist Tabernacle, New York City, brought him prominently before the music-loving public and the churches.

"The sight itself was a thrilling one. A thousand children were seated on a gradually rising platform; about two-thirds of them were girls dressed uniformly in white with white wreath and blue sash; the boys were dressed in jackets with collars turned over in Byronic style. When all were ready, a chord was struck on the piano—the thousand instantly arose and the singing which followed made both sight and sound a thrilling one."

Through these "Festivals" Bradbury stirred the city to a recognition of the necessity of musical instruction in the public schools.

The Origin of Amens and Refrains

In 1583 there appeared a book of original tunes with the following title: *"Seven Sobs of a Sorrowful Soul for Sinne,* comprehending the seven Psalmes of the Princelie Prophet David, commonlie called Penitentiall, framed into a form of familiar praiers and reduced into meeter by William Hunnis, one of the gentlemen of Her Majesties' honourable Chapell, and maister to the children of the same. Whereunto are also annexed his handful of honisuckles; the poore widowes mite; a dialogue between Christ and a sinner; divers godlie and pithie ditties with a Christian Confession of and to the Trinity, newly printed and augmented, 1583."

In this volume appear for the first time "amens" at the end of hymn-tunes, also the "chorus" or "refrain" like the following, repeated seven times after each meditation in his "Widow's Mite":

So shall my soul rejoice, rejoice,
And still for mercy cry,
Peccavi, peccavi,
Miserere mei.

Secular songs before this time carried refrains or "burdens," but these were commonly a mere string of meaningless syllables such as "Hey nonny no."

HOLY, HOLY, HOLY, LORD GOD ALMIGHTY!

1. Holy, holy, holy! Lord God Almighty!
Early in the morning our song shall rise to thee,
Holy, holy, holy, merciful and mighty!
God in three persons, blessed Trinity!

2. Holy, holy, holy! all the saints adore thee,
Casting down their golden crowns around the glassy sea;
Cherubim and seraphim falling down before thee,
Who wert, and art, and evermore shalt be.

3. Holy, holy, holy! though the darkness hide thee,
Though the eye of sinful man thy glory may not see,
Only thou art holy; there is none beside thee,
Perfect in power, in love, and purity.

4. Holy, holy, holy! Lord God Almighty!
All thy works shall praise thy name, in earth, and sky, and sea;
Holy, holy, holy, merciful and mighty!
God in three persons, blessed Trinity!

REGINALD HEBER, 1827.

BIBLICAL TEXT.

Above him stood the seraphim: . . . and one cried unto another and said, Holy, holy, holy, is the Lord of hosts: the whole earth is full of his glory.

ISAIAH 6:2, 3.

And the four living creatures . . . have no rest day and night, saying, Holy, holy, holy, is the Lord God, the Almighty, who was, and who is, and who is to come.

And the elders shall fall down before him that sitteth on the throne, and shall worship him, that liveth forever and ever, and shall cast their crowns before the throne, saying, Worthy art thou, our Lord and our God, to receive the glory and the honor and the power: for thou didst create all things, and because of thy will they were, and were created.

REVELATION 4:8, 10, 11.

LORD GOD ALMIGHTY

"Holy, Holy, Holy," has been designated "The world's greatest hymn," and by no less an authority on true poetry than the late Poet Laureate of England, Alfred, Lord Tennyson!

Seventeen years before the writing of this hymn the young vicar of Hodnet wrote to a London publishing firm: "My psalm-singing continues bad. Can you tell me where I can purchase Cowper's *Olney Hymns* with the music, and in a smaller size, without music, to put into the seats? Some I greatly admire."

This young vicar, only twenty-six years of age, had a vision of the power and value of good congregational singing. He translated that vision into actuality. He appreciated the value of welding sermon, hymnal and liturgy into one unified whole. He began to write hymns appropriate for the various Sundays of the Church Year, and continued thus to enrich the services of the Church until his death in 1826. In the following year fifty-seven of his hymns were collected and published in a volume entitled, *Hymns Written and Adapted to the Weekly Service of the Year.*

Reginald Heber is unique among hymn-writers in that practically all of his hymns are still in use.

The life story of Reginald Heber (1783–1826) is one of thrilling interest and real adventure for the Cross. In early childhood, he evinced courage of the staunchest sort. Once the doctor suggested bleeding him to stop the ravages of whooping-cough. His nurse protested, but the little sufferer settled it with these words: "Send poor nurse downstairs. I won't stir. Don't hold me." And he held out his arm to the lancet.

When off to school, it was necessary to sew up his pocket-money in his pockets, or he gave it away to the first person in distress. Evenings he was the center of a crowd of boys, the story-teller in those stirring times of war with France, of Nelson and Trafalgar. Chivalrous, unselfish, gentle, the servants said of him, "Master Reginald is never in a passion."

With vice prevalent everywhere, Heber preserved his purity and reverence through it all and led many a lad through the fires of temptation. "If his heart," said one, "had no other covering than a glass, its thoughts were so pure, no one need fear to read them."

In Oxford he carried off the University Prize for Latin verse. When only twenty-four years of age he began his work as vicar of Hodnet, where he ministered for sixteen years. To his work during these years Thackeray pays the following high tribute in his *Four Georges:* "The charming poet, the happy possessor of all sorts of gifts and accomplishments—birth, wit, fame, high character, competence—he was the beloved priest in his own home of Hodnet, counselling the people in their troubles, advising them in their difficulties, kneeling often at their sick beds at the hazard of his own life; where there was strife, the peacemaker, where there was want, the free giver."

He was offered the Bishopric of Calcutta on two different occasions, and both times declined the honor, preferring to remain as the parish priest of his home town, Hodnet. The second time he refused it, he felt that the call was one of duty, and retracted the refusal. He sailed for Calcutta in 1823. His diocese included not only all of India, which would have been a sufficiently large parish for any ordinary man, but also the Island of Ceylon and the whole of Australia. Heber thus describes the climate of Calcutta: "It is impossible to sit still under the most favorable circumstances without streaming with perspiration. Our windows are all close shut up, and our rooms darkened to keep out the hot and molten atmosphere, which streams in wherever it can find an entrance, like the breath of a huge blast furnace."

He preached in India only three years. His death came very suddenly in 1826. Leaving his wife and two baby girls in Bombay, he started on what was to be his last journey, visiting Ceylon, Madras, and other parts of Southern India.

To Trichinopoly, rock of the Tree-headed Giant, rising nearly three hundred feet above the plains of Madras, came Bishop Heber. He had journeyed through terrific heat, arriving at midnight. Next morning before eight he began receiving reports, going into conference, writing letters, making numerous visits. What a challenge to this Christian warrior, this center of Dravidic Brahmanism! with the island of heavenly pleasure two miles distant, the vile pagoda of Vishnu, covering four square miles, and on the other side of the city the still viler shrine of Siva. Sunday, April 2, 1826, saw St. John's church crowded with worshippers to hear the Bishop's confirmation address to forty-two native Christians. After the service he visited his sick chaplain, wrote letters, and conducted evening prayers. Monday, his last day on earth, began with four hours of intense work prior to a late Anglo-Indian breakfast in the heat of a Madras April.

He prepared for a swimming bath. The bath held seven feet of water, into which he plunged. Half an hour passed without a sound, when his servant, alarmed, opened the door and saw the body of his master under the water. Resuscitation was impossible. The first shock of the cold water had caused the bursting of a blood vessel in the brain.

Southey's Lines on the Portrait of Heber

"Yes,—such as these were Heber's lineaments;
Such his capacious front,
His comprehensive eye,
His open brow serene.
Such was the gentle countenance which bore
Of generous feeling and of golden truth
Sure Nature's sterling impress; never there
Unruly passion left
Its ominous marks infixed.
Nor the worst die of evil habit set
An inward stain engrained.
Such were the lips whose salient playfulness
Enlivened peaceful hours of private life;

Whose eloquence
Held congregations open eared,
As from the heart it flowed, a living stream
Of Christian wisdom, pure and undefiled.

Yes, to the Christian, to the Heathen world,
Heber, thou art not dead—thou canst not die!
Nor can I think of thee as lost.
A little portion of this little isle
At first divided us; then half the globe;
The same earth held us still; but when,
O Reginald, wert thou so near as now?
'Tis but the falling of the withered leaf,
The breaking of a shell,
The rending of a veil!
O, when that leaf shall fall,
That shell be burst, that veil be rent, may then
My spirit be with thine!"

✣

THE HYMN TUNE. NICÆA, by John Bacchus Dykes (1823–1876), is one of three hundred tunes by this master of the slender and illusive art form of the hymn tune. For a sketch of his life and works see the hymn "Lead, Kindly Light."

MUSICAL INTERPRETATION. The long verse-line of the poetry is peculiarly suited to the expression of repose, adoration, reverence and thoughtfulness.

The hymn should be sung at a moderately slow pace. Attention should be called to the pronunciation of the initial words. Even by singers who should know better, these words are often sung "Ho-lay, ho-lay, ho-lay." Observe the first three commas; it will add a deepened reverence to the hymn to make a slight pause after singing each "holy." One beat in the middle, and one at the end of each long line should be reserved for breathing. This makes it possible to attack the note following with firmness.

Each line of the music should begin with soft tones, increasing in power gradually as the tones rise in the scale, and decreasing as they go lower. This is particularly important (and all too commonly neglected) on the "Holy, holy, holy," at the beginning of each stanza and in the middle of stanzas one and four.

No retard should be allowed at the end of each of the first three stanzas, but in the fourth stanza a gradual retard beginning at the third line adds to the grandeur of the closing stanza. A quiet third stanza, with the fourth, opening majestically, and rising to a veritable shout in the second line, "All thy works shall praise thy name, in earth, and sky, and sea," affords a wonderful contrast and a brilliant ending for the hymn.

This hymn loses greatly in effect if any of the stanzas are omitted. An omission is needless; only three minutes are required for the most effective rendering of the entire hymn.

HOW FIRM A FOUNDATION

1. How firm a foundation, ye saints of the Lord,
Is laid for your faith in his excellent Word;
What more can he say than to you he hath said,
To you who for refuge to Jesus have fled?

2. "Fear not, I am with thee, O be not dismayed;
For I am thy God, I will still give thee aid:
I'll strengthen thee, help thee, and cause thee to stand,
Upheld by my righteous, omnipotent hand."

3. "When through the deep waters I call thee to go,
The rivers of sorrow shall not overflow;
For I will be with thee, thy troubles to bless,
And sanctify to thee thy deepest distress."

4. "When through fiery trials thy pathway shall lie,
My grace, all-sufficient, shall be thy supply;
The flame shall not hurt thee; I only design
Thy dross to consume, and thy gold to refine."

5. "The soul that on Jesus hath leaned for repose,
I will not, I will not desert to his foes;
That soul, though all hell should endeavor to shake,
I'll never, no, never, no, never forsake."

RIPPON'S SELECTION, 1787.

BIBLICAL TEXT.

Now thus saith the Lord that created thee, O Jacob, and he that formed thee, O Israel: Fear not, for I have redeemed thee; I have called thee by thy name, thou art mine. When thou passest through the waters, I will be with thee; and through the rivers, they shall not overflow thee: when thou walkest through the fire, thou shalt not be burned, neither shall the flame kindle upon thee.

ISAIAH 43:1, 2.

I will in no wise fail thee, neither will I in any wise forsake thee.

HEBREWS 13:5.

EXCEEDING GREAT AND PRECIOUS PROMISES

This hymn appeared first in a small collection published by Dr. Rippon, pastor of a Baptist Church in London, in 1787. Its author was designated by the initial "K," all that is positively known about the authorship. However hymnologists are generally agreed that "K" is none other than Robert Keene, a precentor in Dr. Rippon's church.

Is this not a young man's hymn, therefore, written by a song leader who may have been a leader of youth in his day? Note the lively rhythm, "elevens," with accent, not on first syllable, but upon the second, giving forward movement and speed.

Whatever its origin, this hymn has long been a favorite hymn of individual Christians, rich and poor, high and low. Andrew Jackson, ex-President of the United States, in September, 1843, in the course of a conversation at "The Hermitage," remarked: "There is a beautiful hymn on the subject of the exceeding great and precious promises of God to his people. It was a favorite hymn with my dear wife till the day of her death. It commences thus, 'How firm a foundation, ye saints of the Lord.' I wish you would sing it now."

It was a favorite hymn of Robert E. Lee, Theodore Roosevelt, and Woodrow Wilson, and was sung at the funeral service of each of these distinguished Americans.

The stanza,

> "E'en down to old age all my people shall prove
> My sovereign, eternal, unchangeable love;
> And when hoary hairs shall their temples adorn,
> Like lambs they shall still in my bosom be borne."

carries on through all of life the stirring motif of trust.

Frances Willard once wrote: "Mother says that at family prayers in her home they were wont to sing together, 'How firm a foundation,' and her parents used to say it would never wear out because it was so full of Scripture. When mother came back to us after being in her room six weeks, we sang that hymn for her, and she broke in at the verse about "hoary hairs" and said: 'How I enjoyed that for my old grandmother who lived to be ninety-seven, and I enjoyed it for my dear father who was eighty-six when he passed away; and now my daughter enjoys it for me, who am eighty-four, and perhaps she will live to be as old as I, when I feel sure she will have friends who will enjoy it just as tenderly for her."

General Curtis Guild, Jr., tells how this hymn, wedded to the Christmas tune, Adeste Fideles, was sung on a famous Christmas morning. "The Seventh Army Corps was encamped on the hills above Havana, Cuba, on Christmas Eve of 1898—a beautiful tropical night. Suddenly a sentinel from the camp of the Forty-ninth Iowa called, "Number ten; twelve o'clock, and all's well!" A strong voice raised the chorus, and many voices joined in until the whole regiment was singing. Then the Sixth Missouri added its voices, and the Fourth Virginia, and all the rest, till there, on the long ridges above the city whence Spanish tyranny once went forth to enslave the New World, a whole Army corps was singing, 'Fear not, I am with thee, O be not dismayed.' "

Here is an omitted stanza:

In every condition, in sickness, in health,
In poverty's vale, or abounding in wealth;
At home and abroad, on the land, on the sea,
As thy days may demand, shall thy strength ever be.

THE HYMN TUNE. The tune has been erroneously called the PORTUGUESE HYMN, as if originating in Portugal, whereas it is probably English in origin. The Duke of Leeds, hearing this tune for the first time in the "Portuguese Chapel," London, about 1785, and supposing it to be indigenous to Portuguese services, named it the PORTUGUESE HYMN.

Vincent Novello, who was then the organist at the "Portuguese Chapel," London, ascribed the tune to John Reading, the organist of Winchester Cathedral from 1675–1681.

I HEARD THE BELLS

1. I heard the bells on Christmas day
Their old familiar carols play,
And wild and sweet the words repeat
Of peace on earth, good-will to men;

2. And thought how, as the day had come,
The belfries of all Christendom
Had rolled along the unbroken song
Of peace on earth, good-will to men.

3. And in despair I bowed my head:
"There is no peace on earth," I said;
"For hate is strong, and mocks the song
Of peace on earth, good-will to men."

4. Then pealed the bells more loud and deep
"God is not dead, nor doth he sleep;
The wrong shall fail, the right prevail,
With peace on earth, good-will to men."

5. Till, ringing, singing on its way,
The world revolved from night to day,

A voice, a chime, a chant sublime,
Of peace on earth, good-will to men.[1]
HENRY WADSWORTH LONGFELLOW, 1863.

BIBLICAL TEXT.

And suddenly there was with the angel a multitude of the heavenly host, praising God, and saying,

Glory to God in the highest,
And on earth peace, good-will to men.

LUKE 2:13, 14.

If thou hadst known in this day, even thou, the things which belong unto peace! but now they are hid from thine eyes.

LUKE 19:42.

A POET'S SONG OF PEACE

Henry W. Longfellow is remembered chiefly as one of the truly great American poets of the nineteenth century. He is not often thought of as a hymn-writer, but this one hymn of his is included in a number of modern hymnals.

Christmas Day, 1863, in the United States, was anything but a time of "peace on earth, good-will to men." The Civil War was reaching its climax. Six months before had occurred the terrible battle of Gettysburg; close to one hundred and fifty thousand men had fought each other with shot and shell, with sword, saber and bayonet through three long days. The total losses of killed, wounded and missing on both sides in that one battle amounted to more than forty thousand men. In the west Vicksburg had been captured by the Union forces after a prolonged siege, and thirty thousand Confederates had been taken prisoners. At that very time the Union Army had approximately 860,000 men under arms, and the Confederates 480,000: a total of 1,340,000 men engaged in fratricidal strife in a population which amounted in 1860 to only 31,443,321.

No wonder the poet "bowed his head" in despair, and thought, "There is no peace." Hate seemed over-strong at that moment.

Two omitted stanzas, the fourth and fifth, narrate these tragic days in detail:

"Then from each black, accursed mouth
The cannon thundered in the South,
And with the sound the carols drowned
Of peace on earth, good-will to men.

"It was as if an earthquake rent
The hearth-stones of a continent,
And made forlorn, the households born
Of peace on earth, good-will to men."

[1] Copyright by Houghton Mifflin Company.

But it is the privilege of poets to be seers, and Longfellow was in this and other senses a true poet. So the hymn moves toward its climax in these assuring words of the seventh stanza:

"God is not dead, nor doth he sleep;
The wrong shall fail, the right prevail,
With peace on earth, good-will to men."

Henry Wadsworth Longfellow (1807–1882) was born at Portland, Maine, graduated from Bowdoin College, spent four years in travel and study, and returned in 1829 to his alma mater as Professor of Modern Languages. After six years of teaching in Bowdoin, he went to Harvard as Professor of Modern Languages, a position which he retained for nearly twenty years.

Longfellow has had an abiding influence in American literary life, and the memorial to him in "The Poet's Corner," Westminster Abbey, is a permanent testimonial to his influence abroad.

The following excerpt from "The Arsenal at Springfield," published as a hymn, and set to the tune SPRINGFIELD in *The New Hymnal for American Youth,* may be sung or read before or after "I heard the Bells."

"Down the dark future, through long generations,
The sounds of war grow fainter, and then cease;
And like a bell with solemn, sweet vibrations,
I hear once more the voice of Christ say, Peace!

"Peace! and no longer, from its brazen portals,
The blast of war's great organ shakes the skies;
But, beautiful as songs of the immortals,
The holy melodies of love arise."[2]

❖

THE HYMN TUNE. WALTHAM, by John Baptiste Calkin (1827–1905), is the tune commonly used with this hymn, although other tunes are effective such as MAINZER, by Joseph Mainzer (1801–1851), an Alsatian minister and composer. (For comment on WALTHAM, see "Fling out the Banner.")

I HEARD THE VOICE OF JESUS

1. I heard the voice of Jesus say,
"Come unto me and rest;
Lay down, thou weary one, lay down
Thy head upon my breast."

[2] By Henry Wadsworth Longfellow, copyright by Houghton Mifflin Company.

I came to Jesus as I was,
Weary and worn and sad;
I found in him a resting place,
And he has made me glad.

2. I heard the voice of Jesus say,
"Behold, I freely give
The living water, thirsty one,
Stoop down, and drink, and live."
I came to Jesus and I drank
Of that life-giving stream;
My thirst was quenched, my soul revived,
And now I live in him.

3. I heard the voice of Jesus say,
"I am this dark world's light;
Look unto me, thy morn shall rise,
And all thy day be bright."
I looked to Jesus, and I found
In him my star, my sun;
And in that light of life I'll walk,
Till traveling days are done.

HORATIUS BONAR, 1846.

BIBLICAL TEXT.

Come unto me, all ye that labor and are heavy laden, and I will give you rest.

MATTHEW 11:28.

Jesus said unto them, I am the bread of life: he that cometh to me shall not hunger, and he that believeth on me shall never thirst.

JOHN 6:35.

Jesus spake unto them, saying, I am the light of the world: he that followeth me shall not walk in the darkness, but shall have the light of life.

JOHN 8:12.

THE VOICE FROM GALILEE

The author's title for this hymn is "The Voice from Galilee," a most appropriate preface for a hymn in which occurs thrice over the words, "I heard the voice of Jesus say." The weary pilgrim hears the Voice, heeds its invitation, and finds rest. Again, he is a thirsty traveler, in the heat of the day, who hears the Voice and its proclamation of "living water." Thirst is quenched, the soul revived, and life finds new vigor. The sun goes down, the darkness falls, and the traveler is perplexed concerning the road he cannot see. The Voice calls again with its inviting promise of Light. He looks, and lo, in him who speaks from Galilee, he finds his "star," his "sun," in whose light the rest of his journeying shall be brightened and made plain.

Dr. Horatius Bonar (1808–1889) has been called "the prince of Scottish hymn-writers." He was educated at the High School and the University of Edinburgh, and was ordained in 1838 as minister of the North Parish, Kelso. During these years there occurred the great "Disruption" of 1843, which led to the founding of the Free Church of Scotland. Bonar, with his church, went into the Free Kirk, and was for a time a joint editor of *The Border Watch,* a paper in the interests of the Free Kirk.

In response to many calls to leave Kelso for larger parishes, he replied, "Here I am, and here I must remain till my Lord come to me or for me." Finally, after twenty-eight years in Kelso he did accept the larger call, as first minister in the new Chalmers Memorial church, Edinburgh, remaining in this, his home city, until his death in 1881.

"There is nobody like Bonar to sing about heaven," exclaims one of the characters in Mrs. Ward's *Gates Ajar*. His hymns, many at least, were like the monastic hymns of Bernard of Cluny, singing of a wicked world, of a Judge to come, of Jerusalem the golden. "Is Bonar, the hymn-writer, still alive?" questioned one lady of a member of Bonar's Edinburgh congregation, "I always understood he was a medieval saint."

Dr. Benson describes this greatest of Scotch hymn-writers as he saw him two years before his death, "a venerable man in clerical black, bowed down with years and tottering in infirmity, with large frame and head, and the white hair and whiskers around the fresh skin of the face, having even in extreme weakness that look of nobility, which seems so characteristic of the Scotch type of old age." [1]

Dr. Bonar was a man of intense devotion to duty. One said of him that "he was always visiting, another that he was always preaching, another that he was always writing, another that he was always praying." One of the most sacred memories of his household was that of a voice they used to hear for hours together from behind the locked doors of his study, pouring out fervent prayer.

Dr. Bonar's hymn-writing began when he was a student-assistant in the church at Leith. The singing in the Sunday School was very poor. This was not strange, since the children had nothing to sing except the Scottish "Psalms in Meter," and a very few hymns set to the most solemn music. The young assistant wrote new hymns for the Sunday School. "I lay my sins on Jesus" and "I was a wandering

[1] From *Studies of Familiar Hymns,* by Louis F. Benson, copyright by the Westminster Press.

sheep" were among these early hymns. The first one to be written for adults was "Go, labor on."

✣

THE HYMN TUNE. John Bacchus Dykes (1823–1876) has been most successful in his composition of VOX DILECTI. It carries out, in a striking manner, the contrast between the first and the second half of the stanza. The music for the Master's invitation is written in G minor. With the joyous acceptance of the invitation in the second half of the stanza, the music changes to G Major, and mounts to exultant high tones in the last bar, properly emphasizing "found," "resting place" "glad," "light of life," "live in him." This tune does not sing itself. Congregations should be drilled into singing it. In a letter to Dr. Monk, Dykes writes: "You and Stainer and Sir Henry laughed at me the other day for apologizing for setting so many hymns. And I really feel it still needs, if not an apology, at least an explanation. My explanation is simply this—I never think of setting a hymn that is worthily set, where the tune can be got. That would be mere silly caprice, or vanity, or presumption. But if a hymn does not appear to me worthily set, then, I own, I am often induced, I may say, sometimes almost compelled, to try to do my best for it.

"I know so well the teaching power of hymns, if they are happily wedded, that I am very anxious to do my best (as far as God is pleased to help me) to add to the number of those useful and felicitous unions. God forbid that I should make these attempts from any unworthy desire to thrust myself forward. I earnestly pray that this reason may never, never actuate me. My one desire is this—that each hymn should be so set to music (by whomsoever God wills to select for that purpose) that its power of influencing and teaching may be best brought out. All other considerations must be subordinate to that."

I LOVE THY KINGDOM, LORD

1. I love thy kingdom, Lord,
The house of thine abode,
The church our blest Redeemer saved
With his own precious blood.

2. I love thy church, O God;
Her walls before thee stand,
Dear as the apple of thine eye,
And graven on thine hand.

3. For her my tears shall fall,
For her my prayers ascend,
To her my cares and toils be given
Till toils and cares shall end.

4. Beyond my highest joy
I prize her heavenly ways,
Her sweet communion, solemn vows,
Her hymns of love and praise.

5. Sure as thy truth shall last,
To Zion shall be given
The brightest glories earth can yield,
And brighter bliss of heaven.

TIMOTHY DWIGHT, 1800.

BIBLICAL TEXT.
If I forget thee, O Jerusalem,
Let my right hand forget her skill,
Let my tongue cleave to the roof of my mouth,
If I remember thee not;
If I prefer not Jerusalem above my chief joy.

PSALM 137:5, 6.

A COLLEGE PRESIDENT'S HYMN

Able to read Latin when only six years old, a graduate of Yale at seventeen, a tutor in his Alma Mater at nineteen, at twenty the author of a book on *The History, Eloquence and Poetry of the Bible,* Timothy Dwight lived a life which reads like an imagined romance.

Born in Northampton, Massachusetts, the grandson of the famous Jonathan Edwards, he early distinguished himself scholastically, perhaps as a result of his mother's intelligent tutelage. He was so popular as a tutor at Yale that the students unanimously signed a petition requesting the trustees to make him president of the institution, although he was then only twenty-five years old. It was only at Dwight's earnest request that the petition was not presented. He entered the service of the Continental Army in 1777 as a Chaplain, and at once became a favorite with both officers and men. Washington came to know and to greatly admire him. He was an enthusiastic patriot, and no sooner had he entered the army than he began to write songs for the soldiers. His "Ode on the Glory of Columbia" began with the stirring lines:

"Columbia, Columbia, to glory arise,
The queen of the world and child of the skies!
Thy genius commands thee; with rapture behold,
While ages on ages thy splendors unfold."

Paraphrasing Psalm 18, Dwight wrote, with the British in mind:

"Tis by thine aid our troops prevail,
And break united powers,
Or burn their boasted fleets, or scale
The proudest of their towers.
How have we chased them through the fields
And trod them to the ground,
While thy salvation was our shield,
But they no shelter found."

His father's death the next year made it necessary for him to resign his commission and devote himself for the next five years to the management of the farm which was the sole support of his mother, brothers and sisters.

In 1783 he was ordained pastor of the Congregational Church at Greenfield, Connecticut. Here the salary he received, during the twelve years of his pastorate, was so small that he was obliged to found an Academy there and teach in order to support his family.

Called to the Presidency of Yale in 1795 he served that institution until his death, greatly enlarging its usefulness and extending its influence.

It was during the busy years of his presidency of Yale that the Congregationalists of Connecticut felt the imperative necessity for a revision of the hymns of Isaac Watts. The American Revolution had made many of the allusions in Watts' hymns quite out of harmony with the new spirit of independence in the American colonies. Dr. Dwight was chosen for this delicate and difficult task, and performed it admirably. With this revision of Watts' hymns, Dr. Dwight included one of his own, "I love thy kingdom, Lord," which is better known and in more constant use today than any of his revisions of Watts.

Written, doubtless, with the memories of his twelve years' of pastoral service in Greenfield in mind, Dr. Dwight here condenses into twenty lines the ripe scholarship of years, the fire of that poetical genius which had produced an epic poem at twenty-four, and that deep, earnest love for the church which had led him to serve it in every possible way.

✣

THE HYMN TUNE. The tune, ST. THOMAS, by Aaron Williams (1731–1776), gives a fine stateliness to the hymn. Williams was a Welshman, a composer of psalmody, clerk of the Scotch church in London, music engraver and publisher. This tune appeared as the second movement of a four-movement tune in Williams' collection of 1762, which contained pieces by the great masters along with his own.

Old Psalm Tunes sung slowly fell into disfavor. They were "dull, heavy, see-saw, humdrum things," yet when they were first heard by our forefathers they were "Geneva jiggs." "Strange that the very tunes that send us to sleep caused our forefathers to dance." There were veritable hymn-tune battles in those days, keen competition among country choirs as to who should possess the latest and best tunes. Deputations were sent out to hear new tunes and they brought them back intact, whistling them all the time lest they forget, or playing them on the flute.

State Street was composed by Jonathan Call Woodman (1813-1894), a native of Newburyport, Massachusetts. Mr. Woodman had the distinction of having been Dr. Lowell Mason's first assistant in introducing music into the public schools of Boston. He was a brother-in-law of George F. Root. After his removal to Brooklyn he taught music in Rutgers Female Institute, New York, and in the Packer Collegiate Institute, Brooklyn, and served as organist in several New York and Brooklyn churches, also, for a time, as bass soloist in Trinity Church.

I NEED THEE EVERY HOUR

1. I need thee every hour,
Most gracious Lord;
No tender voice like thine
Can peace afford.

Refrain

I need thee, O I need thee,
Every hour I need thee,
O bless me now, my Saviour,
I come to thee.

2. I need thee every hour,
Stay thou near by;
Temptations lose their power
When thou art nigh.

Refrain

3. I need thee every hour,
In joy or pain,
Come quickly and abide,
Or life is vain.

Refrain

4. I need thee every hour,
Teach me thy will;
And thy rich promises,
In me fulfil.

Refrain

5. I need thee every hour,
Most holy One;
O make me thine indeed,
Thou blessed Son.

Refrain

Annie Sherwood Hawks, 1872.

Biblical Text.

Abide in me, and I in you. As the branch cannot bear fruit of itself, except it abide in the vine, so neither can ye, except ye abide in me. I am the vine, ye are the branches. He that abideth in me and I in him, the same beareth much fruit: for apart from me ye can do nothing.

John 15:4, 5.

My God shall supply every need of yours according to his riches in glory in Christ Jesus.

Philippians 4:19.

Let us therefore draw near with boldness unto the throne of grace, that we may receive mercy, and may find grace to help us in time of need.

Hebrews 4:16.

THE DIVINE COMPANIONSHIP

This hymn had its origin in an experience out of which its author, Annie Sherwood Hawks (1835–1918), came to a new realization of the omnipresence of God. She was not in any church, nor engaged in what we ordinarily call "religious service." She was in her home in Brooklyn, New York, busy with the prosaic tasks of ordinary household work. But somehow the rooms around seemed to be like Jacob's hillside long before, none other than "the house of God, and the gate of heaven." Concerning that morning, Mrs. Hawks wrote long years afterward: "I was so filled with a sense of nearness to my Master, that, wondering how one could live without him in either joy or pain, these words, 'I need thee every hour,' were flashed into my mind. Seating myself by the open window in the balmy air of the bright June day, I caught up my pencil and the words were soon committed to paper, almost as they are being sung now. . . . It was not until years after, when the shadow fell over my way, the shadow of a great loss, that I understood something of the comforting power in the words which I had been permitted to give out to others in my hours of sweet security and peace."

The verses were given to her pastor, the Reverend Robert Lowry, who composed for them the tune NEED, adding the refrain. Their first publication was in a little pamphlet of hymns for the National Baptist Sunday School Convention, held at Cincinnati, Ohio, in 1872. The hymn and tune speedily found their way into Sunday School hymn-books, and thence into a large number of our present-day church hymnals.

Mrs. Hawks was born in Hoosick, New York. After her marriage she resided for many years in Brooklyn, where she was a member of the Hanson Place Baptist Church. After the death of her husband in 1888, she resided with her daughter in Bennington, Vermont. Her death occurred there in 1918.

One who was privileged to be a guest in that home and to meet Mrs. Hawks carried away an abiding impression of a quiet, dignified, white-haired lady, whose very presence was a benediction. In her face shone that same sense of the Divine companionship which, more than forty years before, had inspired the hymn which is her great legacy to religion.

Elizabeth Stuart Phelps Ward, in her novel, *A Singular Life,* brings this hymn into the "Church of the Love of Christ in Angel Alley" thus: "The stranger stood packed in, elbow to elbow between an Italian who served the country of his adoption upon the town waterworks, and a dark-browed Portuguese sailor. American fishermen, washed and shaven, in their Sunday clothes, filled the rear seats. Against the wall, lines of rude, red faces crowded like cattle at a spring; men of the sea and of the coast, men without homes or characters; that uninterested and dangerous class which we dismiss in two idle words as the floating population. Some of these men were sober; some were not; others were hovering midway between the two conditions; all were orderly, and a few were listening with evidence of emotion to the hymn, in which by far the greater portion of the audience joined. A girl wearing a Tam o' Shanter and a black fur cape, and singing in a fine, untrained contralto, held her hymn book over the settee to an Italian. 'Come, Tony. Pass it along,' she whispered, 'I can get on without it. Make 'em pile in and sing along the wall, there.'

"With rude, swelling cadences the fishermen sang:

'I need thee every hour,
Most gracious Lord.'

"Their voices and their hearts rose high on one of those plaintive, popular melodies of which music need never be ashamed:—

'I need thee, oh, I need thee,
Every hour I need thee;

Oh, bless me now, my Saviour,
I come to thee.'" [1]

✣

THE HYMN TUNE. NEED was composed by Reverend Robert Lowry, for this hymn, which is made doubly impressive by the refrain, added by Dr. Lowry. Reverend Robert Lowry (1826–1899) was a graduate of Bucknell University, and an honored Baptist pastor in Pennsylvania, New York and New Jersey. While pastor at Lewisburg, he was also Professor of Belles-lettres in Bucknell University there.

On the death of William B. Bradbury in 1868, the Bigelow and Main Company selected Dr. Lowry as the editor of their Sunday School hymn-books. He not only edited a large number of books which had great popularity (one book, *Pure Gold,* sold over a million copies), but composed a great many tunes.

Among the most popular of Dr. Lowry's gospel hymn tunes were those written for "Shall We Gather at the River?" (for which he also wrote the words); "One More Day's Work for Jesus," "All the Way My Saviour Leads Me," "We're Marching to Zion," and "Saviour, Thy Dying Love."

Referring to the inspiration of tunes, Dr. Lowry writes, "Tunes, more vagrant and spontaneous than hymns, often come unbidden, and without being able to account for themselves. They may owe their life to an occasion, a mood, a strain, a chord, a metrical line, and thus take their place in history."

I THINK WHEN I READ THAT SWEET STORY

1. I think when I read that sweet story of old,
When Jesus was here among men,
How he called little children as lambs to his fold,
I should like to have been with them then.

2. I wish that his hands had been placed on my head,
That his arms had been thrown around me,
And that I might have seen his kind look when he said;
"Let the little ones come unto me."

3. Yet still to his foot-stool in prayer I may go,
And ask for a share in his love;
And if I thus earnestly seek him below,
I shall see him and hear him above.

[1] From *A Singular Life,* by Elizabeth Stuart Phelps Ward, copyright by Houghton Mifflin Company.

4. But thousands and thousands who wander and fall,
Never heard of that heavenly home;
I wish they could know there is room for them all,
And that Jesus has bid them to come.

5. I long for the joy of that glorious time,
The sweetest and brightest and best,
When the dear little children of every clime
Shall crowd to his arms and be blest.

JEMIMA LUKE, 1841.

BIBLICAL TEXT.

And they were bringing unto him also their babes, that he should touch them: but when the disciples saw it, they rebuked them. But Jesus called them unto him, saying: Suffer the little children to come unto me, and forbid them not: for to such belongeth the kingdom of God.

LUKE 18: 15, 16.

And other sheep I have, which are not of this fold: them also I must bring, and they shall hear my voice: and they shall become one flock, one shepherd.

JOHN 10: 16.

THE ENCHANTED WORLD OF CHILDREN'S HYMNS

A brisk spring morning, a jogging stage-coach, a solitary passenger inside the coach with plenty of leisure for thinking during the journey, a haunting old Greek melody, and an intense love for the children of an English village school—these were some of the factors which combined to give the world its best known and most widely used Children's Hymn.

In the spring of 1841 Miss Jemima Thompson paid a visit to the Normal Infant School, Gray's Inn Road, to study the system of education in use there. During that visit she listened to a marching piece which was an old Greek air. This tune appealed to the young schoolteacher, and she says: "I searched Watts and Jane Taylor and several other Sunday School hymn books for words to suit the measure, but in vain." Then came the occasion for a trip to the little town of Wellington, a stage-coach journey of about an hour. It was during that journey that the first two stanzas of "I Think When I Read That Sweet Story" were written.

Quite possibly the inspiration of stanzas four and five, which make the hymn so effectively missionary in its scope, may have come from Miss Thompson's contact with Miss Mary Moffatt, daughter of the missionary pioneer in Africa, James Moffatt, and later the wife of David Livingstone, who was a teacher at the Normal Infant School.

Jemima Thompson was a precocious child. When she grew to young womanhood she dedicated her life to the missionary cause, hoping to go to India; but ill health prevented. Her father was much interested in hymn-writing, and at one time offered a prize of twenty pounds for fifty simple hymns suited for cottage prayer-meetings. He was also superintendent of a Sunday School. One Sunday soon after the memorable spring journey to the Normal Infant School, he asked that a hymn be chosen and sung. When it was finished, he turned to his youngest daughter in surprise and said, "Where did that come from? I never heard it before."

"Oh, Jemima made it," was the reply.

In 1843 Miss Thompson was married to Reverend Samuel Luke, pastor of the Congregational Church of Bristol. Always interested in both children and missions, she found for several years the expression of this interest in the editing of *The Missionary Repository*, the first missionary magazine to be published for children. Among the contributors were David Livingstone, James Moffatt, and James Montgomery.

Analysis. This hymn contains, in the first and second stanzas (the ones which were written during the stage-coach journey), a very vivid picture of a scene beside the Perean roadside long ago. Schmid's picture of this incident is less familiar than Plockhorst's, but contains some elements of significant appeal.

The third stanza brings the thought from the distant past and the far-away land of Palestine down to the present and the personal. "Yet still . . . I may go."

The fourth stanza broadens the thought to the inclusion of all the children of missionary lands, and emphasizes the thought that "there is room for all."

Stanza five concludes, as so many of the hymns of that period did, with the joy of that "glorious time" in heaven, when the children "of every clime," shall "crowd to his arms and be blest."

So the hymn links up the distant past in far-away Perea, and the joyous present, with its privileges of prayer and extension of the Saviour's influence to all lands, with the ultimate, glorious future, when all the children shall be blest in him.

✤

The Hymn Tune. The hymn tune is a composite, its first form being the Greek melody or folk-song, called Athens. This is the melody which so fascinated Miss Thompson, when she heard it at the Normal Infant School.

It was reëdited and brought to its present form in 1859 by William Bachelder Bradbury (1816–1868). Mr. Bradbury was born at York, Maine, of musical parents. In 1830 the family moved to Boston where William spent four years in an intensive study of organ, harmony and voice. At the age of eighteen he was an accomplished organist. He became acquainted with Dr. Lowell Mason and George J. Webb, entering Dr. Mason's famous Bowdoin Street Church Choir.

During this time he presided part time at the organ, being paid twenty-five dollars per annum to press the keys down, and to pull them up again to stop the sound. He asked the committee for double pay since his playing required this double duty. For a time he taught in Maine and in St. John, New Brunswick. Then came a call to the First Baptist Church, Brooklyn. A year later he began his significant work as organist and choirmaster in the Baptist Tabernacle, New York City. Here his innovations proved immensely popular. Among these were his Juvenile Singing Classes, his Festivals and his experiments with new types of sacred song. He, with Thomas Hastings, founded Sunday School hymnody. Together they published sixty different books, with a total sale of over two million copies. Bradbury spent two years in Europe studying voice, organ, piano, and harmony with three masters in Leipzig. Bradbury, Lowell Mason and George F. Root were convention specialists and teachers who did much for church and choral music in America.

I WOULD BE TRUE

1. I would be true, for there are those who trust me;
I would be pure, for there are those who care;
I would be strong, for there is much to suffer;
I would be brave, for there is much to dare.

2. I would be friend of all—the foe, the friendless;
I would be giving, and forget the gift;
I would be humble, for I know my weakness;
I would look up, and laugh, and love, and lift.

HOWARD ARNOLD WALTER, 1906.

BIBLICAL TEXT.

Is not this the fast that I have chosen: to loose the bonds of wickedness, to undo the bands of the yoke, and to let the oppressed go free? Is it not to deal thy bread to the hungry, and that thou bring the poor that are cast out to thy house? Then shall thy light break forth as the morning, and thy healing shall spring forth speedily.

ISAIAH 58:6–8.

Whatsoever things are true, whatsoever things are honorable, whatsoever things are just, whatsoever things are pure, whatsoever things are lovely, whatsoever things are of good report; if there be any virtue, and if there be any praise, think on these things.

PHILIPPIANS 4:8.

CRUSADING YOUTH

Here is a hymn which was not written as a hymn at all. It was a personal message from a young man to his mother, sent from Japan to New Britain, Connecticut.

Perhaps one reason why this hymn is so universal in its appeal to young people, and is such a favorite at all gatherings of youth where hymns are sung, is the fact that it is a living message from youth to youth. The author was only twenty-three when he wrote it.

Howard Arnold Walter (1883–1918) was born in New Britain, Connecticut. He graduated from Princeton in 1905, or, as his Seminary Bulletin (Hartford) expresses it: "He romped through Princeton, clutching class and scholastic honors right and left, graduating *cum laude* in 1905 and receiving the Master's degree in 1909. In Hartford Seminary he garnered every prize in sight, including the fellowship, which he used for one year in Glasgow, Edinburgh and Marburg." The year after his graduation from Princeton he spent in Japan, at Waseda University. It was there that he wrote this hymn, on July 1, 1906, and sent it home in a letter to his mother. Feeling that it was too rich a message to be confined to one family, she sent it to Harper's Magazine, in which it was first published.

Mr. Walter was ordained to the Gospel ministry in the Asylum Avenue Congregational Church, Hartford, Connecticut, where he served as Assistant Pastor for two years, 1910–1911. In 1912 he went to India in the service of the Young Men's Christian Association. When he started for India the last time a heart specialist told him that he would probably not live more than five years. His reply was, "That makes it all the more essential that I get back to work at once."

He died there in 1918, only eight years after his ordination and six years after the beginning of his missionary service. His last words were: "O Christ, I am ready." Whatever else he may have accomplished in this short life, Howard Arnold Walter has left to the Christian world a rich legacy and challenge in this single hymn. The key-note is the word which was flashed as a Christmas greeting from General William Booth to every Salvation Army Post in the world, the single word, "Others."

The Hymn Tune. The hymn tune Peek, by Joseph Yates Peek, appears as No. 186 in the *Methodist Sunday School Hymnal,* published in 1911.

It is there printed with a full-page refrain to the words: "Whatsoever things are true, Whatsoever things are pure, Whatsoever things are of good report, Think on these things."

IMMORTAL LOVE, FOREVER FULL

1. Immortal Love, forever full,
Forever flowing free,
Forever shared, forever whole,
A never-ebbing sea.

2. We may not climb the heavenly steeps
To bring the Lord Christ down;
In vain we search the lowest deeps,
For him no depths can drown.

3. But warm, sweet, tender, even yet
A present help is he;
And faith has still its Olivet,
And love its Galilee.

4. The healing of his seamless dress
Is by our beds of pain;
We touch him in life's throng and press,
And we are whole again.

5. Through him the first fond prayers are said
Our lips of childhood frame,
The last low whispers of the dead
Are burdened with his name.

6. O Lord and Master of us all,
Whate'er our name or sign,
We own thy sway, we hear thy call,
We test our lives by thine.

John Greenleaf Whittier, 1866.

Biblical Text.

Lo, I am with you always, even unto the end of the world.

Matthew 28:20.

Peace I leave with you, my peace I give unto you. Let not your heart be troubled, neither let it be fearful.

John 14:27.

And a woman . . . came and touched the border of his garment; for she said within herself, If I do but touch his garment, I shall be made whole. But Jesus, turning and seeing her said, Daughter, be of good cheer; thy faith hath made thee whole. And the woman was made whole from that hour.

MATTHEW 9:20–22.

OUR FRIEND, OUR BROTHER, AND OUR LORD

"A good hymn is the best use to which poetry can be put," according to the New England Quaker poet, John Greenleaf Whittier. However much the average literary man may be inclined to disagree with him, the editors of hymn-books have taken Whittier at his word; for they have chosen here and there from his poems enough verses to make seventy-five hymns.

The Quaker rearing of the poet, his love of nature, and his sense of the nearness of Christ are evident in all of his hymns. In spite of an individual life of turmoil and hardship, Whittier gave many years to the Abolition Movement, and kept through it all a strong conviction of the presence of Christ in the human heart and history. This gave him an inner calm in the midst of difficulties, which makes his poems among the most inspiriting in the hymnal.

The long poem, "Our Master," from which the hymn, "Immortal Love" is taken, was written in 1866, after the more tumultuous days of the poet's life had passed, when the great Cause for which he had worked so ardently had triumphed, and when peace had come again to the land deluged with five years of Civil War. It reflects the poet's deep, abiding faith in the intimate nearness of God, in his present help in all the problems and perplexities of life, and the necessity of sincere and genuine obedience to him as the highest, best expression of devotion. A careful reading of the poem is an essential preparation for a true understanding and appreciation of the hymn. Because of the intimate connection of the six stanzas of the hymn with the thirty-eight of the poem from which they are taken, the following Analysis includes much of the entire poem in its thought.

ANALYSIS. The first stanza is a remarkable tribute to the all-inclusive constancy of the Divine Love. Really to appreciate the significance of the second stanza of the hymn, "We may not climb the heavenly steeps," one needs to read thoughtfully the one immediately preceding it (this is the fifth of the poem),

"Hush every lip, close every book,
The strife of tongues forbear;
Why forward reach, or backward look,
For love that clasps the air?"

If his love "clasps the air," it naturally follows that there is no need to "climb the heavenly steeps," nor to "search the lowest deeps" to find him.

Between stanzas two and three of the hymn are eight in the poem. These eight stanzas emphasize in various ways the fact that in spite of the constant changes in life, the dimness of our hopes, the lack of answers to our questions, yet still,

"The Spirit over-brooding all,
Eternal Love remains."

Much of the rich meaning of the third stanza of the hymn is lost because of its separation from the lines which immediately precede it in the poem:

"No fable old, nor mythic lore,
Nor dream of bards and seers,
No dead fact stranded on the shore
Of the oblivious years;—

"But warm, sweet, tender, even yet
A *present* help is he!"

Not a mere historic Christ, a personage of importance in the dim and distant past, but a living, present, intimately available "help is he!"

The other stanzas of the hymn follow each other in the poem without disturbing omissions. Whittier's broad sympathy with those who expressed their religious convictions in ways different from his own is shown in the beautiful line "Whate'er our name or sign."

The twenty-two stanzas of the poem which follow are a varied and beautiful tribute to the many-sided Christ, an expression of abiding faith in his constant nearness to human life, and a prayer that life may find its highest expression in, "Simply following thee."

✣

THE HYMN TUNE. SERENITY is an arrangement from Wallace's "Ye Winds That Waft," 1836, by Uzziah C. Burnap.

William Vincent Wallace (1824–1865) led a life quite the opposite of this tune name, and quite different from that of the Quaker poet on the New England farm.

Wallace was the son of an Irish bandmaster, and even as a boy, often led the orchestra in the Dublin theater. After hearing Paganini in 1831, he studied the violin with devotion and passion. He gave concerts in Dublin for a time, and then moved to London. When he was only twenty-one he migrated to New South Wales, and later to Australia as a pioneer settler. Adventures of this sort did not satisfy his roving spirit, and he continued his wanderings over the East Indies, South America, Mexico, and the United States. In Australia he once received one hundred sheep as part payment for a concert.

He made a great success of his operas. *Maritana,* in particular, was received everywhere with acclaim. In 1850 he lost everything through the failure of a New York piano factory in which he was interested. In the same year, he narrowly escaped death in a steamboat explosion. He died in France at the age of fifty-one. Though his life was far from serene, in its outward aspects, at least, Wallace's music is appropriately called SERENITY, and has a peculiar fitness for Whittier's consoling lyric.

MUSICAL INTERPRETATION. This music has a sustained quality which is especially adapted to the expression of the words. Hold the four dotted quarter notes to the final limit of time. Sustain! Sustain!

Careful attention should be paid to the punctuation at the ends of the lines. The natural tendency to "drag" hymn tunes should be watched especially in this one, and care should be taken to sing it up to time without making it seem too rapid.

IN CHRIST THERE IS NO EAST OR WEST

1. In Christ there is no East or West,
   In him no South or North;
   But one great fellowship of love
   Throughout the whole wide earth.

2. In him shall true hearts everywhere
   Their high communion find;
   His service is the golden cord
   Close-binding all mankind.

3. Join hands then, brothers of the faith,
   Whate'er your race may be;
   Who serves my Father as a son
   Is surely kin to me.

4. In Christ now meet both East and West,
   In him meet South and North;
   All Christly souls are one in him
   Throughout the whole wide earth.[1]

JOHN OXENHAM, 1908.

BIBLICAL TEXT.

He is our peace, who made both one, and brake down the middle wall of partition . . . through him we both have our access in one Spirit unto

[1] Copyright by John Oxenham.

the Father. So then ye are no more strangers and sojourners, but ye are fellow-citizens with the saints, and of the household of God.

EPHESIANS 2: 14, 18, 19.

Where there cannot be Greek and Jew, circumcision and uncircumcision, barbarian, Scythian, bondman, freeman; but Christ is all, and in all.

COLOSSIANS 3: 11.

A PAGEANT OF DARKNESS AND LIGHT

Two English poets have written of East and West; one sang,

"Oh, East is East, and West is West, and never the twain shall meet,
Till Earth and Sky stand presently at God's great Judgment Seat."

and the other wrote,

"In Christ there is no East or West."

Distances between the nations are gradually and surely lessening by inventions of various sorts. There must be a corresponding lessening of spiritual distances. This is a prophetic hymn of the new day that must be in the world. "Science has made the world a neighborhood; it remains for the Church of Christ to make it a brotherhood."

John Oxenham, a present-day poet and writer of England, received his college training at Victoria University, Manchester. Entering business he traveled extensively, living in France, the United States, and Canada. At one time he visited the South with a view to orange growing and sheep raising. The British "Who's Who" states that he took up writing "as an alleviative and alternative from business and found it much more enjoyable, so dropped business and stuck to writing."

"The High Way" is probably his best known and most often quoted poem (see the musical setting in the New Hymnal for American Youth):

"To every man there openeth
A way, and ways, and a way,
And the high soul climbs the high way,
And the low soul gropes the low;
And in between, on the misty flats,
The rest drift to and fro:
But to every man there openeth
A high way and a low,
And every man decideth
The way his soul shall go." [2]

Another of his poems which bears close resemblance in thought to "In Christ there is no East or West," is "Break Down the Walls":

[2] From *Bees in Amber,* by John Oxenham, copyright by the American Tract Society.

"Break down the hedges that have grown
So thickly all about thy throne,
And clear the paths, that every soul
That seeks thee—of himself alone
May find, and be made whole!—

One church, one all-harmonious voice,
One passion for thy high Employs,
One heart of gold without alloys,
One striving for the higher joys,
One Christ, one Cross, one only Lord,
One living of the Holy Word." [3]

"In Christ there is no East or West" comes from the *Pageant of Darkness and Light,* which was widely produced throughout England and the United States during the years 1908 to 1914. John Oxenham wrote the entire text, which includes such exquisite lines as the Livingstone Lament, the Hindoo prayers, the Hawaiian rhythmic strains and the final Processional of Nations:

"Through tribulations and distress,
They come!
Through perils great and bitterness,
Through persecutions pitiless,
They come!
They come by paths the martyrs trod,
They come from underneath the rod,
Climbing through the darkness up to God,
They come!
Out of mighty tribulation,
With a sound of jubilation,
They come, they come!" [4]

A Responsive Service

Out of Darkness into Light

Minister:

"Lo, in the darkness I wander,
Where is the light?
Nothing know I, but I wonder,
Is there no light?
Lord, in thy vastness I wander,
Where is the way?
How may I reach thee, I wonder,
Is there no way?"

Congregation (singing to "Bethany"):

Though like the wanderer,

[3] Copyright by John Oxenham.
[4] From the *Pageant of Darkness and Light,* copyright by John Oxenham.

The sun gone down,
Darkness be over me,
My rest a stone;
Yet in my dreams I'd be
Nearer my God to thee,
Nearer to thee.

Minister:

"We are the voices of the wandering wind,
Which moan for rest, the rest can never find.
Lo, as the wind is, so is mortal life,
A moan, a sigh, a sob, a storm, a strife.
So many woes we see in many lands,
So many streaming eyes and wringing hands."

Congregation (singing to "Carol"):

And ye beneath life's crushing load,
Whose forms are bending low,
Who toil along the climbing way,
With painful steps and slow;
Look now, for glad and golden hours
Come swiftly on the wing;
O rest beside the weary road,
And hear the angels sing.

Minister:

"Christ the Lord is risen:"
Chant the Easter children,
Their love-moulded faces
Luminous with gladness,
And their costly raiment
Gleaming like the lilies.
But last night I wandered
Where Christ had not risen,
Where love knows no gladness
Where the Lord of Hunger
Leaves no room for lilies
And no time for childhood.[5]

Congregation (singing to "Webb"):

He comes with succor speedy

[5] By Elsa Barker, from *The Frozen Grail and Other Poems,* copyright by Duffield and Company.

To those who suffer wrong,
To help the poor and needy,
And bid the weak be strong;
To give them songs for sighing,
Their darkness turn to light,
Whose souls condemned and dying
Were precious in his sight.

Minister:

God hath made of one blood all nations of men for to dwell on all the face of the earth.

Congregation:

There is one body, and one spirit, one Lord, one faith, one baptism, one God and Father of us all, who is over all, and through all, and in all.

Minister:

Come, kingdom of our God, sweet reign of light and love,
Shed peace and hope and joy abroad, and wisdom from on high.

Congregation (singing to "Ellers"):

Gather us in, thou Love, that fillest all;
Gather our rival faiths within thy fold;
Rend each man's temple veil, and bid it fall,
That we may know that thou hast been of old.
Gather us in, we worship only thee;
In varied names we stretch a common hand,
In diverse forms a common soul we see,
In many ships we seek one spirit-land. Amen.

GEORGE MATHESON.

❖

THE HYMN TUNE. ST. PETER, the tune to which Oxenham's words are ordinarily sung, was composed by Alexander R. Reinagle (1799–1877) for Psalm 118. It was named for the church in Oxford where the composer was the organist for thirty-one years, 1822–1853. It is sometimes given its complete name, ST. PETER'S OXFORD. This is the tune to which John Newton's famous hymn, "How sweet the name of Jesus sounds," is sung.

Alexander Reinagle was the son of a distinguished violoncellist, for a time leader of the orchestra in an Edinburgh theater. He published in 1830 the book of *Psalm Tunes for the Voice and the Pianoforte*, from which this tune is taken.

IN THE CROSS OF CHRIST I GLORY

1. In the cross of Christ I glory,
Towering o'er the wrecks of time;
All the light of sacred story
Gathers round its head sublime.

2. When the woes of life o'ertake me,
Hopes deceive, and fears annoy,
Never shall the cross forsake me;
Lo! it glows with peace and joy.

3. When the sun of bliss is beaming
Light and love upon my way,
From the cross the radiance streaming
Adds new luster to the day.

4. Bane and blessing, pain and pleasure
By the cross are sanctified;
Peace is there that knows no measure,
Joys that through all time abide.

JOHN BOWRING, 1825.

BIBLICAL TEXT.

Christ crucified, unto Jews a stumbling block, and unto Gentiles foolishness; but unto them that are called, both Jews and Greeks, Christ the power of God and the wisdom of God. . . . He that glorieth, let him glory in the Lord.

I CORINTHIANS 1:23, 24, 31.

Far be it from me to glory, save in the cross of our Lord Jesus Christ.

GALATIANS 6:14.

Worthy is the Lamb that hath been slain to receive the power, and riches, and wisdom, and might, and honor, and glory, and blessing.

REVELATION 5:12.

A STATESMAN'S TESTIMONY

The significance of a hymn depends sometimes upon the circumstances under which it was written, sometimes upon the intrinsic worth of the words themselves, and sometimes upon the character and position of the author.

"In the cross of Christ I glory" would be one of the world's great hymns even if nothing at all were known of its author. But when it is remembered that the author of these words was one of the outstanding English statesmen of his day; that he was a linguist of very unusual ability; and that he was intimately acquainted with world politics, the words which he wrote as a young man take on a richer meaning.

Sir John Bowring (1792–1872) was born at Exeter, England. When only thirty-three years of age he was appointed editor of the *Westminster Review.* He was twice a member of Parliament, where he made notable contributions to the cause of prison reform. He served his country in various representative capacities, as Commissioner to France, as Consul at Canton, as Minister Plenipotentiary to China, and as Governor of Hong Kong. He was knighted in 1854.

John Bowring's father, a manufacturer of woolen goods, carried on a successful Spanish and Chinese trade. In preparation for succeeding his father in business John could speak and write before the age of sixteen, Spanish, Italian, Portuguese, French and German. Later he published his *Specimens of Russian Poets,* and later still *Danish and Norwegian Literature.* But he did not stop here; his next ventures in the linguistic field were translations from the Bohemian, Bulgarian, Slavonic, Servian, Polish. "He seems to have touched," says Dr. Duffield," the very nerve centers of language, and to have comprehended by supreme instinct the essence of the poet's thought."

His business prospered too. He carried on a successful Mediterranean trade under the firm name of Bowring and Murdock. He supplied the British army (1814) during the Peninsula campaign. He was elected as a Radical to the House of Commons. His writings include essays on many subjects, anthologies of poetry, political treatises—a total of thirty-six volumes. But he is best remembered by his hymns, three of which, especially, are familiar to most congregations of Christians on both sides of the Atlantic: "In the Cross of Christ I Glory," "Watchman, Tell Us of the Night," and "God is Love, His Mercy Brightens."

ANALYSIS. Against the background of the ruins of purely human efforts in philosophy, religion, art and science, "groping after God, if haply they might feel after him and find him," there stands out the Cross, with its message of consummate love. Sir John had opportunity to study the philosophy, religion and poetry of many peoples, and he recognized the permanent and transcendent value of the Cross and its message.

In a career so varied the author must have seen much of the evil of life. What matter if there be the darkness of overtaking woes, the disappointment of blasted hopes, and the constant annoyance of troublesome fears? All these things vanish in the light of peace and joy from the all-conquering Cross! Too often those upon whom the "sun of bliss is beaming" forget all about the Source of their blessings. The new luster is needed to complete the full beauty of the day of earthly joys. Whatever each day may bring of bane or of blessing the supreme need is that it should be sanctified by that spirit of consummate Love revealed on Calvary; only thus can be found that "peace which passeth understanding," and these joys that "through all time abide."

Dramatization

Fix a large cross at center back. Place back of it an elevation for the Spirit of the Cross to stand on.

Lighting:

First Stanza: Light amber throughout.

Second Stanza: Darkening through red to deep lavender.

Third Stanza: Specially placed light turned on by the suppliant at the word "Light."

Fourth Stanza: White growing brighter through to end.

Characters and Costumes:

1. The suppliant in lavender; being careful to avoid connotations of angels, Greek maidens, etc.
2. The Spirit of the Cross. In white.
3. Symbolic Figure for Woes of Life. Draped in deep purple. Black crêpe over shoulder.

Action: Hymn is played through. During the playing the Spirit of the Cross takes her place back of the Cross.

First Stanza: Suppliant enters. Kneels before the cross. End of the stanza finds her arms lifted, indicating exultation.

Second Stanza: Suppliant gradually relaxes and sinks to floor. Lowest point at close of stanza. Figure No. 3 enters, places black cape on suppliant. She vainly attempts to raise her arms in prayer as before.

Third Stanza: Spirit of the Cross leaves her position, comes down, removes black cape and lets it fall to the floor. Suppliant begins to show joy.

Fourth Stanza: Suppliant very gradually raises arms again. She has been sitting low. Now she rises to knee position. Spirit of the Cross takes position again. Fullest light, highest position, by the end of the last stanza.

Played through again: (Or partly.) Lights out. Characters exeunt.

✣

THE HYMN TUNE. RATHBUN was composed for this hymn by Ithamar Conkey (1815–1867), while he was organist and choir director in the Central Baptist Church, of Norwich, Connecticut.

Dr. Hiscox, pastor of the Central Baptist Church, Norwich, was preaching in 1849 a series of sermons on the "Words on the Cross." One very rainy Sunday Ithamar Conkey, organist and choirmaster of the church, keenly disappointed that so few choir singers reported, closed the organ after the prelude, locked it, slipped out of the choir gallery and went home. He sat down to practice, with the sermon in mind and the words of one particular hymn, "In the cross of Christ I glory," and then and there composed the music "Rathbun," naming it after the leading soprano of his choir, Mrs. Beriah S. Rathbun.

The following year Mr. Conkey moved to New York and became the bass soloist in Calvary Episcopal Church. He took important solo parts in many of the oratorio concerts of the time in New York. His tune was first published in the *Greatorex Collection.* Mr. Greatorex was then the organist at Calvary Church.

IN THE HOUR OF TRIAL

1. In the hour of trial,
Jesus, plead for me,
Lest by base denial
I depart from thee;
When thou see'st me waver,
With a look recall,
Nor, for fear, or favor,
Suffer me to fall.

2. With forbidden pleasures
Would this vain world charm;
Or its sordid treasures
Spread to work me harm;
Bring to my remembrance
Sad Gethsemane,
Or, in darker semblance,
Cross-crowned Calvary.

3. Should thy mercy send me
Sorrow, toil and woe,
Or should pain attend me
On my path below;
Grant that I may never
Fail thy hand to see;
Grant that I may ever
Cast my care on thee.

4. When my last hour cometh,
Fraught with strife and pain,
When my dust returneth
To the dust again;
On thy truth relying,
Through that mortal strife,
Jesus, take me, dying,
To eternal life.

James Montgomery, 1834.

Biblical Text.

Simon, Simon, behold Satan asked to have you, that he might sift you as wheat: but I made supplication for thee, that thy faith fail not.

But Peter said, Man, I know not what thou sayest. . . . And the Lord turned, and looked upon Peter. And Peter remembered the word of the Lord, how that he said unto him, Before the cock crow this day thou shalt deny me thrice. And he went out and wept bitterly.

Luke 22: 31, 32, 60–62.

A LOOK FROM CHRIST

The title that Montgomery gave to this hymn is also a part of its poetry, "The Look from Christ." It is reminiscent of the suffering of Christ in the garden and at the trial. Peter for all his pledges had followed Christ afar off and now sat warming himself by the fire. The first stanza is based upon this, one of the saddest and most vivid of all scenes. When Peter denied that he had ever known Christ, and began to curse and swear, "the Lord turned and looked upon Peter," and Peter remembered and went out and wept bitterly. The second stanza reminds us of Judas. The third stanza remembers that sorrow, toil and pain are sometimes sent by mercy. The fourth recalls Jesus as dying and conquering death.

Harrach has painted in his "Denial of Peter" this self-same hymnic detail. It shows Peter at the courtyard fire, surrounded by his accusers. In the background is an elevated passageway between two sections of Caiaphas' palace. Along this passage the soldiers are conducting Jesus. He pauses long enough to look down for a moment on his erring disciple. As Peter catches that look, he remembers.

James Montgomery (1771–1854) was the son of a Moravian minister. The boy, sent at an early age to the Moravian School at Fulneck, Yorkshire, was delighted with the Moravian hymns, and records that, as soon as he could write and spell, he imitated them. His father's dream that he would become a Moravian minister was not realized, but Montgomery, through his hymns, has made a lasting contribution to the development of the Christian church.

Most of his life was spent as editor and proprietor of the Sheffield

Iris. Writing to a friend during 1807 he said: "When I was a boy I wrote a great many hymns; but as I grew up and my heart degenerated, I directed my talents, such as they were, to other services, and seldom indeed since my fourteenth year have they been employed in the delightful duties of the sanctuary. However, I shall lie in wait for my heart, and when I can string it to the pitch of David's lyre, I will set a psalm 'to the Chief Musician.' "

He evidently found himself able to "string his heart to David's lyre," for although he was enough of a poet to be considered as Laureate, and to have his poems admired by Wordsworth, Southey, Byron and Moore, it is as hymn-writer that Montgomery is chiefly known.

As usually printed in our hymnals, the third and fourth stanzas have been altered by Mrs. Frances A. Hutton. Montgomery's original text seems stronger:

"If, with sore affliction,
Thou in love chastise,
Pour thy benediction
On the sacrifice;
Then upon thine altar,
Freely offered up,
Though the flesh may falter,
Faith shall drink the cup.

"When in dust and ashes,
To the grave I sink,
While heaven's glory flashes
O'er the shelving brink,
On thy truth relying,
Through that mortal strife,
Lord, receive me, dying,
To eternal life."

✣

THE HYMN TUNE. PENITENCE, by Spencer Lane (1843–1903), American composer and manufacturer of musical instruments, was written in 1870 for *Charles L. Hutchins' Hymnal.* It has a yearning note which matches well the longing for guidance expressed in Montgomery's words. It seems to belong particularly to these words, and is seldom, if ever, used for any other hymn.

INTO THE WOODS MY MASTER WENT

1. Into the woods my Master went,
Clean forspent, forspent;
Into the woods my Master came,

Forspent with love and shame.
But the olives they were not blind to him,
The little gray leaves were kind to him,
The thorn-tree had a mind to him,
When into the woods he came.

2. Out of the woods my Master went,
And he was well content;
Out of the woods my Master came,
Content with love and shame.
When death and shame would woo him last,
From under the trees they drew him last;
'Twas on a tree they slew him last,
When out of the woods he came.[1]

SIDNEY LANIER, 1880.

BIBLICAL TEXT.

And they came unto a place which was named Gethsemane: and he saith unto his disciples, Sit ye here, while I pray.

And he went forward a little, and fell on the ground, and prayed that, if it were possible, the hour might pass away from him.

And he said Abba, Father, all things are possible unto thee; remove this cup from me; howbeit, not what I will, but what thou wilt.

Arise, let us be going; behold, he that betrayeth me is at hand.

MARK 14: 32, 35, 36, 42.

A BALLAD OF THE TREES AND THE MASTER

There is the pathos of struggle almost beyond the limit of endurance; the beauty of nature lore; the love of the out-of-doors; and the hush of reverent quiet in the presence of a struggle beyond human comprehension, all of this, and more, in this short poem by that revered poet of the South, Sidney Lanier.

Sidney Lanier (1842–1881) was born at Macon, Georgia, graduated from Oglethorpe College in 1860, and was a tutor there when the Civil War began. As a student he had learned to play the flute, and a silver flute was one of his most prized possessions. When the war opened he took his silver flute and joined the Confederate Army as a private soldier. Among the hardships of the war which he endured was the experience of five months in a Federal Prison. After the war was over he taught school and took up the practice of law. Not neglecting his flute-playing, he also studied literature and music, with the result that he played the flute in a series of concerts with the Peabody Conservatory Orchestra in Baltimore, and in 1877 became Lecturer in English Literature in Johns Hopkins University. Beside his *Poems,* which were published by his widow after his death, he wrote, *The Science of English Verse* and *The English Novel.*

[1] Copyright by Mary O. Lanier and Charles Scribner's Sons.

This little poem about the trees is probably his best-known bit of writing; it is included in most of the modern anthologies of religious poetry, as well as in practically all modern hymnals.

Lanier's thought of the sympathy of the trees for the Master is found in Miss Katharine Lee Bates' recent hymn "Thy Palm Trees Fed with Dew and Sun" (*Hymns for the Living Age* and *The New Hymnal for American Youth*). Basing her poem on the use of palm and willow branches in the Triumphal Entry of Jesus into Jerusalem, she broadens the thought to include the trees of America:

"Thy palm-trees fed with dew and sun,
Thy cedars crowning Lebanon;
Thine olives of Gethsemane,
Lord of Light, all worshipped thee,
Hosanna to the Son of David. Hosanna!

Let oaks and elms take up thy praise,
Let maples, birches, willows raise
Adoring branches in thy sight,
Lord of Beauty, Lord of Light.
Hosanna to the Son of David. Hosanna!

Thou art the vine, to thee we bring
Ourselves thy branches, glad with spring.
By ripening fruit may we be known,
Lord of Light and Love, thine own.
Hosanna to the Son of David. Hosanna!" [2]

✣

THE HYMN TUNE. LANIER was written in 1905 for these words by Peter Christian Lutkin (1858–   ), who was born at Thompsonville, Wisconsin; was a choir boy under Canon Knowles; and began playing church organ at the age of twelve. His musical education went forward in Chicago under Mrs. Regina Watson, Clarence Eddy and Frederick Grant Gleason; in Paris under Moszkowski; in Berlin under August Haupt; and in Vienna under Leschetizky. He was organist and choirmaster in several notable Episcopal churches in Chicago, and in 1895 he became Dean of Northwestern University School of Music, Evanston, Illinois, and a little later Director of the Chicago North Shore Festival.

MINOR TUNES. For centuries the Scotch sang nothing but minor tunes. Three out of every four Methodist tunes of the eighteenth century were minor. The Welsh glory in minor tunes and the richness of their singing rests on this tonality. Note the strength and vigor of the following minor tunes: ABERYSTWYTH, COMMONWEALTH,

[2] Copyright by the Methodist Board of Education, and used by permission.

Dreamers, Ebenezer (Ton-y-botel), Lanier, My Master, Picardy, St. Andrew of Crete, Veni Emmanuel, Vox Dilecti.

IT CAME UPON THE MIDNIGHT CLEAR

1. It came upon the midnight clear,
That glorious song of old,
From angels bending near the earth,
To touch their harps of gold;
"Peace on the earth, good-will to men,
From heaven's all-gracious King;"
The world in solemn stillness lay,
To hear the angels sing.

2. Still through the cloven skies they come,
With peaceful wings unfurled;
And still their heavenly music floats
O'er all the weary world;
Above its sad and lowly plains
They bend on heavenly wing,
And ever o'er its Babel sounds
The blessed angels sing.

(Omitted Stanza)

Yet with the woes of sin and strife
The world hath suffered long;
Beneath the angel-strain have rolled
Two thousand years of wrong;
And man, at war with man, hears not
The love song which they bring:
O hush the noise, ye men of strife,
And hear the angels sing.

3. And ye, beneath life's crushing load,
Whose forms are bending low,
Who toil along the climbing way
With painful steps and slow,
Look now! for glad and golden hours
Come swiftly on the wing;
O rest beside the weary road,
And hear the angels sing.

4. For lo! the days are hastening on,
By prophet-bards foretold,
When, with the ever-circling years
Comes round the age of gold;
When peace shall over all the earth
Its ancient splendors fling,
And the whole world give back the song
Which now the angels sing.

Edmund Hamilton Sears, 1849.

BIBLICAL TEXT.

And suddenly there was with the angel a multitude of the heavenly host praising God, and saying, Glory to God in the highest, and on earth peace among men.

LUKE 2:13, 14.

Come now, and let us reason together, saith the Lord, though your sins be as scarlet, they shall be as white as snow; though they be red like crimson, they shall be as wool. If ye be willing and obedient, ye shall eat the good of the land.

ISAIAH 1:18, 19.

They shall beat their swords into ploughshares, and their spears into pruning-hooks; nation shall not lift up sword against nation, neither shall they learn war any more.

ISAIAH 2:4.

Be not overcome of evil, but overcome evil with good.

ROMANS 12:21.

O, HUSH THE NOISE, YE MEN OF STRIFE

Edmund Hamilton Sears (1810–1876) was born in Sandisfield, among the Berkshire Hills of Massachusetts. He was a lineal descendant of Richard Sears, who came from John Robinson's congregation in Holland to join the Plymouth Colony in 1630, and settled in one of the Cape Cod villages. Except for his college years at Union College, Schenectady, Sears' entire life was spent in Massachusetts. He graduated from college in 1834, and began the study of law, but could not resist the call to the ministry. After completing his theological training at Harvard Divinity School, he held pastorates at Wayland, Lancaster and Weston, all small towns within a short distance of each other in central Massachusetts. He wrote a number of religious books and was co-editor for a time of a religious magazine, but his most enduring fame rests on his two Christmas hymns. The first one, "Calm on the Listening Ear of Night," was written just after his graduation from college at the age of twenty-four, and the other during his second pastorate at Wayland. While nominally a Unitarian, Mr. Sears wrote to Bishop Bickersteth, "Though I was educated in the Unitarian denomination, I believe and preach the Divinity of Christ."

ANALYSIS. It is a mistake to think of this hymn as merely a Christmas hymn and to sing it only during that season. Although written by a village pastor, before the term "Social Service" had been heard of, it is emphatically a thoroughly modern hymn with a present-day social emphasis. The hymn should be carefully and thoughtfully read aloud before singing in order that the complete thought of the words may be clearly grasped.

First stanza: A vivid word-picture of that first Christmas night, with an unusual emphasis on the stillness of the world and its awareness of the angels' song.

Second stanza: The emphasis here should be placed on the first word "Still." The poet would help us sense the significant fact that today, as well as long ago over Bethlehem's plains, "the blessed angels sing." He rightly calls to our attention the difference between the "Babel sounds" of earth, and the heavenly harmony of the angels' song.

(Omitted Stanza): The din of strife, the noise of heartless competition, the injustice of race and social relations have indeed drowned the sweetness of the angels' song. Perhaps in the second quarter of the twentieth century there is needed even more than in the middle of the nineteenth, the challenging summons:

"O hush the noise, ye men of strife,
And hear the angels sing!"

Since this stanza is omitted from most hymnals, the minister should read it before the hymn is sung or after the singing of the second stanza.

Third stanza: What an invitation to rest! How many there are, in our modern, machine-dominated civilization who "toil along the climbing way," with forms bent and minds deadened by "life's crushing load!"

Fourth Stanza: The past, the present and the "glorious golden future" are all included in this final, climactic stanza. It offers an interesting corollary to Isaiah's prophecy included in the Biblical Texts above (Isaiah 2:4), and it is of peculiar interest in this present day of efforts for the outlawry of war.

Social Service Emphasis in Christmas Hymns and Carols

(*It Came upon the Midnight Clear*)
And ye, beneath life's crushing load.

(*Christians, lo, the star*)
Where a life is spent in service
Walking where the Master trod,
There is scattered myrrh most fragrant
For the blessed Christ of God.

(*From the Eastern Mountains*)
Gather in the outcasts,
All who've gone astray;
Throw thy radiance o'er them,
Guide them on their way;

Those who never knew thee,
Those who've wandered far,
Guide them by the brightness
Of thy guiding star.

(*Joy to the World*)

He rules the world with truth and grace,
And makes the nations prove
The glories of his righteousness,
And wonders of his love.

❖

THE HYMN TUNE. Richard Storrs Willis (1819–1900) was a musician and newspaper man, brother of the famous poet, Nathaniel Parker Willis, and son of Deacon N. Willis, who founded the *Youth's Companion*. After his graduation from Yale University, he lived for some time in New York where he edited the *Musical World* and wrote books on church music and other musical subjects. This tune, CAROL, is an arrangement from his "Study No. 23," 1850, by Uzziah C. Burnap.

JERUSALEM THE GOLDEN

1. Jerusalem the golden,
With milk and honey blest,
Beneath thy contemplation
Sink heart and voice oppressed;
I know not, O I know not,
What joys await us there,
What radiancy of glory,
What bliss beyond compare!

2. They stand, those halls of Zion,
All jubilant with song,
And bright with many an angel,
And all the martyr throng;
The Prince is ever in them,
The daylight is serene;
The pastures of the blessed
Are decked in glorious sheen.

3. There is the throne of David;
And there, from care released,
The shout of them that triumph,
The song of them that feast;
And they, who with their Leader,
Have conquered in the fight,
Forever and forever
Are clad in robes of white.

4. O sweet and blessed country,
The home of God's elect!
O sweet and blessed country
That eager hearts expect!
Jesus, in mercy bring us
To that dear land of rest,
Who art, with God the Father
And Spirit, ever blest!

BERNARD OF CLUNY, about 1145,
Translated by John M. Neale, 1851.

BIBLICAL TEXT.

And the city was pure gold, like unto pure glass.

REVELATION 21:18.

And there shall be no curse any more: and the throne of God and of the Lamb shall be therein; and his servants shall serve him; and they shall see his face.

REVELATION 22:3, 4.

Blessed are they that wash their robes, that they may have the right to come to the tree of life, and may enter in by the gates into the city.

REVELATION 22:14.

A SATIRE ON THE WORLD AND A RHAPSODY OF HEAVEN

In England, during the reign of King Stephen (1135–1153) the Anglo-Saxon Chronicler writes: "Never was there more misery and never acted heathen worse. The earth bare no corn, you might as well have tilled the sea, for the land was all ruined by such deeds, and it was said openly that Christ and his Saints slept." Two French monasteries were in their glory at this time; at Clairvaux the plain, simple cloisters of Bernard of the same name, at Cluny the most influential and magnificent establishment in France. It had enormous wealth, its abbot lived in princely state, its furnishings were luxurious, its table incomparable.

Bernard of Clairvaux thundered against Cluny, and why should he not? Outside of its walls were endless war, disease, oppression and poverty. Like England, so the distraught world. A simple monk of Cluny heard the accusations, retired to the magnificent library there, and penned a satire, 3000 lines long, about the whole crazy business. "It is not a rhapsody on heaven; rather is it hot with the fires of hell," says Dr. S. M. Jackson; and further, "At times it is not adapted for family reading." It begins with these warning words, "Little children, it is the last time."

This "prevailing sentiment" is more thoroughly revealed in the lines which were formerly printed in hymn books:

The world is very evil,
The times are waxing late;
Be sober and keep virgil;
The Judge is at the gate.

And now we watch and struggle,
And now we live in hope,
And Zion in her anguish
With Babylon must cope.

The Halls of Heaven are not forgotten, for the author loses himself in the contemplation of the glories of the "Celestial Country." Dr Benson calls it:

"A voice from the cloister, shrining the monastic conception of life, the monk's rapt vision, his longing for release from this vile flesh; and so a part of the Church's unending song." In spite of the pessimism of the first part of the satire, in spite of the monk's conviction that "The world is very evil," he rises in these other parts to the expression of a sublime faith in the ultimate triumph of Christ and a joy in him, far beyond the human mind to comprehend or to express.

Names of Jesus in the hymn (the very center of the glory and joy of heaven):

Jesus, the Gem of Beauty,
True God and Man, they sing:
The never-failing Garden,
The ever-golden Ring:
The Door, the Pledge, the Husband,
The guardian of his Court:
The Day-star of Salvation,
The Porter and the Port.

Dr. Neale says of the poem: "I have no hesitation in saying that I look on these verses of Bernard as the most lovely, in the same manner that the *'Dies Irae'* is the most sublime, and the *'Stabat Mater,'* the most pathetic, of medieval poems."

"Hora Novissima (The times are waxing late)," *"De contemptu Mundi* (Concerning the contempt of the world)," *"O Bona Patria* (For Thee, O dear, dear Country)," *"Urbs Sion aurea* (Jerusalem the golden)" are all titles for different centos of this three thousand line satire. It is an amazing literary production. The rhymes seem to tumble over one another, there being six in every two lines:

Hora Novissima, tempora pessima sunt; vigilemus!
Ecce minaciter, imminet Arbiter, Ille supremus.

No wonder the monk Bernard exclaimed: "Unless that spirit of wisdom and of understanding had been with me, and flowed in upon so difficult a meter, I could not have composed so long a work."

❖

The Hymn Tune. Fortunately, there seems to be a remarkable unanimity of opinion among hymn-book editors as to the one tune for these words, namely, Ewing. This is quite in line with the opinion of the translator, for Dr. Neale wrote: "I have so often been asked to

"Ewing" in Triple Time

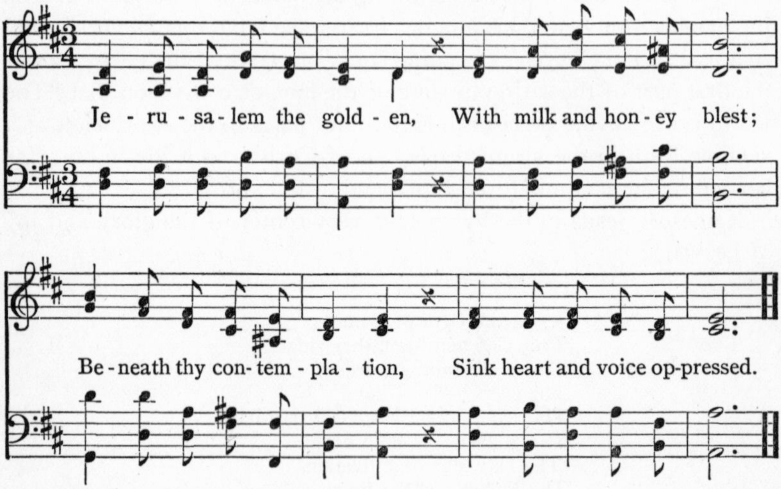
Je - ru - sa - lem the gold - en, With milk and hon - ey blest;
Be - neath thy con - tem - pla - tion, Sink heart and voice op-pressed.

what tune the words of Bernard may be sung that I here mention that of Mr. Ewing, the earliest written, the best known, and with children the most popular; no small proof, in my estimation, of the goodness of Church music."

Alexander Ewing (1830–1895) was born in Aberdeen, Scotland. He was trained as a lawyer, but developed a special love for music and studied the art in Heidelberg. He was a member of the famous Harmonic Choir of Aberdeen. One night in 1853, in the course of a rehearsal of this Choir, he approached the director, William Carnie, with the remark that he had tried his hand at writing a hymn-tune, and asked that the choir might sing it. Handing copies of it to the director, the amateur composer had the pleasure of hearing his new tune sung by the choir of which he was a member. Thus the hymn-tune, Ewing, was launched on its career of association with "Jerusalem the Golden."

Ewing entered the British Army, saw service in the Crimean War, was with "Chinese" Gordon in China, and left the army in 1867 with the rank of Lieutenant Colonel.

The tune was originally in triple time. Colonel Ewing never approved of it in common time, complaining "it now seems to me a good deal like a polka."

JESUS CALLS US, O'ER THE TUMULT

1. Jesus calls us, o'er the tumult
Of our life's wild, restless sea,
Day by day his sweet voice soundeth,
Saying, "Christian, follow me."

2. As of old, St. Andrew heard it
By the Galilean lake,
Turned from home and toil and kindred,
Leaving all for his dear sake.

3. Jesus calls us from the worship
Of the vain world's golden store,
From each idol that would keep us,
Saying, "Christian, love me more."

4. In our joys and in our sorrows,
Days of toil and hours of ease,
Still he calls, in cares and pleasures,
"Christian, love me more than these."

5. Jesus calls us; by thy mercies,
Saviour, may we hear thy call,
Give our hearts to thy obedience,
Serve and love thee best of all.[1]

CECIL FRANCES ALEXANDER, 1852.

BIBLICAL TEXT.

And walking by the Sea of Galilee, he saw two brethren, Simon, who is called Peter, and Andrew his brother, casting a net into the sea; for they were fishers. And he saith unto them, Come ye after me, and I will make you fishers of men. And they straightway left the nets, and followed him.

MATTHEW 4: 18, 19, 20.

He that loveth father or mother more than me is not worthy of me; and he that loveth son or daughter more than me is not worthy of me. And he that doth not take his cross and follow after me, is not worthy of me. He that findeth his life shall lose it; and he that loseth his life for my sake shall find it.

MATTHEW 10: 37–39.

[1] Copyright by Reid Brothers, London.

THE MUSIC OF GALILEE

This hymn is much sung and loved by the younger folk. It has been adopted by the vigorous Brotherhood of St. Andrew as their hymn. It was written for St. Andrew's Day.

Mrs. Cecil Frances Alexander (1823–1895) was a "brilliant and beneficent figure in the life around her," and as the wife of Archbishop Alexander, Primate of Ireland, she was an ardent churchwoman, and exerted a wide influence.

The daughter of Major Humphreys of the Royal Marines, she was born and brought up amidst fine scenery, loving friends, and congenial society in the north of Ireland (Londonderry). She was a "pearl among women" in spite of her nearsightedness and excessive shyness. Two most brilliant men of the times sought her in marriage, Professor Archer Butler and Reverend William Alexander. The latter won her, and she went to live in a parish scattered over miles of mountains and bogs. "Day after day she rode over the wet moorlands in all weathers, carrying food, warm clothing, medical supplies to the impoverished and sick. In one cottage she found a woman in great pain from a bad wound, unattended, and altogether without medical aid. For six weeks every day Mrs. Alexander came to this woman, and herself washed and dressed the wound, until healing set in and she recovered her health."

She continued to write lovely poetry in sight of the shore of Lough Swilly, the next parish, yet she was master in the garden and in farm management. Her husband, coming home late of an afternoon, would quiz her: "Have you sold the cow? Have you shown the gardener how to prune the roses? Have you directed the feeding of the pigs properly? Have you finished that poem? Yes? Then let us come into the study and I will criticize it ferociously."

When her husband became bishop her circle of friends widened to take in Dean Stanley, Matthew Arnold, Mr. Lecky, Bishop Wilberforce, Bishop Wordsworth and a host of others.

Of her hymns Stopford Brooke said: "Charmingly simple and tender, clear in dogma, and of poetical beauty, combining the plainness of Watts with the feeling for and with children of the Taylor sisters, and uniting with both the liturgical associations of the English Prayer Book, they remain unequalled and unapproachable."

People worship God out of what they themselves are. In the hymn, "Thou Power and Peace," we see the reflection of a kindly, gentle soul; in "Jesus calls us," we see a spirit, energetic, alert, resolute.

The writer was impatient of efforts to "improve" her hymns. "You see," she once said, "what I wanted to say is just so, and nothing else." She had the poet's eye to see and depict vivid and significant details of scenery, and the spiritual gift to "consider" when a Christ said, "Consider the lilies of the field." Her hymns contain many charming pictures. In twenty years more than a quarter of a million copies of her *Hymns for Little Children* had been sold. Among her best-known hymns are:

"There is a green hill far away"
"All things bright and beautiful"
"Once in royal David's city"
"I bind myself to thee" (Breastplate of St. Patrick)

A Responsive Service

This familiar and somewhat hackneyed hymn may be given a new meaning and a richer significance to the average congregation by the use of such a simple Responsive Service as the following:

Minister:

And walking by the sea of Galilee, he saw two brothers, Simon, who is called Peter, and Andrew his brother, casting a net into the sea; for they were fishers. And he said unto them, Come ye after me, and I will make you fishers of men. And they straightway left the nets, and followed him.

MATTHEW 4: 18, 19.

Congregation (singing stanza one):

"Jesus calls us" (The emphasis may well be put on the words *us* and *our*).

Minister:

Andrew findeth first his own brother, Simon, and saith unto him, We have found the Messiah (which is, being interpreted, Christ). He brought him unto Jesus.

Congregation (singing second stanza):

"As of old St. Andrew heard it."

Minister:

One thing thou lackest yet: sell all that thou hast, and distribute unto the poor, and thou shalt have treasure in heaven; and come, follow me. But when he heard these things, he became exceeding sorrowful, for he was very rich.

LUKE 18:22, 23.

Congregation (singing stanza three):

"Jesus calls us from the worship."

Minister:

"Enough for me to feel and know
That he in whom the cause and end,
The past and future, meet and blend,
Guards not archangel feet alone,
But deigns to guide and keep my own;
. . . whispers in my spirit's ear,
In tones of love, or warning fear,
A language none beside may hear."

Congregation (singing stanza four):

"In our joys and in our sorrows."

Minister:

"Though heralded with naught of fear,
Or outward sign or show;
Though only to the inward ear
It whispers soft and low;
Though dropping, as the manna fell,
Unseen, yet from above,
Noiseless as dew-fall, heed it well,
Thy Father's call of love!"

Congregation (singing stanza five):

"Jesus calls us; by thy mercies."

(The last line should be sung softly.)

THE HYMN TUNE. GALILEE, appropriately named tune for this hymn, was composed by William Herbert Jude, in 1887. Mr. Jude (1851–1892) was born at Leatherhead, England; was organist of the Blue Coat Hospital, Liverpool; founder of the Purcell Society; editor of the *Monthly Hymnal*. In 1889 he became organist of Stretford Town Hall near Manchester. He lectured on musical subjects in

Great Britain and Australia, and composed operettas and a number of songs.

JESUS, LOVER OF MY SOUL

1. Jesus, Lover of my soul,
Let me to thy bosom fly,
While the nearer waters roll,
While the tempest still is high;
Hide me, O my Saviour, hide,
Till the storm of life be past;
Safe into the haven guide;
O receive my soul at last.

2. Other refuge have I none;
Hangs my helpless soul on thee;
Leave, ah, leave me not alone,
Still support and comfort me.
All my trust on thee is stayed,
All my help from thee I bring;
Cover my defenseless head
With the shadow of thy wing.

3. Thou, O Christ, art all I want,
More than all in thee I find;
Raise the fallen, cheer the faint,
Heal the sick, and lead the blind.
Just and holy is thy name,
I am all unrighteousness;
False and full of sin I am,
Thou art full of truth and grace.

4. Plenteous grace with thee is found,
Grace to cover all my sin;
Let the healing streams abound;
Make and keep me pure within.
Thou of life the fountain art,
Freely let me take of thee;
Spring thou up within my heart,
Rise to all eternity.

CHARLES WESLEY, 1740.

BIBLICAL TEXT.

The eternal God is thy dwelling place, and underneath are the everlasting arms.

DEUTERONOMY 33:27.

Jesus spake unto them, saying, Be of good cheer; it is I; be not afraid.

MATTHEW 14:27.

And immediately Jesus stretched forth his hand, and took hold of him, and saith unto him, O thou of little faith, wherefore didst thou doubt?

MATTHEW 14:31.

A PERFECT AND IMMORTAL SONG

In spite of the poverty and constant parochial difficulties of the Rectory at Epworth, Samuel and Susannah Wesley taught their children to sing. And it may well be that the memories of those early days of Psalm singing in the home helped to inspire the six thousand five hundred hymns which Charles Wesley (1707–1788) wrote.

He received his degree from Oxford in 1728, and was ordained a priest of the Church of England in 1735. That same year he went to Georgia as secretary to Governor Oglethorpe, but returned to England the next year. He dates his conversion May 21, 1738. As an "Anniversary Hymn," on the first anniversary of that important date he wrote, "O for a thousand tongues to sing my dear Redeemer's praise."

From 1739 to 1756 Charles Wesley lived almost as strenuous a life as his brother John. Both were constantly on the move, preaching to great crowds in open-air meetings, riding hundreds of miles each year on horseback, facing hostile mobs, organizing Methodist "Societies." Yet, in spite of all this feverish activity Charles found time to write hymns by the hundreds.

Married in 1749, his wife accompanied him on his itinerating journeys until 1756, when they settled down in Bristol, and Charles gave himself to the task of looking after the Societies in Bristol and London, and of writing hymns for every possible occasion. In 1771 they moved to London which was their home until Wesley's death in 1788. His body was buried in the Marylebone Churchyard, somewhat to the displeasure of his brother John; but in keeping with his expressed wish, "I have lived, and I die, in the communion of the Church of England."

His absorbing interest in hymn-writing is shown in his own record of being thrown from his horse one day: "My companions thought I had broken my neck; but my leg only was bruised, my hand sprained and my head stunned, which spoiled my making hymns until—next day."

"Jesus, Lover of My Soul" is one of the supreme hymns of the world. It has gone to the corners of the earth with the English language, and has been translated into virtually all languages. A thousand legends cluster about it as about the memory of some ancient hero, or of some gentle and famous saint. Countless children through successive generations have learned and cherished its lines; countless men and women have found in it deep refreshment of spirit as from a cool spring and shade by the roadside, and countless ones have passed out of life with these words on their lips.

As literature it has the brevity, melody, intensity, and completeness of the pure lyric. George Saintsbury says of it in his *History of English Prosody:* "The mere word-music of it is fingered throughout in the most absolutely adequate manner." If one reads it without thought of the tune he is still compelled by its inherent melody. And its effects are attained by the simplest and most direct means. Of the two hundred and thirty-six words of the poem, all but thirty-six are monosyllables. The images are vivid and quickly drawn, its movement is swift and melodious, the lines are aglow with life. It is a perfect and immortal song.

It stands today as Wesley made it except that a single word, the subjunctive "be" in line six, is changed to "is"; the Latin vocative "Jesu, Lover," is printed in the English form and the third stanza is omitted. The stanza omitted is as good lyric poetry as the rest, but it is a shade too fervent for the steady hymn-book. Of all the hymns in the book, this one probably has been amended most. There are more than thirty variations in the first stanza: "Refuge," for example, has been substituted for "Lover" and for "bosom." Plural pronouns have been inserted, etc. None of these changes injures the hymn.

LINING OUT THE HYMN: An interesting variation in the use of this hymn, somewhat after the old-fashioned manner of "lining out," is the reading by the minister of the appropriate passages of Scripture as commentaries on the lines of the hymn.

First Stanza

Jesus, Lover of my soul,	Having loved his own that were in the world, he loved them unto the end. JOHN 13:1.
Let me to thy bosom fly;	There was at the table reclining in Jesus' bosom one of his disciples. JOHN 13:23.
While the nearer waters roll,	I am come into deep waters, where the floods overflow me. PSALM 69:2.

While the tempest still is high;	I would haste me to a shelter From the stormy wind and tempest. PSALM 55:8.
Hide me, O my Saviour, hide,	In the day of trouble he will keep me secretly in his pavilion; In the covert of his tabernacle will he hide me. PSALM 27:5.
Till the storm of life is past;	Trust ye in the Lord for ever, for in the Lord, even the Lord, is an everlasting rock. ISAIAH 26:4.
Safe into the haven guide;	Then are they glad because they are quiet; So he bringeth them unto their desired haven. PSALM 107:30.
O receive my soul at last.	And they stoned Stephen, calling upon the Lord, and saying, Lord Jesus, receive my spirit. ACTS 7:59.

Second Stanza

Other refuge have I none;	God is our refuge and strength, A very present help in trouble. PSALM 46:1.
Hangs my helpless soul on thee;	The Lord will not suffer the soul of the righteous to famish. PROVERBS 10:3.
Leave, ah, leave me not alone,	Himself hath said, I will in no wise fail thee, neither will I in any wise forsake thee. HEBREWS 13:5.
Still support and comfort me.	I will give thanks unto thee, O Lord, for . . . thou comfortest me. ISAIAH 12:1.

All my trust on thee is stayed,	Salvation will he appoint for walls and bulwarks. ISAIAH 26:1.
All my help from thee I bring;	Thou wilt keep him in perfect peace whose mind is stayed on thee; because he trusteth in thee. ISAIAH 26:3.
Cover my defenseless head	O Lord, thou hast covered my head in the day of battle. PSALM 140:7.
With the shadow of thy wing.	In the shadow of thy wings will I take refuge. PSALM 57:1.

Third Stanza

Thou, O Christ, art all I want,	Christ is all, and in all. COLOSSIANS 3:11.
More than all in thee I find;	In him dwelleth all the fulness of the Godhead bodily. COLOSSIANS 2:9.
Raise the fallen, cheer the faint,	The Lord upholdeth all that fall, and raiseth up all those that are bowed down. PSALM 145:14.
Heal the sick, and lead the blind.	I will bring the blind by a way that they know not, . . . I will make darkness light before them. ISAIAH 42:16.
Just and holy is thy name,	There is no God else besides me, a just God and a Saviour; ISAIAH 45:21.
I am all unrighteous;	All have sinned, and fall short of the glory of God. ROMANS 3:23.

False, and full of sin I am,	If we say that we have no sin, we deceive ourselves, and the truth is not in us. 1 JOHN 1:8.
Thou art full of truth and grace.	We beheld his glory, glory as of the only begotten from the Father, full of grace and truth. JOHN 1:14.

Fourth Stanza

Plenteous grace with thee is found,	My grace is sufficient for thee. 2 CORINTHIANS 12:9.
Grace to cover all my sin;	Where sin abounded, grace did abound more exceedingly. ROMANS 5:20.
Let the healing streams abound;	Everything shall live whithersoever the river cometh. EZEKIEL 47:9.
Make and keep me pure within;	Create in me a clean heart, O God; And renew a right spirit within me. PSALM 51:10.
Thou of life the fountain art,	In him was life, and the life was the light of men. JOHN 1:4.
Freely let me take of thee;	He that is athirst, let him take the water of life freely. REVELATION 22:17.
Spring thou up within my heart,	The water that I shall give him shall become in him a well of water springing up unto eternal life. JOHN 4:14.
Rise to all eternity.	Whosoever drinketh of the water that I shall give him shall never thirst. JOHN 4:14a.

✣

THE HYMN TUNE. A majority of church hymnals give a choice of at least two tunes for this hymn, HOLLINGSIDE and MARTYN being the favorites. The former is repeated forty-nine times and the latter forty-three in the sixty-odd hymnals examined. REFUGE appears only thirteen times in the church hymnals, and three times in those for the Church School. The English hymnals quite generally place ABERYSTWYTH as the first choice, with HOLLINGSIDE second. Probably a good many Americans will agree with Philo Otis in his *Hymns You Ought to Know,* "Choirmasters and ministers must make their choice. My own is soon made. The tune MARTYN is to me a blessed memory, as I heard it sung by the 'Village Choir' of my childhood." Although not so familiar, REFUGE has a rare beauty when well sung by a company of good singers.

Simeon Butler Marsh (1798–1875) joined a children's choir at the age of seven and at the age of twenty started his career as a singing teacher. For thirty years he taught choirs of adults and children and conducted singing schools in the Albany Presbytery. He also gave free instruction to the children of Schenectady. Knowing the printer's art, he set the type with his own hand for three juvenile singing books. His later life was spent in Sherburne, teaching voice, piano and violin, superintending the Sunday School and leading the choir.

Among his musical compositions was a cantata for boys, "The King of the Forest." He composed MARTYN one morning in the autumn of 1834 while en route from Amsterdam to Johnstown, on his weekly circuit of singing schools. Dismounting his horse he wrote the notes down, using John Newton's words, "Mary at her Saviour's tomb."

JESUS, SAVIOUR, PILOT ME

1. Jesus, Saviour, pilot me,
Over life's tempestuous sea;
Unknown waves before me roll,
Hiding rock and treacherous shoal;
Chart and compass came from thee:
Jesus, Saviour, pilot me.

2. As a mother stills her child,
Thou canst hush the ocean wild;
Boisterous waves obey thy will
When thou say'st to them, "Be still."
Wondrous Sovereign of the sea,
Jesus, Saviour, pilot me.

3. When at last I near the shore,
And the fearful breakers roar

'Twixt me and the peaceful rest,
Then, while leaning on thy breast,
May I hear thee say to me,
"Fear not, I will pilot thee."

EDWARD HOPPER, 1871.

BIBLICAL TEXT.

Behold, there arose a great tempest in the sea, insomuch that the boat was covered with the waves; but he was asleep. And they came to him, and awoke him, saying, Save, Lord, we perish. And he saith unto them, Why are ye fearful, O ye of little faith? Then he arose, and rebuked the winds and the sea; and there was a great calm. And the men marvelled, saying, What manner of man is this, that even the winds and the sea obey him?

MATTHEW 8:24–27.

And seeing them distressed in rowing, for the wind was contrary unto them, about the fourth watch of the night he cometh unto them, walking on the sea; and . . . they were troubled. But he straightway spake with them, and saith unto them, Be of good cheer, it is I, be not afraid. And he went up unto them into the boat; and the wind ceased.

MARK 6:48–51.

A SONG FOR SAILORS

It is quite in line with the general "fitness of things" to find that this hymn, which speaks of the "tempestuous sea," the "ocean wild," and the "fearful breakers" was written by the pastor of a church called "The Church of Sea and Land."

It is obviously a sailor's hymn, written for sailors and published first of all in the April, 1871, issue of *The Sailors' Magazine and Seaman's Friend.*

Edward Hopper (1818–1888) was a Presbyterian minister, born in New York City. His mother was of the heroic Huguenot stock of France. After his graduation from the University of the City of New York and Union Theological Seminary (1842) he served churches in Greenville, New York, and Sag Harbor, Long Island, where he stayed eleven years. From Sag Harbor he returned to New York, where he served the Church of Sea and Land until his death. He did a notable work among the sailors, and was always deeply interested in the men of the sea.

As originally written, this hymn had six stanzas, but for use as a congregational hymn, the author himself selected the first and the last two stanzas as sufficient.

(Omitted Stanzas)

2

When the Apostles' fragile bark
Struggled with the billows dark,

On the stormy Galilee,
Thou didst walk upon the sea;
And when they beheld thy form,
Safe they glided through the storm.

3

Though the sea be smooth and bright,
Sparkling with the stars of night,
And my ship's path be ablaze
With the light of halcyon days,
Still I know my need of thee;
Jesus, Saviour, pilot me.

4

When the darkling heavens frown,
And the wrathful winds come down,
And the fierce waves, tossed on high,
Lash themselves against the sky,
Jesus, Saviour, pilot me,
Over life's tempestuous sea.

❖

THE HYMN TUNE. Tunes are often named for the sentiment of the hymns for which they were composed, or with which they are most commonly associated, as: WATCHWORD, for "Forward, be our watchword"; PENITENCE for "In the hour of trial"; RETREAT, for "From every stormy wind that blows"; CONSOLATION, for "Come, ye disconsolate"; and BENEDICTION, for the dismissal hymn, "Saviour, again to thy dear name."

The only tune with which this hymn is associated also gets its name from the hymn; PILOT, was composed by John Edgar Gould (1822–1875) in 1871 expressly for this hymn. John Gould was the son of Captain Horace Gould. At the age of thirty he opened a music store on Broadway, New York, and later in Philadelphia. While on a European tour during 1874–75, he took sick and died at Algiers.

JESUS SHALL REIGN WHERE'ER THE SUN

1. Jesus shall reign where'er the sun
Does his successive journeys run;
His kingdom stretch from shore to shore,
Till moons shall wax and wane no more.

2. For him shall endless prayer be made,
And praises throng to crown his head;
His name, like sweet perfume, shall rise
With every morning sacrifice.

3. People and realms of every tongue
Dwell on his love with sweetest song,
And infant voices shall proclaim
Their early blessings on his name.

4. Blessings abound where'er he reigns;
The prisoner leaps to lose his chains,
The weary find eternal rest,
And all the sons of want are blest.

5. Let every creature rise and bring
Peculiar honors to our King;
Angels descend with songs again,
And earth repeat the loud Amen!

Isaac Watts, 1719.

Biblical Text.

In his days shall the righteous flourish,
And abundance of peace, till the moon be no more.
He shall have dominion also from sea to sea,
And from the River unto the ends of the earth.
All kings shall fall down before him;
All nations shall serve him. . . .
He will have pity on the poor and needy,
And the souls of the needy he will save.

Psalm 72:7, 8, 11, 13.

Hallelujah: for the Lord our God, the Almighty, reigneth. Let us rejoice and be exceeding glad, and let us give the glory unto him:

Revelation 19:6, 7.

He hath on his garment and on his thigh a name written,
KING OF KINGS AND LORD OF LORDS:

Revelation 19:16.

A PIONEER MISSIONARY HYMN

Back in 1719, "missions" was not the popular subject that it is to-day. The world was a good deal larger, and the interest of the Church in preaching the Gospel "to every creature" had not been aroused by the appeals of Carey and Judson. Count Zinzendorf had not even begun that great work which later made the name "Moravian" synonymous with "missionary." Yet in that year, from his quiet retreat in the beautiful country estate of Sir Thomas Abney, Isaac Watts sent out his clarion call to confidence in the ultimate and entire victory of Jesus, the Christ.

Watts said, concerning the necessity for a newer type of hymnody than the Psalms of David: "We preach the Gospel, and pray in Christ's name, and then check the aroused devotions of the Christians by giving out a song of the old dispensation."

Almost one hundred and fifty years after Watts wrote this "pioneer" missionary hymn, a remarkable use of it occurred in a British dependency on the other side of the globe. On Whitsunday, 1862, the king of the Tonga (Friendly) Islands in the South Pacific, gathered his people about him and read to them a new charter of government, proclaiming that their islands would henceforth be known as a Christian nation. At the conclusion of the proclamation, the crowd of natives burst forth in a glad hymn of praise, none other than Watts' hymn, "Jesus shall reign where'er the sun."

The three omitted stanzas contain much poetic prophecy, although hardly to be appraised as hymnic material:

"Behold the islands with their kings,
And Europe, her best tribute brings;
From North to South the princes meet
To pay their homage at his feet.

"There Persia, glorious to behold,
There India shines in eastern gold,
And barbarous nations at his word
Submit and bow, and own their Lord.

"Where he displays his healing power
Death and the curse are known no more;
In him the tribes of Adam boast
More blessings than their father lost."

These omitted stanzas give an interesting aspect to the matter of hymn revision. Watts, the trail-maker, had not the experience that his followers have, but his hymn sense told him, though not quite emphatically enough, that certain stanzas would not do. Virtually all the hymn books of today have changed or left out all of these stanzas. Why are they not good hymnody? It is not the proper names that are discordant. America, Greenland, Ceylon, India, Africa, China are used in hymns with fine effect; but the "Europe" in these lines does not strike poetic fire. The description of Persia is not convincing, and the idea of "general," "world-wide," which it is meant to give, fails because it is too close to India for that. "For" in stanza two is sometimes printed "To." This is not fanciful criticism; the hymn could not have lived without these main changes.

The hymn is masterful throughout. The idea, developed in ringing, lyric tones, is that the faith taught by Christ will bring about a common civilization, a world-wide unity, and a prevalence of good-will, welfare, happiness; a universal recognition of truth, fulfilment of obligation, and enjoyment of good. No poet could perform a higher service in bringing understanding and good-will, than to plant this idea, vibrant with emotion, in the minds of all sorts of people. If the people get this vision into their songs, they will get it into their ballot-boxes and their general behavior. If the millions who sing this hymn imbibe even half-consciously its spirit of charity and truth, no one can calculate the worth of the hymn-poet as a peacemaker and welfare-worker in human society.

ALTERATIONS IN HYMNS. John Wesley protested: "Many gentlemen have done my brother and me (though without naming us) the honor to reprint many of our hymns. Now they are perfectly free to do so, provided they print them just as they are. But I desire they would not attempt to mend them; for they really are not able. None of them is able to mend either the sense or the verse. Therefore I must beg of them one of these two favors, either let them stand just as they are, to take them for better for worse; or to add the true reading in the margin, or at the bottom of the page, so that we may no longer be accountable, either for the nonsense or for the doggerel (*sic*) of other men."

Concerning hymn-mending, Christophers says: "The Wesleys are seen mending Herbert and Watts; Toplady and Madan are found hashing and recooking Charles Wesley; somebody else is trying to improve Toplady; Heber makes free with Jeremy Taylor; Montgomery is altering—and altered. Keble and Milman and Alford are all pinched and twisted and redressed in turn. Among all these menders, John Wesley was perhaps one of the best. He was positively sure that nobody could mend his own hymns, but he was not scrupulous in mending other people's."

The Arians changed the Trinitarian Doxology to: "Glory be to the Father, *through* the Son, and to the Holy Ghost."

The Seventh Day Adventists chant Watts' opening line: "Joy to the world, the Lord *will* come."

The Roman Catholics altered Wesley's prayer hymn to sing:

> Jesu, Saviour of my soul,
> Let me to thy refuge fly;
> Ave, ave, Jesus mild,
> Deign to hear thy lowly child.

Protestants changed Faber's following stanza to meet their particular needs:

> Faith of our fathers! Mary's prayers
> Shall win our country back to thee:
> And through the truth that comes from God
> England shall then indeed be free.

Unitarians reëdited Trinitarian lines:

God in Three Persons, blessed Trinity.

to

Infinite in power, in love, and purity.

Universalists sing:

When morning gilds the skies,
My heart awaking cries,
Thy name, O God, be praised.

Christian Scientists deftly reword:

Come, ye disconsolate, where'er ye languish,
Here health and peace are found, Life, Truth and Love.

❖

"Duke Street" — Key of G

Je - sus shall reign wher - e'er the sun Does his suc -
ces - sive jour - neys run; His king - dom stretch from
shore to shore, Till moons shall wax and wane no more.

THE HYMN TUNE. One of the most commonly used and universally liked tunes for this hymn is DUKE STREET, composed by John Hatton, who was born at Warrenton, near Liverpool, and who died at St. Helen's in 1793. The tune is named for the street in St. Helen's, township of Windle, on which he lived.

Try singing DUKE STREET in the Key of G, the key in which it was originally written and sung (without accompaniment).

JOYFUL, JOYFUL, WE ADORE THEE

1. Joyful, joyful, we adore thee
God of glory, Lord of love;
Hearts unfold like flowers before thee,
Hail thee as the sun above.
Melt the clouds of sin and sadness;
Drive the dark of doubt away;
Giver of immortal gladness,
Fill us with the light of day.

2. All thy works with joy surround thee,
Earth and heaven reflect thy rays,
Stars and angels sing around thee,
Center of unbroken praise;
Field and forest, vale and mountain,
Blossoming meadow, flashing sea,
Chanting bird, and flowing fountain,
Call us to rejoice in thee.

3. Thou art giving and forgiving,
Ever blessing, ever blest,
Well-spring of the joy of living,
Ocean-depth of happy rest.
Thou our Father, Christ our Brother,
All who live in love are thine;
Teach us how to love each other,
Lift us to the Joy Divine.

4. Mortals, join the mighty chorus,
Which the morning stars began;
Father-love is reigning o'er us,
Brother-love binds man to man.
Ever singing march we onward,
Victors in the midst of strife;
Joyful music lifts us sunward
In the triumph song of life.[1]

HENRY VAN DYKE, 1908.

BIBLICAL TEXT.

All thy works shall give thanks unto thee, O Lord;
And thy saints shall bless thee.

PSALM 145:10

When the morning stars sang together,
And all the sons of God shouted for joy.

JOB 38:7

Oh give thanks unto the Lord; for he is good;
For his lovingkindness endureth forever.
Let the redeemed of the Lord say so.

PSALM 107:1, 2

THE JOY OF LIVING IN GOD'S WORLD

This is a joy-hymn supreme. Every line and every bar of the music express the message of the gladness of the soul in its gratitude to the Creator, who is not only the "God of Glory," but equally the "Lord of Love."

The writer, Dr. Henry van Dyke (1852–   ) is eminent as a preacher, college professor, diplomat and man of letters. He was born in Germantown, Pennsylvania, in 1852. Upon his graduation from Princeton, he served as pastor of the Brick Presbyterian Church of New York City for seventeen busy years. Then he was called to his Alma Mater as Professor of English Literature. After a most successful career at Princeton he served as United States Minister to the Netherlands and Luxemburg, Moderator of the General Assembly of the Presbyterian Church, Commander of the Legion of Honor, and President of the National Institute of Arts and Letters. During recent years he has devoted himself to writing.

His published works have attained world-wide circulation. Among them perhaps the best-loved and most widely known are his prose tales such as *The Blue Flower, The Lost Word, The Other Wise Man, The Lost Boy,* and *The Sad Shepherd.* His collected poems (in one large volume) and his smaller books of poetry, such as *Music* and *The Toiling of Felix,* have made a great appeal to thoughtful people.

A spirit of optimism, courage and faith in God and in his fellowmen, characterizes Dr. van Dyke's writings, both prose and poetry. Among his hymns which may be found in modern hymnals are: "Thy wisdom and thy might appear," "O maker of the Mighty Deep," "Jesus, thou Divine Companion," "O Lord our God, thy mighty hand."

ANALYSIS. First stanza: Every line of this first stanza sounds forth the note of praise and joy. There is rare beauty in the picture of the third line, suggesting the gentle and joyous influence of sunshine on flowers. The seventh line offers a new and most appropriate title for him who is both the "God of glory and Lord of love."

Second stanza: In a most remarkable manner Dr. van Dyke has succeeded in including all of earth and heaven in a universal anthem of praise. Not only "stars and angels" in the realms above, but also and equally, "field and forest," "vale and mountain," "blossoming meadow, flashing sea," "chanting bird and flowing fountain," call on men to join the mighty chorus. Like the old-time singer of Psalm 148, Dr. van Dyke would have man join with the forces of Nature in a glorious song of joy.

Third stanza:

> "Who forgiveth all thine iniquities;
> Who crowneth thee with lovingkindness and tender mercies;
> Who satisfieth thy desire with good things."
>
> PSALM 103:3–5.

There is a very interesting connection between this old-time song and the new-time song of this third stanza. One will search far to find richer poetry or more accurate description of God than that of the third and fourth lines of this stanza. In fact, the entire poem is so very full of beautiful and unusual phrases that it should be read aloud, as well as sung, in order to get the full meaning of these descriptive words.

Fourth stanza: The note of constant victory "in the midst of strife" sounds out most clearly here, while the place and power of music is a vital factor in the development of the Christian life is emphasized in the closing lines.

❖

THE HYMN TUNE. The tune, HYMN TO JOY, was arranged from the Ninth Symphony of Ludwig van Beethoven (1770–1827) by Edward Hodges (1796–1867). Beethoven is one of the most tragic and at the same time one of the most commanding figures of all history; tragic, because of his unequal struggle against misfortune, deafness and a gloomy and irascible disposition; commanding, because of his magnificent accomplishments. His matchless sonatas, choral works, string-quartets, concertos and symphonies express every mood of the human soul. He has been called "the Michelangelo of Music."

Beethoven wrote nine symphonies. When he came to the ninth he seems to have exhausted instrumental colors and effects. He calls on vocal music, the chorus, using the text of Schiller's "Ode to Joy," to give the supreme utterance, the final word.

> "Hail thee, Joy, from heaven descending,
> Daughter from Elysium,
> Ecstasy our hearts inflaming,
> To thy sacred shrine we come."

When this symphony was first produced in Vienna in 1824, the vast audience was intoxicated with delight. People actually shouted for joy. But the deaf composer, facing the orchestra and oblivious alike to the sound of the music and to the uproar of the audience, knew nothing of what was happening until some-one turned him around. Nearly all the people were standing, and now the greater number melted into tears, for the first time recognizing the extent of Beethoven's calamity.

The intimate spirit of union between Beethoven's music and Dr. van Dyke's words is hinted at in the following quotation from Beethoven's words about Nature: "Every tree seems to speak to me of God. How happy am I to wander through the cool paths of the forest. No one can love the country as I do."

Dr. van Dyke's words preserve the exultant spirit of Schiller's poem, with the significant addition that he gives a Christian basis for this holy joy. Note the grandeur and increasing magnitude of the thought as it unfolds, stanza by stanza. How shall we sing such words and such music? Let the tempo be rather quick, but not so hurried as to make the hymn seem trivial. Let there be plenty of organ. Combine organ and piano in order to gain volume and orchestral color.

Edward Hodges, arranger of the hymn-tune from the NINTH SYMPHONY, was an English church composer and organist who spent most of his life in America. In New York he was organist at St. John's Episcopal Church, and later at Trinity. He exerted wide influence on American church music and also on organ construction.

Classic Works in the Hymnal

Among the classic works found in hymnals are the following:

Palestrina's "Gloria Patri et Filio" (Tune—VICTORY)
Mozart's "Kyrie" from the "Twelfth Mass" (Mozart)
Haydn's "The Heavens are Telling" from "The Creation" (CREATION)
Handel's "Comfort Ye," from "The Messiah" (ANTIOCH)
Handel's "I Know that my Redeemer Liveth" from "The Messiah" (BRADFORD)
Beethoven's "Romance in G" (SARDIS)
Beethoven's Ninth Symphony (HYMN TO JOY)
Weber's "Prayer" from "Der Freischuetz" (JEWETT)
Mendelssohn's Song without Words (CONSOLATION)
Haydn's "Introduction to the First Symphony" (HAYDN)
Schumann's Nachtstück, opus 23, No. 4 (CANONBURY)

Five Scores from the Ninth Symphony

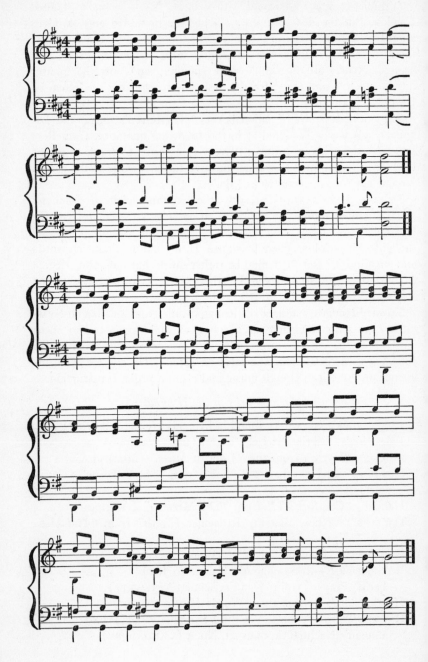

JOY TO THE WORLD

1. Joy to the world; the Lord is come;
Let earth receive her King;
Let every heart prepare him room,
And heaven and nature sing.

2. Joy to the world, the Saviour reigns;
Let men their songs employ;
While fields and floods, rocks, hills and plains
Repeat the sounding joy.

(Omitted Stanza)
No more let sins and sorrows grow,
Nor thorns infest the ground;
He comes to make his blessings flow
Far as the curse is found.

3. He rules the world with truth and grace,
And makes the nations prove
The glories of his righteousness,
And wonders of his love.

ISAAC WATTS, 1719.

BIBLICAL TEXT.

Make a joyful noise unto the Lord, all the earth;
Break forth and sing for joy, yea, sing praises.
Let the sea roar, and the fulness thereof:
The world, and they that dwell therein:
Let the floods clap their hands;
Let the hills sing for joy together
Before the Lord; for he cometh to judge the earth:
He will judge the world with righteousness,
And the peoples with equity.

PSALM 98:4, 7, 8, 9.

Prepare ye in the wilderness the way of the Lord; make level in the desert a highway for our God. Every valley shall be exalted, and every mountain and hill shall be made low; and the uneven shall be made level, and the rough places a plain; and the glory of the Lord shall be revealed, and all flesh shall see it together: for the mouth of the Lord hath spoken it.

ISAIAH 40:3–5.

A CARILLON OF PRAISE

Across more than two centuries of Christian history comes this carillon of praise, in which Christians of all lands and creeds unite, especially at Christmas time, in a great chorus of thanks and gladness.

This hymn is a paraphrase of a portion of Psalm 98, and like its original, is remarkable for its sustained note of exultation. Not merely the Book of Psalms, but many other parts of the Old and New Testaments are full of such rejoicing. In this connection note Isaiah's summons to the exiles to rejoice (Isaiah 40): and Paul's "Letter of the Joy Bells" (Philippians), in which he comes to his climax with the words, "Rejoice in the Lord always; again I will say, "Rejoice." (Philippians 4:4.)

In 1719 Dr. Isaac Watts, already famous for his *Hymns and Spiritual Songs* (1707), published his *Psalms of David Imitated in the Language of the New Testament, and Applied to the Christian State and Worship*. In this work he attempted "to make David speak like an English Christian of the eighteenth century. It is necessary to divest David and Asaph of every other character but that of a Psalmist and a Saint and to make them always speak the common sense of a Christian."

Dr. Benson says of this work of Dr. Watts: "I am looking while I write at a presentation copy of that book to his 'Hon. Uncle' and wondering if any other has been so momentous in the later history of Reformed Churches. It was the bridge across which many of them forced their way, half unconsciously, from the restrictions of an imposed Psalmody to the more open country of which Christ is the Light and the Song."

"He rules the world with truth and grace" is a burst of prophetic triumph and missionary zeal. Note that Watts put that line, as well as "the Savour reigns" in the present tense, even though the great missionary movement of his century had not begun, and in England, says the historian, Green, "religion was never at a lower ebb." Dr. Gillman adds: "Nonconformity, worn out by its long struggle for existence, had lost its virility. Inside the churches fervor was frowned upon, and the preaching was frigid, formal and argumentative." [1]

Against such a background as this, Isaac Watts had the courage and the faith to sing such a carillon as this hymn, and to put its verbs in the present tense.

Handel's Religion

Joy is the key-note of both words and music. Few hymns have been sung to tunes so popular and so well adapted to the words as ANTIOCH is to Watts' radiant lyric.

George Frederick Handel (1685–1759) was blessed with a mother

[1] From Gillman's *Evolution of the English Hymn.* By permission of The Macmillan Company, publishers.

who was intimately acquainted with the Bible and was a woman of deep piety. She was the daughter of a Lutheran clergyman. The influence of her teaching on her son is evidenced in the fact that though both London and Rome tried to induce Handel to change his faith, his reply was that he had "resolved to die a member of the communion in which he had been born and bred."

The practice of certain bishops in sending him from time to time certain Biblical texts to be set to music was taken by Handel to imply that he did not know his Bible. To such he once said, "I know my Bible; I shall choose for myself."

A nobleman at one time complimented Handel on "the noble entertainment he had furnished" in the glorious music of "He was Despised and Rejected." Handel's reply was, "My Lord, I should be sorry if I only entertained you. I wish to make you better."

✣

THE HYMN TUNE. ANTIOCH survives as the best example of a fugue tune. "In spite of its fugue, the tune, apparently by some magic of its own, contrives to enlist the entire voice of a congregation, the bass falling in on the third beat as if by intuition. The truth is, the tune has become the habit of the hymn."

Handel's works have proved a fertile source for hymn tunes. He used over and over again the phrase:

Here the resemblance to the "Lift Up Your Heads" ends, until we reach the second part of the tune which seems to come from the first bars of "Comfort Ye." Lowell Mason (1792–1872) is credited with this arrangement from "The Messiah."

"Antioch" and "Comfort Ye," from "The Messiah"

"COMFORT YE MY PEOPLE," ARIA FROM "THE MESSIAH"

JUST AS I AM, WITHOUT ONE PLEA

1. Just as I am, without one plea,
But that thy blood was shed for me,
And that thou biddest me come to thee.
O Lamb of God, I come.

2. Just as I am, and waiting not
To rid my soul of one dark blot,
To thee, whose blood can cleanse each spot,
O Lamb of God, I come.

3. Just as I am, though tossed about
With many a conflict, many a doubt,
Fightings and fears within, without,
O Lamb of God, I come.

4. Just as I am, poor, wretched, blind,
Sight, riches, healing of the mind,
Yea, all I need in thee to find,
O Lamb of God, I come.

5. Just as I am! thou wilt receive,
Wilt welcome, pardon, cleanse, relieve;
Because thy promise I believe,
O Lamb of God, I come.

6. Just as I am, thy love unknown
Has broken every barrier down,
Now to be thine, yea, thine alone,
O Lamb of God, I come.

CHARLOTTE ELLIOTT, 1836.

BIBLICAL TEXT.

Him that cometh to me I will in no wise cast out.

JOHN 6:37.

And the Spirit and the bride say, Come. And he that heareth, let him say, Come. And he that is athirst, let him come: he that will, let him take the water of life freely.

REVELATION 22:17.

A HYMN THAT TRANSFIGURES LIVES

In spite of changes of method and emphasis in evangelism, there is probably no hymn which has been so constantly in use in evangelistic meetings of all sorts as this one. It has been called the world's "great soul-winning hymn." Many stories are told of its effectiveness in leading individuals all over the world to leave the trivialities of life for the enduring values revealed in the life, teaching and redeeming death of Jesus. The Evangelical or Low Church Party in the Church of England persisted in putting the Gospel first and the Church second. Miss Elliott's parents, two brothers and an uncle were all members of this party; naturally she herself was intensely loyal to the "Church of pardoned sinners."

The story of the writing of the hymn shows the yearning of a soul to break the bonds of its limitations. Charlotte Elliott (1789–1871) was an invalid most of her life. In 1836 her brother, Reverend H. V. Elliott, was raising funds for St. Mary's Hall, at Brighton, England, a college for the daughters of poor clergy. A bazaar was held in Brighton for this purpose and all of the Elliott family were busy, working for it. On the night before the bazaar Charlotte was wakeful much of the night. She was lamenting her inability to do anything. During the day of the bazaar, as she lay on her couch, apparently useless, while all the rest of the family were busy with the work, there came back to her mind the words of a clergyman, Dr. Cesar Malan, of Geneva, who had visited her home, fourteen years before. He had been urging Miss Elliott to "give her heart to Christ, and become a useful worker for him." At first she had resented the suggestion, but later had said, "But I do not know how to find Christ." Dr. Malan had replied, "Come to him just as you are."

Lying there alone on her couch, the invalid wrote "Just as I am." It was published first of all in *The Christian Remembrancer* which Miss Elliott edited. A lady who admired it reprinted it in leaflet form, evidently without the author's name. A copy came into the hands of Miss Elliott's physician, and one day he gave it to her, thinking it would prove a comfort to her. He was surprised indeed to learn that he was presenting the hymn to its author. Amos Wells tells this incident in his *A Treasure of Hymns:* "John B. Gough was once placed in a pew with a man so repulsive that he moved to the farther end of the seat. The congregation began to sing 'Just as I am,' and the man joined in so heartily that Mr. Gough decided that he could not be so disagreeable after all, and moved up nearer, though the man's singing 'was positively awful.' At the end of the third stanza, while the organ was playing the interlude, the man leaned toward Mr. Gough and whispered: 'Won't you please give me the first line of the next verse?' Mr. Gough replied, 'Just as I am, poor, wretched, blind,' and the man replied, 'That's it; and I am blind—God help me; and I am a paralytic.' Then as he tried with his poor twitching lips to make music of the glorious words, Mr. Gough thought that never in his life had he heard music so beautiful as the blundering singing of that hymn by the paralytic." [1]

✣

THE HYMN TUNE. Bradbury's tune WOODWORTH, as do his other tunes, marks the transition from Lowell Mason's more churchly tunes to the livelier gospel songs that followed. Nothwithstanding, WOODWORTH appears in the New Hymnal (Episcopal) sanctioned by such committeemen as Frank Damrosch, Jr., Walter Henry Hall, Horatio Parker, T. Tertius Noble, Peter Christian Lutkin and Wallace Goodrich.

William Bachelder Bradbury (1816–1868) will be remembered as editor, singing-master, and pianoforte manufacturer.

LEAD, KINDLY LIGHT

1. Lead, kindly Light, amid th' encircling gloom,
Lead thou me on;
The night is dark, and I am far from home,

[1] From *A Treasure of Hymns,* by Amos Wells, copyright by the United Society of Christian Endeavor.

Lead thou me on;
Keep thou my feet; I do not ask to see
The distant scene, one step enough for me.

2. I was not ever thus, nor prayed that thou
Shouldst lead me on;
I loved to choose and see my path; but now
Lead thou me on:
I loved the garish day, and, spite of fears,
Pride ruled my will; remember not past years.

3. So long thy power hath blest me, sure it still
Will lead me on,
O'er moor and fen, o'er crag and torrent, till
The night is gone;
And with the morn those angel faces smile,
Which I have loved long since, and lost awhile.

JOHN HENRY NEWMAN, 1833.

BIBLICAL TEXT.

In the day-time also he led them with a cloud,
And all the night with a light of fire.

PSALM 78: 14.

I will instruct thee and teach thee in the way which thou shalt go:
I will counsel thee with mine eye upon thee.

PSALM 32: 8.

Behold, the eye of the Lord is upon them that fear him,
Upon them that hope in his lovingkindness;
To deliver their soul from death,
And to keep them alive in famine.

PSALM 33: 18, 19.

LIGHT IN DARKNESS

It was June in the Mediterranean, and there was a dead calm. No breezes blew to stir the sails of the orange boat which was bearing a passenger on the first stage of his journey from Rome to his home in Oxford, England. He had been ill for three weeks, and now was away from all his friends. That calm lasted. There was nothing for the passangers to do but wait, and think and pray. One of them was not only ill in body, but sick of soul as well. A young minister in the Church of England, he had long been heart-sick at the conditions of religious life there, and especially at the lack of spiritual vitality in the established Church of England. One of the purposes of this tour of Europe had been to escape from it all and get a new perspective. He had just visited Rome, had met and talked with a Cardinal of the Roman Church; his soul was stirred with conflict: which was right, the Church of England, or the Church of Rome?

Everything seemed dark to the young minister as he drifted aboard the orange boat on the calm waters of the Mediterranean through that interminable week. He could only pray and hope for light and guidance. One other thing he did during that week, and that one thing has made the name of John Henry Newman known and honored around the world, wherever Christian song has gone. He voiced his prayer for light and guidance in a hymn. Though he became an author of note, though he was later honored with the Cardinal's hat, the one special thing for which he is remembered with gratitude by Christians of every name and race is the writing of "Lead, Kindly Light."

"John Henry Newman was the leader of the Oxford Movement of the nineteenth century, as John Wesley was the leader of the Oxford Movement of the eighteenth century. Both men were sons of God-fearing Evangelistical parents. Both went to Oxford and became Fellows of colleges. Both were ordained clergymen of the Church of England, and both agreed that real Christianity consists in a living personal fellowship with a living personal God. Yet how different were their aims and teachings. The aim of these Oxford men, for example, was to make the Church live again before the eyes and the minds of men, as in times past. They strove against religious indifferences and worldiness; they loved a powerful episcopacy, the use of the surplice and other sacerdotal vestments, the celebration of all the church festivals, the communion-table set altar-wise, the antiphonal chanting of choirs, the efficacy of frequent communion and all other Sacraments." [1]

These men were fascinated by the spell of the historic past. They went too far. "The Oxford lamp was antique, ornate, and fair to behold, but its many-colored glass dimmed the Light of Life."

John Henry Newman (1801–1890) grew up in London, in a home of marked evangelical piety.

"I was brought up from a child," he writes, "to take delight in reading the Bible. Of course I had a perfect knowledge of my catechism. I used to wish the Arabian Nights were true; my imagination ran on magical powers and talismans. I thought life might be a dream, or I an angel. I was very superstitious, and for some months previous to my conversion (when I was fifteen) used constantly to cross myself on going into the dark."

He was graduated with honors from Trinity College, Oxford, in 1820, and ordained to the ministry of the Church of England in 1824. Four years later he was appointed to St. Mary's, Oxford, where his

[1] From "Songs of the Church," by Lady M'Dougall, copyright by Robert Culley, London.

sermons had a powerful influence on the University. William Ewart Gladstone, England's "Grand Old Man," was an undergraduate in Oxford at that time. He later wrote of Newman as a preacher: "He was much respected for his character and known ability. His sermons were read, and his eyes were always bent on his book; and all that, you will say, is against efficiency in preaching. Yes, but you must take the man as a whole; there was a stamp and a seal upon him; there was a solemn sweetness and music in the tone; there was a completeness in the figure, which made his delivery singularly attractive."

Newman preached his last sermon as an Anglican in September, 1843, and in 1845 was formally received into the Roman Catholic Church. After spending many years in the secluded life of the Oratory of St. Philip Neri at Birmingham, his abilities at last won recognition, and he was made a Cardinal in 1879.

Moffatt says of him: "He leaves the memory of a religious poet of slender but high achievement, a master of the purest, and most melodious English prose, a spiritual force of almost the first magnitude, albeit misdirected and largely wasted, a great Englishman, and a great saint." [2]

His one outstanding hymn was written twelve years before he became a Catholic and forty years before Pope Leo XIII made him a Cardinal. It is the record of his own personal struggle in the darkness and uncertainty of doubt as to which pathway he should take. Perhaps the very intensity of that struggle is one of the reasons why the hymn has become so popular;—it reflects the conditions of struggle common to human hearts everywhere. His own title for it was "Light in Darkness"; it has been a messenger of Light to millions of darkened souls. It was written by a young man—Newman was thirty-two at the time. " 'Lead, Kindly Light,' serene, inspired poetry, needs no words spelled in capitals nor exclamation points at the end. And there is nothing of wrangling in the religion of this hymn. Its mood of fervent, humble prayer and the lyric charm of its words and rhythms have carried this hymn to the heart of Christendom. The difficulty of the half line, 'I loved the garish day,' wherein is an unhappy figure suggesting preference of a torch at night to broad open day to travel by—this slight infelicity is submerged like a stone in the brook by the full swift current of the poetry. The line describing the trials and hardships of life by 'moor and fen and crag and torrent' is richly suggestive of the wild beauty of old romance; and what a poetic im-

[2] From the *Handbook of the Church Hymnary,* by James Moffatt, copyright by the Oxford University Press.

agining of this troubled life! The last two lines are a triumph of lyric art and at the same time of Christian hope." [3]

Another of the reasons for its universal appeal to folk of all sorts and shades of belief, or lack of it, is its sublime confidence in the final dawn. That note runs, like an ever-recurring theme of a great symphony, through all the poem. In the first stanza it finds expression in the adjective applied to the Light; it is a "kindly" Light; and in the thought of light enough for the next step, embodied in the last line. In the second stanza it is voiced in the contrast between the former wilful choosing of "my path," and the present willingness to be led entirely by the "kindly light." In the climactic third stanza it shines with rare beauty in the memorable lines,

> ". . . till the night is gone;
> And with the morn those angel faces smile
> Which I have loved long since, and lost awhile."

✣

THE HYMN TUNE. LUX BENIGNA is one of those all-too-few instances of a perfect marriage of hymn and tune. It was composed by the great hymn-tune composer, John Bacchus Dykes, in 1868, especially for this hymn. Dykes himself is authority for the statement that the tune came to him while walking along the Strand in London. Thus the hymn, written amid the quietness of a becalmed sea, and the tune, coming out of the midst of the roar of traffic on London's busiest street, meet and blend in a perfectly harmonious union.

Concerning the tune, we are fortunate enough to have the opinion of Newman himself. Reverend George Huntington tells of a visit to Newman, after he had been made a Cardinal. When congratulated on being the author of a hymn "treasured wherever English-speaking Christians are to be found," Newman replied, "But you see it is not the hymn, but the tune, that has gained the popularity. The tune is Dyke's, and Dr. Dykes was a great master."

John Bacchus Dykes (1823–1876) was a clergyman of the Church of England, but it is as a composer of hymn-tunes that he is chiefly known. Born in Hull, educated at Cambridge, he began his musical career early in life, playing the organ in his grandfather's church when only ten years old, and helping to found the University Musical Society at Cambridge while still a student there. He was ordained in 1847, and served for a number of years as Minor Canon and Precentor

[3] From *The Hymn in History and Literature,* by J. B. Reeves, copyright by The Century Co.

in Durham Cathedral. For fourteen years he was Vicar of St. Oswald's, Durham. It was there that many of his hymn-tunes were composed. It is said that on Sunday evenings his own family and a few friends frequently spent the evening trying over new tunes which Dykes had composed, offering their criticisms or approbation.

Dykes received the degree of Mus.D., 1861, from Durham University. He composed nearly three hundred hymn-tunes. Our modern hymnals contain from twenty to fifty hymns, set to Dr. Dykes' tunes—a significant testimony to their commendable "singableness."

LEAD ON, O KING ETERNAL

1. Lead on, O King Eternal,
The day of march has come;
Henceforth in fields of conquest
Thy tents shall be our home;
Through days of preparation
Thy grace has made us strong,
And now, O King Eternal,
We lift our battle-song.

2. Lead on, O King Eternal,
Till sin's fierce war shall cease,
And holiness shall whisper
The sweet Amen of peace;
For not with swords loud clashing,
Nor roll of stirring drums;
With deeds of love and mercy,
The heavenly kingdom comes.

3. Lead on, O King Eternal,
We follow, not with fears,
For gladness breaks like morning
Where'er thy face appears;
Thy cross is lifted o'er us,
We journey in its light;
The crown awaits the conquest;
Lead on, O God of might.

Ernest W. Shurtleff, 1888.

Biblical Text.

I saw the Lord sitting upon a throne, high and lifted up: then said I, Woe is me! for I am undone; because I am a man of unclean lips, and I dwell in the midst of a people of unclean lips: for mine eyes have seen the King, the Lord of hosts. . . . And I heard the voice of the Lord, saying, Whom shall I send, and who will go for us? Then said I, Here am I; send me.

Isaiah 6: 1, 5, 8.

Behold, I send you forth. . . .

He that doth not take his cross and follow after me, is not worthy of me. He that findeth his life shall lose it; and he that loseth his life for my sake shall find it. He that receiveth you receiveth me, and he that receiveth me receiveth him that sent me.

MATTHEW 10: 16, 38–40.

A STUDENT'S GRADUATION HYMN

The Class of 1888 at Andover Theological Seminary had the unusual distinction of having a poet within its ranks, a poet who had already published two volumes of verse. It was quite the natural thing, then, to ask Ernest W. Shurtleff to write a graduation hymn for the class, which he did.

It persists a universal favorite in conventions and conferences of youth, as is quite the natural thing, since it was written by a young man for young men.

Ernest Warburton Shurtleff (1862–1917) was a Congregational minister, who held important pastorates at Buenaventura, California, Plymouth, Massachusetts, and Minneapolis, Minnesota, before going to Europe for the crowning work of his life. In 1895 he organized the American Church at Frankfort-on-the-Main, Germany, and from 1906 to his death in 1917 he had charge of the Students' Atelier Reunions, Academy Vitti, Paris.

The setting of this hymn, the graduation of a group of young men from the Seminary into the active work of the Christian ministry, illuminates the references to the "days of preparation," and the "fields of conquest" in the first stanza.

This hymn has the martial air without the militaristic note of "Onward, Christian Soldiers." The second stanza was written forty years before the signing of the Kellogg Treaty for the renunciation of war among the nations, but it sets forth the same great truth of the futility of "swords loud clashing" embodied in the solemn agreement of that significant document. There is a sublime courage and a glorious optimism in the third stanza which may account for the appeal of of this hymn to youth. It faces the unknown future as a glorious opportunity for service.

The hymn as a whole sings a very hearty belief that the forces of enlightenment and justice and good-will are moving forward and that there is a steady advance of God's Kingdom on earth. It sings a wholehearted committal of mind, soul and body to the guidance of Jesus. The words have the poetic flow and fervor of a true hymn.

✣

THE HYMN TUNE. The tune LANCASHIRE seems to be the ideal vehicle for these challenging words. It was composed by Henry Smart in 1836, for "From Greenland's Icy Mountains," and was first sung at a musical festival at Blackburn, where Smart was organist of the parish church, in celebration of the tercentenary of the Reformation.

The tune has a daring melody and forward movement eminently fitting for such marching words. It has quickness and vigor enough to make an instant appeal to youth, and with them—a rare combination—genuine dignity and melodic surety.

SINGING WITH EXPRESSION. The first stanza of this hymn should receive the same bold, broad treatment that any first stanza should receive in order to overcome at the outset any inertia, timidity and uncertainty resident in individuals or the congregation *in toto*. The second stanza should grow softer and softer through "and holiness shall whisper the sweet Amen of peace," continuing to the end thoughtfully and quietly as in the spirit of "deeds of love and mercy." The third stanza is full of glowing pictures, calling for marked movement, brilliance and increasing volume of tone, with the ringing utterance of such phrases as "gladness breaks like morning," "thy cross is lifted," and "the crown awaits the conquest."

LET THERE BE LIGHT, LORD GOD OF HOSTS

1. Let there be light, Lord God of Hosts,
Let there be wisdom on the earth;
Let broad humanity have birth,
Let there be deeds instead of boasts.

2. Within our passioned hearts instill
The calm that endeth strain and strife;
Make us thy ministers of life;
Purge us from lusts that curse and kill.

3. Give us the peace of vision clear
To see our brothers' good our own,
To joy and suffer not alone,
The love that casteth out all fear.

4. Let woe and waste of warfare cease,
That useful labor yet may build
Its homes with love and laughter filled;
God give thy wayward children peace.[1]

WILLIAM MERRILL VORIES, 1908.

[1] Copyright by the American Peace Society.

BIBLICAL TEXT.

He maketh wars to cease unto the end of the earth;
He breaketh the bow, and cutteth the spear in sunder;
He burneth the chariots in the fire.

PSALM 46:9.

And the work of righteousness shall be peace; and the effect of righteousness quietness and confidence forever. And my people shall abide in a peaceful habitation, and in safe dwellings and in quiet resting-places.

ISAIAH 32:17, 18.

A PEACE HYMN FROM LAKE BEWA, JAPAN

The author of this hymn believes in a lived religion. In 1905, three years before he wrote this hymn, he founded "The Omi Mission" in Omi Province in the interior of Japan. This mission is significantly described as "An Experiment in the establishing of the Kingdom of God in the Province of Omi, Japan. Interdenominational, international, supported by voluntary contributions."

In a personal letter to the author, Mr. Vories says concerning the origin of this hymn, "I wrote it in 1908, together with some verses about War. These I did in an ironical vein, and the hymn came as a reaction or relief. I have always been interested in hymnology, and am a strong believer in the power of hymns to affect the lives of people. I began a collection of hymnals when a high-school boy."

The hymn was published the same year in which it was written, in *The Advocate of Peace,* the journal of the American Peace Society. Not long afterward, it was reprinted by a Chicago newspaper, accompanied by editorial comment to the effect that "as most hymnals are lacking in peace or brotherhood hymns, some one ought to set this hymn to music for general use." This is one of the few instances in which a daily newspaper opened the way into the singing church for a new hymn. In the issue of January 3, 1914, *The Survey* published the best one hundred hymns in the English language on Social Service. Among the hundred, a very few were selected for special printing in this issue, a hymn to a page, with an ornamental border. The Vories hymn was one of the few thus honored.

Prayer for the Breaking Down of Barriers

"King of the whole earth,
Break down, we beseech thee, by thy great power,
All those barriers which do now keep mankind asunder:
Overcome the hindrance of race, of custom, and of prejudice:
Drive out all those adverse influences,
Which now mar our union.
Foster throughout the world
Every movement of thought, of activity, of good-will,

Which tends, for whatever motive and in whatever sphere,
To break down isolation and exclusiveness,
To unite men in common enterprise and service,
To build up coöperation and interdependence."[2]

The Family of Nations in the Hymn Book

(A Congregational Song Service for Missionary or Peace Sunday, Armistice Day or Christmastide.)

Germany—When morning gilds the skies
(to be sung as a choir processional)
Japan—Let there be light, Lord God of hosts
(to be sung as a congregational hymn)
Egypt—Shepherd of tender youth
(to be sung as a congregational hymn)
Palestine—Art thou weary, art thou languid?
(to be read responsively as a Scripture selection)
Italy—Welcome, happy morning
(to be sung as an antiphonal choir selection)
Austria—Silent night, holy night
(to be sung softly or hummed by all)
America—Where cross the crowded ways of life
(to be sung as a solo)
England—In Christ there is no East or West
(to be sung as a congregational hymn)

✣

THE HYMN TUNE. Although the author of the hymn has also composed a tune for his own words, the words had, as he himself says, "gone out first, and were reprinted in several places." They are most commonly associated with PENTECOST, by William Boyd (1847–1927).

LET US WITH A GLADSOME MIND

1. Let us with a gladsome mind
Praise the Lord, for he is kind;
For his mercies aye endure,
Ever faithful, ever sure.

2. Let us blaze his name abroad,
For of gods he is the God;
Who by all-commanding might,
Filled the new-made world with light.

[2] From *A Book of Prayers,* by John Hoyland. By permission of W. Heffer and Sons, Ltd., Cambridge, England.

3. He the golden-tressed sun
Caused all day his course to run;
Th' horned moon to shine by night,
'Mid her spangled sisters bright.

4. All things living he doth feed,
His full hand supplies their need;
For his mercies aye endure,
Ever faithful, ever sure.

JOHN MILTON, 1623 (Altered).

BIBLICAL TEXT.

Oh give thanks unto the Lord; for he is good;
For his lovingkindness endureth forever.
Oh give thanks unto the God of gods;
For his lovingkindness endureth forever.
To him who alone doeth great wonders;
For his lovingkindness endureth forever.
To him that by understanding made the heavens;
For his lovingkindness endureth forever.
To him that made great lights;
For his lovingkindness endureth forever.
The sun to rule by day;
For his lovingkindness endureth forever.
The moon and stars to rule by night;
For his lovingkindness endureth forever.
Who giveth food to all flesh;
For his lovingkindness endureth forever.
Oh give thanks unto the God of heaven;
For his lovingkindness endureth forever.

PSALM 136: 1, 2, 4, 5, 7, 8, 9, 25, 26.

SINGING YOUTH OF THE WORLD

The boy, Milton, aged fifteen and attending St. Paul's School, London, wrote this Psalm paraphrase. It shows the trace of a boyish pen, yet hand in hand with the wealth of youthful imagination goes the promise of unfolding powers. Milton translated nine of the Psalms into meter, holding faithfully to the original. The complete paraphrase contains twenty-four stanzas. He lived and wrote at a time when "human composures" were very strenuously objected to by the ecclesiastical "powers that be." Hymn singing in that day meant Psalm singing. Hence Milton did not attempt an original poem. He was concerned only to put the Psalms into the language of his own day, in a metrical arrangement. What might not Milton, with his genius, have written, had he lived in the free hymn-writing days of Watts and Wesley!

What a century was the seventeenth to write one thing and to live another—an artificial glamour over all, a play of the intellect and imagination on subjects outside of truth, experience, conviction. Sincere and sublime in that world of sham, towered John Milton (1608–1674), best known as the author of *Paradise Lost* and *Paradise Regained.* Both were written after he had been smitten with blindness at the age of forty-four. The publisher, who accepted them, paid Milton the munificent sum of five pounds for the manuscript. In the generosity of his heart, however, he agreed to pay a royalty of an additional five pounds for every fifteen hundred copies sold. As a total of three editions were disposed of in a period of seven years, the poet was paid a total sum of fifteen pounds ($75) for his greatest work.

Youthful Poets in the Hymn Book

The Christian Church has always had her troubadours, her singing horsemen, her teen age poets and tune writers. How is it that we have accustomed ourselves to think of hymns as coming only from old age, from invalidism, from ecclesiastical rigidness, when Watts and Wesley were young men, Newman was thirty-two when he wrote "Lead, Kindly Light," and Palmer, just out of Yale, and twenty-two, was the author of "My Faith Looks up to Thee"?

Ten Youthful Hymn-Writers

"Behold a Stranger at the door," Joseph Grigg, 10 years of age.
"Jesus, and shall it ever be," Joseph Grigg, 10 years of age.
"Let us with a gladsome mind," John Milton, 15 years of age.
"Work, for the night is coming," Anna L. Coghill, 18 years of age.
"When marshaled on the nightly plain," Henry K. White, 19 years of age.
"O where are kings and empires now?" Arthur C. Coxe, 21 years of age.
"My faith looks up to thee," Ray Palmer, 22 years of age.
"Come thou Fount of every blessing," Robert Robinson, 23 years of age.
"I would be true," Howard A. Walter, 23 years of age.
"My country, 'tis of thee," Samuel F. Smith, 24 years of age.
"The church's one foundation," Samuel John Stone, 26 years of age.

Some of the greatest musicians of the world have also done some of their finest work in youth. The story of Handel's learning to play the clavichord as a child, by himself in the attic at night, is a familiar one, illustrated by Miss Dicksee's famous painting. He played the organ in the private chapel of the Duke when only seven, and published his first Oratorio at nineteen, his first Opera at twenty.

Mendelssohn composed the Nocturne to Midsummer Night's Dream when only sixteen, and wrote his first Symphony two years earlier. Haydn composed an Opera at twenty; Beethoven composed his first Sonata at twenty-five, and Schubert wrote "The Unfinished Symphony" at twenty-five. Mozart, of all composers, the most surprising prodigy, accomplished the most Herculean musical tasks before he was ten, and wrote his symphonies, string quartets, sonatas in his early twenties.

✣

THE HYMN TUNE. The tune INNOCENTS was first discovered in a magazine for the advancement of church music, *The Parish Choir* (1846–1849). It was appointed to be sung to a hymn for "Innocents' Day"; hence its name. The hymn was called "Little Flowers of Martyrdom," and referred to the Massacre of the Innocents. (See Matthew 2:16.)

This tune is attributed to Handel because of its similarity to "CHRISTMAS." It is also traced to a Joseph Smith tune book of the early nineteenth century. This tune is in two parts and is called, "THE SUN."

The Sun (*The original "Innocents"*)

Who am I with no - ble face, Shin - ing in a clear blue space?
If to look at me you try, I shall blind your lit - tle eye.

LIFE OF AGES, RICHLY POURED

1. Life of ages, richly poured,
Love of God, unspent and free,
Flowing in the prophet's word,
And the people's liberty.

2. Never was to chosen race
That unstinted tide confined;
Thine is every time and place,
Fountain sweet of heart and mind.

3. Breathing in the thinker's creed,
Pulsing in the hero's blood,
Nerving simplest thought and deed,
Freshening time with truth and good.

4. Consecrating art and song,
Holy book and pilgrim track,
Hurling floods of tyrant wrong
From the sacred limits back.

5. Life of ages, richly poured,
Love of God, unspent and free,
Flow still in the prophet's word
And the people's liberty.

SAMUEL JOHNSON, 1864.

BIBLICAL TEXT.

God is no respecter of persons: but in every nation he that feareth him, and worketh righteousness, is acceptable to him.

ACTS 10: 34, 35.

Thy word is a lamp unto my feet,
And light unto my path.

PSALM 119: 105.

It is not ye that speak, but the Spirit of your Father that speaketh in you.

MATTHEW 10: 20.

PROPHET'S WORD AND PEOPLE'S LIBERTY

The author of this hymn was a man of the broadest thinking. He has been called "the apostle of individualism." He would not accept a pastorate within the bounds of any organized denomination, and finally organized at Lynn, Massachusetts, an Independent Church, which he served for seventeen years as its pastor. From 1870 to his death in 1882, he lived in Salem, Massachusetts, and devoted himself entirely to literary work.

Samuel Johnson (1822–1882) was an intimate friend of Samuel Longfellow, brother of the poet, and his classmate in Harvard Divinity School. While they were together in Divinity School they conceived the idea of the publication of a new hymnal for the Unitarian churches which should be literary in quality and liberal in spirit. They searched everywhere for material which should be of the highest literary merit. Finding a poem, "Lead, Kindly Light," in a newspaper, they included it in their hymnal, though they had no knowledge of its author. They also included poems by Whittier, Harriet Beecher Stowe, Ralph Waldo Emerson, James Russell Lowell, and other poets of that period, material never before used in public worship.

In 1864 Longfellow and Johnson published another hymn-book, *Hymns of the Spirit*. It was for this book that Mr. Johnson wrote "Life of Ages."

ANALYSIS. Naturally, a spirit so broadly independent as Mr. Johnson's, would be impatient with the old idea of the exclusive revelation of God to the Hebrews. Accordingly it is not surprising that the emphasis in the second stanza should be on the "unstinted tide" of the "Life of ages," too torrential to have been confined to one "chosen race."

The thought of the continuing presence and inspiration of God in all of life is admirably expressed in the third stanza, where the author links "the thinker's creed," "the hero's blood," the "simplest thought" with quiet deed, and finds Divinity in all of them.

All too few are the hymn-book's references to the spiritual values of art and music. Here in this hymn is one of the very best. This fourth stanza finds God in "art and song," in "holy book and pilgrim track." And all these manifestations of God through the varying expressions of the human spirit are for the one united purpose of "Hurling floods of tyrant wrong from the sacred limits back."

The poem originally had nine stanzas. The four omitted stanzas follow:

"Secret of the morning stars,
Motion of the oldest hours,
Pledge through elemental wars
Of the coming spirit's powers!

"Rolling planet, flaming sun,
Stand in nobler man complete;
Prescient laws thine errands run,
Frame the shrine for Godhead meet.

"Homeward led, the wondering eye,
Upward yearned in joy or awe,
Found the love that waited nigh,
Guidance of thy guardian law.

"In the touch of earth it thrilled;
Down from mystic skies it burned;
Right obeyed and passion stilled,
Its eternal gladness earned."

Some New England Hymns and Hymn-Writers

John Greenleaf Adams, of Portsmouth,
"Heaven is here, where hymns of gladness."
William Cullen Bryant, of Great Barrington and New York City,
"O North, with all thy vales of green."
Leonard Bacon, of New Haven,
"O God, beneath thy guiding hand."
Katharine Lee Bates, of Wellesley,
"O beautiful for spacious skies."
John White Chadwick, of Marblehead,
"Eternal Ruler of the ceaseless round."
Allen Eastman Cross, of Milford and Manchester,
"Wild roars the blast, the Storm is high."
Timothy Dwight, of New Haven,
"I love thy kingdom, Lord."
William C. Gannett, of Boston,
"Bring, O morn, thy music."
Frederick L. Hosmer, of Framingham and Berkeley,
"Forward through the ages."
Oliver Wendell Holmes, of Dartmouth and Boston,
"Lord of all being, throned afar."
John Haynes Holmes, of Malden,
"God of the nations, near and far."
Julia Ward Howe, of Boston,
"Mine eyes have seen the glory."
Samuel Johnson, of Salem and Lynn,
"Life of ages, richly poured."
Shepherd Knapp, of Worcester,
"Lord God of Hosts, whose purpose."
James Russell Lowell, of Cambridge,
"Once to every man and nation."
Henry Wadsworth Longfellow, of Bowdoin and Cambridge,
"I heard the Bells on Christmas Day."
Samuel Longfellow, of Cambridge,
"God's trumpet wakes the slumbering world."
Lucy Larcom, of Boston,
"Draw thou my soul, O Christ."
Edwin Pond Parker, of New Haven,
"Master, no offering, costly and sweet."
Theodore Parker, of Boston,

"O thou great friend to all the sons of men."
Daniel C. Roberts, of Brandon, Vermont,
"God of our fathers, whose almighty hand."
Edmund Hamilton Sears, of Wayland and Weston,
"It came upon the midnight clear."
Samuel Frances Smith, of Newton Centre,
"My country, 'tis of thee."
John Greenleaf Whittier, of Amesbury,
"Dear Lord and Father of mankind."

THE HYMN TUNE. The hymn tune, POSEN was composed by George Christopher Strattner (1650–1705) and published in 1691 in the composer's edition of "Neander's *Bundes-lieder*."

ELLINGHAM, by Nathaniel S. Godfrey (1817–1883), is an acceptable alternative tune.

LORD, DISMISS US WITH THY BLESSING

1. Lord, dismiss us with thy blessing;
Fill our hearts with joy and peace;
Let us each, thy love possessing,
Triumph in redeeming grace:
O refresh us,
Travelling through this wilderness.

2. Thanks we give and adoration
For thy gospel's joyful sound:
May the fruits of thy salvation
In our hearts and lives abound:
Ever faithful,
To the truth may we be found.

JOHN FAWCETT, 1773.

BIBLICAL TEXT.

The grace of the Lord Jesus Christ, and the love of God, and the communion of the Holy Spirit, be with you all.

2 CORINTHIANS 13: 14.

Now unto him that is able to guard you from stumbling, and to set you before the presence of his glory without blemish in exceeding joy, to the only God our Saviour, through Jesus Christ our Lord, be glory, majesty, dominion and power, before all time, and now, and for evermore. Amen.

JUDE 1: 24, 25.

A HYMN FOR THE CLOSE OF WORSHIP

Reverend John Fawcett (1740–1817), pastor of the Baptist Church at Wainsgate, England, author of "Blest be the tie that binds," published in 1782 a hymn-book containing one hundred and twenty-six hymns of his own.

"Lord, dismiss us" was written for the close of the service, a prayer of appreciation and gratitude for the blessings of the service of worship just closing; for the "redeeming grace" of which it has reminded them; for the inspiration and helpfulness of the sermon to which they have listened—"For thy gospel's joyful sound." It is more than this; while very properly a reference to the service just closing, it is a united prayer for the immediate, and even for the distant, future. As Dr. Julian intimates, Fawcett is nothing if not practical, and he gives a very prominent place in his hymn to the thought of the "fruits of thy salvation." He implies that the congregation has here, in God's house, received a rich blessing in the implanted word; now they should go out into the common tasks of daily life to "bring forth fruits worthy of repentance."

There is a tendency in certain quarters to disparage the older hymns, especially those of the eighteenth century, as being too much concerned with "other-worldliness." Surely a careful reading of this hymn, with that closing prayer of the second stanza properly emphasized, will help "moderns" to realize that the preachers and hymn-writers of the latter years of the eighteenth century were very practical folk, who believed in squaring the life of Monday and Tuesday and the other week-days, with the teachings and the worship of Sunday and the Lord's house.

To be sure, there is a third stanza, generally omitted now, which does carry on the thought to its ultimate conclusion in the fellowship of the Christian with Christ, in realms of "Endless Day!"

> "So, whene'er the signal's given
> Us from earth to call away,
> Borne on angels' wings to heaven,
> Glad the summons to obey,
> May we ever
> Reign with Christ in endless Day."

Some Hymns of the Seventeenth Century

"All my heart this night rejoices"
"All praise to thee, my God"
"Fairest Lord Jesus"

"Let all the world in every corner"
"Let us with a gladsome mind"
"Now thank we all our God"
"O come, all ye faithful"

Some Hymns of the Eighteenth Century

"All hail the power of Jesus' name"
"Awake, my soul, stretch every nerve"
"Blest be the tie that binds"
"Christ the Lord is risen today"
"Come, thou almighty King"
"Glorious things of thee are spoken"
"Hark! the herald angels sing"
"How firm a foundation, ye saints"
"Jesus, lover of my soul"
"Jesus shall reign where'er the sun"
"Joy to the world! the Lord is come"
"Let saints on earth in concert sing"
"Lord, dismiss us with thy blessing"
"Love divine, all love excelling"
"Our God, our help in ages past"
"Praise to God, immortal praise"
"Rock of Ages, cleft for me"
"We plough the fields, and scatter"
"When I survey the wondrous cross"

✣

THE HYMN TUNE. SICILIAN MARINERS seems to have no connection with Sicily, except its name. It may possibly have come originally from there, but it is unknown in Sicily today. Southern France is named as one of the possible sources for this tune, which appeared first in hymn-books about 1794 in connection with Tattersall's musical edition of Merrick's Psalms. Here it was arranged for two soprano voices, and set to the words:

O Sanctissima, O Purissima,
Dulcis Virgo Maria,
Mater amata, intemerata
Ora pro nobis.

O most holy one,
O most lowly one,
Dearest Virgin, Maria.

Mother of fair love
Home of the Spirit Dove,
Ora, ora pro nobis.

Help us in sadness drear,
Port of gladness near,
Virgin Mother, Maria,
In pity heeding,
Hear thou our pleading,
Ora, ora pro nobis.

Even today, on Saint Mary's Day, the gondoliers in Venice sing this hymn as they row their gondolas through the canals of the "Bride of the Sea."

LORD OF ALL BEING, THRONED AFAR

1. Lord of all being, throned afar,
Thy glory flames from sun and star;
Center and soul of every sphere,
Yet to each loving heart how near!

2. Sun of our life, thy quickening ray
Sheds on our path the glow of day;
Star of our hope, thy softened light
Cheers the long watches of the night.

3. Our midnight is thy smile withdrawn;
Our noon-tide is thy gracious dawn;
Our rainbow arch, thy mercy's sign;
All, save the clouds of sin, are thine.

4. Lord of all life, below, above,
Whose light is truth, whose warmth is love,
Before thy ever-blazing throne,
We ask no luster of our own.

5. Grant us thy truth to make us free,
And kindling hearts that burn for thee!
Till all thy living altars claim
One holy light, one heavenly flame!

Oliver Wendell Holmes, 1848.

Biblical Text.

The heavens declare the glory of God; and the firmament showeth his handiwork.

Psalm 19:1.

In him was life, and the life was the light of men. And the light shineth in the darkness, and the darkness apprehended it not.

John 1:4, 5.

THE OMNIPRESENCE OF GOD

This hymn was written not for a hymnal, but for a magazine, *The Atlantic Monthly*. The author, Dr. Oliver Wendell Holmes, was writing what later became one of his most famous books, *The Professor at the Breakfast Table*. He closed the chapter for the December issue of the magazine with these words: "And so my year's record is finished. Thanks to the friends who from time to time have sent their messages of kindly recognition and fellow-feeling. Peace to all such as may have been vexed in spirit by any utterance the pages may have repeated. They will doubtless forget for the moment the difference in the hues of truth we look at through our human prisms, and join in singing (inwardly) this hymn to the Source of light we all need to lead us and the warmth which can make us all brothers." The hymn followed—"Lord of all being, throned afar."

Oliver Wendell Holmes (1809–1894) was one of the famous group of New England men of letters to which Longfellow, Bryant, Lowell and Whittier belonged. He was born in 1809, in Cambridge, Massachusetts. In that same year occurred the birth of Tennyson, Mrs. Browning, Darwin, Gladstone and Lincoln. After graduating from Harvard, he made a special study of medicine both in this country and abroad. He spent two years in Europe, going first to the surgical schools in Paris. "Of Lisfranc I can say little," he wrote, "except that he was a great drawer of blood and hewer of members." (He always ordered a wholesale bleeding of his patient.) Returning to Boston, Holmes steadily built up a practice, became Professor of Anatomy at Dartmouth, and later at Harvard, holding the latter post for thirty-five years. His special field in which he held consultations and lectured (delivering over one hundred each year) was intermittent and contagious fevers. Problems of heredity and ante-natal influences fascinated him. Does not his fine literary work show the observant eye of the physician? He was too sympathetic to practise medicine. He knew that vivisection was necessary, but in his heart he hated it. His assistant tells that when it became necessary to have a freshly killed rabbit for his lecture, he always ran out of the room, left him to chloroform it, and besought him not to let it squeak.

Another relates: "Into all his professional studies he carries the same kindly, tender heart. Thirty years afterward there is still a sob in his throat when he speaks of the little child in the hospital cot, whose fresh voice yet rang in his ears." In old age he said to a friend,

"Outside I laugh; inside I never laugh. It is impossible; the world is too sad."

When the Civil war broke out Dr. Holmes was mightily aroused, and wrote the "Puritan War Song" to be sung by troops marching south:

"Where are you going, soldiers,
With banner, gun and sword?
We're marching South to Canaan
To battle for the Lord."

When his son, Justice Oliver Wendell Holmes, responded to the call, his father wrote:

"O Lord of Hosts! Almighty King!
Behold the sacrifice we bring!
To every arm thy strength impart,
Thy spirit shed through every heart."

As the war increased, and his son among others was wounded at Balls Bluff, Antietam and Fredericksburg, he wrote other stanzas:

"Father of mercies, heavenly Friend,
We seek thy gracious throne;
To thee our faltering prayers ascend,
Our fainting hearts are known.

From blasts that chill, from suns that smite,
From every plague that harms;
In camp and march, in siege and fight,
Protect our men-at-arms."

On the death of Dr. Holmes at the ripe age of eighty-five, these lines appeared in Punch:

"Was there one who ever took
From its shelf by chance a book
Penned by you,
But was fast your friend for life,
With one refuge from its strife
Safe and true?

From that Boston breakfast-table
Wit and wisdom, fun and fable,
Radiated
Through all English-speaking places;
When were Science and the Graces
So well mated?"

In closing this study of this hymn and of its author, what more fitting lines than these from his "Chambered Nautilus":

"Build thee more stately mansions, O my soul,
As the swift seasons roll!
Leave thy low-vaulted past!
Let each new temple, nobler than the last,
Shut thee from heaven with a dome more vast,
Till thou at length art free,
Leaving thine outgrown shell by life's unresting sea!"[1]

✣

THE HYMN TUNE. Virgil Corydon Taylor (1817–1891) traced his ancestry back to William Brewster, who drew up the compact on the *Mayflower*. In his old home in Connecticut, he early learned to play the church organ. His subsequent life was given entirely to music, as organist, private teacher, organizer of singing schools and institutes. From Hartford, his last Connecticut habitat, he moved to Poughkeepsie to take the leadership of the Union Musical Association there. He was also organist and choirmaster at the Central Baptist Church and his wife the soprano soloist. His next moves were to the Strong Place Baptist Church, Brooklyn, then to Niagara Falls, and finally to Des Moines, Iowa, where he served St. Paul's Church, and where he died at the age of seventy-four.

LOUVAN was first used with Thomas Moore's text:

"There's nothing bright above, below
From flowers that bloom to stars that glow,
But in its light my soul shall see
Some feature of thy Deity."

A stronger tune for the Holmes hymn, with accent of word and note synchronized, is ST. CRISPIN, by George J. Elvey (1816–1893).

LORD, SPEAK TO ME, THAT I MAY SPEAK

1. Lord, speak to me, that I may speak
In living echoes of thy tone;
As thou has sought, so let me seek
Thy erring children lost and lone.

2. O lead me, Lord, that I may lead
The wandering and the wavering feet;
O feed me, Lord, that I may feed
Thy hungering ones with manna sweet.

3. O strengthen me, that while I stand
Firm on the Rock, and strong in thee,
I may stretch out a loving hand
To wrestlers with the troubled sea.

[1] From Oliver Wendell Holmes' "The Chambered Nautilus," copyright by Houghton Mifflin Company.

4. O teach me, Lord, that I may teach
The precious things thou dost impart;
And wing my words, that they may reach
The hidden depths of many a heart.

5. O fill me with thy fulness, Lord,
Until my very heart o'erflow
In kindling thought and glowing word,
Thy love to tell, thy praise to show.

FRANCES RIDLEY HAVERGAL, 1872.

BIBLICAL TEXT.

These words, which I command thee this day, shall be upon thy heart; and thou shalt teach them diligently unto thy children, and shalt talk of them when thou sittest in thy house, and when thou walkest by the way, and when thou liest down, and when thou risest up.

DEUTERONOMY 6:6, 7.

Blessed art thou, O Lord; teach me thy statutes.
With my lips have I declared all the ordinances of thy mouth.
I have rejoiced in the way of thy testimonies, as much as in all riches.

PSALM 119:12-14.

A WORKER'S PRAYER

This was a singularly appropriate caption which Miss Havergal herself gave to this hymn for its first publication. And with the title she referred to Paul's words in Romans 14:7: "For none of us liveth to himself."

The hymn is an expression of high Christian ambition, such as the saints, apostles, prophets, martyrs have had, and such as Christian workers, teachers, parents and ministers should have. One must search far for finer poetry and deeper devotion.

Elizabeth Barrett Browning has enduringly expressed the place of woman in relation to the Christian message in the familiar lines:

"Not she with traitorous kiss her Saviour stung;
Not she denied him with unholy tongue;
She, while apostles shrank, could danger brave,
Last at his Cross, and earliest at his Grave."

Woman has right of way in singing the songs of the redemption story, for with the coming of Christ came new life, greater hope and a grander mission in the world for women.

Miss Frances Ridley Havergal (1836-1879) showed early promise of an unusual career, first as a linguist, for she was most proficient in Latin, Greek and Hebrew, also French, German and Italian. She was also very musical, having decided talents as composer, singer and brilliant piano player. Her performance of the Beethoven Moonlight Sonata was in that day almost unrivaled.

She was often sought after for concert singing. But she turned from these to "love and service," her ideals. She spent her life in writing letters, leaflets and books, teaching in Sunday School, conducting religious meetings, and making public addresses. The time, thought and labor demanded of her gradually broke her down in health, and so wore her spirit out at times, that she said she hoped "the angels would have orders to let her alone a bit when she first got to heaven."

Miss Havergal belonged to the Evangelical School within the Church of England, as did Charlotte Elliott, author of "Just as I am." She has been called the "most voluminous, most diffuse, and best loved of the Evangelical school." Concerning her confirmation in Worcester Cathedral, she wrote: "My feelings when the bishop's hands were laid on my head I cannot describe; they were too confused; but when the words, 'Defend, O Lord, this child with thy heavenly grace' were solemnly pronounced, if ever my heart followed a prayer it did then; if ever it thrilled with earnest longing not unmixed with joy, it did at the words, 'Thine forever.'"

She has said concerning her poems (which were so many that they filled six volumes) that they came to her without effort. "I can never set myself to write verse. I believe my King suggests a thought and whispers me a musical line or two, and then I look up and thank him delightedly, and go on with it."

Among her more familiar hymns are: "Another year is dawning," "I could not do without thee," "Take my life, and let it be," "True-hearted, whole-hearted," "O Saviour, Precious Saviour," "I gave my life for thee," "I am trusting thee, Lord Jesus," "Who is on the Lord's side?" and "Standing at the portal of the opening year." What masculine strength in these hymns; no hint of bodily infirmity, of constant pain and suffering, of a short, fragile life! but strong virile phrases, exultant bursts of praise!

The hymn "Lord, speak to me" resolves itself into a study of verbs:—"speak," "lead," "feed," "strengthen," "teach," "fill," "tell," "show." There is nowhere in it a single selfish thought. The first personal pronoun is prominent in this hymn, but it is sharply differentiated from many modern evangelistic songs with similar emphasis on "I" and "me," by the fact that none of the blessings sought in this "Worker's Prayer" are for the benefit of the individual. All of it is directed toward the achievement of a better, more complete helpfulness for others.

A text for reading, or an anthem which may be effectively sung with this hymn, is "God be in my head," by Walford Davies, an English musician of considerable reputation. The words are:

"God be in my head, and in my understanding;
God be in mine eyes, and in my looking;
God be in my mouth, and in my speaking;
God be in my heart, and in my thinking;
God be in mine end, and at my departing."

✣

THE HYMN TUNE. ROCKINGHAM is by Edward Miller (1735–1807), an Anglican, and one of the first to profit by the enthusiastic singing of the Methodists through the eighteenth century. He realized that the old Psalm tunes must be supplemented by hymn-tunes. His *Psalms of David Hymn and Tune Book* was a great success and was adopted by over one hundred churches. King George III sent Miller twenty-five pounds as a recognition of this work. Miller was a fine literary scholar, in spite of the fact that he was brought up at his father's trade, that of stone mason. He studied music in London, played the German flute in Handel's orchestra, was an organist for fifty-six years. ROCKINGHAM is named after the Marquis of Rockingham, patron and friend of Miller, well-known Whig statesman of the period, and thrice Prime Minister. This tune was an arrangement by Miller from an older tune—TUNBRIDGE.

CANONBURY, by Robert Alexander Schumann (1810–1856), is an arrangement from "Nachtstück, Opus 23, No. 4." Robert was brought up among books, for his father was an author and a bookseller. At the age of ten we find him leader of a school orchestra of two violinists, two flutists, two clarinetists, two horn players, himself at the piano. All through these school years he played portraits of his school fellows, making the piano tell the merry pranks of one or the solemn studiousness of another.

When his father died Robert was fifteen, and then it was that they tried to make him a lawyer at the Universities of Leipzig, and Heidelberg, but without success. His passion and genius for music drove him forward into playing and composing. At the age of forty he won his wife, his playmate through the years, Clara Wieck, and then during a year of supreme happiness he wrote song after song, his finest *Lieder*. His married life was a happy one until his mind failed him and his last years were spent in an insane asylum. He died there at the early age of forty-six. He is one of the Immortals with his four symphonies, his overtures, concertos, string-quartets and violin sonatas. His rich piano literature, his superb songs, and his choral and dramatic works stamp him as the preëminent leader of the Romantic movement in music. In all his writings he is poetic, imaginative, "mentally programatic."

LORD, WHILE FOR ALL MANKIND WE PRAY

1. Lord, while for all mankind we pray,
Of every clime and coast,
O hear us for our native land,
The land we love the most.

2. O guard our shores from every foe;
With peace our borders bless;
With prosperous times our cities crown,
Our fields with plenteousness.

3. Unite us in the sacred love
Of knowledge, truth, and thee;
And let our hills and valleys shout
The songs of liberty.

4. Lord of the nations, thus to thee
Our country we commend;
Be thou her refuge and her trust,
Her everlasting friend.

John R. Wreford, 1837.

Biblical Text.

When our sons shall be as plants grown up in their youth,
And our daughters as corner-stones hewn after the fashion of a palace;
When our garners are full, affording all manner of store,
And our sheep bring forth thousands and ten thousands in our fields;
When our oxen are well laden;
When there is no breaking in and no going forth,
And no outcry in our streets;
Happy is the people that is in such a case;
Yea, happy is the people whose God is the Lord.

Psalm 144: 12–15.

Thou art my God and I will give thanks unto thee;
Thou art my God, I will exalt thee.
Ō give thanks unto the Lord; for he is good;
For his lovingkindness endureth forever.

Psalm 118: 28, 29.

LAYS OF LOYALTY TO QUEEN VICTORIA

Though written by an Englishman almost a century ago, and included in his *Lays of Loyalty* in honor of the accession of Queen Victoria to the throne of England, 1837, this hymn finds an honored place in the hymnals of America as well as of England.

It is a prayer of patriotism, recognizing, as do the Psalms quoted above, the necessity for the guidance of God in the affairs of nations. One stanza, omitted here, is a clear declaration of this belief:

"Here may religion, pure and mild,
Smile on our Sabbath hours;
And piety and virtue bless
The home of us and ours."

John Reynell Wreford (1800–1881) was educated at Manchester College, York, and became, in 1826, the Unitarian co-pastor of the New Meeting, Birmingham, England. He wrote extensively on theology and church history, and was the author of several volumes of verse, mainly devotional. After five years' service in the New Meeting, he was obliged to resign on account of serious difficulty with his voice. With another clergyman, he founded a school at Egbaston.

Dr. Wreford did not belong to the modern school of Unitarians, but considered himself connected with the body of "English Presbyterians, who always carefully repudiated all sectarian names and doctrinal distinctions."

Hymns Written for Great Occasions

The Queen Victoria Jubilee of 1897 called forth such hymns as Kipling's "Recessional," and Bishop How's "O King of kings, whose reign of old."

In America, Anniversary Odes and Occasional or Festival Hymns are even more common. Bryant wrote "Thou, whose unmeasured temple stands" for the dedication of one of New York's finest churches in the thirties, and "Look from thy sphere of endless day" for the Home Missionary National Gathering of 1840. Leonard Bacon wrote "O God, beneath thy guiding hand" for the Bicentenary of the city of New Haven, as did Bishop Doane "Ancient of days" for the Bicentennial of the city of Albany, 1886. James Russell Lowell wrote the *Crisis,* from which comes "Once to every man and nation," at the beginning of the War with Mexico, protesting against this war as unjust and untimely. Whittier wrote anniversary poems for the opening of the Centennial in Philadelphia, 1876, for the American Horticultural Society Meeting, 1882, for the opening of Plymouth Church, St. Paul, etc.

✣

THE HYMN TUNE. There seems to be a wider variation among hymnal editors in the choice of a tune for these words than on almost any other hymn. An examination of thirteen church hymnals in current use reveals the fact that nine different tunes are set to these words.

DALEHURST, however, by Arthur Cottman (1842–1879), seems to have the preference. Mr. Cottman was a solicitor and amateur musician. He died at the early age of thirty-seven.

LOVE DIVINE, ALL LOVE EXCELLING

1. Love divine, all love excelling,
Joy of heaven, to earth come down;
Fix in us thy humble dwelling,
All thy faithful mercies crown;
Jesus, thou art all compassion,
Pure, unbounded love thou art;
Visit us with thy salvation,
Enter every trembling heart.

2. Breathe, O breathe thy loving Spirit
Into every troubled breast;
Let us all in thee inherit,
Let us find the promised rest;
Take away the love of sinning;
Alpha and Omega be;
End of faith, as its beginning,
Set our hearts at liberty.

3. Come, Almighty to deliver,
Let us all thy life receive;
Suddenly return, and never,
Never more thy temples leave.
Thee we would be always blessing,
Serve thee as thy hosts above,
Pray and praise thee without ceasing,
Glory in thy perfect love.

4. Finish, then, thy new creation;
Pure and spotless let us be;
Let us see thy great salvation
Perfectly restored in thee;
Changed from glory into glory
Till in heaven we take our place,
Till we cast our crowns before thee,
Lost in wonder, love and praise.

CHARLES WESLEY, 1747.

BIBLICAL TEXT.

We love, because he first loved us.

I JOHN 4: 19.

God is love, and he that abideth in love abideth in God.

I JOHN 4: 16.

Come unto me, all ye that labor and are heavy laden, and I will give you rest.

Take my yoke upon you, and learn of me; for I am meek and lowly in heart: and ye shall find rest unto your souls.

MATTHEW 11:28, 29.

Behold what manner of love the Father hath bestowed upon us, that we should be called children of God.

I JOHN 3:1.

THE SINGER OF DIVINE LOVE

England in the days of the Wesleys was unbelievably wicked. The clergy were idle, remiss in their labors, corrupt in practice. Among men of fashion, drunkenness and vile talk were marks of distinction. In the playhouses the manners and morals depicted were incredible even in our day. Among working people, there was brutality and bestial torture of animals. On holidays Cockneys were permitted, on paying twopence, to go through Bethlehem Hospital, and amuse themselves at the expense of the lunatics. In London signs in the gin shops invited passers-by to get "drunk for a penny, or dead drunk for twopence." Cruel penal laws held sway. Hanging was meted out to robbers of hen-roosts, writers of threatening letters, thieves who stole to the value of five shillings. Twenty young men were strung up one morning in front of Newgate.

Into this world were ushered John and Charles Wesley. They changed the face of England, they begot in the nation a new enthusiasm for the service of suffering humanity. Hospitals, churches, the visitation of criminals, missions to the heathen, the abolition of the slave-trade—all these came with the Revival of Religion. "What St. Francis was to Europe in the thirteenth century, the Wesleys were to the English of the eighteenth century."

Out of a pamphlet collection of "Hymns for Those that Seek and Those that have Found Redemption," published by Charles Wesley in 1747, comes this hymn of superlative joy, expressing the sublime confidence of the Christian in that transfiguring love through which "we are called the children of God." This is the chief note in Wesley's songs, sounding constantly in and through all the other motifs. Some of his references to this Divine love are: "Love divine," "Pure, unbounded love," "Infinite love," "Everlasting love," "Redeeming love," "My Lord, my love," "Glorious love," "O unexampled love," "The heart-renewing love," and "Jesus, lover of my soul."

ANALYSIS. So very familiar is this hymn to all church-goers, so constantly is it sung in all sorts of churches, that it might seem that any attempt at "analysis" of it would be superfluous. Yet, is it not possible that its very familiarity may be the cause of indifference to its beauty and depth of meaning? Is it not possible that, knowing the words as one does, one may often sing the hymn thoughtlessly?

First stanza: As Wesley wrote the first line it read, "Love divine, all *loves* excelling." Today, the "s" is usually dropped. What Wesley evidently meant to say was that the Divine love goes far beyond all earthly loves, precious and dear as those may be.

Second stanza: "the promised rest"—another change from the original, which had "that second rest"—an allusion to the double promise of Jesus in Matthew 11:28, "I will give you rest," "Ye shall find rest."

Third stanza: Is it for the "life beyond" for which Wesley prays here, or for this present life of the here and now? "Thee we would be always blessing." When? After death, amid the glories of heaven, or now, in the midst of toil and testing and trouble?

Fourth stanza: Note the progression of thought! Through the seeking and finding of salvation a "new creation" has begun; but it is not completed in a day; the singer prays that Christ who has begun the work will carry it on to completion.

✣

THE HYMN TUNE. The tune to which these words are most commonly sung in America is appropriately called BEECHER, because its composer, John Zundel (1815–1882) was the assistant musical editor of the famous "Plymouth Collection," prepared for Henry Ward Beecher's Plymouth Church in Brooklyn. He wrote twenty-eight tunes for the book.

Zundel was German-born, though most of his life was spent in America. His first positions in America were in the First Unitarian Church, Brooklyn, and in St. George's Church, New York. In 1850 he became organist in Plymouth Church, then at the height of its glory under the leadership of Dr. Beecher. Although Dr. Beecher was not a musician, he appreciated the value of congregational singing. He says concerning good tunes: "Let a true tune be sung, and every person of sensibility, every person of feeling, every child even is aroused and touched. The melody clings to them. On the way home, snatches of it will be heard on this side and on that; and when, the next Sabbath, the same song is heard, one and another of the people fall in, and the volume grows with each verse, until at length, the song, breaking forth as a many-rilled stream from the hills, grows deeper and flows on, broad as a mighty river. Such tunes are never forgotten. They cling to us through our whole life. We carry them with us upon our journey. We sing them in the forest. The workman follows the plow with sacred songs. Children catch them, and singing only for the joy it gives them now, are yet laying up for all their life, food of the sweetest joy. Such tunes give new harmony and sweetness even to the hymns which float upon their current. And when some celestial hymn of Wesley, or of the scarcely less inspired Watts, is wafted upon such music, the soul is lifted up above all its ailments, and rises unto the very presence of God, with joys no longer unspeakable, though full of glory."

In 1851 Beecher appealed to his choir director, Mr. Darius E. Jones, to make a hymn-book. The result was *Temple Melodies,* which appeared at a time when probably not over twenty churches in all America were supplied with hymn-books, "lining out" being still the prevalent fashion. In 1855 appeared the *Plymouth Collection* which aroused a storm of protest among Protestants because it contained some hymns by Roman Catholic authors.

Zundel remained at Plymouth Church as organist for twenty years or more. His last position in America was in the Central Methodist Church, Detroit. A most unusual leader of congregational singing, he lifted Plymouth Church to a position of acknowledged primacy in genuine worship music. Many have been the famous musicians who have presided at the organ, led the choir and sung at Plymouth Church; among them Emma Thursby, Antoinette Sterling, Leopold Damrosch, Reinald Werrenrath and John Spencer Camp.

MINE EYES HAVE SEEN THE GLORY

1. Mine eyes have seen the glory of the coming of the Lord;
He is trampling out the vintage where the grapes of wrath are stored;
He hath loosed the fateful lightning of his terrible swift sword;
His truth is marching on.

Refrain

Glory! glory! Hallelujah! Glory! glory! Hallelujah!
Glory! glory! Hallelujah! His truth is marching on!

2. I have seen him in the watch-fires of a hundred circling camps;
They have builded him an altar in the evening dews and damps;
I can read his righteous sentence by the dim and flaring lamps;
His day is marching on.

Refrain

3. I have read a fiery gospel, writ in burnished rows of steel:
"As ye deal with my contemners, so with you my grace shall deal;

Let the Hero, born of woman, crush the serpent with his heel";
Our God is marching on.
Refrain

4. He has sounded forth the trumpet that shall never call retreat;
He is sifting out the hearts of men before his judgment seat;
O be swift, my soul, to answer him, be jubilant, my feet!
Our God is marching on.
Refrain

5. In the beauty of the lilies Christ was born across the sea,
With a glory in his bosom that transfigures you and me;
As he died to make men holy, let us die to make men free,
While God is marching on.
Refrain

JULIA WARD HOWE, 1861.

BIBLICAL TEXT.

Jehovah, when thou wentest forth out of Seir,
When thou marchedst out of the field of Edom,
The earth trembled, the heavens also dropped. . . .
The mountains quaked at the presence of the Lord,
Even yon Sinai at the presence of the Lord, the God of Israel.
The Lord came down for me against the mighty.
The kings came and fought;
Then fought the kings of Canaan. . . .
They took no gain of money.
From heaven fought the stars,
From their courses they fought against Sisera.

JUDGES 5:4, 5, 13, 19, 20.

The Son of man came not to be ministered unto, but to minister, and to give his life a ransom for many.

MATTHEW 20:28.

THE SONG OF A GREAT CRUSADER

The days of Crusaders are by no means confined to the eleventh and twelfth centuries, to the stalwart, armor-clad men who strove to wrest the Holy Sepulcher from the control of the Saracen. Modern times as well have their Crusades and their Crusaders, and women as well as men have qualified.

To this noble group belongs Julia Ward Howe (1819–1910), "Crusader" through the years of a long life for many a cause of truth and righteousness. Julia Ward's talents began to flower early in life; she contributed to literary magazines before she was seventeen, and had published a volume of essays and poems before she was twenty-one. Her marriage in 1843 to Dr. Samuel G. Howe, head of the Perkins Institute for the Blind, was a union of kindred spirits. Their honeymoon in Europe opened to them friendships with Dickens, Carlyle, Wordsworth and other literary leaders, through Dr. Howe's intimate acquaintance with Lord Byron, formed during their work together for Greek independence.

During the fifties both Dr. and Mrs. Howe threw themselves heartily into the abolitionist cause. Editing the Boston *Commonwealth,* they were friends of William Lloyd Garrison and Wendell Phillips.

In the days of the Civil War Dr. Howe was an officer of the Sanitary Commission. In the autumn of 1861 Mrs. Howe, with her husband, her pastor, Reverend James Freeman Clarke of Boston, and Governor John A. Andrew of Massachusetts, visited the Army of the Potomac. One day they rode out from Washington to witness a review of the troops. The review was broken up by a sudden movement of the enemy. On their way back to Washington the road was filled with infantry. As they passed in their carriage Mrs. Howe and her party heard the soldiers singing popular songs of the day. Among those songs was "John Brown's Body." When they finished that song, Dr. Clarke turned to Mrs. Howe with the remark, "Mrs. Howe, why do you not write some good words to that stirring tune?"

"I went to bed that night as usual," she records, "and slept according to my wont quite soundly. I awoke in the gray of the morning twilight; and as I lay waiting for the dawn, the long lines of the desired poem began to twine themselves in my mind. Having thought out all the stanzas I said to myself, 'I must get up and write these verses down lest I fall asleep again and forget them.' So with a sudden effort I sprang out of bed, and found in the dimness an old stump of a pen which I remembered to have used the day before. I scrawled the verses almost without looking at the paper. . . . I feared to have recourse to a light lest I should wake the baby, who slept with me."

It was published in the *Atlantic Monthly* in 1862. The famous Chaplain McCabe helped it spring into public favor. Thus was written the greatest of the songs of the Civil War period; a song which found new use and new meaning during the World War; a song which has found its way into practically every American hymnal, and even into some of those published abroad. Rudyard Kipling always referred to it as the "Terrible Battle Hymn of the Republic."

Following the war, Mrs. Howe continued her "crusading," first for the then unpopular cause of Woman Suffrage, and later for World Peace. For the latter cause she made in 1872 a lecture tour of England urging arbitration as the ideal means for settling international disputes.

Mrs. Howe lived to the extreme age of ninety-one. On October 5, 1910, she visited Smith College to receive in person the honorary degree of Doctor of Laws. Twelve days later came her graduation to the ranks of "the immortals."

A truly "Great Crusader," Julia Ward Howe deserves to be remembered as author, poet, lecturer. But she is, and will continue to be, remembered chiefly as the author of "Mine eyes have seen the glory of the coming of the Lord."

The Battle Hymn of the Revolution

A song written by William Billings and sung to his own tune of CHESTER, was called the "Battle Hymn of the Revolution," and was almost as famous in its day as the "Battle Hymn of the Republic" at a later time.

Everywhere, in church and home, by the children and the aged,

The Battle Hymn of the Revolution

"CHESTER"

these words were sung with passionate fervor. The soldiers knew them by heart, and to the sound of fife and drum they sang them as they advanced to meet the foe. This Battle Hymn contributed not a little to the winning of the Revolutionary War.

✣

THE HYMN TUNE. The origin of the familiar and famous tune BATTLE HYMN OF THE REPUBLIC seems to be shrouded in mystery. One account traces it to John William Steffe, of Richmond, Virginia, who composed it as a Camp Meeting song. Louis C. Elson, in *The History of American Music* says of its popularity in the South before the Civil War: "The song was used at many a Southern camp meeting before the war, and was also employed in many of the colored congregations. It even made its way into the Methodist hymnals at the North."

The following arrangement shows its original use with the words, "Say, Brothers, will you Meet Us?"

Say, Brothers, Will You Meet Us?

1. Say, broth-ers, will you meet us? Say, broth-ers, will you
2. By the grace of God we'll meet you, By the grace of God we'll
3. Je - sus lives and reigns for - ev - er, Je - sus lives and reigns for-
meet us? Say, broth - ers, will you
meet you, By the grace of God we'll
ev - er, Je - sus lives and reigns for -
meet us, On Ca - naan's hap - py shore?
meet you, Where part - ing is no more.
ev - er, On Ca - naan's hap - py shore.

MORE LIGHT SHALL BREAK

1. More light shall break from out thy word
For pilgrim followers of the gleam,

Till, led by thy free spirit, Lord,
We see and share the pilgrim dream.

2. What mighty hopes are in our care,
What holy dreams of brotherhood;
God of our Fathers, help us dare
Their passion for the common good.

3. Wild roars the blast, the storm is high;
Above the storm are shining still
The lights by which we live and die;
Our peace is ever in thy will.

4. The ancient stars, the ancient faith,
Defend us till our voyage is done;
Across the floods of fear and death
The Mayflower still is sailing on.

Allen Eastman Cross, 1920.

Biblical Text.

The Spirit of truth . . . shall guide you into all the truth.

John 16 : 13.

Brethren, I count not myself yet to have laid hold: but one thing I do . . . I press on toward the goal unto the prize of the high calling of God in Christ Jesus.

Philippians 3: 13, 14.

The Lord hath more truth and light yet to break forth out of his Holy Word. (*Pastor Robinson's farewell to the Mayflower Pilgrims.*)

A HYMN OF TWENTIETH CENTURY PILGRIMS

This hymn flowered out of the three hundredth anniversary of the coming of the Pilgrims. It was first sung in the Old South Church in Boston at the International Council of Congregational Churches in 1920. If the Pilgrim faith is to prevail in our day, it must have a voice. This hymn is such a voice! It puts the mighty compulsion and the iron strength of ancient law behind the gospel of freedom and fellowship. It emphasizes and puts into a deathless line what was so signally brought out in the celebration of the Pilgrim spirit in 1920, "Their passion for the common good."

It has besides this, three other unforgettable lines; in the first line of the first verse, the paraphrase of Pastor Robinson's farewell words to the Mayflower Pilgrims: "The Lord hath more truth and light yet to break forth out of his Holy Word." In the third verse there is the adapted translation of what has been called Dante's greatest line in the Divina Commedia, *"In sua voluntate, nostra pax"*—"In his will is our peace!" In the last verse, like a morning reveille, is the assertion of the Pilgrim faith and life in the words, "The Mayflower still is sailing on!"

If Plymouth Rock be the corner-stone of the Republic, then may this interpretation of the Pilgrim faith be sung by all America. It has been illustrated by picture films, and employed in Thanksgiving and Forefathers' Day Services. It was repeatedly used at the anniversary services of 1920 in both America and England. It will be always appropriate as a sequel and supplement to Leonard Bacon's famous hymn, such as he himself might approve: "O God, beneath thy guiding hand."

Allen Eastman Cross, the author of this modern pilgrim hymn, was born at Manchester, New Hampshire, in 1864. He was educated at Phillips Andover, Amherst College and the Andover Theological Seminary. For ten years he was the associate pastor of the Old South Church, Boston, with Dr. George A. Gordon. In 1914 he became pastor of the First Congregational Church, Milford, Massachusetts, and served that church for eleven years. Since 1925 he has resided in the ancestral home in Manchester, New Hampshire, where he devotes his time to writing. The late Dr. Gordon, with whom he was associated so long, said of him: "Dr. Cross had a distinctive literary gift much appreciated by many of our people; he was and is a poet as well as a preacher."

Among the significantly modern hymns by Dr. Cross which are found in our present-day hymnals are: "America, America, the shouts of war shall cease," "The gray hills taught me patience," "Young and radiant," "The hidden years at Nazareth," "Jesus, kneel beside me."

A Related Hymn

In December, 1924, while Dr. Cross was pastor at Milford, the State Y. M. C. A. Older Boys' Conference was held in Newton. One of its features was the kindling of an electric torch, to be carried by boys from place to place and from group to group throughout Massachusetts and Rhode Island. Accompanying the torch were three messages—two from Governors—and a hymn for the torch-bearers, written by Dr. Cross. By the following May the torch had been carried on foot a distance of five hundred and thirty-four miles by over five hundred boys through fifty-one cities. Dr. Cross's hymn for these boys in the regions of the Pilgrims and the Puritans is as follows:

"Pass on the torch, pass on the flame;
Remember whence the glory came,

And eyes are on you as you run,
Beyond the shining of the sun.

"Lord Christ, we take the torch from thee;
We must be true, we will be free;
And clean of heart and strong of soul,
To bear the Glory to its goal.

"America, God hear the prayer—
America for God, we dare,
With Lincoln's heart and Lincoln's hand,
To fling a flame across the land.

"O Lord of life, to thee we kneel;
Maker of men, our purpose seal;
We will, for honor of thy name,
Pass on the torch, pass on the flame."

❖

THE HYMN TUNE. Two tunes are in common use with this hymn, TRURO, by Charles Burney (1726–1814), and DUKE STREET, by John Hatton (?–1793). (For the latter, see "Jesus Shall Reign.")

TRURO is from *Psalmodia Evangelica,* 1790, and assigned to Charles Burney, the son of an organist, who received the Mus.D. degree from Oxford in 1769, wrote many volumes on music, including a four-volume *General History of Music,* which is said to mark an epoch in English musical literature; was the composer of violin concertos, sonatas, piano trios, as well as a few hymn tunes. He made his home during the closing years of his life in Chelsea, where he was organist at Chelsea College. He traveled extensively on the continent, and was regarded as one of the outstanding musical critics of his day.

MY COUNTRY, 'TIS OF THEE

1. My country, 'tis of thee,
Sweet land of liberty,
Of thee I sing;
Land where my fathers died,
Land of the pilgrims' pride,
From every mountain side
Let freedom ring.

2. My native country, thee,
Land of the noble free,
Thy name I love;
I love thy rocks and rills,
Thy woods and templed hills;
My heart with rapture thrills,
Like that above.

3. Let music swell the breeze,
And ring from all the trees
Sweet freedom's song;
Let mortal tongues awake;
Let all that breathe partake;
Let rocks their silence break,
The sound prolong.

4. Our fathers' God, to thee,
Author of liberty,
To thee we sing;
Long may our land be bright
With freedom's holy light;
Protect us by thy might,
Great God, our King.

SAMUEL FRANCES SMITH, 1832.

BIBLICAL TEXT.

Proclaim liberty throughout the land unto all the inhabitants thereof.
LEVITICUS 25:10a.

Fear not, O land, be glad and rejoice; for the Lord hath done great things.
JOEL 2:21.

And he brought forth his people with joy,
And his chosen with singing. . . .
That they might keep his statutes,
And observe his laws.

PSALM 105:43, 45.

THE NATIONAL HYMN OF AMERICA

Dr. Frank W. Gunsaulus of Chicago, witty orator and popular preacher of the last generation, writing in the Chicago Record-Herald concerning a new National Anthem, said in his inimitable style: "Let us be ready gratefully to welcome a new National Anthem when it comes. But let it *come*. It must not be fetched. If it comes, it will arrive in the course of the night and wake with us in the morning. It is with songs of immortal breath as with the grace of God; they spring out of the elemental as the wind bloweth where it listeth. The soul of a National Anthem cannot be gotten on demand.

" 'America' will be sung anyhow. . . . It will always be sung, for it is a simple, easily understood song. It is an endearing song—it frankly says that the land of liberty is 'sweet.' This is not sugary, but blossomy sweetness. . . . This hymn 'America' embodies the soul that righted the fallen republic. . . . Its tune may be English, but this discloses the sturdy root which furnished our primitive sap. All English-speaking nations may rally round that tune some day. It is well to keep it on the lips of both England and America. . . . The hymn is the republic's very spirit transcending in song any party, sect, scheme or man. . . . Strong in simplicity and deep in its trust in God, children and philosophers can repeat it together. Every crisis will hear it above the storm."

Samuel Frances Smith (1808–1895) was born in a little house on one of the narrow streets in the "twisted North End" of Boston. Graduating from Harvard in the famous Class of 1829, with Oliver Wendell Holmes and many other noted men, he prepared for the ministry at Andover Theological Seminary. His first pastorate was in Waterville, Maine, where he also served as Professor of Modern Languages in Colby College. From 1842 to 1854 he was pastor of the First Baptist Church of Newton Centre, Massachusetts, resigning this work in order to devote his entire time to secretarial and editorial work for the American Baptist Missionary Union. He continued to reside in Newton Centre until his death.

"My country, 'tis of thee" was written while Dr. Smith was still a student at Andover. His friend, Dr. Lowell Mason, had received a number of German hymn books, and not being able to read German himself, had given them to Smith to look over. One afternoon in February, 1832, as the young student was leafing over one of these books, he came upon the tune which is now known as "America." It appealed to him by reason of its spirited movement, and noting that the words in German were patriotic, he says, "I instantly felt the impulse to write a patriotic hymn of my own, adapted to the tune. Picking up a scrap of waste paper which lay near me, I wrote at once, probably within half an hour, the hymn 'America' as it is now known everywhere. The whole hymn stands today as it stood on the bit of waste paper."

He gave it to his friend Dr. Mason, and forgot it. Much to his surprise, Dr. Mason brought it out at a children's celebration on the Fourth of July of that year, in Park Street Church, Boston. So the children of Boston had the privilege of singing first of all the hymn which Dr. Gunsaulus prophesies will "always be sung" as America's "National Anthem."

On Dr. Smith's eightieth birthday, his old college classmate, Oliver Wendell Holmes, sent him the following tribute in verse:

"Full many a poet's labored lines
A century's creeping waves shall hide,—
The verse a people's love enshrines
Stands like a rock that breasts the tide.

"Time wrecks the proudest piles we raise,
The towers, the domes, the temples fall,

The fortress crumbles and decays,—
One breath of song outlasts them all."

Dr. Smith's hymn has sometimes been criticized as too exclusively New England in its tone and pictures. To remedy that "defect," no less a poet than Dr. Henry van Dyke once wrote some supplementary stanzas; decidedly Western and Southern in thought:

"I love thine inland seas,
Thy groves of giant trees
Thy rolling plains;
Thy mighty rivers' sweep,
Majestic canyons deep,
Thy mountains wild and steep,
All thy domains.

"Thy silver eastern strands,
Thy Golden Gate that stands
Fronting the West;
Thy flowing southland fair,
Thy sweet and crystal air,—
O land beyond compare,
Thee I love best." [1]

Less profound and rich than Katharine Lee Bates' "America the Beautiful," it is more popular. Less flamboyant and pugnacious than "The Star-Spangled Banner," it is a more fitting hymn for a right and peace-loving nation. For its easy grace, its directness and simplicity, its zealous patriotism, its fervent piety, and its insistent note of liberty "America" has become the favorite national hymn.

✣

THE HYMN TUNE. Printed in *Thesaurus Musicus,* 1740, AMERICA was brought to the attention of England by Henry Carey, who sang it, with the words, "God Save the King" at a dinner to celebrate the capture of Portobello by the English. Dr. Julian is authority for the statement that the tune became known on the continent in the later years of the eighteenth century, and was used as a national air in Denmark, Prussia, Saxony, and other North German states.

F. J. Metcalf, in *Stories of Hymn Tunes* (1928), says that "its first use as a hymn tune was probably in an American book—James Lyon's *Urania,* 1761—where it is set to the words 'Come thou Almighty King.' "

Dr. Smith's own comment on the use of this tune by both England and America was: "I deem it a new and beautiful bond of union between the mother country and her daughter."

[1] Copyright by Charles Scribner's Sons.

MY FAITH LOOKS UP TO THEE

1. My faith looks up to thee,
Thou Lamb of Calvary,
  Saviour Divine.
Now hear me while I pray,
Take all my guilt away,
O let me from this day
  Be wholly thine.

2. May thy rich grace impart
Strength to my fainting heart,
My zeal inspire;
As thou hast died for me,
O may my love to thee,
Pure, warm, and changeless be,
  A living fire.

3. While life's dark maze I tread,
And griefs around me spread,
  Be thou my guide;
Bid darkness turn to day;
Wipe sorrow's tears away,
Nor let me ever stray
  From thee aside.

4. When ends life's transient dream,
When death's cold, sullen stream
Shall o'er me roll;
Blest Saviour, then, in love,
Fear and distrust remove;
O bear me safe above,
  A ransomed soul!

RAY PALMER, 1830.

BIBLICAL TEXT.

The righteous shall live by faith.

ROMANS 1:17.

By faith in his name hath his name made this man strong.

ACTS 3:16.

We walk by faith, not by sight.

II CORINTHIANS 5:7.

A YOUNG MAN'S VISION OF CHRIST

New York City in 1830 was not a terrifying metropolis, but it was large enough to give a young man just out of college reasons for feeling lonely and discouraged. Ray Palmer (1808–1887) was twenty-two when he landed in New York City fresh from Yale. Added to his loneliness was ill health and a feeling of religious uncertainty.

This is not the sort of soil out of which one would expect one of the rarest blooms of American hymnology to grow and flower. Yet it was out of just these discouraging circumstances that Ray Palmer had the vision of faith which inspired the writing of "My Faith Looks Up to Thee."

He had been translating two verses from a German poem. They told of a suppliant at the cross. With these German verses freshly in mind, there came to him a vision of Christ, "an hour," as he himself describes it, "when Christ in the riches of his grace and love, was so vividly apprehended as to fill the soul with deep emotion." In that hour "My Faith Looks Up to Thee" was written.

The author copied it into his pocket note-book, but with no thought at all of writing for anyone else, "least of all," he says, "of writing a hymn for Christian worship. The stanzas came with little effort. I recall that I wrote them with very tender emotion, and penned the last stanza in tears."

Born in Little Compton, Rhode Island, Ray Palmer (1808–1887) attended Phillips Andover Academy, where he was a classmate of Oliver Wendell Holmes. After graduation from Yale, in 1830, he taught for a time in a girls' school in New York City. Ordained as a Congregational minister in 1835, he served two long pastorates in Bath, Maine, and Albany, New York. For twelve years he served as the Secretary of the Congregational Union. His last years were spent in literary work.

❖

THE HYMN TUNE. Had it not been for a "chance" meeting on a Boston street, Dr. Palmer's hymn might have remained hidden away in his personal note-book. Two years after the writing of "My Faith Looks Up to Thee," he was stopped on the street in Boston by Lowell Mason (1792–1872) who asked him to write something for a hymn-book which he and Thomas Hastings were soon to publish. It was then that young Palmer drew out his little note-book and brought to light one of the world's great hymns. They stepped into a store and the hymn was copied. Reading it over at home Mason wrote the lovely air OLIVET with which the hymn is associated all over the Western world. Two or three days later Mason again met Palmer on the street, and said to him, "You may live many years and do many good things, but I think you will be best known to posterity as the author of 'My Faith Looks Up to Thee.'"

MY GOD, I THANK THEE

1. My God, I thank thee who hast made
The earth so bright,
So full of splendor and of joy,
Beauty and light;
So many glorious things are here,
Noble and right.

2. I thank thee, too, that thou hast made
Joy to abound;
So many gentle thoughts and deeds
Circling us round;
That in the darkest spot of earth
Some love is found.

3. I thank thee more that all our joy
Is touched with pain;
That shadows fall on brightest hours;
That thorns remain;
So that earth's bliss may be our guide,
And not our chain.

4. I thank thee, Lord, that thou hast kept
The best in store;
We have enough, yet not too much
To long for more;
A yearning for a deeper peace,
Not known before.

5. I thank thee, Lord, that here our souls
Though amply blest,
Can never find, although they seek,
A perfect rest;
Nor ever shall, until they lean
On Jesus' breast.

Adelaide Anne Procter, 1858.

Biblical Text.

Oh give thanks unto the Lord, call upon his name;
Make known among the peoples his doings.
Sing unto him, sing praises unto him;
Talk ye of all his marvellous works.

Psalm 105: 1, 2.

Beloved, now are we children of God, and it is not yet made manifest, what we shall be. We know that, if he shall be manifested, we shall be like him; for we shall see him even as he is.

I John 3:2.

LEGENDS AND LYRICS OF AN INVALID

For a year and a half, about the middle of the nineteenth century, Charles Dickens, as editor of *Household Words,* accepted and published poem after poem from an unknown contributor. Even though the author continued to keep her identity concealed, Dickens gladly accepted the contributions because of their uniformly high literary quality. Imagine his surprise, after a year and a half, to discover that the poems were the work of the daughter of an intimate friend. The poet, Miss Adelaide Anne Procter, gives the following reason for concealing her identity: "If I send him, in my own name, verses that he does not honestly like, either it will be very painful for him to return them, or he will print them for papa's sake and not for their own. So I have made up my mind to take my chance fairly with the unknown volunteers."

Such modesty and thoughtfulness received its reward when in 1858, on the publication of a volume of Miss Procter's verse under the title, "Legends and Lyrics," Dickens wrote a most complimentary introduction. It is from this volume of "Legends and Lyrics" that the hymn "My God, I Thank Thee" is taken. In this same volume are two other poems familiar as hymns in some modern hymnals: "One by one the sands are flowing" and "The Shadows of the Evening Hours." The enlarged edition of 1862 contained among other new poems, "I do not ask, O Lord, that life may be a pleasant road."

Adelaide Procter was the "Golden-tressed Adelaide" of one of her father's best poems. "Mrs. Procter talked to me a great deal about her little daughter Adelaide, who must be a wonderful creature, a beautiful girl, delicate, gentle and pensive, looking as if she knew she was a poet's child." Frail in body and intimately acquainted with suffering, she was triumphant in soul. Her habitual cheeriness of disposition and buoyant sense of humor shine through her poems.

The demand for Miss Procter's poems about 1877, thirteen years after her death, exceeded that of any other writer except Tennyson. We will not forget that she wrote the "Legend of Bregenz" and "The Lost Chord":

"Seated one day at the organ,
I was weary and ill at ease,
And my fingers wandered idly
Over the noisy keys.
I know not what I was playing,
Or what I was dreaming then,
But I struck one chord of music,
Like the sound of a great Amen."

ANALYSIS. The opening line of this hymn strikes a new note in the hymnody of the time in which it was written. It was one of the first hymns to break away from the plaintive other-worldliness of the eighteenth century, and to thank God for his beneficent activity in this present world.

The hymn is remarkably inclusive in its thought. While it is placed by most hymn-book editors in the "Nature" section, one puts it, with equal appropriateness, in the section devoted to "The Christian Life, Love and Gratitude." There is here praise for God's thoughtfulness in making the present world so wondrously fair; praise for the abundance of joy in common life; praise for the promise of the future, in a richer joy, a "deeper peace" and a more "perfect rest" than any afforded by the present.

One of the most significant stanzas is the third, in which the author even finds reason for gratitude for pain. That closing line of this stanza, "earth's bliss may be our guide, and not our chain," is a poetic gem "of purest ray serene."

Interpretative Reading and Singing

The Minister:

"The Lord God planted a garden
In the first white days of the world,
And he set there an angel warden
In a garment of light enfurled.

"So near to the peace of Heaven,
That the hawk might nest with the wren,
For there in the cool of the even
God walked with the first of men.

"And I dream that those garden closes
With their shade and their sun-flecked sod
And their lilies and bowers of roses,
Were laid by the hand of God."

DOROTHY FRANCES GURNEY.

Soloist, choir or congregation—First Stanza "My God, I thank thee, thou hast made."

The Minister:

"The little cares that fretted me
I lost them yesterday,
Among the fields above the sea,
Among the winds at play,
Among the lowing of the herds,
The rustling of the trees,
Among the singing of the birds,
The humming of the bees.

"The foolish fears of what might happen,
I cast them all away

Among the clover-scented grass,
Among the new-mown hay,
Among the husking of the corn,
Where the drowsy poppies nod
Where ill thoughts die and good are born,
Out in the fields with God."

MRS. BROWNING.

Soloist, choir, or congregation—Second Stanza.

The Minister:

"If all the skies were sunshine,
Our faces would be fain
To feel once more upon them
The cooling splash of rain.

"If all the world were music,
Our hearts would often long
For one sweet strain of silence,
To break the endless song.

"If life were always merry,
Our souls would seek relief,
And rest from weary laughter
In the quiet arms of grief." [1]

HENRY VAN DYKE.

Soloist, choir or congregation—Third Stanza.

The Minister:

"Thou hast made the flowers to bloom
And the stars to shine;
Hid rare gems of richest ore
In the tunneled mine;

"But chief of all thy wondrous works
Supreme of all thy plan,
Thou hast put an upward reach
Into the heart of man." [2]

HARRY KEMP.

Soloist, choir, or congregation—Fourth Stanza.

The Minister:

"Beyond the last horizon's rim,
Beyond adventure's farthest quest,
Somewhere they rise, serene and dim,
The happy, happy, Hills of Rest.

"Sweet hours we did not live go by
To soothing note, on scented wing;
In golden-lettered volumes lie
The songs we tried in vain to sing.

"They all are there; the days of dream
That built the inner lives of men;

[1] From the Poems of Henry van Dyke, copyright by Charles Scribner's Sons, and used by permission.
[2] Copyright by Brentanos, publishers.

'The might be' and the 'might have been'!
The silent, sacred years we deem

"Some evening when the sky is gold
I'll follow day into the west;
Nor pause, nor heed, till I behold
The happy, happy, Hills of Rest." [3]

ALBERT BIGELOW PAINE.

Soloist, choir, or congregation—Fifth Stanza.

✣

THE HYMN TUNE. WENTWORTH was composed by Frederick C. Maker (1844–1927). Mr. Maker was born at Bristol. He was chorister in Bristol Cathedral, and later, organist at the Milk Street Methodist Free Church, the Clifton Downs Congregational Church, and the Redlands Park Congregational Church. He composed a cantata "Moses in the Bulrushes," contributed tunes to the Bristol Tune Book, and issued an original collection of tunes and anthems.

NEARER, MY GOD, TO THEE

1. Nearer, my God, to thee,
Nearer to thee!
E'en though it be a cross
That raiseth me;
Still all my song shall be,
Nearer, my God, to thee,
Nearer to thee.

2. Though like the wanderer,
The sun gone down,
Darkness be over me,
My rest a stone;
Yet in my dreams I'd be
Nearer, my God, to thee,
Nearer to thee.

3. There let the way appear
Steps unto heaven;
All that thou sendest me
In mercy given;
Angels to beckon me
Nearer, my God, to thee,
Nearer to thee.

4. Then, with my waking thoughts
Bright with thy praise,
Out of my stony griefs,
Bethel I'll raise;
So by my woes to be

[3] Copyright by Albert Bigelow Paine.

Nearer, my God, to thee,
Nearer to thee.

5. Or if on joyful wing,
Cleaving the sky,
Sun, moon, and stars forgot,
Upward I fly,
Still all my song shall be,
Nearer, my God, to thee,
Nearer to thee.

SARAH FLOWER ADAMS, 1841.

BIBLICAL TEXT.

And he lighted on a certain place, and tarried there all night, and he took one of the stones of the place, and put it under his head, and lay down to sleep. And he dreamed; and behold, a ladder set up on the earth, and the top of it reached to heaven, and behold, the angels of God ascending and descending on it. . . . This is none other than the house of God, and this is the gate of heaven.

GENESIS 28:11, 17.

Verily, verily, I say unto you, Ye shall see the heaven opened and the angels of God ascending and descending upon the Son of man.

JOHN 1:51.

SURELY THE LORD IS IN THIS PLACE

Played by the ship's band in the last moments of the great *Titanic* disaster, a favorite of the martyred President McKinley, and greatly beloved by Theodore Roosevelt, this hymn is a mighty expression of trust and triumph in the crises of life. It is also a prayer of aspiration in the humdrum gray of common experience.

Three or four years before the writing of this hymn, Mrs. Sarah Flower Adams (1805–1848) had realized the dream of her heart, a dramatic triumph as "Lady Macbeth," and the beginning of a successful career in drama. But ill health developed suddenly and forced her to give up the stage. She turned to literature and became a frequent contributor to magazines. She published a long dramatic poem, *"Vivia Perpetua,"* on the sufferings of the martyrs of early Christian Centuries. She is remembered, however, chiefly as the author of one hymn, "Nearer, my God, to thee." Perhaps "the cross that raiseth me" may have been the closed door to her life ambition.

This hymn should be read or sung with the experience of Jacob at Bethel freshly in mind. As vivid and speedy as a modern motion picture play runs the story:—a crafty cunning which secures the birthright; a plot to deceive the blind old father; a blessing falsely obtained; an injured and revengeful brother; a shrewd mother in the background; a hurried flight from the brother's wrath; a lonely, desolate hillside; a bed on the ground, with a stone for a pillow. And then a dream! And in the morning a sense of awe, and a new name for the place of vision, "Bethel, The House of God."

So the hymn, starting with the cross "that raiseth me," goes through the darkness and the dream to the consciousness that even this difficult, hard way may be "steps unto heaven."

Omit any one of these stanzas, and the delicate web of thought is rudely broken. On through the fourth stanza, with its reference to the dedication of the "Memorial Stone," and its realization that even by our woes we may be lifted nearer to God, on goes the hymn to a triumphant climax.

Whether lifted by a cross, or in the midst of woes, or in soaring joy "cleaving the sky," the prayer and song of all of life must be "Nearer, my God, to thee, nearer to thee!"

Eventually twentieth-century singers of all nations join with this nineteenth-century English poet, and the Old Testament Hebrew hero in Jacob's important realization!

> "Surely the Lord is in this place. . . .
> This is none other than the house of God,
> And this is the gate of heaven."

❖

THE HYMN TUNE. Lowell Mason (1792–1872), composer of BETHANY, was born in Medfield, Massachusetts, and began his musical work there as a young man, leading the local church choir. For fifteen years he lived in Savannah, Georgia, working in a bank, and developing his musical leadership. His first collection of music, made during these years, was offered in vain to publishers in Boston and Philadelphia. It was finally published by the Handel and Haydn Society of Boston as the product of the Society, in 1822. It went through seventeen editions, fifty thousand copies being sold in thirty-five years. In 1827 he returned to Boston, becoming president of the Handel and Haydn Society, and Director of music in the Bowdoin Square Church. It was here that he began his work with the children, which later resulted in a grudging permission from the School Committee of Boston to try an experiment with one class of school children provided he did it at his own expense. So successful was the experiment that in 1838, under his direction, the teaching of music was introduced into all the schools of Boston. This was the beginning of Public School Music in America.

In 1855 Mr. Mason was honored with the degree of Doctor of

Music by the University of New York, the first award of that degree in this country. The MISSIONARY HYMN or HEBER for "From Greenland's Icy Mountains," was his first published hymn tune, 1823.

Concerning BETHANY, Dr. Benson says, "What started the hymn on its free course in America was the tune BETHANY, which Lowell Mason wrote for it and published in 1856. And when the hymn, set to this taking tune, appeared in 1859 in the wonderfully successful *Sabbath Hymn and Tune Book* of the professors of Andover Seminary, its general use became assured." Dr. Benson also affirms that Mr. Mason based it on "Oft in the Stilly Night."

Oft in the Stilly Night

JOHN STEVENSON

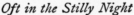

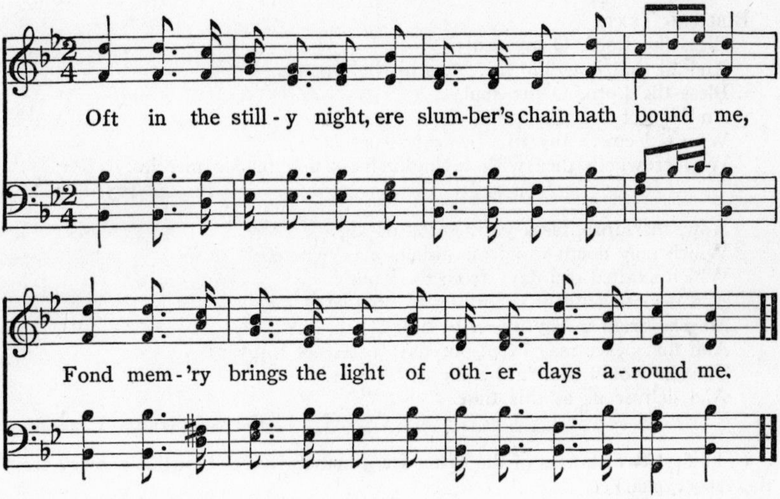
Oft in the still - y night, ere slum-ber's chain hath bound me,
Fond mem - 'ry brings the light of oth - er days a - round me.

NOW THANK WE ALL OUR GOD

1. Now thank we all our God,
With heart and hands and voices,
Who wondrous things hath done,
In whom his world rejoices;
Who, from our mothers' arms,
Hath blessed us on our way
With countless gifts of love,
And still is ours today.

2. O may this bounteous God,
Through all our life be near us,
With ever joyful hearts

And blessed peace to cheer us;
And keep us in his grace,
And guide us when perplexed,
And free us from all ills,
In this world and the next.

3. All praise and thanks to God,
The Father, now be given,
The Son and him who reigns
With them in highest heaven;
The one eternal God,
Whom earth and heaven adore;
For thus it was, is now,
And shall be evermore.

MARTIN RINKART, 1636,
Translated by Catherine Winkworth, 1858.

BIBLICAL TEXT.
Bless the Lord, O my soul;
And all that is within me, bless his holy name.
Bless the Lord, O my soul,
And forget not all his benefits.
Who redeemeth thy life from destruction;
Who crowneth thee with lovingkindness and tender mercies.

PSALM 103: 1, 2, 4.

Now, therefore, bless ye the God of all,
Which only doeth wondrous things everywhere,
Which exalted our days from the womb,
And dealeth with us according to his mercy.
May he grant us joyfulness of heart,
And that peace may be in our days in Israel forever:
That he would confirm his mercy with us,
And deliver us at this time.

ECCLESIASTICUS 1: 22–24.

(The first two stanzas of the hymn are a metrical version of this passage from the Apocrypha.)

THE "TE DEUM" OF GERMANY

Out of the horror and suffering, the struggle and turmoil, the conflict and pain of the "Thirty Years' War" comes this hymn of praise to a "Bounteous God."

Martin Rinkart (1586–1649), its author, was poet, musician, dramatist, scholar, patriot and faithful pastor. After his graduation from the University of Leipzig he became pastor of the Lutheran Church in his home town of Eilenberg, Saxony. There he served during all the strenuous days of the Thirty Years' War. Into that walled city swept the refugees from the surrounding country, with famine and plague at their heels. In the single year of 1637 as many as eight thousand people are said to have died of the fever in Eilenberg. Rinkart, the only pastor left in the town, buried four thousand people in one terrible year.

He surely evinced that "Faith that will not shrink, though pressed by every foe, that will not tremble on the brink of any earthly woe"; for this remarkable "Te Deum" was written in Eilenberg, either during or just after those days of suffering. It seems a strange background for such triumphant words as: "Who from our mothers' arms, hath blessed us on our way."

The hymn was published in 1647 and was first used as a grace at table. It is reckoned, next to *"Ein Feste Burg,"* the favorite hymn of the German people. Among the notable occasions on which it has been used are the completion of the great Cathedral of Cologne, in 1887, the Diamond Jubilee of Queen Victoria, in 1897, and the laying of the foundation-stone of the new Reichstag Building in Berlin by Emperor William I, 1884.

✣

The Hymn Tune. The tune, Nun Danket, is one of the noble German Chorales. It is found in the 1648 edition of Johann Cruger's *Praxis Pietatis Melica* ("Tunes of Devotion, Sweet as Honey"). This book was first issued in 1645 and went through sixty editions in one hundred years. Because of its presence in Cruger's book, the tune is often attributed to him, although Miss Winkworth, the translator of the hymn says: "This simple, but noble expression of trust and praise, with its fine chorale, was composed by Martin Rinkart in 1644 when the hope of a general peace was dawning on the country."

NOW THE DAY IS OVER

1. Now the day is over,
Night is drawing nigh;
Shadows of the evening
Steal across the sky.

2. Jesus, give the weary
Calm and sweet repose;
With thy tenderest blessing
May our eyelids close.

3. Grant to little children
Visions bright of thee;
Guard the sailors tossing
On the deep, blue sea.

4. Comfort every sufferer
Watching late in pain;
Those who plan some evil
From their sins restrain.

5. Through the long night watches
May thine angels spread
Their white wings above me,
Watching round my bed.

6. When the morning wakens,
Then may I arise
Pure, and fresh, and sinless
In thy holy eyes.

SABINE BARING-GOULD, 1865.

BIBLICAL TEXT.

In peace will I both lay me down and sleep;
For thou, Lord, alone makest me dwell in safety.

The "Evening Hymn," PSALM 4:8.

When thou liest down, thou shalt not be afraid;
Yea, thou shalt lie down, and thy sleep shall be sweet.

PROVERBS 3:24.

THE CHORUS OF CHILDREN'S SONG

Sabine Baring-Gould wrote this hymn for the children of England, even as he did that other famous hymn, "Onward, Christian Soldiers."

The one stanza in which the author "condescended" to write to the supposed level of children was speedily dropped and is now entirely forgotten:

"Now the darkness gathers,
Stars begin to peep,
Birds and beasts and flowers
Soon will be asleep."

True children's hymns, like Luther's "Cradle Song," Watts' "Hush, my dear, lie still and slumber," Wesley's "Gentle Jesus, meek and mild," and Alexander's "Jesus calls us, o'er the tumult," are more than children's hymns, although hymns for children only are rarely hymns for anybody.

The best hymns, if given a chance, quickly become favorites with the children. It is mistaken zeal that stamps on the early memory of children so-called "Children's Hymns," inane, foolish stuff which the growing child is ashamed to know and would be glad to forget.

Juvenile Song Through the Ages

From the monastic period, for the use of school children to assist them in learning their alphabet, comes this Criss-Cross Prayer:

Christie's Cross be my speed
In all virtue to proceed,
A b c d e f g h i j k l m n o p q r s and t
Double-u, v x with y ezod,
And per se con per se title title, Amen.
When you have done, begin againe, begin againe;
Christie's Cross be my speed
In all virtue to proceed.

The first noteworthy attempt at writing hymns for children dates back to 1715 and to Isaac Watts who dedicated to Sir Thomas Abney and his family, with whom he lived for thirty-seven years, his *Divine and Moral Songs for Children.* This collection reached enormous sales and sang itself into every corner of the globe.

"Let dogs delight to bark and bite,
For God hath made them so;
Let bears and lions growl and fight,
For 'tis their nature too."

"How doth the little busy bee
Improve each shining hour;
And gather honey all the day,
From ev'ry opening flower."

"'Tis the voice of sluggard; I heard him complain,
You have waked me too soon, I must slumber again;
As the door on its hinges, so he on his bed,
Turns his sides, and his shoulders, and his heavy head."

"Hush! my dear, lie still and slumber,
Holy angels guard thy bed;
Heavenly blessings, without number,
Gently falling on thy head."

Twenty years later John Wesley wrote: "There are two ways of writing or speaking to children: the one is to let ourselves down to them: the other to lift them up to us. Dr. Watts wrote in the former way, and has succeeded admirably well, speaking to children as children, and leaving them as he found them. The following hymns are written on the other plan; they contain strong and manly sense, yet expressed in such plain and easy language, as even children may understand. But when they do understand them, they will be children no longer, only in years and stature." After Watts follow the Charles Wesley hymns for children, among them, "Gentle Jesus, meek and mild." Note the number of hymns and carols that have been written primarily for children:

"Away in a Manger"
"Fairest Lord Jesus"
"Fling out the banner"
"I think when I read that sweet story"
"Jesus calls us o'er the tumult"
"My country, 'tis of thee"
"Now the day is over"
"Onward, Christian soldiers"
"O little town of Bethlehem"
"Saviour, like a Shepherd lead us."

THE HYMN TUNE. "Now the Day is Over" is charmingly interpreted by MERRIAL, by Joseph Barnby (1838–1896). The even flow of the melody and the low-pitched tones make it fitting for an evening prayer. Barnby attempted unusual things in music, and splendid evidence of his success is found here. The sun is just sinking out of sight, when there is a final flash of glory—a "sunburst"—and the tenor rises in bright suddenness on "Night is drawing nigh." The "Shadows of the evening" then "Steal across the sky," and the bass part accompanies the setting sun in a close procession of descending notes, down to its rest.

Barnby himself said, "I prefer to imitate the old writers in their independent method of working rather than in their works." He wished to write his tunes in a style that would be a natural expression of his feelings.

Baring-Gould himself wrote a hymn tune to go with his words: EUDOXIA, which is used in *Hymns Ancient and Modern* and other hymnals in preference to MERRIAL.

O BEAUTIFUL FOR SPACIOUS SKIES

1. O beautiful for spacious skies,
For amber waves of grain,
For purple mountain majesties
Above the fruited plain!
America! America!
God shed his grace on thee,
And crown thy good with brotherhood
From sea to shining sea.

2. O beautiful for pilgrim feet,
Whose stern, impassioned stress
A thoroughfare for freedom beat
Across the wilderness!
America! America!
God mend thine every flaw,
Confirm thy soul in self-control,
Thy liberty in law.

3. O beautiful for heroes proved
In liberating strife,
Who more than self their country loved,
And mercy more than life!
America! America!
May God thy gold refine,
Till all success be nobleness,
And every gain divine.

4. O beautiful for patriot dream
That sees beyond the years
Thine alabaster cities gleam,
Undimmed by human tears!
America! America!
God shed his grace on thee,
And crown thy good with brotherhood
From sea to shining sea![1]

KATHARINE LEE BATES, 1893, Revised, 1904.

BIBLICAL TEXT.

Walk about Zion, and go round about her;
Number the towers thereof;
Mark ye well her bulwarks;
Consider her palaces;
That ye may tell it to the generation following.
For this God is our God for ever and ever:
He will be our guide even unto death.

PSALM 48: 12, 13, 14.

A MOUNTAIN-TOP VISION OF AMERICA

One summer day in 1893 a company of teachers, mostly from Eastern colleges stood at the summit of Pike's Peak, Colorado, and "gazed in wordless rapture over the far expanse of mountain ranges and sea-like sweep of plain." So writes Katharine Lee Bates, who was one of that group of Eastern professors teaching in the new summer school at Colorado Springs. Fortunately for America, there was something more than "wordless rapture," for, Miss Bates continues, "It was then and there that the opening lines of 'America the Beautiful' sprang into being." That evening in Colorado Springs the hymn was written out.

Back of that day on Pike's Peak was Professor Bates' visit to the

[1] Copyright by the estate of Katharine Lee Bates.

Columbian Exposition, Chicago, with its fair "White City," set in gardens of beautiful green; her first journey to the West, and her first glimpse of the great, far-stretching fields of golden grain.

Miss Bates herself tells the story in a recent issue of the *Journal* of the National Education Association: "My friend took me to the great World's Fair, whose White City made such strong appeal to patriotic feeling that it was in no small degree responsible for at least the last stanza of 'America the Beautiful.' It was with this quickened and deepened sense of America that we went on, my New England eyes delighting in the wind-waved gold of the vast wheat-fields."

Thus, out of the first visit of this New England teacher and poet to the far-stretching plains and the "purple mountain majesties" of the West, there came the hymn which has already taken its place with "The Star-Spangled Banner" and "America," as one of our great national hymns. It unites, in a remarkably clear manner, the Pilgrim of 1620 with the pilgrims of later days who together made "a thoroughfare for freedom, across the wilderness." It glimpses the heroism and self-sacrifice of Civil War days. And it voices the "dream that sees beyond the years," and would make the temporary beauty of World's Fair buildings into true and permanent "alabaster cities" "undimmed by human tears."

Best of all, "America the Beautiful" is a true hymn, and has a rightful place in the hymnal, because it recognizes so clearly and emphasizes so fully, the fact that America alone and unaided cannot make this dream come true. It is only God who can "shed his grace" and "crown good with brotherhood." So the hymn is a prayer, a confession and a declaration of confidence in God's guidance.

A Correlated Poem

Miss Bates wrote a lyrical description of the impression made upon her by the Chicago World's Fair, of which the following stanzas are a significant commentary upon "America the Beautiful":

"For through all stress of the material strife,
The greed, the clash, the coarse, unlovely fashion,
America bears on to sweeter life
    And purer passion.
Oh, sting our souls with this diviner need
And, ere thou fadest, take our high decision
To make thy radiant dream immortal deed,
    Year of the Vision."

✤

THE HYMN TUNE. MATERNA, by Samuel Augustus Ward (1847–1903), was composed in 1882 for the hymn, "O Mother dear, Jerusalem." Hence its name MATERNA or "Mother." Ward was an American composer and conductor, residing at Newark, New Jersey, where he operated a successful music business and was for fourteen years the director of the Orpheus Club.

O BROTHER MAN, FOLD TO THY HEART THY BROTHER

1. O brother man, fold to thy heart thy brother;
Where pity dwells, the peace of God is there;
To worship rightly is to love each other,
Each smile a hymn, each kindly deed a prayer.

2. For he whom Jesus loved has truly spoken,
The holier worship which he deigns to bless
Restores the lost, and binds the spirit broken,
And feeds the widow and the fatherless.

3. Follow with reverent steps the great example
Of him whose holy work was "doing good";
So shall the wide earth seem our Father's temple,
Each loving life a psalm of gratitude.

4. Then shall all shackles fall; the stormy clangor
Of wild war music o'er the earth shall cease;
Love shall tread out the baleful fire of anger,
And in its ashes plant the tree of peace!

JOHN GREENLEAF WHITTIER, 1848.

BIBLICAL TEXT.

Pure religion and undefiled before our God and Father is this, to visit the fatherless and widows in their affliction, and to keep one's self unspotted from the world.

JAMES 1:27.

Verily I say unto you, Inasmuch as ye did it unto one of these, my brethren, even these least, ye did it unto me."

MATTHEW 25:40.

A POET'S DEFINITION OF WORSHIP

To appreciate this important hymn by the Quaker poet, Whittier, it is necessary to read the entire poem from which it is taken. Stanzas one, three, and four of the hymn are next to the end of the long poem entitled "Worship," written in the year that saw the end of the Mexican War, 1848, and stanza two comes about the middle of the poem.

John Greenleaf Whittier (1807–1892) was a Quaker by birth and rearing, but, as H. E. Scudder, editor of his *Complete Poetical Works,* says, "Whittier was not a Quaker in any conventional sense, but by birthright, conviction, and growing consciousness of communion with God."

This "consciousness of communion with God" is evident in this poem, "Worship," as he traces what are to him mistaken efforts to worship God.

Referring first to "Pagan myths and ghosts of old Beliefs," he speaks of the martyrs of the "Blind Faith" of those early days when human sacrifice was thought to be the supreme act of worship. He speaks of "red altars" beneath "the cruel eye of lawless Power and sanguinary Terror"; of how "Man's oblation was his fear and woe." Then, with genuine Quaker disregard of cathedral beauty as an aid to worship, he flays the "dismal moaning of dirge-like music and sepulchral prayer," the mocking hypocrisy of "feet red from war-fields" treading holy aisles, and the "oppressor there," to crush human hearts "beneath his knee of prayer." From that prelude he rises to heights of poetic fervor with the stanzas:

"As if the pomp of rituals, and the savor
Of gums and spices could the Unseen One please;
As if his ear could bend, with childish favor,
To the poor flattery of the organ keys!

Not such the service the benignant Father
Requireth at his earthly children's hands:
Not the poor offering of vain rites, but rather
The simple duty man from man demands."

It is a significant testimony to the prophetic element in Whittier's poetry, that in at least one modern hymnal, this hymn written in 1848 finds place alongside hymns of "Service and Brotherhood" written in 1906 and 1911.

This poem was written the year after Whittier accepted the position of Corresponding Editor of "The National Era," the organ of the American and Foreign Anti-Slavery Society, already famous in its first year as the vehicle for the publication of "Uncle Tom's Cabin."

Garrison, writing to Whittier in 1833, says: "The cause is worthy of Gabriel—yea, the God of hosts places himself at its head. Whittier, enlist. Your talent, zeal, influence—all are needed." In those days before the Civil War the Abolitionists were hailed as anarchists. The churches, colleges and courts were against them. Whittier's keen un-

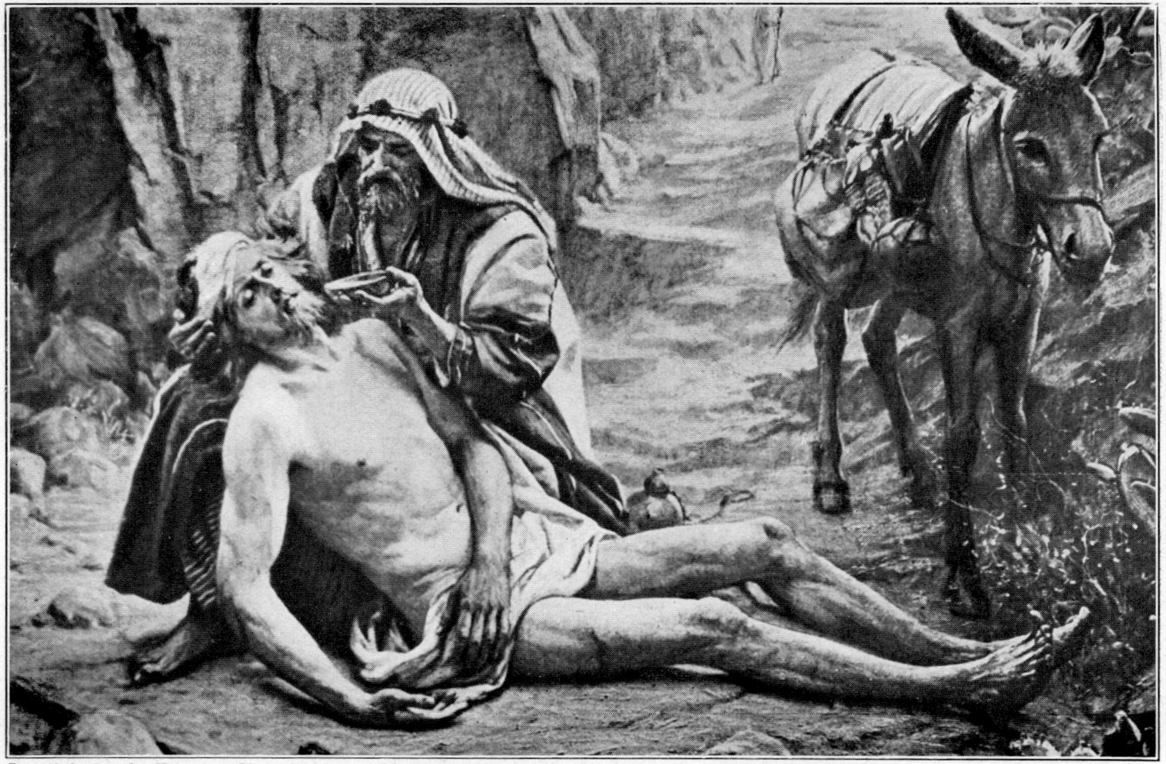

THE GOOD SAMARITAN

"Where Pity dwells, the Love of God is there!"

derstanding of public opinion showed him perfectly what company he was to keep. To be an active Abolitionist was to join the outcasts. Poverty, chastity and obedience were his portion in this life. By the road of renunciation he entered into his spiritual freedom.

✣

THE HYMN TUNE. It seems that the ideal tune for this hymn has not yet been found, as various tunes are in use with it, hardly one of them being the choice of two editors.

WINDSOR, by Joseph Barnby (1838–1896), which is used for Harriet Beecher Stowe's words, "Still, still with thee," is equally appropriate for Whittier's. Joseph Barnby was trained at the Royal Academy, London, and was for forty years one of England's leading organists and conductors. In addition to serving as organist in several churches, he was adviser for the publishing house of Novello; was the first conductor of the London Musical Society (1878–1866); precentor at Eton; and, from 1892, head of the Guildhall School of Music, London. He was knighted in 1892. Among his compositions, in addition to a number of hymn-tunes, were a large number of services, anthems, part-songs, and the cantata "Rebekah."

Sir Joseph Barnby maintained that music is the servant of religion and that its influence in helping the spiritual life is a first consideration. He wrote: "The evil of making the musical part of the service a means of counteracting the deficiencies of the rest, strikes at the very root of church morals. No one, I am sure, will suspect me of depreciating my art, or of holding music in anything but the highest honor. But for that very reason I should wish music to occupy its rightful place, and no other; nor can I see aught but disadvantage and ultimate failure in the attempt to make the musical part of the church service more than an accessory, to be regulated by the precept that enjoins the doing of all things connected with public worship 'decently and in order.'"

The hymn tune, STRENGTH AND STAY, by John Bacchus Dykes (1823–1876), was written in 1875 for a translation of St. Ambrose' hymn, "*Rerum Deus tenax Vigor*":

"O strength and stay, upholding all creation,
Whoever dost thyself unmoved abide,
Yet day by day the light in due gradation,
From hour to hour through all its changes guide."

O COME, ALL YE FAITHFUL

1. O come, all ye faithful, joyful and triumphant,
O come ye, O come ye to Bethlehem;
Come and behold him, born the King of angels:

Refrain

O come, let us adore him,
O come, let us adore him,
O come, let us adore him, Christ the Lord.

2. Sing, choirs of angels, sing in exultation,
O sing, all ye citizens of heaven above;
Glory to God, all glory in the highest:

Refrain

3. Yea, Lord, we greet thee, born this happy morning,
Jesus, to thee be all glory given;
Word of the Father, now in flesh appearing:

Refrain

LATIN HYMN, EIGHTEENTH CENTURY,
Translated by Frederick Oakeley, 1841.

BIBLICAL TEXT.

Let us now go even unto Bethlehem.

And the shepherds returned, glorifying and praising God for all the things that they had heard and seen, even as it was spoken unto them.

LUKE 2:15, 20.

In the beginning was the Word, and the Word was with God, and the Word was God. . . . And the Word became flesh, and dwelt among us (and we beheld his glory, glory as of the only begotten from the Father) full of grace and truth.

JOHN 1:1, 14.

THITHER BEND YOUR JOYFUL FOOTSTEPS

"Adeste Fideles" was written by an unknown hymnist of France in the early part of the eighteenth century, probably in the private chapel of some wealthy Roman Catholic family. The first publication of this hymn was in a collection by John Francis Wade, priest of a private chapel in Lancashire, entitled *"Cantus Diversi pro Dominicis et Festis per annum."* This was in 1751, and the hymn was in Latin. Over forty different English translations have been made. That in most common use is by Frederick Oakley (1802–1880), and was made in 1841. Canon Oakley was educated at Christ Church, Oxford, winning special honors in Latin. While at Oxford he was actively interested in the Tractarian Movement, with John Keble, John Henry

Newman, Frederick William Faber and others. After serving in the Church of England for nineteen years, he followed his friends Newman and Faber into the priesthood of the Roman Catholic Church, and became a canon of the district of Westminster in 1852.

(Omitted Stanzas)

"See how the shepherds, summoned to his cradle,
Leaving their flocks, draw nigh with lowly fear;
We too will thither bend our joyful footsteps:

"Lo, star-led chieftains, Magi, Christ adoring,
Offer his incense, gold, and myrrh;
We to the Christ Child bring our hearts' oblations:

"Child, for us sinners poor and in a manger,
Fain would we embrace thee, with awe and love;
Who would not love thee, loving us so dearly?"

Each in His Own Tongue

O Come All Ye Faithful in Latin:

Adeste, fideles, læti triumphantes;
Venite, venite in Bethlehem;
Natum videte regem angelorum:

Refrain

Venite, adoremus,
Venite, adoremus,
Venite, adoremus Dominum.

Cantet nunc Io! chorus angelorum;
Cantet nunc aula caelestium,
Gloria in excelsis Deo:

Refrain

Ergo qui natus die hodierna:
Jesu, tibi sit gloria,
Patris aeterni Verbum caro factum:

Refrain

A Christmas Carol in the German:

Stille Nacht, heilige Nacht!
Alles schläft, einsam wacht,
Nur das heilige Eltern-paar,
Das in Stalle zu Bethlehem war,
Bei dem himmlischen Kind,
Bei dem himmlischen Kind.

Stille Nacht, heilige Nacht!
Hirten erst kund gemacht;
Durch der Engel Halleluja
Tönt es laut von fern und nah:
Christ der Retter ist da,
Christ der Retter ist da.

Stille Nacht, heilige Nacht!
Gottes sohn, O wie lacht
Lieb aus deinem holdseligen Mund,
Da uns schlägt die rettende Stund,
Christ in deiner Geburt,
Christ in deiner Geburt.

JOSEPH MOHR, 1818.

A Christmas Carol in the French:

Un flambeau, Jeannette, Isabelle!
Un flambeau-Courons au berceau.
C'est Jésus, bonnes gens du hameau;
Le Christ est né, Marie appelle.
Ah! Ah! Ah! que la Mère est belle!
Ah! Ah! Ah! que l'Enfant est beau!

C'est un tort quand l'Enfant sommeille,
C'est un tort De crier si fort.
Taisez-vous, l'un et l'autre, d'abord!
Au moindre bruit, Jésus s'éveille.
Chut! Chut! Chut! il dort à merveille.
Chut! Chut! Chut! voyez comme il dort!

✣

THE HYMN TUNE. The earliest text and tune yet discovered is in a manuscript written in 1751 by John Wade, a priest who often acted as a music transcriber. At this time he was a pensioner in the house of Nicholas King in Lancashire, and he copied for his employer ADESTE FIDELES. It is concluded that the hymn and tune came into use together, being first used among the Roman Catholics in the early eighteenth century, at a period when many Catholic families had their own private chapels and the custom prevailed of priests going from house to house copying music for general use. In 1782 this tune appears in an Essay on the "Church Plain-Chant" for general use. The Duke of Leeds heard it sung at the Portuguese Chapel in London and immediately spread its fame as THE PORTUGUESE HYMN, arranged in its present form by Vincent Novello, organist at the Portuguese Chapel. It is an anonymous hymn coming from the eighteenth century Evening Office ("whilst the Benediction is offered, is sung ADESTE FIDELES") of the Catholic Church.

The natural structure of the hymn and tune suggests the following arrangement for the refrain:

First, "O come, let us adore him"—sopranos;
Second, "O come, let us adore him"—sopranos and alto;
Third, "O come, let us adore him"—all parts, ff.

O COME, O COME, EMMANUEL

1. O come, O come, Emmanuel,
And ransom captive Israel;
That mourns in lonely exile here,
Until the Son of God appear.

Refrain

Rejoice! Rejoice!
Emmanuel shall come to thee,
O Israel!

2. O come, thou Wisdom from on high,
And order all things, far and nigh;
To us the path of knowledge show,
And cause us in her ways to go.

Refrain

3. O come, Desire of Nations, bind
All peoples in one heart and mind;
Bid envy, strife and quarrels cease;
Fill the whole world with heaven's peace.

Refrain

Based on Ancient Latin Antiphons,
Translated by John M. Neale, 1851.
Henry S. Coffin, 1916.

Biblical Text.

And they shall call his name Emmanuel; which, being interpreted, is God with us.

Matthew 1:23.

Take counsel together, and it shall be brought to nought; speak the word, and it shall not stand: for God is with us.

Isaiah 8: 10.

PREPARING FOR CHRISTMAS IN THE NINTH CENTURY

By the ninth century the Catholic Church had begun singing the Greater Antiphons or short anthem-verses at Vespers from December seventeenth onwards; they were sung before and after the Magnificat. Five of the Seven original Antiphons are herewith reproduced, this being the full form and also the older form of "O come, O come, Emmanuel." They are strikingly poetical in thought and rich in Scripture allusions.

O come, O come, Emmanuel,
And ransom captive Israel,
That mourns in lonely exile here,
Until the Son of God appear.
Rejoice! Rejoice! Emmanuel
Shall come to thee, O Israel.

O Emmanuel, our king and lawgiver, the expectations of all nations and their Saviour: come and save us, O Lord, our God.

O come, thou Rod of Jesse, free
Thine own from Satan's tyranny;
From depths of hell thy peoples save,
And give them victory o'er the grave.
Rejoice! Rejoice! Emmanuel
Shall come to thee, O Israel.

O Root of Jesse, who standest as the ensign of the people, before whom kings shall not open their lips; to whom the Gentiles shall pray: come and deliver us, tarry now no more.

O come, thou Dayspring, from on high,
And cheer us by thy drawing nigh;
Disperse the gloomy clouds of night,
And death's dark shadows put to flight.
Rejoice! Rejoice! Emmanuel
Shall come to thee, O Israel.

O Orient Splendor of the Eternal Light, and Sun of Justice: come and enlighten them that sit in darkness and in the shadow of death.

O come, thou Key of David, come
And open wide our heavenly home;
Make safe the way that leads on high
And close the path of misery.
Rejoice! Rejoice! Emmanuel
Shall come to thee, O Israel.

O Key of David, and Scepter of the House of Israel; who openest, and no man shutteth; who shuttest, and no man openeth: come and lead the captive from the prison-house, and him that sitteth in darkness and in the shadow of death.

O come, Adonai, Lord of might,
Who to thy tribes, on Sinai's height,
In ancient time didst give the law
In cloud and majesty and awe.
Rejoice! Rejoice! Emmanuel
Shall come to thee, O Israel.

O Adonai, and Leader of the House of Israel, who didst appear unto Moses in the burning bush, and gavest him the Law on Sinai: come and redeem us by thy outstretched arm.

John Mason Neale (1818–1866) was a clergyman of the Church of England, but in spite of evident talent, he failed to gain preferment in that Church. In fact, he was at one time forbidden by the Bishop of Chichester to officiate in the churches of his diocese. He was feared as a Romanist in disguise, and at times severely persecuted. Twenty of the twenty-four years of his ministry were spent in the obscure post of Warden of "Sackville College," East Grinstead, which was not a college at all, but an almshouse, sheltering some thirty poor and aged householders. Here he received the munificent stipend of twenty-seven pounds per year.

It was during these years at East Grinstead that Neale did his life-work of translating many of the old Greek and Latin hymns into English. Julian calls his translations, "preëminent, unique, having an ear for melody which prevented him from spoiling rhythm by too servile imitation of originals, yet spirited and preserving spring and dash even in translations." [1]

Dr. Brownlie says of him: "His work was that of a discoverer and

[1] From the *Dictionary of Hymnology,* by John Julian, copyright by John Murray.

a scientist. Neale mapped the territory through which he passed, took the height of its mountains, traced its rivers, and sounded its lakes. Dr. Neale stands forth par excellence the interpreter of the praise literature of the early and the medieval church."

"In a patient study of the past, uniting a monk's love for an old missal to a scholar's evaluation of the treasures of antiquity, he unearthed and discovered jewels of great price—the crown jewels of the church." [2]

Dr. Neale's literary work was enormous and comes under four heads: Theological; Hymnological; Tales and Books for Children; Miscellaneous. Harvard College conferred on him the Degree of D.D. It is to Dr. Neale that we are indebted for "Jerusalem the Golden," "Christian, dost thou see them?" "The Day of Resurrection," "Come, ye faithful, raise the strain," "Art thou weary, art thou languid?" and many other gems of hymnody.

In the arrangement given above, the first stanza is Neale's translation; the other two are by Dr. Henry Sloane Coffin (1877–   ); the latter are more acceptable than Neale's in their greater freedom and spiritual kinship with the modern church.

THE HYMN TUNE. The tune, VENI, EMMANUEL, is an adaption of an ancient plain-song Kyrie of the thirteenth century. This tune, like the proverbial plain-song, does not follow the pretty curves of modern melodies, but what it lacks in grace it makes up in freedom and vigor. It is particularly suited for congregational use. It should be sung in unison and with great freedom of rhythm. The church would do well to cultivate this ecclesiastical song form.

O DAY OF REST AND GLADNESS

1. O day of rest and gladness,
O day of joy and light,
O balm of care and sadness,
Most beautiful, most bright;
On thee, the high and lowly,
Bending before the throne,
Sing Holy, holy, holy,
To the great God Triune.

2. On thee, at the creation,
The light first had its birth;

[2] From *Hymns and Hymn Writers of the Church Hymnary,* by John Brownlie, copyright by Henry Frowde.

On thee, for our salvation,
Christ rose from depths of earth;
On thee, our Lord, victorious,
The Spirit sent from heaven;
And thus on thee, most glorious,
A triple light was given.

3. Today on weary nations
The heavenly manna falls;
To holy convocations
The silver trumpet calls,
Where gospel light is glowing
With pure and radiant beams,
And living water flowing
With soul refreshing streams.

4. New graces ever gaining
From this our day of rest,
We reach the rest remaining
To spirits of the blest;
To Holy Ghost be praises,
To Father, and to Son;
The Church her voice upraises
To thee, blest Three in One.

CHRISTOPHER WORDSWORTH, 1862.

BIBLICAL TEXT.

This is the day which the Lord hath made;
We will rejoice and be glad in it.

PSALM 118:24.

There remaineth therefore a sabbath rest for the people of God.

HEBREWS 4:9.

A TRIUMPHANT SONG TO THE DAY OF REST

A triumphant burst of praise dedicated to the Day of Rest! It contains the hush of Sabbath peace, and at the same time lifts the soul of the singer to glad recognition of the "great God Triune." The emotional feeling it generates is not allowed to spread itself in useless repetition, but is concentrated into a single crystal-clear glorification of God's day. The Scripture content is superb—the Creation, the Resurrection, and the gift of the Holy Spirit.

Christopher Wordsworth (1807–1885) was an honor graduate of Trinity College, Cambridge, Headmaster of Harrow School, Canon of Westminster for nineteen years and Bishop of London for fifteen years. He was successful not only in scholarship but in athletics, gaining so many prizes and honors that he was known as "the Great Christopher." He did his most scholarly work while on duty nineteen years at a country charge which had the striking name of Stanfordin-the-Vale-cum-Goosey. He therefore belongs to that splendid line of English clergymen such as Herrick, Herbert, Vaughan, Heber, and Keble who, living in obscure country places, not only maintained a rich comeliness of life but made important contributions to the world's literature.

He was a nephew of the poet Wordsworth, and kept intimately in touch with him; this may account for his love of poetry, passionate but discriminating. He was a man of wide literary attainments, the author of *Pompeian Inscriptions, Greece, Pictorial and Descriptive,* a *Commentary on the Whole Bible,* and *The Holy Year,* a collection of hymns for the services of the Church.

Bishop Wordsworth held that the materials for Christian hymns should be sought in Scripture, in the writings of Christian antiquity and in the poetry of the Ancient Church. He wrote one hundred and twenty-seven hymns of which "O Day of Rest," and "O Lord of heaven and earth and sea," are practically the only survivals in our modern hymnals.

(Omitted Stanzas)

"Thou art a port protected
From storms that round us ride;
A garden intersected
With streams of Paradise.
Thou art a cooling fountain
In life's dry, dreary sand;
From thee, like Pisgah's mountain
We view the Promised Land.

"Thou art a holy ladder,
Where angels go and come;
Each Sunday finds us gladder,
Nearer to heaven our home.
A day of sweet refection
Thou art, a day of love,
A day of resurrection
From earth to things above."

✣

THE HYMN TUNE. MENDEBRAS is an arrangement by Lowell Mason from a German folk-song. Concerning these folk-songs, John Stuart Blackie says: "Many of these melodies, though used on convivial occasions, have a solemnity about them, in virtue of which they are well fitted for the service of the sanctuary."

The custom has always been of using secular melodies to foster a religious cause. It was natural to provide well-known tunes that people might heartily join in singing. Clement Marot used hunting and love songs of the Court of Francis I. Luther used secular tunes. The Wesleys did the same. The Salvation Army follows the vogue to-day.

David and other choristers used secular song to sacred Psalm as for example Psalm 8, "set to a vintage melody," Psalm 22 to the tune "Deer of the Dawn," Psalm 45 to the tune of "The Lilies—an ode or love song." The following tunes, in general church use to-day, once carried secular words: "POLAND" by Koschat carries the words "The Lord is my Shepherd," and not "Forsaken, forsaken"; LYNDE was once sung with "How can I leave thee?" but now it is "Thou art my Shepherd"; the "Londonderry Air" to many a secular text is increasingly coming into intimate association with such words as "O Son of man, our Hero strong and tender." The old "Passion Chorale" now indissolubly used with "O sacred head now wounded" was originally *"Mein G'müt ist mir verwirret."*

The alternative tune ROTTERDAM, by Berthold Tours (1838–1897), vies with AURELIA and the AUSTRIAN HYMN as a pure hymn-tune, singable, strong and inspiriting.

O JESUS, I HAVE PROMISED

1. O Jesus, I have promised
To serve thee to the end;
Be thou forever near me,
My Master and my Friend;
I shall not fear the battle
If thou art by my side,
Nor wander from the pathway,
If thou wilt be my Guide.

2. O let me feel thee near me,
The world is ever near;
I see the sights that dazzle,
The tempting sounds I hear:
My foes are ever near me,
Around me and within;
But, Jesus, draw thou nearer,
And shield my soul from sin.

3. O let me hear thee speaking
In accents clear and still;
Above the storms of passion,
The murmurs of self-will;
O speak to reassure me,
To hasten or control;
O speak, and make me listen,
Thou Guardian of my soul.

4. O Jesus, thou hast promised
To all who follow thee,
That where thou art in glory
There shall thy servant be;
And, Jesus, I have promised
To serve thee to the end;
O give me grace to follow,
My Master and my Friend.

JOHN E. BODE, 1868.

BIBLICAL TEXT.

Teacher, I will follow thee whithersoever thou goest.

MATTHEW 8:19.

If any man serve me, let him follow me; and where I am, there shall also my servant be.

JOHN 12:26.

If any man would come after me, let him deny himself, and take up his cross, and follow me.

MARK 8:34.

THE DEDICATION OF YOUTH TO CHRISTIAN SERVICE

John Ernest Bode (1816–1874) was born in London, educated at Eton, and Christ Church, Oxford. He was a Fellow and Tutor of Christ Church for six years, then rector of Westwell, Oxfordshire, and from 1860 to his death, rector of Castle Camps, Cambridgeshire. He delivered the Bampton Lectures at Oxford in 1855, and was the author of several volumes of hymns and other verse.

"O Jesus, I have promised" was written by Mr. Bode on the occasion of the confirmation of his daughter and two sons in his own church at Castle Camps, 1869. The original form of the hymn had six eight-line stanzas, the first of the following "Omitted Stanzas" appearing as stanza three, and the second as stanza six.

(Omitted Stanzas)

"O let me see thy features,
The look that once could make
So many a true disciple
Leave all things for thy sake;
The look that beamed on Peter
When he thy name denied;
The look that draws thy loved ones
Close to thy pierced side.

"O let me see thy foot-marks,
And in them plant mine own;
My hope to follow duly
Is in thy strength alone;
O guide me, call me, draw me,

Uphold me to the end;
And then in heaven receive me,
My Saviour and my Friend."

A Service of Dedication for Youth [1]

Leader:

"Christ wants the best! He in far-off ages
Once claimed the firstling of the flock, the finest of the wheat;
And still he asks his own with gentlest pleading
To lay their highest hopes and brightest talents at his feet.
Though he will not refuse the feeblest, humblest love,
He asks that of our stores we give to him the best we have."

Hymn (Tune—All Saints New):

"O Jesus, Prince of life and truth,
Beneath thy banner bright,
We dedicate our strength and youth
To battle for the right;
We give our lives with glad intent
To serve the world and thee,
To die, to suffer and be spent
To set our brothers free."

Youth's Commitment to Service:

We believe in the work to which Jesus Christ devoted his life. We desire to commit ourselves to the tasks which were to him of supreme importance: to preach the gospel to the poor; to bind up the broken-hearted; to set at liberty them that are bruised; to comfort those who mourn, to give them beauty for ashes, the garment of praise for the spirit of heaviness; that they may be called trees of righteousness, the planting of the Lord, that he may be glorified.

The vision lures us forth into the field of religious service, the place, for us, of all places most high and holy.

Hymn (Tune—All Saints New):

"In serried ranks, with fearless tread,
O Captain of us all,
Thy glory on our banners shed,
We answer to thy call;
And where the fiercest battles press

[1] *A Service of Dedication,* from the School of Religious Education and Social Service, Boston University.

Against the hosts of sin,
To rescue those in dire distress
We gladly enter in."

Leader:

Remember the words of the Lord Jesus:
Ye have not chosen me, but I have chosen you, and ordained you,
That ye should go and bring forth fruit, and that your fruit should remain;
That whatsoever ye shall ask of the Father in my name, he may give it you.

Choir (Tune—Elmhurst):

"Send thou, O Lord, to every place
Swift messengers before thy face,
The heralds of thy wondrous grace,
Where thou, thyself, wilt come.

Send men whose eyes have seen the King,
Men in whose ears his sweet words ring;
Send such thy lost ones home to bring;
Send them where thou wilt come."

Youth's Consecration:

"Send me, O Lord, I ask not how, or where,
To those who on this earth, called by thy name,
Have never found thee 'neath the grinding care
Of mine, or wood, or field, or furnace flame.
Lead me to those in south, or west, or north,
Who need thee most; the vision sends me forth;
I pledge my life to thee, to them, and here."

Hymn (Tune—All Saints New):

"O thou who dost the vision send,
And gives to each his task,
And with the task, sufficient strength,
Show us thy will, we ask;
Give us a conscience bold and good,
Give us a purpose true,
That it may be our highest joy,
Our Father's work to do."

✣

THE HYMN TUNE. ANGEL'S STORY is named from the first lines of a hymn by Emily Huntington Miller,

"I love to hear the story
Which angel voices tell."

It was written in 1881 by Arthur Henry Mann (1850–1929) who was born in Norwich, England, and was trained as a choir boy in the Cathedral of his native city by Dr. Zechariah Buck. His most distinguished service was performed as organist and choirmaster at King's College, Cambridge, famous for its superb choral music.

He was also music master of the Leys school there. He was an acknowledged authority on the music of Handel. He and Ebenezer Prout made the discovery in 1894 at the Foundling Hospital of the original wind parts of the Messiah. He edited the famous motet of Tallis for forty voices, and was musical editor of the Church of England hymnal.

O JESUS, THOU ART STANDING

1. O Jesus, thou art standing
Outside the fast-closed door,
In lowly patience waiting
To pass the threshold o'er;
Shame on us, Christian brothers,
His name and sign we bear,
O shame, thrice shame upon us,
To keep him standing there.

2. O Jesus, thou art knocking;
And lo! that hand is scarred,
And thorns thy brow encircle,
And tears thy face have marred;
O love that passeth knowledge,
So patiently to wait;
O sin that hath no equal,
So fast to bar the gate.

3. O Jesus, thou art pleading
In accents meek and low,
"I died for you, my children,
And will ye treat me so?"
O Lord, with shame and sorrow,
We open now the door;
Dear Saviour, enter, enter,
And leave us nevermore!

WILLIAM WALSHAM HOW, 1867.

Biblical Text.

Behold, I stand at the door and knock; if any man hear my voice and open the door, I will come in to him, and will sup with him, and he with me.

Revelation 3:20.

Jesus stood in the midst, and saith unto them, Peace be unto you. And . . . he showed unto them his hands and his side. The disciples therefore were glad, when they saw the Lord.

John 20:19, 20.

THE LIGHT OF THE WORLD

The island of Patmos, in the Ægean Sea, an English fishing village, the slums of East London, a Bishop's palace and an artist's studio would seem to have little or no connection. Yet it was the vision which came to John on Patmos and the words of the Risen Redeemer, "Behold, I stand at the door and knock," which inspired a sermon in an English fishing village. Jean Ingelow wove the sermon's message into a poem, "Brothers and a Sermon." To William Walsham How, then honorary Canon of St. Asaph's Cathedral, and later Suffragan Bishop of East London, came the poem. He says of it: "The pathos of the verses impressed me very forcibly at the time. I read them over and over again, and finally closing the book, I scribbled on an odd scrap of paper my first idea of the verses beginning, 'O Jesus, thou art standing.' I altered them a good deal subsequently, but I am fortunate in being able to say that after the hymn left my hands it was never revised or altered in any way."

This was in 1867. Thirteen years earlier William Holman Hunt, the artist, had painted a picture which he called "The Light of the World," suggested by this same message of the Risen Redeemer in John's vision. It is very likely that Bishop How had seen the original, and was acquainted with both the popular disapproval of it at first, and Ruskin's subsequent defense of the artist. "The Light of the World" produced the greatest effect of any religious painting of the century. "For the first time in England a picture became a subject of conversation and general interest from one end of the Island to the other."

Hunt's own words to his friend John Everett Millais at the beginning of his work on "The Light of the World" are illuminating: "There is a text in Revelation, 'Behold, I stand at the door and knock.' Nothing is said about the night, but I wish to accentuate the point of its meaning by making it the time of darkness, and that brings us to the need of the lantern in Christ's hand, He being the bearer of the light to the sinner within. I shall have a door choked up with weeds, to show that it has not been opened for a long time, and in the background there will be an orchard."

So Patmos and its vision, a village and a poem, the needs of the teeming millions of London and an artist's vivid picture, united to give to the Christian world one of her noblest hymns.

Bishop William Walsham How (1823–1879) was a "most unselfish, lovable man, with a tender fondness for children." Shepherd of Souls in teeming East London, his was a life of the ideal minister, whom Bishop How himself once characterized:

"A man pure, holy and spotless in life;
a man of much prayer;
in character meek, lowly and infinitely compassionate;
of tenderest love to all;
full of sympathy for every pain and sorrow, and devoting his days and nights to lightening the burdens of humanity;
utterly patient of insult and enmity;
ever ready to answer every call, to go wherever bidden, in order to do good;
wholly without thought of self;
making himself the servant of all;
patient, gentle, and untiring in dealing with the souls he would save;
bearing with ignorance, wilfulness, slowness, cowardice, in those of whom he expects most;
sacrificing all, even life itself, if need be, to save some."

Unlike many of our hymn-writers and religious leaders, How was not a brilliant student. His learning came with effort and he confesses to having been "nonplussed" by a science examination at Oxford. Perhaps this and other experiences made him sympathetic with those who plod along life's highway, the ordinary folk who lived in East London or East Anywhere. The words engraved upon his pastoral staff were those of St. Bernard, *"Pasce verbo, Pasce vita."* Bishop How's ambition was "not to be remembered, but to be helpful." He gave free use of his hymns to every one at all times. His was ample reward if he could enlarge the thanksgiving of the church or minister to the souls of men through song. His simple, direct, earnest, reverent hymns will never be forgotten:

"O Jesus, thou art standing"
"O Word of God incarnate"
"For all the saints who from their labors rest"
"We give thee but thine own"
"Summer suns are glowing"
"Behold the Master passeth by."

The year of Bishop How's birth, 1823, was also the natal year of this galaxy of hymn writers: James Drummond Burns, Cecil Frances

Alexander, Thomas Hughes, Henry Twells, Godfrey Thring, and Fanny Crosby.

A Lenten Meditation

(But equally appropriate at other seasons)

The Minister:

"And I saw in the midst of the candlesticks one like unto a son of man, clothed with a garment down to the foot, and girt about at the breasts with a golden girdle. And his head and his hair were white as white wool, white as snow; and his eyes were as a flame of fire; and his voice as the voice of many waters. And he said, 'Fear not, I am the first and the last and the Living One; and I was dead, and behold, I am alive forevermore, and I have the keys of death and of Hades.

" 'Behold, I stand at the door and knock; if any man hear my voice and open the door, I will come in to him, and will sup with him, and he with me.' "

REVELATION 1:13–15, 17–19; 3:20.

Solo (Contralto):

"O Jesus, thou art standing
Outside the fast-closed door,
In lowly patience waiting
To pass the threshold o'er":

Congregation:

"Shame on us, Christian brothers,
His name and sign we bear,
O shame, thrice shame upon us,
To keep him standing there."

Minister:

"Open the door with shame if ye have sinned;
If ye be sorry, open it with sighs.
Albeit the place be bare for poverty,
And comfortless for lack of plenishing
Be not abashed for that, but open it,
And take him in that comes to sup with thee:
'Behold,' he saith, 'I stand at the door and knock!' "

JEAN INGELOW.

Solo:

"O Jesus, thou art knocking;
And lo! that hand is scarred,
And thorns thy brow encircle,
And tears thy face have marred."

Congregation (singing):

"For God so loved the world, that he gave his only begotten Son, that whosoever believeth on him should not perish, but have eternal life."

Congregation (led by the Minister):

"O love that passeth knowledge,
So patiently to wait;
O sin that hath no equal,
So fast to bar the gate."

Minister:

"Speak then, O rich and strong;
Open, O happy young, ere the hand
Of him that knocks, wearied at last, forbear;
The patient foot its thankless quest refrain,
The wounded heart forevermore withdraw."

JEAN INGELOW.

Solo:

"O Jesus, thou art pleading
In accents meek and low,
'I died for you, my children,
And will ye treat me so?'"

Congregation:

"O Lord, with shame and sorrow,
We open now the door;
Dear Saviour, enter, enter,
And leave us nevermore!"

Correlation with Art

Among the pictures which may wisely be used with this hymn Holman Hunt's "Light of the World" is preëminent. Others leading up to this as a climax are:

Stanza One, first half: "Behold, I stand at the door," Overbeck.
Second half: "Christ Knocking at the door," Schönherr.

Stanza Two, first half: *"Ecce Homo,"* Guido Reni.
Second half: "Christ knocking at the door," Hofmann.
Stanza Three, first half: "Christ on Calvary," Munkacsy.
Second half: "Light of the World," Hunt.

❖

THE HYMN TUNE. ST. HILDA is an adaptation (1871) by Reverend Edward Husband (1843–1908) from a melody by Justin Heinrich Knecht (1752–1817), who was a musician of considerable importance in the eighteenth century. He was born at Biberach, Swabia, and early learned to play flute, oboe, trumpet, violin and the organ. He became Professor of Belles-lettres and director of music in his native town. He was called to Stuttgart at the age of fifty-five to conduct the court and theater orchestra there where he continued for ten years.

Reverend Edward Husband, amateur organist and composer, was Vicar of St. Michael's in Folkstone. He composed much vocal music and lectured widely on church music.

O LITTLE TOWN OF BETHLEHEM

1. O little town of Bethlehem,
How still we see thee lie!
Above thy deep and dreamless sleep
The silent stars go by;
Yet in thy dark streets shineth
The everlasting Light;
The hopes and fears of all the years
Are met in thee to-night.

2. For Christ is born of Mary,
And gathered all above,
While mortals sleep, the angels keep
Their watch of wondering love.
O morning stars, together
Proclaim the holy birth,
And praises sing to God the King,
And peace to men on earth!

3. How silently, how silently,
The wondrous gift is given!
So God imparts to human hearts
The blessings of his heaven.
No ear may hear his coming,
But in this world of sin,
Where meek souls will receive him, still
The dear Christ enters in.

4. O holy child of Bethlehem,
Descend to us, we pray;
Cast out our sin, and enter in;
Be born in us today.
We hear the Christmas angels
The great glad tidings tell;
O come to us, abide with us,
Our Lord Emmanuel!

PHILLIPS BROOKS, 1868.

BIBLICAL TEXT.

And they shall call his name Emmanuel; which is, being interpreted, God with us.

MATTHEW 1:23.

The people that walked in darkness have seen a great light; they that dwelt in the land of the shadow of death, upon them hath the light shined.

ISAIAH 9:2.

OUR LORD EMMANUEL

Phillips Brooks (1835–1893), prince among American preachers, has three most significant memorials. Two of them are to be found in the city of Boston! Trinity Church, with its active and far-reaching ministry in its splendid building, erected during Phillips Brooks' rectorship, and beside the building, close to the street "where cross the crowded ways of life," the second memorial, the famous St. Gaudens statue of Phillips Brooks. Behind the stalwart figure of the preacher stands the Christ, the preacher's inspiration. The third of the enduring memorials to Phillips Brooks is found everywhere. Wherever the Gospel of Christ has gone on the wings of song, wherever the Festival of the Christ-Child is observed, there is Phillips Brooks remembered, there hearts are lifted on the wings of his deathless words in praise of "Our Lord Emmanuel."

The building may some day be torn down to make room for a still larger and more beautiful church; the statue may be removed, and forgotten, even by lovers of art; but the song will continue to be sung each Christmas in an ever-increasing number of churches and homes, and around Community Christmas Trees, as one of the Church's finest tributes of praise to God for the wonderful gift so silently given in the "Little Town of Bethlehem."

Phillips Brooks (1835–1893) was born in Boston, graduated from Harvard and from the Alexandria Seminary, in Virginia. He served as rector at the Church of the Holy Trinity, Philadelphia, and later at Trinity Church, Boston. He came to Trinity at a time when Boston was the center of the Unitarian movement. Many who were turning from the austere preaching of the Evangelicals of that day listened to Phillips Brooks with delight. The Evangelical faith came to have secure status once more in Boston.

Something of the remarkable power of Brooks as a preacher and a Christian may be gathered from the tributes paid: "I have never heard preaching like it, and you know how slow I am to praise preachers. So much thought and so much life combined, so much reach of mind and such depth of insight and soul: I was electrified. I could have got up and shouted." Phillips Brooks' life and ministry centered in Jesus Christ. Boston-born, Harvard-trained, giant in mind and heart, he commanded attention and dared to preach Jesus Christ; not Christ the wrathful judge, sweeping sinners to hell, but Christ altogether lovely. Here it is in this carol:

"The earth has grown old with its burden of care,
But at Christmas it always is young,
The heart of the jewel burns lustrous and fair,
And its soul full of music breaks forth on the air,
When the song of the Angels is sung.

"It is coming, old earth, it is coming to-night,
On the snowflakes which cover thy sod,
The feet of the Christ child fall gently and white,
And the voice of the Christ child tells out with delight
That mankind are the children of God.

"On the sad and the lonely, the wretched and poor,
That voice of the Christ child shall fall;
And to every blind wanderer opens the door
Of a hope which he dared not to dream of before,
With a sunshine of welcome for all.

"The feet of the humblest may walk in the field
Where the feet of the holiest have trod,
This, this is the marvel of mortals revealed,
When the silvery trumpets of Christmas have pealed,
That mankind are the children of God."

The boy Phillips came up through a musical home where memorizing and reciting hymns was the order of the day. He had committed to memory two hundred hymns up to his college years. The Brooks household knew when Phillips was up in the morning, because he was always singing and humming tunes.

On his voyage to Japan in 1889 he wrote some of his best carols, this Easter one for example:

"Tomb, thou shalt not hold him longer;
Death is strong, but Life is stronger;

Stronger than the dark the light;
Stronger than the wrong, the right.
Faith and Hope triumphant say,
Christ will rise on Easter Day."

Phillips Brooks had no real home of his own, so he loved the children of others with a very tender love, especially those of his brother, William. Romps were always expected with this six-foot-four prince among men. Several dolls were kept at the rectory for the entertainment of the young. Writing to his Sunday-school children in Philadelphia he says: "I do not mind telling you (though of course I should not like to have you speak of it to any of the older people of the church) that I am much afraid the younger part of my congregation has more than its share of my thoughts and interest. I cannot tell you how many Sunday mornings since I left you I have seemed to stand in the midst of our crowded classroom again, and look about and know every face and every class just as I used to." It is in this and other carols that he shows his love for children and skill in immediate and winsome address to them. Many of his letters, written abroad, were addressed to his brother's children.

"Everywhere, everywhere, Christmas to-night!
Christmas in lands of the fir tree and pine,
Christmas in lands of the palm tree and vine,
Christmas where snow peaks stand solemn and white,
Christmas where cornfields lie sunny and bright:

"Christmas where children are hopeful and gay,
Christmas where old men are patient and gray,
Christmas, where peace, like a dove in his flight,
Broods o'er brave men, in the thick of the fight;
Everywhere, everywhere, Christmas to-night:
For the Christ-child who comes is the Master of all;
No palace too great and no cottage too small:

"Then let every heart keep its Christmas within,
Christ's pity for sorrow, Christ's hatred of sin,
Christ's care for the weakest, Christ's courage for right,
Christ's dread of the darkness, Christ's love of the light;
Everywhere, everywhere, Christmas to-night."

While Rector in Philadelphia Phillips Brooks was given a year's leave of absence to tour Europe and the Near East. Writing home, Christmas week of 1865, he says: "After an early dinner, we took our horses and rode to Bethlehem. It was only about two hours when we came to the town, situated on an Eastern ridge of a range of hills, surrounded by its terraced gardens. Before dark, we rode out of town to the field where they say the shepherds saw the star. It is a fenced piece of ground with a cave in it, in which, strangely enough, they put the shepherds. The story is absurd, but somewhere in those fields we rode through the shepherds must have been. As we passed, the shepherds were still 'keeping watch over their flocks,' or 'leading them home to fold.'" Two years later at the age of thirty-two Phillips Brooks wrote the carol, which was at once used in the Christmas service of his Sunday School, in Philadelphia.

THE HYMN TUNE. ST. LOUIS was written by Lewis Redner (1831–1908), organist of the church, superintendent of the Sunday School, and teacher of one of the classes. As Christmas approached the rector told his organist he had written a simple carol for which he (Redner) was asked to write the tune. It was done in great haste on Saturday night before Christmas. Redner was aroused from sleep by a melody which chimed in his heart. He wrote it down (the melody of ST. LOUIS) and in the morning he filled in the harmony. For over twenty years it remained a stranger to hymnals, congregations, Christmas carol services. About 1890 it came into use and since then it has swept over the world.

O LOVE THAT WILT NOT LET ME GO

1. O Love that wilt not let me go,
I rest my weary soul in thee;
I give thee back the life I owe,
That in thine ocean depths its flow
May richer, fuller be.

2. O Light that followest all my way,
I yield my flickering torch to thee;
My heart restores its borrowed ray,
That in thy sunshine's blaze its day
May brighter, fairer be.

3. O Joy that seekest me through pain,
I cannot close my heart to thee;
I trace the rainbow through the rain,
And feel the promise is not vain
That morn shall tearless be.

4. O Cross that liftest up my head,
I dare not ask to fly from thee;
I lay in dust life's glory dead,
And from the ground there blossoms red
Life that shall endless be.[1]

GEORGE MATHESON, 1882.

[1] Copyright by Novello & Co., Ltd.

BIBLICAL TEXT.

When Israel was a child, then I loved him, and called my son out of Egypt. I taught Ephraim to walk; I took them on my arms; but they knew not that I healed them. I drew them with bands of love; how shall I give thee up, Ephraim? How shall I cast thee off, Israel?

HOSEA 11: 1, 3, 4, 8.

I am persuaded, that neither death, nor life, . . . nor height, nor depth, nor any other creature, shall be able to separate us from the love of God, which is in Christ Jesus our Lord.

ROMANS 8: 38, 39.

THE FRUIT OF PAIN

This is the phrase by which the author himself describes this hymn. Fortunately Dr. Matheson's own account of the writing of this world-famous hymn is available. "My hymn was composed in the manse of Innellan, on the evening of June 6, 1882. I was at that time alone. It was the day of my sister's marriage, and the rest of the family were staying over night in Glasgow. Something had happened to me, which was known only to myself, and which caused me the most severe mental suffering. The hymn was the fruit of that suffering. It was the quickest bit of work I ever did in my life. I had the impression rather of having it dictated to me by some inward voice than of working it out myself. I am quite sure that the whole work was completed in five minutes, and equally sure that it never received at my hands any retouching or correction."

He also describes its writing as "a unique experience," and modestly says, "I have no natural gift of rhythm. All the other verses I have written are manufactured articles; this came like a dayspring from on high. I have never been able to gain once more the same fervor in verse."

George Matheson (1842–1906) was one of Scotland's outstanding preachers, and one of the world's greatest devotional writers. In spite of the fact that he became totally blind soon after he entered the University of Glasgow, he graduated at nineteen, and entered the ministry of the Church of Scotland in 1866. His first parish was Innellan, on the Firth of the Clyde. Here he remained for eighteen years, winning all hearts by his attractive personality and constantly growing in power as a preacher. While pastor here, he had once the high honor of being summoned to preach at Balmoral before Queen Victoria. She expressed herself as "immensely delighted with the sermon and the prayers" and presented Matheson with a small bust of herself.

At the age of forty-four, in the height of his powers, he was called to St. Bernard's Parish Church in Edinburgh. Here he reached the zenith of his power and influence. Great crowds attended his services. Here also he wrote some of his famous theological works.

The closing years of his life were spent in retirement, and in the writing of books which are among the richest treasures of the world's devotional literature, notably *Rests by the River, Searchings in the Silence,* and *Moments on the Mount.*

Dr. Charles Parkhurst, one of New York's famous preachers of the last generation, said of Dr. Matheson, after hearing him preach in St. Bernard's: "Announcing a Psalm, he takes his verses without the mistake of a word, and throughout the service, calling for several hymns and Scripture references with chapter and verse, he never made an error. Then he prays, and such a prayer! It seems profane to write about it. Though his sight is eclipsed, he does see God, he does see into the hearts of his people. For forty minutes he preached. We were instructed, refreshed, inspired."

A supreme expression of Christian renunciation and hope, this hymn has as its major theme the Parable of the Lost Sheep and of the Lost Coin—the pursuit of the human soul by the Spirit of God (Francis Thompson's *The Hound of Heaven* is an eloquent elaboration of the idea). It is a hymn of sorrow; but the ascription of Deity, like that of the early Greek Hymns, is "Love," "Light," "Joy." It portrays the ever-seeking spirit "That wilt not let me go," and the soul in its Godlike quality of being free to evade or to receive the Love, the Light, the Joy, the Cross. The soul in the hymn is like the lost sheep, heartily ready to be found.

This hymn is the autobiography of a rare soul. Written twenty years after the author went blind, and not immediately after his rejection by his fiancée because of that misfortune, it chronicles a life time of enduring pain rather than the sudden, poignant, sentimental suffering of the current legend. But even in the midst of blindness, loneliness and suffering, Matheson could and did conceive of God as the Love that clings, the Light that "followest *all* my way," the truest Joy that brings rainbows through the rain, and, best of all, Life, "the sacrificial life which blossoms by shedding itself." He is said to have remarked in this connection, "White is the blossom of prosperity, red of self-sacrificing love."

✣

THE HYMN TUNE. The tune, like the words, seems to have had an unusual origin. The story of it is that Dr. Albert Lister Peace (1844–

1912), then organist of Glasgow Cathedral and musical editor of *The Scottish Hymnal of 1885,* used to carry about with him the words of hymns for which tunes were needed, and record the tune as the melody came to him. Sitting one day on the sands of Arran, an island off the coast of Scotland, he read over the words of Dr. Matheson's hymn. Instantly the music came to him. The transcription of the tune, like the writing of the words, took only a few minutes.

Albert L. Peace developed musical ability very early; at the age of nine he was playing a church organ. He was born in Huddersfield, England, but spent much of his life in Scotland. He was only thirty-five years old when called to be organist of the Cathedral, Glasgow, a position which he held for sixteen years, and from which he went to St. George's Hall, Liverpool. He received the degree of Mus.D. from Oxford in 1875. He composed the cantata of St. John the Baptist, three organ-sonatas, and many other musical works.

O MASTER, LET ME WALK WITH THEE

1. O Master, let me walk with thee
In lowly paths of service free;
Tell me thy secret; help me bear
The strain of toil, the fret of care.

2. Help me the slow of heart to move
By some clear, winning word of love;
Teach me the wayward feet to stay,
And guide them in the homeward way.

3. Teach me thy patience; still with thee
In closer, dearer company,
In work that keeps faith sweet and strong,
In trust that triumphs over wrong.

4. In hope that sends a shining ray
Far down the future's broadening way;
In peace that only thou canst give,
With thee, O Master, let me live.

WASHINGTON GLADDEN, 1879.

BIBLICAL TEXT.

Have this mind in you, which was also in Christ Jesus: who, existing in the form of God, counted not the being on an equality with God a thing to be grasped, but emptied himself, taking the form of a servant, being made in the likeness of men; and being found in fashion as a man, he humbled himself, becoming obedient even unto death, yea, the death of the cross.

PHILIPPIANS 2: 5–8.

WALKING WITH GOD

Washington Gladden (1836–1918) was born at Pottsgrove, Pennsylvania, and reared on a farm. He studied at Oswego Academy where he learned the printers' trade. He went to Williams College, graduating in 1859. He was ordained to the Congregational ministry in 1860, and held pastorates successively at Brooklyn and Morrisania, N. Y., and at North Adams and Springfield, Massachusetts. He was an editor of the *Independent* for four years. While at Springfield he edited a paper, *Sunday Afternoon*. He was pastor for thirty-two years in Columbus, Ohio. He was a great believer in his country and its democratic institutions and was a leader in the awakening of a new social conscience, and in the Church's movements for social service.

The above hymn was written in 1879 for the devotional section of his *Sunday Afternoon,* called "The Still Hour." He said of it, "It had no liturgical purpose and no theological significance, but it was an honest cry of human need, of the need of divine companionship." It was published in Charles H. Richards' *Songs of Praise* (1880), the following stanza, the second, being omitted.

"O Master, let me walk with thee
Before the taunting Pharisee;
Help me to bear the sting of spite,
The hate of men who hide the light,
The sore distress of souls sincere
Who cannot read thy judgments clear,
The dulness of the multitude
Who dimly guess that thou art good."

This hymn reflects very clearly the conflicts of the days in which the author wrote and the life of Dr. Gladden himself. The first two four-line stanzas, while an ideal expression of the normal Christian life, nevertheless reveal his sense of responsibility as pastor. And the present-day emphasis on service is there; this is no hymn of a monk in his cell, but of a man at grips with the problems of life. The first eight lines may be paraphrased in prose: Master, may I learn to serve in comradeship with thee; teach me how to endure hard work and responsibility. Help me to speak in clearness and love that I may win the irresponsive ones. Show me how to hold the straying and turn them back to thee. The omitted eight lines seem to reveal something of the sore trials that must have been his as he bravely faced truth and duty in an age of changing standards, when his interest in the social and labor problems might win him scorn and distrust from vested interests and such as are always fearful of change, and when his revised and open thinking on religious problems would bring upon him the open attacks of some of his brother ministers and the fearful misunderstanding of many who, though vague in their understanding of God, felt that he was undermining all. Master, help me in thy spirit to bear the taunts of the self-righteous, the bitterness and hate of those who will not or dare not face new truth, the fearful distrust of me in those who do not understand, the slowness of the many who but vaguely reach out to God. In the last eight lines he comes back to a warm expression of faith and comradeship with the Master: Teach me like thee to be patient, working in a trustful comradeship with thee that wins against all evil. Lord, may I ever live in this fellowship with thee, strong in a hope that lights the unknown future, and in such peace as comes only from thee.

There is a danger that this hymn may be spoiled, or at least robbed of some of its deeper meaning, by over-use or use at wrong times. The section of *Sunday Afternoon* in which it was published was a devotional column called "The Still Hour." This very fact is a hint as to the place and time where the hymn should be used. To sing it at times of large crowds and volatile enthusiasms is seriously to misinterpret its purpose and mar its meaning. It is distinctively a prayer hymn (and, as such, should always be concluded with the Amen) and a prayer of dedication to service. It is admirably adapted to moments of quiet consecration, when the congregation or the group is in the hushed, reverent mood of prayer and dedication.

✣

THE HYMN TUNE. MARYTON or SUN OF MY SOUL, the tune to which Dr. Gladden preferred that his hymn be set, was composed by Canon Henry Percy Smith (1825–1898) for the hymn, "Sun of my Soul." It was first published in *Church Hymns with Tunes,* in 1874. The quiet earnest measure of MARYTON makes a beautiful devotional response for a social prayer.

The composer, Henry Percy Smith, was not a famous musician, but a clergyman of the Church of England. He served for two years as curate at Eversley, under Charles Kingsley. He was Canon of Gibraltar from 1892 to his death.

O MASTER WORKMAN OF THE RACE

1. O Master workman of the race,
Thou man of Galilee,

Who with the eyes of early youth
Eternal things did see;
We thank thee for thy boyhood faith
That shone thy whole life through;
"Did ye not know it is my work
My Father's work to do?"

2. O Carpenter of Nazareth,
Builder of life divine,
Who shapest man to God's own law,
Thyself the fair design;
Build us a tower of Christlike height,
That we the land may view,
And see like thee our noblest work
Our Father's work to do.

3. O thou who dost the vision send
And gives to each his task,
And with the task sufficient strength,
Show us thy will, we ask;
Give us a conscience bold and good,
Give us a purpose true,
That it may be our highest joy,
Our Father's work to do.[1]

JAY THOMAS STOCKING, 1912.

BIBLICAL TEXT.

And they found him in the temple, sitting in the midst of the teachers, both hearing them, and asking them questions.

And his mother said unto him, Son, why hast thou thus dealt with us? Behold, thy father and I sought thee sorrowing. And he said unto them: How is it that ye sought me? knew ye not that I must be in my Father's house?

And Jesus advanced in wisdom and stature, and in favor with God and man.

LUKE 2:46, 48, 49, 52.

A HYMN OF BOYHOOD FAITH AND MANHOOD WORK

This hymn carries one back to Jerusalem and its Temple, to Nazareth and a carpenter shop, but it does not leave us there. Vividly and beautifully it gives us reverent glimpses of the Boy in the temple, sitting among the teachers with shining eyes; of the Youth and the Man at work at the homely tasks of the carpenter shop. But, with equal reverence and startling vividness, it brings one back from his journey to these far places to his own home and his own tasks in the challenging life of the present. And there it makes him see that, like the Boy and the Carpenter of old, it is the noblest work, our Father's will to do.

Jay Thomas Stocking (1870–   ) is a prominent Congregational

[1] Copyright by The Pilgrim Press.

clergyman. After graduation from Amherst in 1895 he taught English in Lawrenceville School, took his theological course at Yale Divinity School, studied in the University of Berlin; served churches in Bellows Falls, Vermont, in Newtonville, Massachusetts, in Washington, D. C., in Upper Montclair, New Jersey, and since 1927 he has been pastor of the Pilgrim Congregational Church, St. Louis, Missouri. He is the author of *The Dearest Spot on Earth, The City That Never Was Reached,* and *The Golden Goblet.* He has been a leader on the missionary boards of his denomination, has served on the Committee on International Justice and Good-Will of the Federal Council of Churches, and is a member of the Executive Committee of the American Peace Society.

A Tragedy in the Boyhood of Jesus

The Home-Coming

The Roman net grips land and sea,
Roman hearts are stones,
And on many a hill of Galilee
Shudders the bitter felon tree,
Whose fruit cries out and moans.

"Get forth the supper," bade Joseph;
"Is not the day far spent?"
Weary he came from his workshop,
His heavy shoulders bent.

One daughter spread the rich-hued mat
And brought the wooden tray;
Another poured water on his hands
From a cruse of tawny clay;

Another fetched the stoup of wine
And the thin round cakes of bread,
The dish of herbs and the cheeses,
And after the prayer was said

James and Joses and Simon
Around the tray with him
Sat on the floor like Arabs,
While Juda ran to trim

The lamp and see that the floating
Wick on the oil burned clean,
For he might not sit with the men-folk
Till his years had touched thirteen.

But our Lady Mary tarried,
Leaning out over the sill

Of the door till she heard the steps she loved
Climbing Nazareth hill.

"Welcome, my Ever-Truant,
My Slip-away-under-the-stars.
Have you brought me fresh rose-laurel
For the mouths of our water-jars?"

But the face of the world's desire,
Was pale as a poplar leaf;
The young face framed in the open door
Was wan and wild as never before,
A face acquainted with grief.

"You are long away," quoth Joseph,
But his tone might not condemn
The firstborn son of his household,
Remembering Bethlehem;

"We have labored from dawn to even
With many a fruitless wish
For our master-servant, yet sit at board
And dip your hand in the dish."

Still Jesus stood in the doorway,
His eyes dark pools of pain;
Muffled in purple cloak, he seemed
The shadow of a dream that dreamed
Divinely and in vain.

His sisters drew off his sandals
And washed and dried his feet,
While his touch on their bowed heads blessed them
For their service deft and sweet.

"There is blood on his sleeve," cried Simon,
But Joses laughed: "Such flings
The knife when it cuts a creature's throat.
He has chanced on the slaying of sheep or goat,
He who sickens at common things."

"Nay," chided James, uprising,
Leal Brother of our Lord;
"He has met the men of Herod the Fox,
Hunting the rebels from out their rocks.
Of Galilee under the sword."

"Have they hurt you?" sobbed little Juda,
"Hurt you whom the smallest bird
Will not flutter away from?" But Jesus
Answered never a word.

How could Love find speech for the horror
No beauty should henceforth hide?
How could Pity forevermore forget

Those feet he had kissed, still red and wet,
Of a young Jew crucified? [2]

✣

THE HYMN TUNE. Dr. Stocking's hymn is usually set to either AMESBURY, by Uzziah Christopher Burnap; or to MATERNA, by Samuel Ward. The latter is, of course, the more familiar, owing to its constant use with "America the Beautiful." (See that hymn.)

U. C. Burnap (1834–1900) was an American organist, a resident of Brooklyn, New York.

O SACRED HEAD, NOW WOUNDED

1. O sacred Head, now wounded,
With grief and shame weighed down,
Now scornfully surrounded
With thorns, thy only crown;
How art thou pale with anguish,
With sore abuse and scorn;
How does that visage languish,
Which once was bright as morn!

2. What language shall I borrow
To thank thee, dearest Friend,
For this, thy dying sorrow,
Thy pity without end?
O make me thine forever;
And should I fainting be,
Lord, let me never, never,
Outlive my love to thee.

3. Be near when I am dying,
O show thy cross to me;
And for my succor flying,
Come, Lord, and set me free.
These eyes, new faith receiving,
From Jesus shall not move,
For he who dies believing,
Dies safely through thy love.

BERNARD OF CLAIRVAUX (1091–1153),
or ARNULF VON LOEWEN (1200–1250).
Translated into German by Paul Gerhardt, 1656.
Translated into English by James Waddell Alexander, 1830.

BIBLICAL TEXT.

And platting a crown of thorns, they put it on him; and they began to salute him, Hail, King of the Jews! And they smote his head with a reed,

[2] From *The Pilgrim Ship,* by Katharine Lee Bates, copyright by The Woman's Press.

and spat upon him, and bowing their knees worshipped him. And when they had mocked him . . . they led him out to crucify him.

MARK 15: 17–20.

THE VALE OF WORMWOOD BECOMES THE VALLEY OF LIGHT

The story of the life of Bernard of Clairvaux (1091–1153) is one of the thrilling romances of the history of the Medieval Church. Nothing sums it up quite so significantly as the change in the name of the valley in which he established his monastery in 1112. He and the eleven monks associated with him in the project, built their abbey in a valley whose name meant "Wormwood"—bitter; but so remarkable was Bernard's leadership, and so spiritual his life, that soon there were one hundred and twenty monks, and the name of the valley was changed to "Clairvaux," Valley of Light.

Those were stirring times in Europe. Bernard was only a boy when Peter the Hermit preached his *"Deus Vult!"* and aroused all Europe to the enthusiasm of the First Crusade. Bernard himself sounded forth the summons to kings and emperors, to princes and knights, to join in the Second Crusade. In all the turmoil and upheaval of those critical years Bernard stood out as the man of destiny. It has even been said that he ruled the world from Clairvaux; for kings and rulers of state, bishops, cardinals and even popes sought his wisdom and counsel.

The Church tried to win him to its highest honors. Milan vehemently declared him to be the only fit successor to the illustrious Ambrose, and Rheims, noblest city in France, was equally eager to place him on its arch-episcopal throne. But Bernard chose to continue as Abbot of Clairvaux, influencing the Christian world through his visits and his writings.

It is easy to imagine him, alone in his narrow cell, with its floor of stone, gazing with rapture upon the Cross and its figure of the Saviour, and thinking of the agony and suffering there portrayed. Thus he writes his Passion Hymn, fifty lines each, addressed to the sacred head, hands, feet, knees, breast, side and heart of Jesus as he hangs on the cross, three hundred and fifty lines altogether.

Salve mundi salutare (to the Feet)
Salve Jesu, Rex sanctorum (to the Knees)
Salve Jesu, pastor bone (to the Hands)
Salve Jesu, summe bonus (to the Side)
Salve salus mea, Deus (to the Breast)

Summi Regis cor aveto (to the Heart)
Salve caput cruentatum (to the Face)

From the hymn to the Sacred Feet comes this stanza:

"With the deepest adoration
Humbly at thy feet I lie,
And with fervent supplication
Unto thee for succor fly:
My petition kindly hear;
Say in answer to my prayer,
'I will change thy grief and sadness
Into comfort, joy and gladness.'"

It is from the section addressed to the head, *"Salve Caput Cruentatum,"* that our English hymn is taken.

The first stanza is a vivid description of that Sacred Head, with its crown of thorns. The second is a prayer clearly suggesting the poverty of language in expressing the gratitude of the human heart for a "love so amazing, so divine." The third voices the everlasting confidence of the believer in the completeness and redemption wrought through Jesus' death both for here-and-now and hereafter.

"Bernard's original is powerful and searching, but Gerhardt's hymn is still more powerful and profound, as redrawn from the deeper spring of evangelical Lutheran, Scriptural knowledge, and fervency of faith. Thus this classic hymn expresses in three languages, the Latin, the German and the English, and in three confessions, the Roman, the Lutheran and the Anglican, the confidence of the believer in the Christ of Calvary."

"While Francis of Assisi moved the hearts of the people like Jesus," says Raby, "Bernard was rather another Ambrose, a terror to evil-doers and heretics, and a doctor whose lips distilled honey." Bernard says in one of his sermons: "Jesus is honey to the lips, in the ear melody, in the heart joy. Medicine also is that name. Is any sad? Let Jesus come into his heart, and thence leap to his tongue."

St. Bernard regulated the chanting at Citeaux: "It is necessary that men sing in a virile manner and not with voices shrill and artificial like the voices of women, or in a manner lascivious and nimble like actors." He added cautions that singers should "manage their respiration" and not sing through the nose. The words of St. Bernard indicate pretty clearly that the male soprano was already employed in the church choir.

✤

The Hymn Tune. This famous Passion Chorale was composed by Hans Leo Hassler (1564–1612), a German organist, for some amatory stanzas, beginning *"Mein G'müt ist mir verwirret."* The melody was considerably altered by Bach who uses it five different times in his St. Matthew Passion music. Fifty years ago this solemn, poignant text was sung to Thalberg's "Amid the Greenwood smiling."

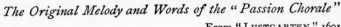

The Original Melody and Words of the "Passion Chorale"

From "Lustgarten," 1601

Mein Gemüht ist mir ver-wir - ret, Das macht ein' Jungfrau zart, Bin
ganz und gar ver - ir - ret, Mein Herz das kräncktsich
hart. Hab Tag und Nacht kein' Ruh, Für all Zeit gros - se Klag',
Tu' stets seufs-tzen und wei - nen in trau - ren schier Ver - zag.

O WORD OF GOD INCARNATE

1. O Word of God incarnate,
O Wisdom from on high,
O Truth, unchanged, unchanging,
O Light of our dark sky!
We praise thee for the radiance
That from the hallowed page,

A lantern to our footsteps,
Shines on from age to age.

2. The Church from her dear Master
Received the gift divine,
And still that light she lifteth
O'er all the earth to shine.
It is the golden casket,
Where gems of truth are stored;
It is the heaven-drawn picture
Of Christ, the living Word.

3. It floateth like a banner
Before God's host unfurled;
It shineth like a beacon
Above the darkling world;
It is the chart and compass
That o'er life's surging sea,
'Mid mists and rocks and darkness,
Still guides, O Christ, to thee.

4. O make thy Church, dear Saviour,
A lamp of purest gold,
To bear before the nations
Thy true light, as of old.
O teach thy wandering pilgrims
By this their path to trace,
Till, clouds and darkness ended,
They see thee face to face.

WILLIAM WALSHAM HOW, 1867.

BIBLICAL TEXT.

Thy word is a lamp unto my feet, and light unto my path.

PSALM 119: 105.

Ye are seen as lights in the world, holding forth the word of life.

PHILIPPIANS 2: 15, 16.

I am the light of the world; he that followeth me shall not walk in the darkness, but shall have the light of life.

JOHN 8: 12.

A MIGHTY DECADE OF HYMN WRITING

The decade of 1860–1870 was a strategic time for a hymnic renaissance. In these years Jacob Chamberlain began his notable work among the Telugus; political and social revolution in Japan marked the beginning of the opening of that country to Christian missionaries; Bishop Patterson served his heroic ten years in Melanesia; Father Damien began his self-sacrificing work among the lepers of Molokai; and John G. Paton was demonstrating the power of faith in the New Hebrides.

In England, William Walsham How (1823–1897) was rapidly reaching the height of his powers as a clergyman and writer. During this decade he served part of the time as select preacher at Oxford. He was a master of the technique of hymn-making. He expresses basic truths in simple, forceful diction, with a combination of vivid detail and bold, broad strokes.

The crowning tribute to Bishop How's ability as a poet came in the closing year of his life, when he was honored as the poet to write a national hymn for the British Empire's observance of Queen Victoria's Jubilee in 1897. (Kipling wrote "The Recessional" for the London *Times* on the same occasion.) The third stanza of Bishop How's hymn reads:

"O royal heart, with wide embrace
For all her happy children yearning;
O happy realm, such mother-grace
With loyal love returning.
Where England's flag flies wide unfurled,
All tyrant wrongs repelling,
God made the world a better world
For man's brief earthly dwelling."

Study the Scripture sources of the titles given to Christ in this hymn, such as:

"Word of God," John 1:1, Revelation 19:13; "Wisdom," I Corinthians, 1:30; "Truth," John 14:6; "Light," John 12:35, 8:12, 9:5, 1:9; "Master," Matthew 23:10; "Christ," Matthew 16:16; "Saviour," Luke 2:11.

The different figures of speech for the written Word of God are as interesting as the different titles for the Incarnate Word. The allusions indicate the author's intimate knowledge of the Bible: "lantern," "gift divine," "golden casket," "heaven-drawn picture," "banner," "beacon," "chart and compass."

✣

THE HYMN TUNE. MUNICH is an old German chorale from the *Meiningen Gesang Buch,* published in 1693. It was first sung to *"O Gott, Du frommer Gott"* in this earlier form of melody and rhythm.

It was known in Germany as the "Koenigsberg Chorale." Mendelssohn adapted and harmonized it for use in *Elijah* (see music).

Kahn in his *Die Melodien der deutschen evangelischen Kirchenlieder* traces MUNICH back to melodies in *Lobsingende Harffe,* published in 1682.

"Munich" as arranged by Mendelssohn in his "Elijah"

"Munich"—First Form

O WORSHIP THE KING, ALL GLORIOUS ABOVE

1. O worship the King, all glorious above,
O gratefully sing his power and his love;
Our Shield and Defender, the Ancient of Days,
Pavilioned in splendor, and girded with praise.

2. O tell of his might, O sing of his grace,
Whose robe is the light, whose canopy space;
His chariots of wrath the deep thunder-clouds form,
And dark is his path on the wings of the storm.

3. Thy bountiful care what tongue can recite?
It breathes in the air, it shines in the light;
It streams from the hills, it descends to the plain,
And sweetly distills in the dew and the rain.

4. Frail children of dust, and feeble as frail,
In thee do we trust, nor find thee to fail;
Thy mercies how tender, how firm to the end,
Our Maker, Defender, Redeemer, and Friend!

Robert Grant, 1833.

Biblical Text.
O Lord my God, thou art very great;
Thou art clothed with honor and majesty:
Who coverest thyself with light as with a garment;
Who walketh upon the wings of the wind;

Who maketh winds his messengers;
Flames of fire his ministers. . . .
These wait all for thee,
That thou mayest give them their food in due season.

PSALM 104: 1, 2, 3, 4, 27.

A HYMN STORY OF THE SIX DAYS OF CREATION

Sir Robert Grant (1785–1838) is remembered, perhaps, as the member of Parliament, from Inverness, Scotland, who introduced a bill granting rights to the Jew in favor of which Macaulay, the historian, made his first speech. He was Governor of Bombay from 1834 to 1838.

It is as a hymn-writer that he will chiefly be remembered. While he wrote only twelve hymns, one of them lives, and is universally and constantly used. It is a metrical version of a portion of Psalm 104, which Dr. Moulton called, "The Hymn of the World Without." Compare Grant's words with those of the quaint old English paraphrase in the Anglo-Genevan Psalter of 1561.

"My soule praise the Lord, speake good of his name;
O Lord, our greate God, how doest thou appeare,
So passing in glorie, that great is thy fame,
Honour and majestie, in thee shine most cleare.

"His chamber beams lie in the clouds full sure,
Which as his chariot, are made him to beare,
And there with much swiftness his course doth endure:
Upon the wings riding, of winds in the aire."

Two stanzas of Robert Grant's hymn are usually omitted:

"The earth with its stores of wonders untold,
Almighty, thy power hath founded of old,
Hath stablished it fast by a changeless decree,
And round it hath cast, like a mantle, the sea.

"O measureless might, ineffable love,
While angels delight to hymn thee above,
The humble creation, though feeble their lays,
With true adoration shall lisp to thy praise."

Rewarding would be an inquiry into the scriptural sources for the names of Deity used in the first and last stanzas of this hymn: "King," "Shield," "Defender," "Ancient of Days," "Maker," "Redeemer," "Friend." Note the development from the thought of a distant Creator, "whose robe is the light, whose canopy, space," to that of an intimate, tender Friend.

This hymn may well be linked with "Ancient of Days," because of the use of the phrase, Ancient of Days, in stanza one of each hymn. What is there about the phrase that calls forth the majesty that is so evident in each of these hymns?

A Metrical Commentary on the Days of Creation

Psalm 104 and "O Worship the King" are a metrical commentary on the Six Days of Creation in Genesis one. It may be used as an Antiphonal Service.

The First Day

Minister:

And God said, Let there be light: and there was light.

GENESIS 1:3.

Reader:

Who coverest thyself with light as with a garment.

PSALM 104:2.

Congregation or choir:

O tell of his might, O sing of his grace,
Whose robe is the light, whose canopy space.

The Second Day

Minister:

And God said, Let there be a firmament in the midst of the waters, and let it divide the waters from the waters.

GENESIS 1:6.

Reader:

Who stretchest out the heavens like a curtain;
Who layeth the beams of his chambers in the waters;
Who maketh the clouds his chariot;
Who walketh upon the wings of the wind.

PSALM 104:2, 3.

Congregation or Choir:

"His chariots of wrath the deep thunder-clouds form,
And dark is his path on the wings of the storm."

The Third Day

Minister:

And God said, Let the waters under the heavens be gathered together unto one place, and let the dry land appear: and it was so.

And God said, Let the earth put forth grass, herbs yielding seed, and fruit-trees bearing fruit.

GENESIS 1:9, 11.

Reader:

Thou coveredst it with the deep as with a vesture:
The waters stood above the mountains.
At thy rebuke they fled; . . .
He causeth the grass to grow for the cattle,
And herb for the service of man;
That he may bring forth food out of the earth.

PSALM 104:6, 7, 14.

Congregation or Choir:

"The earth with its stores of wonders untold,
Almighty, thy power hath founded of old;
Hath stablished it fast by a changeless decree,
And round it hath cast, like a mantle, the sea."

The Fourth Day

Minister:

And God said, Let there be lights in the firmament of heaven . . . the greater light to rule the day, and the lesser light to rule the night.

GENESIS 1:14, 16.

Reader:

He appointed the moon for seasons;
The sun knoweth his going down.

PSALM 104:19.

Congregation or Choir:

"Thy bountiful care, what tongue can recite?
It breathes in the air, it shines in the light."

The Fifth Day

Minister:

And God said, Let the waters swarm with swarms of living creatures, and let birds fly above the earth.

GENESIS 1:20.

Reader:

Wherein all the beasts of the forest creep forth . . .
And seek their food from God.
Yonder is the sea, great and wide,
Wherein are things creeping innumerable,
Both small and great beasts. . . .
These wait all for thee.

PSALM 104:20, 21, 25, 27.

Congregation or Choir:

"The humble creation, though feeble their lays,
With true adoration shall lisp to thy praise."

The Sixth Day

Minister:

And God said, Let us make man in our image, after our likeness. . . . And God created man in his own image, in the image of God created he him.

GENESIS 1:26, 27.

Reader:

Man goeth forth to his work
And to his labor until the evening.
O Lord, how manifold are thy works!
In wisdom hast thou made them all,
The earth is full of thy riches.

Congregation or Choir:

"O worship the King, all glorious above,
And gratefully sing his power and his love.
Thy mercies how tender, how firm to the end,
Our Maker, Defender, Redeemer, and Friend."

The Hymn Visualized

This hymn and Psalm may further be illuminated by the use of stereopticon slides or prints of the Burns-Jones panels, "The Six Days of Creation." Some of the Michelangelo "Creation" pictures in the Sistine Chapel should furnish additional visual material.

✣

THE HYMN TUNE. The tune LYONS is arranged from the music of Johann Michael Haydn (1737–1806). Michael Haydn was a less distinguished musician than his brother Joseph. He was an Austrian; first known as a boy soprano, then as a violinst, and a pianist, and later, as an organist and chorister. The year of his death was that of Robert Grant's graduation from Cambridge University. Haydn's best work is found among his religious compositions, twenty masses, many offertories and one hundred and fourteen graduals.

Free Rhythms for Congregational Singing

The medieval craftsman, whether he was making tunes or sculpture, hated anything like mechanical exactitude of outline. He wanted to produce forms that would tell of the endless variety of life, and must, therefore, not contain many formal iterations. Plain-song was thus constructed on this principle of free rhythm.

Hymn tunes like LYONS, OLD HUNDREDTH, and ST. ANNE, being essentially akin to the old plain-song, should be sung with the same free rhythm and occasional pauses. They should not be sung with hurry-up, catch-breath liveliness, but in the free, hearty traditional style. (See example.)

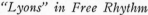

"Lyons" in Free Rhythm

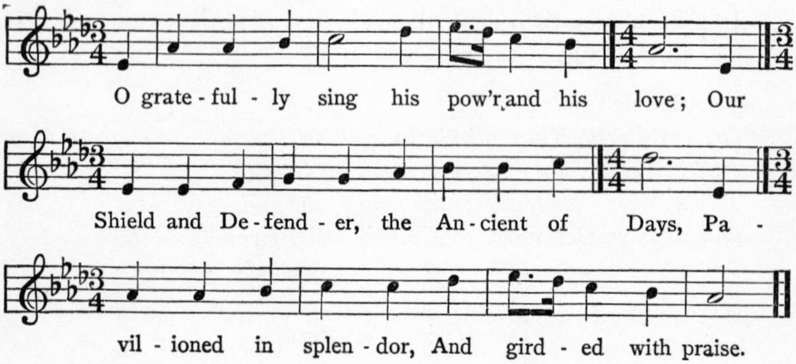
O grate-ful-ly sing his pow'r and his love; Our
Shield and De-fend-er, the An-cient of Days, Pa-
vil-ioned in splen-dor, And gird-ed with praise.

O ZION, HASTE, THY MISSION HIGH FULFILLING

1. O Zion, haste, thy mission high fulfilling,
To tell to all the world that God is light;
That he who made all nations is not willing
One soul should perish, lost in shades of night.

Refrain

Publish glad tidings, tidings of peace,
Tidings of Jesus, redemption and release.

2. Behold how many thousands still are lying
Bound in the darksome prison house of sin,
With none to tell them of the Saviour's dying,
Or of the life he died for them to win.

Refrain

3. Proclaim to every people, tongue and nation,
That God, in whom they live and move, is love;

Tell how he stooped to save his lost creation,
And died on earth that man might live above.

Refrain

4. Give of thy sons to bear the message glorious;
Give of thy wealth to speed them on their way;
Pour out thy soul for them in prayer victorious;
And all thou spendest Jesus will repay.

Refrain

5. He comes again: O Zion, ere thou meet him,
Make known to every heart his saving grace;
Let none whom he has ransomed fail to greet him,
Through thy neglect, unfit to see his face.

Refrain

MARY ANN THOMSON, 1870.

BIBLICAL TEXT.

And he called the twelve together . . . and sent them forth to preach the kingdom of God.

LUKE 9: 1, 2.

How then shall they call on him in whom they have not believed? And how shall they believe in him whom they have not heard? and how shall they hear without a preacher? and how shall they preach, except they be sent even as it is written, How beautiful are the feet of them that bring glad tidings of good things!

ROMANS 10: 14, 15.

THE HIGH MISSION OF THE CHURCH

It is a tribute to the redeeming power of faith that it is so frequently the aftermath of fear as it was in the experience which gave rise to this hymn. A mother, watching all night by the bed of a feverish child, suddenly realizes the widespread evil of suffering; also the equal universality of comfort always available in the enduring spirit of Jesus. She gives voice to her vision in a poem recalling the Church to its "high mission" of consolation and redemption.

Mrs. Mary Ann Thomson (1834–1923), a native of London, was the wife of John Thomson, Librarian of the Philadelphia Free Library, and Accounting Warden of the Church of the Annunciation. She was the author of some forty hymns, of which four are included in the Episcopal Hymnal of 1894.

This is a great hymn of missions, full of force and beauty. In prophetic style, it keeps a notable balance between stateliness and enthusiasm.

(*An Omitted Stanza*)

'Tis thine to save from peril of perdition
The souls for whom the Lord his life laid down;

Beware lest, slothful to fulfil thy mission,
Thou lose one jewel that should deck his crown.

Forgotten Stanzas of Famous Hymns.

When the apostles' fragile bark
Struggled with the billows dark
On the stormy Galilee,
Thou didst walk upon the sea;
And when they beheld thy form,
Safe they glided through the storm.

(*Jesus, Saviour, pilot me*)

Stand up, stand up for Jesus,
The solemn watchward hear;
If, while ye sleep, he suffers,
Away with shame and fear;
Where'er ye meet with evil,
Within you or without,
Charge for the God of battles,
And put the foe to rout.

(*Stand up, stand up for Jesus*)

Where children pure and happy,
Pray to the blessed child;
Where misery cries out to thee,
Son of the undefiled;
Where charity stands watching
And faith holds wide the door,
The dark night wakes, the glory breaks,
And Christmas comes once more.

(*O little Town of Bethlehem*)

Within thy gates nothinge doth come
That is not passinge cleane;
Noe spider's web, no durt, no dust,
Noe filthe may there be seen.
In thee noe sickness may be seene,
No hurt, noe ache, noe sore;
There is no deathe, nor ugly devill,
But life forever more.

(*Jerusalem, my happy home*)

Thou art a holy ladder,
Where angels go and come;
Each Sunday finds us gladder,
Nearer to heaven, our home.
A day of sweet refection,
Thou art a day of love,
A day of resurrection
From earth to things above.

(*O Day of Rest and Gladness*)

Wilt thou not regard my call?
Will thou not accept my prayer?

Lo—I sink, I faint, I fall,
Lo—on thee I cast my care.
Reach me out thy gracious hand,
While I of thy strength receive,
Hoping against hope I stand,
Dying, and behold I live.

(*Jesus, Lover of my Soul*)

Haste, ye females, from your fright,
Take to Galilee your flight;
To his sad disciples say—
Jesus Christ is risen today.

(*Jesus Christ is risen today*)

THE HYMN TUNE. The author tells us that she wrote these words to fit the tune of "Hark, hark, my soul, angelic songs are swelling." But she adds: "I do not think my hymn is ever sung to the tune for which I wrote it. Mr. Anketell told me, and I am sure he was right, that it is better for a hymn to have a tune of its own and I feel much indebted to the author of the tune TIDINGS for writing such inspiring music to my words."

However, TIDINGS was composed by James Walch (1837–1901), in 1876, for "Hark, hark, my soul," not Mrs. Thomson's words. Walch was an English organist and composer.

ON OUR WAY REJOICING

1. On our way rejoicing,
As we homeward move,
Hearken to our praises,
O thou God of love.
Is there grief or sadness?
Thine it cannot be;
Is our sky beclouded?
Clouds are not from thee.

Refrain

On our way rejoicing
As we homeward move,
Hearken to our praises,
O thou God of love.

2. If with honest-hearted
Love for God and man,
Day by day thou find us
Doing all we can,
Thou who givest the seed-time
Wilt give large increase,

Crown the head with blessings,
Fill the heart with peace.

Refrain

3. On our way rejoicing
Gladly let us go;
Victor is our Leader,
Vanquished is the foe;
Christ without, our safety;
Christ within, our joy;
Who, if we be faithful,
Can our hope destroy?

Refrain

4. Unto God the Father
Joyful songs we sing;
Unto God the Saviour
Thankful hearts we bring;
Unto God the Spirit
Bow we and adore;
On our way rejoicing
Now and evermore.

John S. B. Monsell, 1863.

Biblical Text.

He went on his way rejoicing.

Acts 8:39.

Rejoicing in hope; patient in tribulation.

Romans 12:12.

Rejoice in the Lord always; again I will say, Rejoice.

Philippians 4:4.

LET YOUR HOPE BE A SONG TO YOU

John Samuel Bowley Monsell, LL.D. (1811–1875), was born in Ireland, the son of an Archdeacon. He was educated for the ministry at Trinity College, Dublin, and was ordained at twenty-three years of age. Most of his ministry as a clergyman of the Church of England was spent in Egham, England. His last post was at Guilford, Surrey, where he was Rector of the Church of St. Nicholas. It was there that the tragic accident occurred which caused his death at the age of fifty-four. During some repairs to his church, the Rector, being very much interested in the progress of the work, was standing in the church watching the workmen, when suddenly a great mass of stone fell from the roof, striking him on the head. He was carried unconscious to the Rectory, where he died soon afterward. The hymn he wrote for the rebuilding fund had this singularly ominous stanza:

Dear body, thou and I must part;
Thy busy head, thy throbbing heart
Must cease to work and cease to play,
For me at no far distant day.

His home at Guildford was "quite an ideal household, full of the beauty of holiness, with genial brightness and gaiety playing like sunshine over all the troubles of life."

"More fervent and joyous," he insisted our hymns should be. "We are too distant and reserved in our praises; we sing not as we should sing to him and of him who is Chief among ten thousand, the Altogether Lovely."

Edwin Hodder has written of him as a preacher: "Many a time have I listened to the words of life from his lips. Standing there in the pulpit, with a small Bible in his hand, unencumbered with notes or sermon-book, the preacher has held his audience spellbound, while in plain, simple language, yet full of tender poetic thought, he has told them the sweet story of eternal love."

This hymn was first published in *Hymns of Love and Praise,* in 1863. Ten years later, in the *Parish Hymnal,* it was adapted for processional use by adding the first four lines of stanza one, as a refrain.

✣

THE HYMN TUNE. Frances Ridley Havergal (1836–1879) appears in the list of authors of hymns as a matter of fact. But as a composer of tunes she is a delightful surprise. She was born at Astley, Worcestershire, where her father, W. H. Havergal, was Rector. She was especially gifted in literature and music. During much of her life Miss Havergal suffered greatly from ill health, but she was noted for her courage and good cheer. Her father has been called one of the pioneers of modern hymnody. She worked much with him in the preparation of both hymns, texts and tunes.

The name of this tune, HERMAS, is taken from Paul's friend in Rome, to whom he wished to be remembered. (See Romans 16: 14.) It was originally set to another of Dr. Monsell's hymns, "Earth below is teeming," and was published in *Havergal's Psalmody,* in 1871.

The tune has a rapid movement which fits the thought of the hymn and gives ample opportunity for emphasis on the significant word "rejoicing."

ONCE TO EVERY MAN AND NATION

1. Once to every man and nation
Comes the moment to decide,
In the strife of truth with falsehood,
For the good or evil side;
Some great cause, God's new Messiah,
Offering each the bloom or blight,
And the choice goes by forever
'Twixt that darkness and that light.

2. Then to side with truth is noble,
When we share her wretched crust,
Ere her cause bring fame and profit,
And 'tis prosperous to be just;
Then it is the brave man chooses,
While the coward stands aside
Till the multitude make virtue
Of the faith they had denied.

3. By the light of burning martyrs,
Jesus' bleeding feet I track,
Toiling up new Calvaries ever
With the cross that turns not back;
New occasions teach new duties,
Time makes ancient good uncouth;
They must upward still and onward,
Who would keep abreast of truth.

4. Though the cause of evil prosper,
Yet 'tis truth alone is strong;
Truth forever on the scaffold,
Wrong forever on the throne;
Yet that scaffold sways the future,
And, behind the dim unknown,
Standeth God within the shadow
Keeping watch above his own.

JAMES RUSSELL LOWELL, 1844.

BIBLICAL TEXT.

Blessed are they that have been persecuted for righteousness' sake; for theirs is the kingdom of heaven. Blessed are ye, when men shall reproach you, and persecute you, and say all manner of evil against you falsely, for my sake. Rejoice, and be exceeding glad; for great is your reward in heaven; for so persecuted they the prophets that were before you.

MATTHEW 5: 10–12.

If ye abide in my word . . . ye shall know the truth, and the truth shall make you free.

JOHN 8: 31, 32.

A PROTEST AGAINST THE MEXICAN WAR

Although written eighty-seven years ago, this hymn has a decidedly "modern" ring. It is a hymn of warning, of challenge, and of stinging scorn. It is a powerful admonition to nobility of life; a ringing call to go forward, and a stalwart affirmation of sure faith in the ultimate triumph of Truth.

A careful comparison of the hymn with the complete poem is almost essential to a real appreciation of the strength and the ominous quality of the hymn. The four stanzas as printed above are the ones usually given, and in this order, in hymnals. Two of the stanzas of the poem which may not be good hymnody, and therefore are rightfully omitted, but which are surely most challenging poetry, are:

"'Tis as easy to be heroes as to sit the idle slaves
Of a legendary virtue carved upon our fathers' graves;
Worshippers of light ancestral make the present light a crime;—
Was the Mayflower launched by cowards, steered by men behind their time?
Turn those tracks toward Past or Future, that make Plymouth Rock sublime?

. . . .

Shall we make their creed our jailer? shall we in our haste to slay,
From the tombs of the old prophets steal the funeral lamps away
To light up the martyr-fagots round the prophets of today?

. . . .

Lo, before us gleam her camp-fires! we ourselves must Pilgrims be,
Launch our Mayflower, and steer boldly through the desperate winter sea,
Nor attempt the Future's portal with the Past's blood-rusted key."

James Russell Lowell (1819–1891), true New Englander, genuine patriot, lover of America and believer in her destiny, poet, professor, editor and diplomat, was one of the outstanding men of letters of the nineteenth century. Born in Cambridge, his life was centered in that University city and its neighbor, Boston. He was the successor of Henry W. Longfellow as Professor of Belles-lettres in Harvard; the first editor of the *Atlantic Monthly* (1857–1859), co-editor with Charles Eliot Norton of the *North American Review;* United States Minister to Spain (1877–1880), and then the representative of our government at the Court of St. James's (1880–1885). He is known as a poet, but his prose writings are more voluminous than his poetry. He was a writer with a forward look, as this hymn so clearly proves. "There is a sense of intellectual and imaginative dawn to be found in Lowell's essays and verse, a dawn that is to gladden the granite and pines of his native land. With a loving admiration for the old literature, there is a loyal national pride in the new."

Lowell had a great love for justice and the brotherhood of man. He once expressed the yearning of his heart in the following words taken from a letter to a friend: "It seems as if my heart would break in pouring out one glorious song that should be the gospel of Reform, full of consolation and strength to the oppressed, yet falling gently and restoringly as dew on the withered youth-flowers of the oppressor."

The Roaring Forties

This red-letter decade, the roaring forties, saw feverish activity in every department of American life. There were great inventions like the plow, the reaper, and the threshing-machine which made America a paradise for farmers and encouraged a mighty western movement. The sewing-machine, and the telegraph added new zest to business and to home living. Wars and rumors of wars there were—the Mexican War against which Lowell hurled his "Present Crisis," the impending anti-slavery struggle which split the Methodist Church North and South, and the Indian wars and massacres. The gold rush to California and the tide of immigration which reached the amazing total of three hundred and ten thousand by 1850, further started the caldron boiling. Out of such a period poets penned noble, ominous, ringing messages, and many of our finest hymns:

"We are living, we are dwelling,
In a grand and awful time,
In an age on ages telling;
To be living is sublime.
Hark! the waking up of nations,
Gog and Magog to the fray;
Hark! what soundeth is creation
Groaning for the latter day."

ARTHUR CLEVELAND COX.

"Look from the spheres of endless day,
O God of mercy and of might!
In pity look on those who stray,
Benighted, in this land of light.
In peopled vale, in lonely glen,
In crowded mart, by stream or sea,
How many of the sons of men
Hear not the message sent from thee!"

WILLIAM CULLEN BRYANT.

"Then shall all shackles fall; the stormy clangor
Of wild war's music o'er the earth shall cease;
Love shall tread out the baleful fire of anger,
And in its ashes plant the tree of life."

JOHN GREENLEAF WHITTIER.

"For not like kingdoms of the world
Thy holy church, O God;
Though earthquake shocks are threatening her,
And tempests are abroad;

Unshaken as eternal hills,
Immovable she stands,
A mountain that shall fill the earth,
A house not made by hands."

ARTHUR CLEVELAND COX.

THE HYMN TUNE. TON-Y-BOTEL or EBENEZER arr. by Thomas John Williams (1869–), resident of Yursmeudwy, Swansea Valley, Wales. Organist and choir-master of churches in Llanelly, he has written many hymn-tunes and anthems. TON-Y-BOTEL comes from a widely credited story that the tune was found in a bottle washed ashore in a storm on the Welsh coast. It is an old Welsh melody.

ONWARD, CHRISTIAN SOLDIERS

1. Onward, Christian soldiers,
Marching as to war,
With the cross of Jesus
Going on before;
Christ, the royal Master,
Leads against the foe;
Forward into battle
See, his banners go.

Refrain

Onward, Christian soldiers,
Marching as to war,
With the cross of Jesus
Going on before.

2. At the sign of triumph
Satan's host doth flee;
On then, Christian soldiers,
On to victory!
Hell's foundations quiver
At the shout of praise;
Brothers, lift your voices,
Loud your anthems raise.

Refrain

3. Like a mighty army
Moves the church of God;
Brothers, we are treading
Where the saints have trod;
We are not divided,
All one body we,
One in hope and doctrine,
One in charity.

Refrain

4. Crowns and thrones may perish,
Kingdoms rise and wane,
But the church of Jesus
Constant will remain;
Gates of hell can never
'Gainst that church prevail;
We have Christ's own promise,
And that cannot fail.

Refrain

5. Onward, then, ye people,
Join our happy throng;
Blend with ours your voices
In the triumph song;
Glory, laud, and honor
Unto Christ, the King;
This, through countless ages
Men and angels sing.[1]

Refrain

SABINE BARING-GOULD, 1865.

BIBLICAL TEXT.

The kingdom of the world is become the kingdom of our Lord, and of his Christ; and he shall reign for ever and ever.

REVELATION 11:15.

Now is come the salvation, and the power, and the kingdom of our God, and the authority of his Christ.

REVELATION 12:10.

A PROCESSION WITH CROSS AND BANNERS

Sabine Baring-Gould (1834–1924) was born in Exeter, England, and was graduated from Clare College, Cambridge, A.B. 1854, and M.A. 1856. He was ordained in 1864 and became curate at Horbury. In 1881 he was rector of Lew Trenchard, Devonshire. Here he was Rector, squire and lord of the manor. There were fewer than three hundred people in the parish, while the net income was only one hundred and seventeen pounds. However he made his parish as wide as the world by writing books. He was the author of a prodigious number of books such as *Lives of the Saints* (15 vols.), *Curious Myths of the Middle Ages, Yorkshire Oddities, Folklore,* a great number of novels, translations from the Danish, and two volumes of original hymns, including one of the most robust of hymns, "Onward, Christian Soldiers," and one of the gentlest and sweetest, "Now the Day Is Over." He says concerning his ability to work so effectively, "The secret is simply that I stick to a task when I begin it." And "It would never do to wait from day to day for some moments which might seem favorable for work." He was a deeply religious man. He was a

[1] Copyright by Novello & Co., Ltd.

notably vigorous, earnest, and independent-minded man established in his ways and very outspoken.

A lovely story about Baring-Gould is his courtship and marriage. At Horbury he fell in love with Grace Taylor, daughter of a mill-hand. With the consent of her parents he sent her away to be educated. On her returning from college they were married, Baring-Gould himself pronouncing the marriage vows. It was a most happy union. At her death eight years before his own, he had inscribed on her tomb: "Half of my soul."

The editors of *Hymns Ancient and Modern* recognized hard facts instead of idealistic theory, for they changed the line "We are not divided" to read, "Though divisions harass." In this connection some sentences from Baring-Gould's writings are significant:

"If we were to take the religions of the world and spread them out before us, and tabulate their characteristics, we should be able to form a register of the corresponding wants of the human spirit. Every religion marks the existence of a want. And every reformation indicates the awakening, the assertion, of a new one."

"To bring this down to our own experience and our own days. How is it that England teems with sects? Simply because the Established Church does not meet every religious requirement of Christian souls. True wisdom would seek to make her bands elastic, and vary her methods to embrace and satisfy all, and not seek to stamp and stiffen and solidify her, as the martyr Geronimo was kneaded into a bed of concrete."

"Much better endow the Church of England with centripetal than with centrifugal force; and this can only be done by allowing to grow together in luxuriance objective worship and subjective mysticism; by giving to those who want on either side with full hand, instead of measuring to each in grudged pinches."

❖

THE HYMN TUNE. "Music is bound up with daily life and is a necessity of existence," wrote Sir Arthur Sullivan, the composer of ST. GERTRUDE, the familiar music to which "Onward, Christian Soldiers" is set.

The tune was written in 1871, at the home of Mrs. Gertrude Clay-Ker-Seymer, in Dorsetshire, while Sir Arthur was a guest there. Mrs. Clay-Ker-Seymer writes of it: "I remember that we sang it in the private chapel attached to the house, Sir Arthur playing the harmonium, and having taught us the tune, as we had not the music."

There is an interesting similarity between the first singing of this hymn by the little company of choir boys marching from Horbury Bridge, and the first singing of the tune, which is now so inseparably linked with it, by a company of friends in a private chapel of a country home.

Sir Arthur himself has related this incident in connection with his writing of the tune: "It is perhaps a curious fact that one of my best known hymn tunes was written as the result of a quarrel. The quarrel was between the proprietors of *Hymns Ancient and Modern* and the firm of Novello who printed it, and who then gave way to Messrs. Clowes, who still print it. Novello's then proceeded to compile a collection of hymns, and for that Hymnary I wrote 'Onward, Christian Soldiers,' which, as you see, was thus the indirect outcome of a quarrel." The tune was published first in the *Musical Times* for December, 1871, and then in the *Church Hymnary,* the following year.

This is an excellent tune for modulating, stanza by stanza, into higher keys, D, E flat, E, and F. It was first sung to the slow movement of Haydn's Symphony in D.

OUR GOD, OUR HELP IN AGES PAST

1. Our God, our help in ages past,
Our hope for years to come,
Our shelter from the stormy blast,
And our eternal home.

2. Before the hills in order stood,
Or earth received her frame,
From everlasting thou art God,
To endless years the same.

3. A thousand ages in thy sight
Are like an evening gone;
Short as the watch that ends the night
Before the rising sun.

4. Time, like an ever-rolling stream,
Bears all its sons away;
They fly forgotten, as a dream
Dies at the opening day.

5. Our God, our help in ages past,
Our hope for years to come,
Be thou our guard while life shall last,
And our eternal home.

ISAAC WATTS, 1719.

BIBLICAL TEXT.

Lord, thou hast been our dwelling-place
In all generations.
Before the mountains were brought forth,
Or ever thou hadst formed the earth and the world,
Even from everlasting to everlasting, thou art God,
For a thousand years in thy sight
Are but as yesterday when it is past,
And as a watch in the night.
So teach us to number our days,
That we may get us a heart of wisdom.
Let the favor of the Lord our God be upon us;
And establish thou the work of our hands upon us:
Yea, the work of our hands establish thou it.

PSALM 90: 1, 2, 4, 12, 17.

MAN FRAIL AND GOD ETERNAL

The above words formed the title of this hymn in the book in which it was first published, Watts' "Psalms of David," 1719. They suggest the ninetieth Psalm of which the hymn is a paraphrase.

The hymn is the best known and most universally used of all the six hundred hymns and paraphrases written by this gifted "father of English hymnody."

The important place of Isaac Watts in our hymnals is indicated by the researches of Reverend James King in the hymnody of the Anglican Church. He examined fifty-two representative hymnals of the Anglican Church, published in England, Scotland, America and the Colonies between 1863 and 1885, and listed "the three hundred and twenty-five hymns of highest merit according to the verdict of the whole Anglican Church." In this list, Charles Wesley ranks first, with twenty-two hymns: Isaac Watts is a close second, with twenty-one.

It was John Wesley who was responsible for the change of the opening word of the hymn from Watts' "Our" to the frequently used "O."

This hymn is a favorite among English-speaking peoples for use on national and special occasions. It was sung at the thanksgiving for peace after the World War, and at the funeral of the Unknown Soldier in Westminster Abbey. Like the Psalm, which is its original, it is a majestic, serene, deep-moving hymn of faith, one of the race's supreme expressions of beauty and religion. "It swells like the ocean: it sobs out the grief of centuries," says Prof. Warmingham.

(*Some Omitted Stanzas*)

"Under the shadow of thy throne
Still may we dwell secure;
Sufficient is thine arm alone,
And our defense is sure.

"The busy tribes of flesh and blood,
With all their cares and fears,
Are carried downward with the flood,
And lost in following years."

✣

THE HYMN TUNE. The tune, ST. ANNE, was composed by William Croft (1678–1727) and was originally set to the Forty-second Psalm, "As pants the hart for cooling streams." It made no headway with the Methodists or Dissenters until the end of the eighteenth century, although HANOVER, by the same composer, came into instant favor.

Grave discussions there were in those days: (1) Whether it was proper for one to sing while others joined in spirit only, uniting in an audible Amen at the close of the tune. (2) Whether women as well as men, or men alone should sing. (3) Whether the unconverted should join in the Psalm tune. (4) Whether it was lawful to sing psalms at all, in tunes devised by man. (5) Whether it was proper to learn new tunes which were "uninspired." If a new tune were introduced in fifty years it became an event, for the whole church had to pass upon it.

The Strand, busiest of London's thoroughfares, hears ST. ANNE every day, played by the chimes of St. Clement's Church.

The Speed of Hymn-Tunes

English traditions should not be treated slightingly in setting the speed-rate of hymn-tunes. A noted authority gives the following metronome marks for certain familiar tunes:

ST. ANNE—"Our God, our help in ages past"	66
OLD HUNDREDTH—"Praise God from whom all blessings flow"	80
ST. GEORGE'S WINDSOR—"Come, ye thankful people, come"	92
AURELIA—"The Church's one foundation"	96
EVENTIDE—"Abide with me"	100
EWING—"Jerusalem the Golden"	100
ELLERS—(Benediction) "Saviour, again to thy dear name"	104
ST. GERTRUDE—"Onward, Christian Soldiers"	104

PRAISE GOD FROM WHOM ALL BLESSINGS FLOW

Praise God from whom all blessings flow;
Praise him, all creatures here below;
Praise him above, ye heavenly host;
Praise Father, Son, and Holy Ghost.

THOMAS KEN, 1695.

BIBLICAL TEXT.

Bless the Lord, O my soul;
And all that is within me, bless his holy name.

PSALM 103:1.

Praise ye the Lord from the heavens;
Praise ye him, all his angels:
Praise ye him, all his host.
Praise the Lord from the earth,
Kings of the earth and all peoples;
Both young men and virgins;
Old men and children;
Let them praise the name of the Lord;
For his name alone is exalted;
His glory is above the earth and the heavens.

PSALM 148:1, 2, 7, 11–13.

THE IMMORTAL SONG OF THE WINCHESTER SCHOOL BOYS

If there were to be selected one stanza of all Christian hymnody most universally known and most constantly used, the choice would be these four lines of Bishop Ken's. It is entirely probable that no words ever written outside the sacred Scriptures themselves, have been so continually repeated as this ascription of praise to the Triune God.

This is "The Doxology" of the Christian Church in all the world, sung Sunday by Sunday in many lands, in many tongues. So familiar is it that no minister of any denomination would for a moment think of announcing the number of the Doxology in the hymnal and waiting for the congregation to "find the place."

But, with all its familiarity, a comparatively small number of Christians have sensed the real significance of these words in their original setting. These four lines form the concluding stanza of each of Bishop Ken's three hymns, "The Morning Hymn," "The Evening Hymn," and "The Midnight Hymn." These were written when Bishop Ken was especially interested in the young men of Winchester College. It is said that the three hymns were printed first of all on broadsheets, so that they might be posted over the scholars' beds. His own directions regarding their use merit careful reading: "As soon as you wake in the morning, good Philotheus, strive as much as you can to keep all worldly thoughts out of your mind, till you have presented the first-fruits of the day to God; which will be an excellent preparation to make you spend the rest of it better; and therefore, be sure to sing the Morning and Evening Hymns in your chamber, devoutly remembering that the Psalmist, from happy experience, assures you that it is a very good thing to tell of the lovingkindness of God in the morning and of his truth in the night season."

The "Morning Hymn" has fourteen four-line stanzas, of which five are usually included in our hymnals, under the title, "Awake, my soul, and with the sun."

The "Evening Hymn" (found in hymnals under the title "All Praise to thee, my God, this night") has twelve stanzas.

The life story of Thomas Ken (1637–1711) is one of thrilling interest, of devotion to duty and loyalty to conviction. Ken was early left an orphan, and grew up in the home of his sister Anne, who married Izaak Walton, of *The Compleat Angler* fame. Walton's influence upon the young Ken is summed up by his biographer, Dean Plumptre: "The surroundings of the home in which Ken found a refuge after his father's death left an indelible impression on his character; and determined the direction of his mental and moral growth. . . . The companionship of such a man as Walton was invaluable. Every page of the *Angler* shows how he watched the habits of everything that lives, the adaptation of their structure to their environment, the things in which they fore-shadow the self-seeking or the altruism of humanity. I am drawing no imaginary picture in assuming that these influences contributed to Ken's after character."

He was educated at Winchester and at New College, Oxford. In 1666 he returned to Winchester as Fellow of the College. Appointed in 1679 Chaplain to Princess Mary at The Hague, he lost this position because of his outspoken remonstrance against immorality. Later he refused his house to Nell Gwynne, the favorite of Charles II. The King so admired his loyalty to conviction and outspoken courage that he made him Bishop of Bath and Wells.

In 1688 James the Second issued the Declaration of Indulgence and seven bishops, among them Bishop Ken, were committed to the London Tower. People were everywhere aroused to their danger. Beginning on the west coast men banded together to march upon the Tower of London. Grim was their war song:

"And shall Trelawny die, and must Trelawny die?
Then twenty thousand Cornishmen shall know the reason why."

This mighty army, entering London, went on singing:

"And shall the Bishops die, and must the Bishops die?
Then a hundred thousand Englishmen shall know the reason why."

The last days of Thomas Ken were full of suffering, from a very painful disease, depriving him of rest, and making sleep almost impossible.

His character is summed up by the historian Macaulay in these words: "He approached as near as human infirmity permits to the ideal perfection of Christian virtue."

Dryden wrote of Ken:

"Letting down the golden chain from high,
He drew his audience upward to the sky;
And oft with holy hymns he charmed their ears,
(A music more melodious than the spheres),
For David left him, when he went to rest,
His lyre; and after him he sung the best."

"In Church and State (1644–1700) every difference became a dispute; the electricity which, in calm weather, quickened life, and exploded into thunderstorms. Yet, amidst the din, the old psalmody flowed on, piercing with its music all the clamor. George Herbert, ministering to the poor and borne to his grave with cathedral chants; blind John Milton, secretary of the Protector, and scorn of the court of the Restoration; Richard Baxter, true pastor of the flock of Christ, so basely brow-beaten by Judge Jeffreys; Bishop Ken, the non-juror —these are the voices which carried on the song of peace through the time of strife."[1]

Doxologies and "The Doxology"

Doxologies have been used from the very earliest times, to conclude sermons, addresses, psalms, hymns and chants. The "GLORIA IN EXCELSIS" is known as "The Greater Doxology" and the "GLORIA PATRI" as "The Lesser Doxology." Watts felt their importance so fully that he closed his *Hymns and Spiritual Songs* with twenty versions of the Doxology, saying, "I cannot persuade myself to put a full period to these divine hymns till I have addressed a special song of Glory to God the Father, the Son and the Holy Spirit."

Ken's Doxology is a masterpiece at once of amplification and compression: of amplification on the thought, "Praise God," repeated in every line; of compression, by including, in the short space of four

[1] From *Christian Life in Song,* by Mrs. Rundel Charles, copyright by the Society for the Promotion of Christian Knowledge.

lines, God as the object of praise for all his blessings, by every creature, above, below, and in each of his manifestations as Father, Son and Holy Ghost.

❖

THE HYMN TUNE. OLD HUNDREDTH (formerly "Old One Hundred Thirty-fourth," since it was originally used with Psalm 134) is a legacy of Calvin's days in Geneva. Dissatisfied with the type of music used in Germany, Calvin entrusted the composition of new tunes for the *Genevan Psalter* largely to Louis Bourgeois (1500–1561), who had followed him to Geneva from Paris. Calvin insisted on two general principles for the music; the tune must be sung in unison, and there must be only one note to each syllable.

This tune is found in a *Huguenot Psalter,* published in Geneva in 1551, set to Psalm 134. Whether it was composed entirely by Bourgeois, or adapted by him, perhaps from some secular source, cannot be definitely stated.

The Puritan refugees, returning to England, after the death of Mary, brought with them the *Genevan Psalter,* and thus OLD HUNDREDTH was introduced into England.

A Cycle of Doxologies

(A Responsive Service in the language of Praise)

Minister (reading):

Praise God from whom all Blessings flow.

Choir (Tune—INNOCENTS):

Let us with a gladsome mind,
Praise the Lord, for he is kind;
For his mercies, aye, endure,
Ever faithful, ever sure.

MILTON.

All (singing. Tune—OLD HUNDREDTH):

Praise God, our Maker and our Friend;
Praise him through time, till time shall end;
Till Psalm and song his name adore
Through heaven's great day of Evermore.

PALGRAVE.

Minister (reading):

Praise Him, all creatures here below.

Choir (singing. Tune—ROLAND):

Warriors, fighting for the Lord,
Prophets burning with his word,
Men and women, young and old,
Raise the anthem manifold.
And let children's happy hearts
In this worship bear their parts:
Holy, Holy, Holy, cry!
Glory be to God on high!

S. A. BROOKE.

All (singing. Tune—OLD HUNDREDTH):

O Lord of earth and sea and skies,
To whom our reverent praises rise,
With light and love our spirits fill,
As we go forth to do thy will.

EDWIN RALPH.

Minister (reading):

Praise Him above, ye heavenly host.

Choir (Tune—CREATION):

Soon as the evening shades prevail,
The moon takes up the wondrous tale,
And nightly to the listening earth
Repeats the story of her birth;
Whilst all the stars that round her burn,
And all the planets in their turn,
Confirm the tidings as they roll,
And spread the truth from pole to pole.

ADDISON.

All (singing. Tune—OLD HUNDREDTH):

Lo, God is here, him day and night,
United choirs of angels sing;
To him enthroned above all height,
Heaven's host their noblest praises bring.

TERSTEEGEN.

Minister (reading):

Praise Father, Son, and Holy Ghost.

All (singing. Tune—ITALIAN HYMN):

To the great One in Three,
Eternal praises be
Hence evermore.

His sovereign majesty,
May we in glory see,
And to eternity,
Love and adore.

ANONYMOUS.

REJOICE, YE PURE IN HEART

1. Rejoice, ye pure in heart,
Rejoice, give thanks and sing;
Your festal banner wave on high,
The cross of Christ your King;

Refrain

Rejoice, rejoice,
Rejoice, give thanks and sing.

2. Bright youth and snow-crowned age,
Strong men and maidens fair,
Raise high your free, exulting song,
God's wondrous praise declare.

Refrain

3. With all the angel choirs,
With all the saints on earth,
Pour out the strains of joy and bliss,
True rapture, noblest mirth.

Refrain

4. With voice as full and strong
As ocean's surging praise,
Send forth the hymns our fathers loved,
The psalms of ancient days.

Refrain

5. Yes, on through life's long path,
Still chanting as ye go;
From youth to age, by night and day,
In gladness and in woe.

Refrain

6. Still lift your standard high,
Still march in firm array,
As warriors through the darkness toil
Till dawns the golden day.

Refrain

7. At last the march shall end,
The wearied ones shall rest,
The pilgrims find their Father's house,
Jerusalem the blest.

Refrain

EDWARD H. PLUMPTRE, 1865.

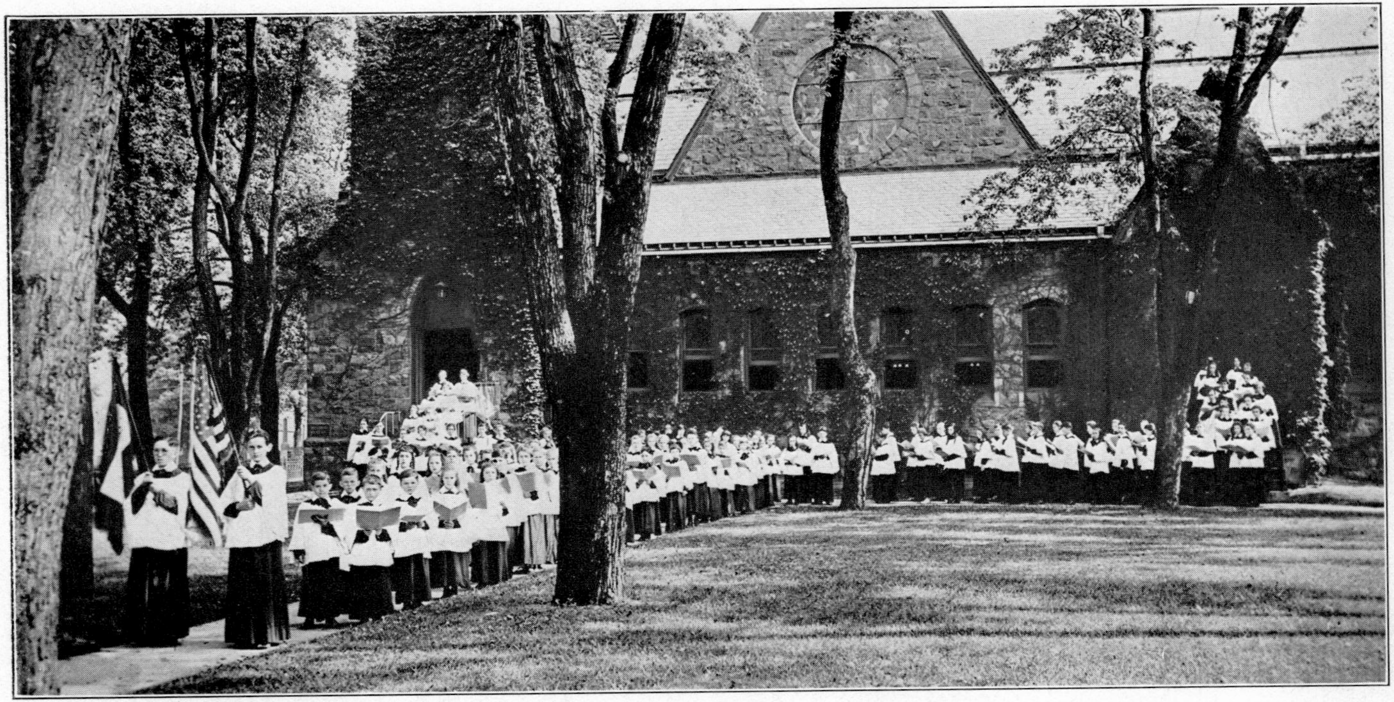

By permission of E. P. Greisamer, photographer, Flemington, N. J.

THE FLEMINGTON (NEW JERSEY) CHOIRS, MISS ELIZABETH VOSSELLER, DIRECTOR

The noble choir traditions of Messiter at Trinity are upheld in the non-liturgic churches to-day.

Biblical Text.

Praise ye the Lord:
For it is good to sing praises unto our God;
For it is pleasant, and praise is comely.

Psalm 147:1.

Rejoice in the Lord always: again I will say, Rejoice.

Philippians 4:4.

THROUGH CHURCH AND CHANCEL, AISLE AND TRANSEPT DEEP

Many of the hymns that have lived through the years were called forth by some special event, such as the choir boys' march out of Horbury Bridge, which occasioned "Onward, Christian soldiers." "Rejoice, ye pure in heart" was written for a Choir Festival in Peterborough Cathedral in May, 1865, and is peculiarly adapted to a Processional.

In a remarkable way the hymn makes the thought of joy, with which it begins, increasingly meaningful. One can easily picture the processions of choirs as they marched into the stately cathedral, and sang with hearty enthusiasm these joyous words. But it is not limited to the members of the choir—it is all-inclusive in its outreach and meaning, embracing even the "angel choirs" above, and "all the saints" below.

Edward H. Plumptre (1821–1891) was an outstanding leader in the Church of England. Educated at King's College, London, and University College, Oxford, he was Prebendary of St. Paul's, London; Rector of Pluckley; Vicar of Bickley; Professor of New Testament Exegesis, King's College, London; Special Lecturer at Oxford; a member of the Old Testament Committee of the Revisers of the Bible, and Dean of Wells Cathedral from 1881 to his death. His literary productions have been important and varied, including classics, history, the biography of Thomas Ken, Biblical criticism and poetry. This hymn was published in a collection of poems entitled *Lazarus, and Other Poems* (1865). Dr. Julian says of his hymns: "The rhythm of his verse has a special attraction for musicians, its poetry for the cultured, and its stately simplicity for the devout and earnest-minded."

✣

The Hymn Tune. "Rejoice, ye pure in heart" is one of the hymns upon the musical setting of which there seems to be general agreement. The tune Marion is found for Dean Plumptre's hymn in practically all hymnals, and, what is even more remarkable, this tune is used only for this hymn.

Marion was composed by Arthur H. Messiter (1831–1903), in 1883. Mr. Messiter was born in Frome, Somersetshire, England, and studied music there. He came to America about 1855 and from 1866 to 1897 was the organist and choirmaster at Trinity Church, New York. He prepared a new edition of *The Psalter* for use in Trinity Church, and also wrote a history of the music and choir of that church.

RIDE ON, RIDE ON IN MAJESTY

1. Ride on, ride on in majesty!
Hark! all the tribes "Hosanna" cry;
O Saviour meek, pursue thy road,
With palms and scattered garments strowed.

2. Ride on, ride on in majesty!
In lowly pomp ride on to die;
O Christ, thy triumphs now begin
O'er captive death and conquered sin.

3. Ride on, ride on in majesty!
The winged squadrons of the sky
Look down with sad and wondering eyes
To see th' approaching sacrifice.

4. Ride on, ride on in majesty!
The last and fiercest strife is nigh;
Bow thy meek head to mortal pain,
Then take, O Christ, thy power and reign.

Henry H. Milman, 1827.

Biblical Text.

Behold, thy king cometh unto thee; he is just and having salvation; lowly, and riding upon an ass.

Zechariah 9:9.

And the multitude that went before him, and that followed, cried, saying, Hosanna to the son of David: Blessed is he that cometh in the name of the Lord; Hosanna in the highest. And when he was come into Jerusalem, all the city was stirred, saying, Who is this?

Matthew 21:9, 10.

"Friendless and faint, with martyred steps and slow,
Faint for the flesh, but for the spirit free,
Stung by the mob that came to see the show,
The Master toiled along to Calvary;
We jibed him, as he went, with houndish glee,
Till his dim eyes for us did overflow;
We cursed his vengeless hands thrice wretchedly,—
And this was nineteen hundred years ago.

"But after nineteen hundred years the shame
Still clings, and we have not made good the loss
That outraged faith has entered in his name.

Ah, when shall come love's courage to be strong!
Tell me, O Lord—tell me, O Lord, how long
Are we to keep Christ writhing on the cross!"[1]

JERUSALEM AND THE PASSOVER PILGRIMS

The more one studies the hymnody of the Church, the more one is amazed at its marvelous variety. In it one finds the work of humble, obscure folk, whose one single contribution bursts out of the commonplace of everyday life with all the suddenness of a sheet of flame. And alongside these sudden bursts of lyric beauty from humble, unknown poets, one finds the productions of the master minds of the world in literature, statesmanship and the church.

To this latter class belongs the brilliant author of "Ride on, ride on in majesty." Henry Hart Milman (1791–1868) was poet, scholar, playwright, historian, theologian, professor at Oxford, and Dean of St. Paul's Cathedral, London.

Even in his college and university days his talents won for him many honors, among them the coveted Newdigate Prize.

"His lines on Apollo
Beat all the rest hollow,
And gained him the Newdigate prize."

His first drama, written when a student, was an unquestioned stage success in England and America. It did stand in his way however during his first parish work, as there was prejudice against any dominie who was a playwright. Later three religious dramas crowned his career as poet and dramatist—"The Fall of Jerusalem," "The Martyr of Antioch," and "Belshazzar," for the copyrights of which he received $2500 each.

It was through the invitation of Bishop Heber that Milman became a hymn-writer. In 1820 Heber planned to issue a new hymn book and looked about to see what poets he could enlist in securing new hymns for his book. Keats, Shelley, Byron, Coleridge, Wordsworth, Campbell, Moore, Southey, Scott and Milman were all living and writing. Scott and Southey promised to write hymns for him, but failed to send any. Heber was not discouraged by this, for when he received "Ride on in majesty" and eleven others from Milman, he wrote back: "A few more such hymns, and I shall neither need nor wait for the aid of Scott and Southey."

Milman was not only a hymn-writer and playwright; he became a distinguished historian; his *History of the Jews* was the first attempt

[1] From the poem "Calvary" by Edwin Arlington Robinson, copyright by Charles Scribner's Sons, and used by permission.

to read the Bible in the light of historical criticism. His greatest work, *Latin Christianity,* was published while he was Dean of St. Paul's.

His life in London from 1849, when he was made Dean of St. Paul's Cathedral, to his death in 1868 was one of intense activity. He was everywhere sought after for his brilliant scholarship, his social charm and his straightforward Christianity. It was during his Deanship that the interior of St. Paul's was decorated and the famous Sunday evening services were begun. As a boy he had witnessed the burial of Nelson from St. Paul's, and, as its Dean, he officiated at the funeral of the Duke of Wellington.

His style was like Heber's, full of lyric grace and literary finesse, as might be expected from a man who had held the chair of Poetry in Oxford.

A City That Lost Its Chance

And do you know what happened on the evening of this day? Jesus sat on one of the hills overlooking the city. It was dark now and all the shadows were long and heavy, almost as long and heavy as the soul of him who sat there and looked. The shouts of the multitude were still ringing in his ears, but they had changed from the sounds like those of golden bells to the sounds of clanging brass. That was why Jesus wept as he sat there. That was why he said: "O Jerusalem, If thou hadst known, even thou, at least in this thy day, the things which belong unto thy peace. But now they are hid from thine eyes." A city had lost its chance!

"Ride on, ride on in majesty" is full of dramatic movement and vivid pictures. As we sing it, we see again the Passover Pilgrims, enthusiastically waving their palm branches in the air, carpeting his pathway with their garments, and loudly acclaiming him "Son of David," and "Lord." The picture darkens, the voices are hushed; we realize that he who thus rides "in lowly pomp," "rides on to die." We hear his voice in tones of most passionate yearning, weeping over the city.

The hymn goes on through the thought of sacrifice and strife to the ultimate and certain triumph, and closes with the picture of the "Son of David," victorious by reigning.

A hint of Milman's poetic ability is given in the following quotation from his description of the Pipe Organ in the Cathedral:

"When beneath the nave
High arching, the cathedral organ 'gins
Its prelude, lingeringly exquisite

Within, retired, the bashful sweetness dwells;
Anon like sunlight, or the floodgate rush
Of waters, bursts it forth—clear, solemn, full,
It breaks upon the mazy fretted roof;
It coils up round the clustering pillars tall;
It leaps into the cell-like chapels; strikes
Beneath the pavement sepulchres; at once
The living temple is instinct, ablaze
With the uncontrolled exuberance of sound."

✣

The Hymn Tune. St. Drostane, by John Bacchus Dykes (1823–1876), is one of this master's finest tunes, written specifically for these words thirty-five years after the words were written by Milman. Naturally, other tunes have been used with Milman's text, such as Winchester New and Park Street, but St. Drostane, composed especially for these words, carries them, it seems, with peculiar appropriateness, through awe and grief to the high rapture of redemption. Dr. Dykes had his troubles with his Bishop, who was willing to license Dr. Dykes as Curate only on these conditions: That Dr. Dykes shall never wear a colored stoll; never have anything to do with incense; shall never stand with his back to the congregation except when ordering the Bread. Dr. Dykes lost his case in court. He never recovered from the shock, but died three years later.

RING OUT, WILD BELLS

1. Ring out, wild bells, to the wild sky,
The flying cloud, the frosty light;
The year is dying in the night;
Ring out, wild bells, and let him die.

2. Ring out the old, ring in the new,
Ring, happy bells, across the snow;
The year is going, let him go;
Ring out the false, ring in the true.

3. Ring out a slowly dying cause,
And ancient forms of party strife,
Ring in the nobler modes of life,
With sweeter manners, purer laws.

4. Ring out old shapes of foul disease;
Ring out the narrowing lust of gold;
Ring out the thousand wars of old,
Ring in the thousand years of peace.

5. Ring in the valiant man and free,
The larger heart, the kindlier hand;

Ring out the darkness of the land,
Ring in the Christ that is to be.

ALFRED TENNYSON, 1849.

BIBLICAL TEXT.

Remember ye not the former things, neither consider the things of old.

Behold, I will do a new thing; now shall it spring forth; shall ye not know it?

I will even make a way in the wilderness, and rivers in the desert.

ISAIAH 43: 18, 19.

For, behold, I create new heavens and a new earth; and the former things shall not be remembered, nor come into mind.

But be ye glad and rejoice forever in that which I create; for, behold, I create Jerusalem a rejoicing, and her people, a joy.

And I will rejoice in Jerusalem, and joy in my people; and there shall be heard in her no more the voice of weeping and the voice of crying;

The wolf and the lamb shall feed together, and the lion shall eat straw like the ox;

They shall not hurt nor destroy in all my holy mountain, saith the Lord.

ISAIAH 65: 17–19, 25.

RING OUT THE OLD, RING IN THE NEW

A truly great poet, honored by England as Wordsworth's successor as Poet Laureate in 1850, made a peer of the realm in 1884 (after he had twice declined such honor), Alfred Tennyson (1809–1892) might have been expected to write hymns. But he is represented in the hymnal by only three hymns. His own statement about hymn-writing is significant: "A good hymn is the most difficult thing in the world to write." It was not until almost the end of his lifetime of writing that Tennyson achieved his one really great hymn; that came to him suddenly, as an inspiration, when he was in his eighty-first year —"Sunset and Evening Star." Tennyson felt its greatness and directed that it should be placed at the end of all editions of his poems.

His other two hymns are "Ring out, wild bells," and "Strong Son of God, Immortal Love." Both are taken from "In Memoriam," a lament for the poet's dead friend, one of the great elegies of the world; it is also a profound study of philosophy, and fights through the battle of science and religion. Hallam's death had occurred in 1833. "In Memoriam" is the result of seventeen years of pondering, sorrowing and writing. It is described by Eugene Parsons as his best reflective poem and favorite work. Into it he poured the consecrated fragrance of his genius.

"Ring out, wild bells" is section CVI of this poem. Of the eight stanzas of this section, five are usually printed as the hymn. Occasionally a sixth is added.

(Omitted Stanzas)

"Ring out the grief that saps the mind,
For those that here we see no more;
Ring out the feud of rich and poor,
Ring in redress to all mankind.

Ring out the want, the care, the sin,
The faithless coldness of the times;
Ring out, ring out, my mournful rhymes,
But ring the fuller minstrel in.

Ring out false pride in place and blood,
The civic slander and the spite;
Ring in the love of truth and right,
Ring in the common love of good."

Alfred Tennyson was the son of the rector of Somersby. He was educated at Louth Grammar School and Trinity College, Cambridge. His first book of poems was published (in coöperation with his brother Charles) when he was only eighteen. A second volume followed, three years later, and in 1842 *Poems by Alfred Tennyson* placed him in the front rank of English poets. This volume included "Morte d'Arthur," "Locksley Hall," "The Talking Oak," and "Sir Galahad."

He lived at Freshwater, Isle of Wight, and Aldworth, Surrey, but spent much time in travel. In 1865 he declined a baronetcy offered by the Queen, and again in 1868 a similar honor tendered by Disraeli. But he was at last persuaded by Gladstone, and on Jan. 24, 1884, was made a peer of the realm, with the title of Baron of Aldworth and Farringford.

He lived to be eighty-one years of age, active to the last, even dictating "The Silent Voices" on his deathbed. He was buried in the Poets' Corner, Westminster Abbey.

There is a splendid forward look in this hymn, a sublime confidence in the glory of the new day which should be far better than the former ones. It is too commonly limited to use at the New Year season; for, while it sings of the old year's going, it sings of changing conditions which fit any season. It is a vibrant hymn for youth, with its courage, optimism and enthusiasm for the new and challenging.

THE HYMN TUNE. WILD BELLS comes from an anthem by Henry Lahee (1826–1912), an English organist and pianist, who presided at the organ in Holy Trinity Church, Brompton, for twenty-two years. He wrote the cantatas, "The Building of the Ship," "The Blessing of the Children," "The Sleeping Beauty," and many part-songs and glees.

His son, Henry Charles Lahee (1856–), came to Boston in 1883, where he was for eight years secretary of the New England Conservatory of Music.

"Ring out, wild bells" is also set to the tune WALTHAM, composed by J. Baptiste Calkin. The beauty of the words can be greatly augmented by a chime accompaniment. The hymn should be sung lightly and clearly in order to bring out the contrast of the old sordid era which is to be rung out and the new glorious age which the bells are to usher in. If the third stanza is sung softly, the last stanza is made more effective, and can be brought to a vibrant climax on the words "The Christ that is to be."

RISE UP, O MEN OF GOD

1. Rise up, O men of God,
Have done with lesser things;
Give heart and soul and mind and strength
To serve the King of kings.

2. Rise up, O men of God,
His kingdom tarries long;
Bring in the day of brotherhood
And end the night of wrong.

3. Rise up, O men of God,
The Church for you doth wait,
Her strength unequal to her task;
Rise up, and make her great.

4. Lift high the cross of Christ,
Tread where his feet have trod;
As brothers of the Son of man
Rise up, O men of God! [1]

WILLIAM PIERSON MERRILL, 1911.

BIBLICAL TEXT.

Awake, awake, put on thy strength, O Zion.

ISAIAH 52: 1.

Arise, shine; for thy light is come, and the glory of the Lord is risen upon thee.

ISAIAH 60: 1.

Watch ye, stand fast in the faith, quit you like men, be strong.

I CORINTHIANS 16: 13.

THE MUSIC OF THE CITY

William Pierson Merrill (1867–) is one of the outstanding preachers and writers of present-day America. He has been since October 1, 1911, the pastor of the Brick Presbyterian Church, Fifth Avenue, New York City. Before coming back to New York, where

[1] Copyright by William Pierson Merrill.

he graduated from Union Theological Seminary in 1890, he served as pastor of the Sixth Presbyterian Church, Chicago, for sixteen years and Trinity Church, Chestnut Hill, Philadelphia, for five years.

Among his books are *Footings for Faith, Christian Internationalism, The Common Creed of Christians, The Freedom of the Preacher,* and *Liberal Christianity.*

Since 1915 he has been president of the Board of Trustees of the Church Peace Union, and is one of the active leaders in many movements for civic betterment.

This hymn was written in the year in which he began his New York pastorate. It is a stirring challenge to men of the Church in New York, Chicago, Philadelphia, Boston, everywhere, to "have done with lesser things," and give of their time, talents and energy to the advent of "the day of brotherhood."

Hymns of City Life and Industrial Relations

Many hymns stress Christian living in terms of city life. Hymns call to the voter to build an upright city. Modern artists like Flandrin have caught this modern viewpoint, and Christ is pictured by him, not as weeping over Jerusalem of old with pinnacled temples, massive gates, alabaster in the Oriental sunlight, but rather over a modern industrial center, with tenement houses filling the foreground, chimneys belching smoke, and crowded and grimy streets leading nowhere in particular.

Vocational Hymn Lines:

> My Master was a worker with daily work to do.
> O Master of the callous hand, the workshop, bench and plane.
> We are builders of that city.
> Give these that teach pure hearts and wise.
> The Master of our schools.
> Comrades known in marches many.
> Guard the sailor tossing on the deep blue sea.
> When the soldier on the field lifts his heart to thee.
> When the shepherd on the moor.
> Watchman, tell us of the night.
> Traveler, lo, the Prince of Peace.
> When the man of toil and care in the city crowd.
> When the stranger asks a home.

> From street and square, from hill and glen,
> Of this vast world beyond my door,
> I hear the tread of marching men,
> The patient armies of the poor.

> The bondmen of the forge and shaft
> Whose tasks are never done.

Ring out a slowly dying cause,
And ancient forms of party strife.
Ring in the nobler modes of life,
With sweeter manners, purer laws.

Where cross the crowded ways of life,
Where sound the cries of race and clan.

Give us, O God, the strength to build
The city that hath stood
Too long a dream, whose laws are love,
Whose ways are brotherhood.

Famous City Centers of Hymn-writing: Alexandria, Egypt; Edessa, Mesopotamia; Constantinople, Turkey; Geneva, Switzerland; Bristol, Oxford, Olney and London, England; Boston and New York City.

✣

THE HYMN TUNE. ST. THOMAS is also frequently used with Watts' hymn, "Come we who love the Lord." It has the sturdy forward movement so necessary for "Rise up, O men of God." See the account of this tune under "I love thy Kingdom, Lord."

ROCK OF AGES, CLEFT FOR ME

1. Rock of Ages, cleft for me,
Let me hide myself in thee;
Let the water and the blood,
From thy riven side which flowed,
Be of sin the double cure,
Cleanse me from its guilt and power.

2. Could my zeal no respite know,
Could my tears forever flow,
All for sin could not atone,
Thou must save, and thou alone;
Nothing in my hand I bring,
Simply to thy cross I cling.

3. While I draw this fleeting breath,
When my eyelids close in death,
When I soar to worlds unknown,
See thee on thy judgment throne,
Rock of Ages, cleft for me,
Let me hide myself in thee.

AUGUSTUS M. TOPLADY, 1776.

BIBLICAL TEXT.

In that day there shall be a fountain opened to the house of David and to the inhabitants of Jerusalem, for sin and for uncleanness.

ZECHARIAH 13:1.

Be thou to me a strong rock,
A house of defense to save me.

PSALM 31:2.

From the end of the earth will I call unto thee, when my heart is overwhelmed:
Lead me to the rock that is higher than I.

PSALM 61:2.

For by grace have ye been saved through faith, and that not of yourselves, it is the gift of God.

EPHESIANS 2:8.

A LIVING AND DYING PRAYER FOR THE HOLIEST BELIEVER IN THE WORLD

Theological controversies arise and pass, even that between Calvinism and Arminianism, but this hymn, which was inspired by just that sort of controversy, seems to be enduring. The fervor of the controversy and the warmth of the debate are suggested by the lengthy title above, which is exactly as it was worded by the author for the first publication of the hymn in *The Gospel Magazine,* March, 1776.

Toplady and John Wesley were stout theological opponents. Since Peter and Paul disagreed so hotly, Christian leaders have found it necessary to fight not only the world, the flesh, and the devil, but sometimes one another. A controversy between these brother priests of the Church of England over the dogma of Election seems partly to have fired the emotion that blazed out in one of the greatest hymns of the world, "Rock of Ages." Toplady had published a hymn beginning:

My name from the palm of his hand
Eternity cannot erase;
Impressed on his heart it remains
In marks of indelible grace.

Wesley called him a "vain boaster," and the two exchanged arguments peppered with invective.

This famous hymn was written as a part of this long and acrimonious debate. Comparing a man's "debt of sin" to the National Debt, Toplady showed that, at the rate of one sin per second, every man at twenty years is guilty of the total of 630,720,000 sins; at fifty, of 1,576,800,000; and at eighty, of 2,522,880,000. Then he asks "When shall we be able to pay off this debt?" and answers, "Never. But Christ has redeemed us from the curse of the Law and his Blood cleanseth from all sin. We must bless God the Father for electing us, God the Son for assuming our debts, God the Holy Spirit for his gift of faith in

Christ." Then follows the title, as given above, and the four stanzas of the hymn.

And so the cold and storm of disputation with the ironic thrust even in the title of the poem, changes to lyric sunshine with the first line of the hymn. It is a grand hymn. Few poems are more familiar and more treasured in the affections of the people than this. For example, at the hundredth anniversary of its writing, ten thousand people gathered on the wild hillside, where tradition says it was written. What other poem has had ten thousand as pilgrims to its shrine to celebrate its birthday? The fact that the Prince Consort Albert repeated its lines as he died helped of course to spread its fame over the British Empire; but that is a detail only of its history, a symbol of its hold upon the world.

Augustus Toplady (1740–1778) was born at Farnham in Surrey, son of Major Richard Toplady, of the British Army, who was killed at Carthagena, 1741. He was sent to the Westminster School in London. Going with his mother to Ireland he entered Trinity College, Dublin. He was the Vicar of Broadhernbury in Devonshire from 1768 until his death. He published a volume of Psalms and Hymns in 1766. Troubled with weak lungs, he sought to exchange his vicarage in Devonshire for one in a dryer climate, but without success. Going to London in 1775 he became minister of a church of French Colonists in Leicester Fields, but lived only a short time after this. At his death he said, "O my dear sir, I cannot tell you the comforts I feel in my soul; they are past expression. My prayers are all converted into praise."

Oliver Wendell Holmes wrote to Harriet Beecher Stowe concerning this hymn: "I recognize its wonderful power and solemnity. If you asked me what is the secret of it, I should say that of all the Protestant hymns I remember, it is the richest in material imagery. . . . It is the Protestant *Dies Iræ*."

✣

THE HYMN TUNE. Appropriately named TOPLADY, the tune by Thomas Hastings is thoroughly wedded to this hymn. Thomas Hastings (1784–1872) was born in Washington, Connecticut. When he was twelve years old his family moved to Clinton, New York, where six years later he was leading the village choir. In 1828 he went to Utica, where he stayed four years, editing a weekly religious paper, *The Western Recorder*. Subsequently, the New York City churches combined to secure his leadership for their choirs. New York recognized his musical ability; for the University of the City of New York gave him in 1858 the degree of Mus.D.

He is said to have written as many as six hundred hymns, composed a thousand hymn-tunes, and published fifty volumes of music. Julian's Dictionary lists over fifty of his hymns as in common use (1892). Probably his most familiar hymn is "Hail to the brightness of Zion's glad morning," although "He that goeth forth with weeping" is a close second.

With Lowell Mason and W. B. Bradbury, Hastings may be said to have helped to mold the musical taste of American churches.

SAVIOUR, AGAIN TO THY DEAR NAME WE RAISE

1. Saviour, again to thy dear name we raise,
With one accord our parting hymn of praise;
We stand to bless thee ere our worship cease;
Then, lowly kneeling, wait thy word of peace.

2. Grant us thy peace, upon our homeward way;
With thee began, with thee shall end the day:
Guard thou the lips from sin, the hearts from shame,
That in this house have called upon thy name.

3. Grant us thy peace, Lord, through the coming night;
Turn thou for us its darkness into light;
From harm and danger keep thy children free,
For dark and light are both alike to thee.

4. Grant us thy peace throughout our earthly life,
Our balm in sorrow, and our stay in strife;
Then, when thy voice shall bid our conflict cease,
Call us, O Lord, to thine eternal peace.

John Ellerton, 1866.

Biblical Text.

Lord, lift thou up the light of thy countenance upon us.
In peace will I both lay me down and sleep;
For thou, Lord, alone makest me to dwell in safety.

Psalm 4:6, 8.

Peace I leave with you; my peace I give unto you. . . . Let not your heart be troubled, neither let it be fearful.

John 14:27.

Jesus came and stood in the midst, and saith unto them, Peace be unto you. And when he had said this, he showed unto them his hands and his side. The disciples therefore were glad, when they saw the Lord.

John 20:19, 20.

A SONG OF THE EVER-PRESENT GOD

This hymn ought to be a special favorite with church choirs, for it was written for them. John Ellerton (1826–1893), then Vicar of Crewe Green in the English Midlands, was so firm a believer in the value of church music that he organized an association of church choirs in the Midlands. This Festival of the Malpas, Middlewich and Nantwich Choral Association was an important occasion, important enough, so it seemed to the Vicar of Crewe Green, to deserve a special hymn.

"Saviour, again to thy dear name" was published in *Thorn's Collection,* and later reviewed and abridged by Ellerton himself for the Appendix to *Hymns Ancient and Modern,* in 1868.

A stanza usually omitted follows:

> "Grant us thy peace—the peace thou didst bestow
> On thine apostles, in thine hour of woe;
> The peace thou broughtest, when at eventide
> They saw thy pierced hands, thy wounded side."

Canon John Ellerton was one of the brilliant English hymn-writers of the nineteenth century. Among the more familiar of his hymns found in modern hymnals are:

> "Our day of praise is done"
> "This is the day of light"
> "The day Thou gavest, Lord, is ended"
> "Behold us, Lord, a little space"

and also his translation of Fortunatus' Easter hymn of the sixth century, "Welcome, happy morning."

❖

THE HYMN TUNE. ELLERS, or BENEDICTION, was written by Edward J. Hopkins (1818–1901) for these words of Ellerton's. The melody rises persistently through twenty notes of the first half of the tune as if to dramatize "standing to bless" and "raising a parting hymn of praise"; then as consistently it moves downward through twenty notes of the last half to say in music what is uttered in the text "lowly kneeling," "wait thy word of peace." The tune, but for one inflected note at the end of the second line, is in the Mixo-Lydian mode, the mode of the fifth of the scale, that in which "Scots, wha hae" is composed. It was designedly written in this mode by Dr. Hopkins, and the melody derives much of its freshness and charm from this novel construction.

The tune was first published in the *Supplemental Hymn and Tune Book,* compiled by the Reverend R. Brown-Borthwick, in 1869. It was arranged for voices in unison, with an organ accompaniment which was different for each stanza. This was a concession to cathedral organists who improvised all manner of delightful harmonies, while the voices carried the air in unison. But in England and America the usual four-part version is preferred, and Dr. Hopkins was requested to provide ELLERS with a standard harmonization for four voices.

"The tune," says Dr. Hopkins, "should be the offspring of particular words, and should be consecrated to them."

SAVIOUR, BREATHE AN EVENING BLESSING

1. Saviour, breathe an evening blessing,
Ere repose our spirits seal;
Sin and want we come confessing;
Thou canst save, and thou canst heal.

2. Though the night be dark and dreary,
Darkness cannot hide from thee;
Thou art he who, never weary,
Watchest where thy people be.

3. Though destruction walk around us,
Though the arrow past us fly,
Angel-guards from thee surround us,
We are safe if thou art nigh.

4. Should swift death this night o'ertake us,
And our couch become our tomb,
May the morn in heaven awake us,
Clad in light and deathless bloom.

JAMES EDMESTON, 1820.

BIBLICAL TEXT.

The darkness hideth not from thee,
But the night shineth as the day:
The darkness and the light are both alike to thee.

PSALM 139: 12.

There shall no evil befall thee,
Neither shall any plague come nigh thy tent.
For he will give his angels charge over thee,
To keep thee in all thy ways.

PSALM 91: 10, 11.

OUT OF THE STORM OF THE BOXER UPRISING

During the Boxer uprising in China a company of beleaguered missionaries were gathered at a meeting-place just outside of Shanghai, where there was a semblance of safety. One of that company describes the scene: "Separated from home and friends, facing death in a far-off land, and full of tenderest feelings, we lifted our hearts in song:

'Though destruction walk around us,
Though the arrow past us fly:
Angel-guards from thee surround us:
We are safe if thou art nigh.'

"Out of the storm, each soul, renewing its strength, mounted up with wings as eagles and found peace in the secret of his presence. Our Saviour breathed, in very deed, 'an evening blessing,' the fragrance of which remains even unto this day. The last verse of the hymn, 'Should swift death this night o'ertake us,' was omitted. It seemed too probable that it might. We wanted only to think of the safe-keeping, and such, thank God, it proved to be."

A layman who "builded better than he knew" was James Edmeston (1791–1867), an English architect. How many of the buildings he planned have lasted through the years few people know or care, but many remember him as the author of one of the supreme evening hymns of the church.

The writing of hymns, especially for children, seems to have been Mr. Edmeston's avocation. He wrote nearly two thousand of them. Two of them have survived and are commonly used today, "Saviour, breathe an evening blessing," and "Lead us, heavenly Father, lead us."

Edmeston, interested in missions, was much impressed by an account of a night on the desert, described in Salte's "Travels in Abyssinia at Night." The writer says, "their short evening hymn, *'Jesu Mahaxaroo,'* 'Jesus forgive us,' stole through the camp." Edmeston made this his hymn theme.

Bishop Bickersteth added an eight-line stanza which is sometimes used:

"Father, to thy holy keeping
Humbly we ourselves resign;
Saviour, who hast slept thy sleeping,
Make our slumbers pure as thine;
Blessed Spirit, brooding o'er us,
Chase the darkness of our night,

Till the perfect day before us
Breaks in everlasting light."

✣

THE HYMN TUNE. This hymn has been set to several tunes, but none has been so popular on the American continent as EVENING PRAYER, by George C. Stebbins (1846–).

Mr. Stebbins' early life was spent on a farm in Orleans County, New York. His musical career began in Chicago, as Musical Director at the First Baptist Church. In the fall of 1876 he began an association with Dwight L. Moody, and Ira D. Sankey, which lasted throughout the lives of these two men. He organized the choir for their campaign of 1876 in Chicago.

Later, Mr. Stebbins assumed the leadership of the music in Tremont Temple, Boston. It was there that the tune, EVENING PRAYER, was composed and rendered on several occasions by the Temple Quartet, in which Stebbins himself sang the tenor.

Mr. Stebbins was one of the editors of *Gospel Hymns* and the sole editor of the *Northfield Hymnal*. His own tunes are of pleasing melody and have attained wide use. He is probably the best of the writers of Gospel Hymn tunes.

SEND DOWN THY TRUTH, O GOD

1. Send down thy truth, O God;
Too long the shadows frown,
Too long the darkened way we've trod,
Thy truth, O Lord, send down.

2. Send down thy spirit free,
Till wilderness and town
One temple for thy worship be,
Thy spirit, O send down.

3. Send down thy love, thy life,
Our lesser lives to crown,
And cleanse them of their hate and strife,
Thy living love send down.

4. Send down thy peace, O Lord;
Earth's bitter voices drown
In one deep ocean of accord,
Thy peace, O God, send down.

EDWARD ROWLAND SILL, 1867.

BIBLICAL TEXT.

O send out thy light and thy truth; let them lead me;

Let them bring me to thy holy hill,
And to thy tabernacles.

PSALM 43:3.

If there is therefore any exhortation in Christ, if any consolation of love, if any fellowship of the Spirit, if any tender mercies and compassions. make full my joy, that ye be of the same mind, having the same love, being of one accord, of one mind; doing nothing through faction or vain-glory;

PHILIPPIANS 2:1–3.

A PRAYER FOR AMERICA EMERGING FROM CIVIL WAR

Edward Rowland Sill (1841–1887) was born at Windsor, Connecticut, and graduated at Yale. He went west in 1874 to become professor of English in the University of California. He was author of two volumes of verse, *The Hermitage,* 1867, and *Venus of Milo,* 1883, He is perhaps most widely known by a single short poem, "The Fool's Prayer," a masterpiece of grace and wisdom, and by the above hymn which appeared in *The Hermitage*. It is a chastened, penitent and longing hymn that might well have been sung itself at the close of the Civil War, which now seems so senseless and so devoid of the graces of mind and heart the hymn pleads for. "Send down thy truth, O God"—it might have been different if even in the limited sense the common folk of the north and the south had known more of the truth about each other instead of so discounting each others' spiritual and material powers. The hymn pleads for the free spirit of religion and for love, contemplating what those gifts will do for the country, remembering what their reverse has brought over the land. Their lives, especially after those long years of fighting and bloodshed and devastation, needed to be "cleansed of their hate and strife." There was emphatic need of that "living love" which comes only from the deeper springs of being. So the hymn fitted the day of its writing, since it grew out of the conditions of its time.

True and great hymns are timeless as well as timely. There is still reason to sing "Send down thy spirit free," for town and wilderness have not yet become "one temple for thy worship"; and the world is not yet united in "accord." There is need of God's peace everywhere. His hymn pleads for the spirit of religion and love, contemplating what those gifts will do for nations and remembering what their opposites, bitterness and hate, have brought upon a country, broken by civil strife.

Following are Professor Sill's well-known lines from "Life":

"Forenoon and afternoon and night,—Forenoon
And afternoon, and night,—

Forenoon, and—what!
The empty song repeats itself, no more?
Yea, that is life: make this forenoon sublime,
This afternoon a psalm, this night a prayer,
And Time is conquered, and thy crown is won."

✣

THE HYMN TUNE. GARDEN CITY was the work of Horatio W. Parker (1863–1919), noted American composer. He was born in Auburndale, Massachusetts. His father was a distinguished architect; his mother a musician of very considerable ability. Young Parker did not care for music until he was fourteen years old, when his mother says he spent "literally whole days at the piano." She was his first teacher of piano and organ, and in two years' time he had mastered the organ sufficiently to play for church services. He studied under Chadwick in Boston, and under Rheinberger in Munich.

After graduating from the Munich Conservatory at the age of twenty-two, he returned to America and became Director of Music at St. Paul's and St. Mary's Schools, Garden City, Long Island, whence the title of this tune.

In 1894 he became professor of music at Yale, and held that position until his death. He was honored with the opportunity of directing his oratorio, *"Hora Novissima,"* at the Worcester (England) Festival in 1899, the first English music festival at which the work of an American composer was produced. His success was so great that he was invited to compose a work for the Hereford Festival of 1900, and wrote "The Wanderer's Psalm." From 1893 to 1901 he was organist of Trinity Church, Boston, in addition to his duties at Yale.

Among his compositions are two operas, *Mona,* produced in 1912 in the Metropolitan Opera House, New York, and *Fairyland;* three oratorios, *Hora Novissima, The Legend of St. Christopher,* and *Morven and the Grail;* a large number of cantatas and much solo and orchestra music.

Dr. Benson says of him: "He had no instinctive sympathy with congregational singing, which he found inartistic; and he had an idealist's contempt for the common level and for popularity. One of his earlier tunes, GARDEN CITY, that attained wide vogue, became an offense to him. He told me he would recall his tune if he could. And yet effectiveness need not be a bugbear to an artist. . . . Certainly Parker's 'Mount Sion' is, within its limits, as good music as his prize opera *Mona.* And one can imagine the hymn-tune being sung on church occasions till the end of time, while it is doubtful if the profoundly accomplished opera . . . will again be performed." [1]

SHEPHERD OF TENDER YOUTH

1. Shepherd of tender youth,
Guiding in love and truth,
Through devious ways;
Christ, our triumphant King,
We come thy name to sing,
And here our children bring
To shout thy praise.

2. Thou art our holy Lord,
The all-subduing Word,
Healer of strife;
Thou didst thyself abase,
That from sin's deep disgrace
Thou mightest save our race,
And give us life.

(*Omitted Stanza*)

Thou art the great High Priest;
Thou hast prepared the feast
Of heavenly love;
In all our mortal pain
None call on thee in vain;
Help thou didst not disdain,
Help from above.

3. Ever be thou our Guide,
Our Shepherd and our Pride,
Our Staff and Song;
Jesus, thou Christ of God,
By thy perennial Word,
Lead us where thou hast trod,
Make our faith strong.

4. So now, and till we die,
Sound we thy praises high,
And joyful sing;
Let all the holy throng,
Who to thy Church belong,
Unite and swell the song
To Christ, our King.

CLEMENT OF ALEXANDRIA, about 220 A. D.
Translated by Henry M. Dexter, 1846.

[1] From *The Hymnody of the Christian Church,* by Louis F. Benson, copyright by Richard R. Smith.

BIBLICAL TEXT.

I am the good shepherd: the good shepherd layeth down his life for the sheep.

JOHN 10: 11.

The Lord is my shepherd; I shall not want . . .
Thou preparest a table before me in the presence of mine enemies.

PSALM 23: 1, 5.

Unto him that sitteth on the throne, and unto the Lamb, be the blessing, and the honor, and the glory, and the dominion, for ever and ever. Amen.

REVELATION 5: 13.

THE OLDEST CHRISTIAN HYMN

This hymn, a free translation from the Greek, is often called the oldest Christian hymn; written over seventeen hundred years ago by Clement of Alexandria.

Relatively little is known of Clement, except that he was from about 190 A. D. to 203 A. D. the head of the Catechetical School in Alexandria. It is supposed that he was born in Athens about 140, and grew up in the philosophical atmosphere of that city. Failing to find satisfaction of soul in Greek philosophy, he is said to have tried Assyrian, Egyptian and Jewish teachers. At last he came in touch with Pantænus, the head of this Christian Catechetical School in Alexandria, and through him, found in Christ the "All in All," he had been seeking. When Pantænus left Alexandria to become a missionary, Clement took his place. In the persecution under Severus, in 203, he was obliged to leave Alexandria; the date or place of his death is unknown.

Among his writings is a work called *The Pedagogue* (or Tutor), in three books. The first describes the Tutor, Christ, the children whom he trains, and his general method of instruction. The second gives general admonitions as to daily life; the third condemns extravagance. With this work are two poems, one, "The Hymn of the Saviour," and the other, an address "To the Tutor." It is from the former that this hymn is taken.

Henry Martyn Dexter (1821–1890) was an American Congregational minister, a graduate of Yale, and Andover Theological Seminary. His pastorates were in Manchester, New Hampshire, and Boston. In 1867 he became editor of *The Congregationalist,* and remained in that position until his death.

While a pastor in Manchester, Doctor Dexter preached a sermon on "Some prominent characteristics of the early Christians." In connection with this sermon he thought to emphasize its message by making an English hymn out of the old Greek poem by Clement. "I transfused as much of its language and spirit as I could into the hymn." So the choir of a Manchester, New Hampshire, Congregational Church was the first, in this country, at least, to bring to light this old poem which had lain buried for sixteen and a half centuries. There are a great number and variety of English translations of this hymn. The original describes Christ as the supreme Teacher, in a series of bold metaphors—"bridle for unbroken colt," "wing of sure-flying bird," "rudder, girdle and shepherd."

One writer has described it in these words: "Through all the images here so quaintly interwoven, like a stained glass window, of which the eye loses the design in the complication of colors, we may surely trace, as in quaint old letters on a scroll winding through all the mosaic of tints, 'Christ all in all.' "

The first stanza of the poem, literally rendered and construed, is as follows:

"Bridle of untaught foals,
Wing of unwandering birds,
Helm and Girdle of babes,
Shepherd of royal lambs,
Assemble thy simple children
To praise holily,
To hymn guilelessly
With innocent mouths
Christ, the guide of children."

Another literal translation reads:

"O Saviour Jesus, Shepherd, Husbandman,
Helm thou to guide, and Bridle to restrain,
Wing of the holy flock that heaven would gain,
Thou art, O Christ, the living heavenly Way,
The everflowing Word, unchanging Day,
Eternal Light, and Mercy's healthful Spring."

Symbolism in Hymns

God is a fisherman, in a hymn translated by Dr. Neale:

"Fisher, the Father is: this world, the sea;
Christ's flesh the bait, the Hook his Deity,
The line his generation. Satan took
The offered bait; and perished by the hook."

Another hymn represents Christ as the nut; the Cross is the bitter hull; the Body is the shell; and his Godhead the fruit. The forerunner of Rock of Ages is this Prudentius hymn:

"Ah! how wondrous was the fountain flowing from his pierced side,
Whence the blood and water mingled in a strange and sacred tide—
Water, sign of mystic cleansing; blood, the martyr's crown of pride."

Another symbol is the cock at dawn waking the sleeper and being regarded as a symbol of Christ waking the soul to life, and this hymn about the true priest caring for his own like the cock:

"Cock, he findeth grains of wheat,
And his hens he calleth,
Giving to the dearer ones
What to each befalleth:
'Midst his people thus the clerk
Scripture nurture shareth,
And for sick, and poor, and maimed
Providently careth."

Samuel Medley wrote:

"A filthy dog I am by sin;
A furious dog, dear Lord, I've been;
A greedy dog in evil ways,
And a dumb dog to all thy praise."

✣

THE HYMN TUNE. While a number of tunes are in use for these words, the one frequently preferred is KIRBY BEDON, composed by Edward Bunnett (1834–1923) in 1887. (For the life of the composer see the hymn, "Christ in his word draws near.")

SILENT NIGHT, HOLY NIGHT

1. Silent night, holy night,
All is calm, all is bright,
Round yon Virgin Mother and Child,
Holy Infant so tender and mild,
Sleep in heavenly peace,
Sleep in heavenly peace.

2. Silent night, holy night,
Darkness flies, all is light;
Shepherds hear the angels sing,
"Alleluia! hail the King!
Christ the Saviour is born,
Christ the Saviour is born."

3. Silent night, holy night,
Guiding Star, lend thy light;
See the eastern wise men bring
Gifts and homage to our King!
Christ the Saviour is born,
Christ the Saviour is born.

4. Silent night, holy night,
Wondrous Star, lend thy light;
With the angels let us sing
Alleluia to our King!
Christ the Saviour is born,
Christ the Saviour is born.

Translated from Joseph Mohr, 1818.

Biblical Text.

And there were shepherds in the same country, abiding in the field, and keeping watch by night over their flock.

Luke 2:8.

And they came with haste, and found both Mary and Joseph, and the babe lying in the manger.

Luke 2: 16.

Wise-men from the east came to Jerusalem, saying, Where is he that is born King of the Jews? for we saw his star in the east, and are come to worship him.

And lo, the star . . . went before them, till it came and stood over where the young child was. And when they saw the star, they rejoiced with exceeding great joy.

Matthew 2: 1, 2, 9, 10.

A CHRISTMAS CAROL OF WANDERING TYROLESE

In 1818 Joseph Mohr (1792–1848) was assistant pastor at Oberdorf, near Arnsdorf. On Christmas Eve he attended a meeting at the Arnsdorf school-house, where he was greeted by Franz Gruber. Two sisters named Strasser were among those who were present on this occasion. During some of the preparations for the Christmas celebration Mohr withdrew for a time, and when he was later called into the room for the presentation of the Christmas gift, he carried a folded sheet of paper as his gift to his friend, Franz Gruber. When Gruber opened it, he read aloud the poem which has become one of the world's best-loved and most widely used Christmas carols, "Silent night, holy night."

Thus it was that a personal gift to an intimate friend at Christmas time more than a century ago, in an obscure German village, has resulted in a world-chorus of praise at Christmas time. Wandering Tyrolese singers made this hymn known and loved over wide areas of Germany and Austria.

Analysis. In the thought of this hymn, there is a beautiful progression which should be carefully noted in every use of it.

First, the quiet of the night, the darkness everywhere, except that one light which shines in the cave of the Khan where the weary travelers from Nazareth had found shelter when "there was no room for them in the inn."

Then, the sudden flood of the glory-light from heaven, and the appearance to those humble shepherds on the hillside of the Angelic Messenger and his accompanying "Heavenly Host," and the joyous rapture of their "Alleluia" anthem of praise to "God in the highest," and proclamation of "Peace on earth, good-will among men."

The scene changes. We now see those strange and kingly figures on their long journey from the Eastern country, following the light of that "Guiding Star." Not empty-handed do they come, nor with mere objective gifts of gold, frankincense and myrrh, but with sincere "homage" and genuine devotion do they kneel in the presence of the Infant King.

Finally the hymn mounts to its climax with a prayer that we, too, may be guided to the Manger-Cradle-Throne, there to bow in sincere adoration and worship, and to lift our voices with the Angel Choir in praise to him who is both Saviour and King.

✣

THE HYMN TUNE. Later, on that same Christmas Eve of 1818, when Joseph Mohr had presented the poem as his gift to his friend Franz Gruber, and Mohr had retired to his own rooms, he was surprised to hear his own hymn being sung to a beautiful melody. He hurried to thank his friends: Gruber's greeting was: "Indeed, has not the song become a beautiful tune! One cannot do anything else at once but sing your beautiful song. Therefore the sound at once came to me, and while you were gone I played it to my friends, the Strassers, and we together have composed it." Author and composer then sang it together, Mohr singing the melody (tenor) and accompanying on the guitar, composer Gruber singing the bass.

Thus it appears that both the words and the music of this familiar and most beautiful Christmas carol were the spontaneous inspiration of the Christmas atmosphere and the Christmas thought and spirit.

Franz Gruber (1787–1863) was a schoolmaster, song-writer and organist. *"Stille Nacht"* is, however, the only one of his compositions commonly found in our modern hymnals.

The custom in Germany of naming hymn-tunes by the first lines of the hymns they fit, is indicated by this one, which is called STILLE NACHT, and also by EIN FESTE BERG, and NUN DANKET ALLE GOTT.

SPIRIT OF GOD, DESCEND UPON MY HEART

1. Spirit of God, descend upon my heart;
Wean it from earth; through all its pulses move;
Stoop to my weakness, mighty as thou art,
And make me love thee as I ought to love.

2. I ask no dream, no prophet-ecstasies,
No sudden rending of the veil of clay,
No angel visitant, no opening skies;
But take the dimness of my soul away.

3. Teach me to feel that thou art always nigh;
Teach me the struggles of the soul to bear,
To check the rising doubt, the rebel sigh;
Teach me the patience of unanswered prayer.

4. Teach me to love thee as thine angels love,
One holy passion filling all my frame,
The baptism of the heaven-descended Dove,
My heart an altar, and thy love the flame.

GEORGE CROLY, 1854.

BIBLICAL TEXT.

And Jesus, when he was baptized, went up straightway from the water; and lo, the heavens were opened unto him, and he saw the Spirit of God descending as a dove, and coming upon him; and lo, a voice out of the heavens, saying, This is my beloved Son, in whom I am well-pleased.

MATTHEW 3:16, 17.

If we live by the Spirit, by the Spirit let us also walk.

GALATIANS 5:25.

A PRAYER-HYMN FOR EVERYDAY HOLINESS

This is a hymn of the spiritual life, expressing in forceful and colorful language one of the very real needs of modern life. There is a danger that present-day living may be so filled with "doing" that there shall be little time or thought left for the "being" from which the "doing" must proceed if it is to be really effective.

This is not the type of hymn which could be called "popular," yet because of its very evident spirituality it has come to the front. There is a deep meaning in that last line of the third stanza, "Teach me the patience of unanswered prayer."

The following omitted stanza is placed in the original setting as the third:

"Hast thou not bid us love thee, God and King?
All, all thine own, soul, heart, strength and mind,
I see thy cross—there teach my heart to cling:
O let me seek thee, and O let me find."

George Croly, a clergyman of the Church of England (1780–1860), was born in Dublin, and graduated from Dublin University. He served churches in Ireland until 1810, when he went to London to take up literary work. He was a frequent contributor to *Blackwell's Magazine,* was the editor of the *Universal Review,* and wrote the leading articles of *Britannia,* a Conservative newspaper. He was the author of forty books, among them a novel, *Salathiel.* In 1854 he published, at the request of his people, a hymn-book entitled "Psalms and Hymns for Public Worship," containing twenty-five psalms, fifty hymns and six longer pieces on Scriptural subjects. Ten of the psalm versions and ten of the hymns were by Croly himself. The hymn above was included in this volume.

He is described by a writer of the period as: "A man of vast power, possessed of a mind of gigantic grasp, prodigiously energetic, but he is not a great preacher. Listening to him was like reading scenes from his own gorgeous-flashes of lightning."

The following stanzas may well be used with this hymn as a closing prayer following the singing:

"As some rare perfume in a vase of clay
Pervades it with a fragrance not its own,
So then thou dwellest in the human soul
All heaven's sweetness seems about it thrown.

"The soul alone like a neglected harp
Grows out of tune and needs thy hand divine.
Dwell thou within it, time it, touch its chords,
Till every note and string shall answer, 'Thine'!"

✣

THE HYMN TUNE. MORECAMBE was composed in 1880 by Frederick Cook Atkinson (1841–1897) for the hymn "Abide with Me."

STAND UP, STAND UP FOR JESUS

1. Stand up, stand up for Jesus,
Ye soldiers of the cross;
Lift high his royal banner,
It must not suffer loss;
From victory unto victory
His army he shall lead,
Till every foe is vanquished,
And Christ is Lord indeed.

2. Stand up, stand up for Jesus,
The trumpet call obey;

Forth to the mighty conflict
In this his glorious day;
Ye that are men now serve him
Against unnumbered foes;
Let courage rise with danger,
And strength to strength oppose.

3. Stand up, stand up for Jesus,
Stand in his strength alone;
The arm of flesh will fail you,
Ye dare not trust your own;
Put on the gospel armor,
Each piece put on with prayer;
Where duty calls, or danger,
Be never wanting there.

4. Stand up, stand up for Jesus,
The strife will not be long;
This day the noise of battle,
The next the victor's song:
To him that overcometh
A crown of life shall be;
He with the King of Glory
Shall reign eternally.

George Duffield, 1858.

Biblical Text.

Finally, be strong in the Lord, and in the strength of his might. Put on the whole armor of God, that ye may be able to stand against the wiles of the devil.

Stand therefore, having girded your loins with truth, and having put on the breastplate of righteousness, and having shod your feet with the preparation of the gospel of peace; withal taking up the shield of faith. . . . And take the helmet of salvation, and the sword of the Spirit, which is the word of God; with all prayer and supplication.

Ephesians 6: 10, 11, 14–18.

A RINGING CALL TO COURAGEOUS SERVICE

"Go now, ye that are men, and serve the Lord."

(Exodus 10: 11.)

These words formed the text of a sermon preached in Jaynes' Hall, Philadelphia, on March 30, 1858, by Reverend Dudley A. Tyng, to an audience of five thousand men. It was the time of the revival of 1857–58, and the city of Philadelphia was aroused.

Mr. Tyng, rector of the Protestant Episcopal Church of the Epiphany, was a young man of evangelical fervor and broad sympathies. Three weeks after that sermon, Mr. Tyng died as the result of an accident. His last words were a message to his fellow-workers and the men to whom he had been preaching: "Tell them, 'Let us all stand up for Jesus.' "

On the day of his funeral, his intimate friend and fellow-worker, Reverend George Duffield (1818–1888), went home from the service with those words ringing in his mind. They shaped themselves into verse, and on the following Sunday he preached from the text, "Stand therefore" (Ephesians 6: 10), and closed his sermon with the poem, "Stand up for Jesus." Little thinking that it would ever become one of the outstanding American hymns, he gave a copy of it to his Sunday School Superintendent, who had it printed on a leaflet and sung by the Sunday School. In the seventy-odd years since its writing it has gone around the world with its clarion call to courage and to service.

An Omitted Stanza

Duffield wrote the hymn with six stanzas. While only the four printed above are in common use one of the omitted ones is of special interest, considering the loss of Dr. Tyng at the beginning of the revival campaign:

"Stand up, stand up for Jesus,
Each soldier to his post;
Close up the broken column,
And shout through all the host:
Make good the loss so heavy,
In those that still remain,
And prove to all around you,
That death itself is gain."

The Reverend George Duffield was a Presbyterian clergyman. He held important pastorates in Brooklyn, Bloomfield (New Jersey), Philadelphia, Galesburg (Illinois), and Adrian, Ann Arbor and Lansing (Michigan). He wrote other hymns, including "Blessed Saviour, Thee I Love," but none of them has attained the popularity of "Stand up for Jesus." His son, Samuel Willoughby Duffield, was a noted writer on hymnology.

✣

THE HYMN TUNE. The tune, WEBB, was composed by George J. Webb (1803–1887), in 1837. Webb was born at Rushmore Lodge, Wiltshire, near Salisbury, England, and received his education in England. In 1830 he came to Boston, where he lived for forty years, associated with Dr. Lowell Mason in his spread of musical education through the public schools, the Boston Academy of Music, the Handel and Haydn Society (of which he was president and conductor), and other organizations. In 1870 he followed Dr. Mason to Orange, New Jersey, and was active in musical circles in New York.

WEBB, composed for secular words, " 'Tis dawn, the lark is singing," was included in 1850 in *Cantica Laudis* published by Mason and Webb, as the setting for Samuel F. Smith's "The Morning Light is Breaking." The tune name then was GOODWIN.

STILL, STILL WITH THEE

1. Still, still with thee, when purple morning breaketh,
When the bird waketh, and the shadows flee;
Fairer than morning, lovelier than the daylight,
Dawns the sweet consciousness, I am with thee.

2. Alone with thee, amid the mystic shadows,
The solemn hush of nature newly born;
Alone with thee in breathless adoration,
In the calm dew and freshness of the morn.

(*Omitted Stanza*)

Still, still with thee; as to each new-born morning
A fresh and solemn splendor still is given,
So doth this blessed consciousness, awaking,
Breathe, each day, nearness unto thee and heaven.

3. When sinks the soul, subdued by toil, to slumber,
Its closing eye looks up to thee in prayer;
Sweet the repose beneath thy wings o'er-shading,
But sweeter still to wake and find thee there.

4. So shall it be at last, in that bright morning,
When the soul waketh, and life's shadows flee;
O in that hour, fairer than daylight dawning,
Shall rise the glorious thought, I am with thee.

HARRIET BEECHER STOWE, 1855.

BIBLICAL TEXT.

I laid me down and slept;
I awaked; for the Lord sustained me.

PSALM 3: 5.

When I awake, I am still with thee
If I take the wings of the morning,
And dwell in the uttermost parts of the sea;
Even there shall thy hand lead me,
And thy right hand shall hold me.

PSALM 139: 9, 10, 18.

A HYMN OF SUNRISE BEAUTY

So vivid, clear-cut and beautiful are the word-pictures of this hymn, that even city-dwellers who seldom see the dawn can enjoy its glory through this poem.

It was evidently written in "the calm dew and freshness of the morn" by one who was accustomed to rise early that she might not miss a single facet of the "jeweled morning."

Harriet Beecher Stowe (1812–1896) spent her girlhood in the Litchfield hills of western Connecticut, a location which offered rare delights of sunrise over bird-thronged hills and valleys. She is known chiefly as a writer of fiction, particularly, *Uncle Tom's Cabin;* but the hymnody of America has been greatly enriched by her hymns: "Abide with me, O Lord, and I in thee," "When winds are raging o'er the upper ocean," "Knocking, knocking, who is there?"

Mrs. Stowe was a woman of singularly sincere religious feeling.

On one occasion she challenged a visiting friend to enjoy the dewy loveliness of morning with her. The next morning they went out together and in the "solemn hush of nature newly born" she read for the first time the verses which had been written under the spell of another dawn-time meditation.

This hymn was published with two others by Mrs. Stowe in her brother's, Henry Ward Beecher's, *Plymouth Collection* of 1855.

✣

THE HYMN TUNE. Several tunes are used with Mrs. Stowe's beautiful words. Mendelssohn's CONSOLATION, WINDSOR by Joseph Barnby, and OBERLIN by John Arthur Demuth (1848–1920).

STRONG SON OF GOD, IMMORTAL LOVE

1. Strong Son of God, immortal Love,
Whom we, that have not seen thy face,
By faith, and faith alone, embrace,
Believing where we cannot prove.

2. Thou seemest human and divine,
The highest, holiest manhood, thou;
Our wills are ours, we know not how;
Our wills are ours, to make them thine.

3. Our little systems have their day;
They have their day and cease to be;

They are but broken lights of thee,
And thou, O Lord, art more than they.

4. We have but faith: we cannot know,
For knowledge is of things we see;
And yet we trust it comes from thee,
A beam in darkness: let it grow.

5. Let knowledge grow from more to more,
But more of reverence in us dwell:
That mind and soul, according well,
May make one music as before.

ALFRED TENNYSON, 1850.

BIBLICAL TEXT.

Whom, having not seen ye love; on whom, though now ye see him not, yet believing, ye rejoice greatly with joy unspeakable and full of glory.

I PETER 1:8.

Now faith is assurance of things hoped for, a conviction of things not seen.

HEBREWS 11:1.

And Simon Peter answered and said, Thou art the Christ, the Son of the living God.

MATTHEW 16:16.

AN AFFIRMATION OF FAITH

Through the dust and confusion of theological and scientific dispute; through the gloom of a soul-baffling bereavement, Alfred Tennyson, one of the strongest and finest spirits of England, fought his way to light and peace in the magnificent elegy, "In Memoriam." This hymn states the result of that memorable battle.

The stanzas of the hymn are taken from the introduction to "In Memoriam," which is really the summary, or conclusion, of the whole series of elegies, written at intervals in the seventeen years between Hallam's death and their publication in 1850. Tennyson dated the Introduction 1849.

In the first line he states the Key, the Explanation, the Way of Life. It is a tremendously rich and enlightening expression of religious faith. If at Oxford there was a group of earnest souls meditating on the result of "The Oxford Movement," there was also a group at Cambridge, Tennyson, Jowett, Gladstone and others, who were to be towers of strength in a confused age. Notice how, in the last stanza, Tennyson faces the light; there is no abnegation of intellect; daylight is not "garish day," as Newman had beautifully, but sadly, sung. Rather, "let knowledge grow from more to more," and with it, "more of reverence in us dwell"; then, in joyous, radiant faith, "mind and soul" shall indeed "make one music, as before"—but vaster.

This is one of the truly great hymns of faith. It should be regarded as one of the outstanding "Heritage Hymns" of the ages, and should be learned by youth when doubts arise, sung in manhood's struggles and disappointment; and softly chanted when age seems lonely and friends have gone. It should always be seen against its background and recognized for the triumphant chime of faith's victory over disillusionment and grief.

✣

THE HYMN TUNE. ST. CRISPIN, to which Tennyson's words are set in a number of hymnals, was composed in 1862 by George J. Elvey. It was first published in *A Selection of Psalm and Hymn Tunes,* edited by E. H. Thorne, 1863. It was composed for the hymn, "Just as I am," and is also used for Bishop How's hymn, "Behold the Master passeth by." This tune was used at the funeral of the composer.

SUN OF MY SOUL, THOU SAVIOUR DEAR

1. Sun of my soul, thou Saviour dear,
It is not night if thou be near;
O may no earth-born cloud arise
To hide thee from thy servant's eyes.

2. When the soft dews of kindly sleep
My wearied eyelids gently steep,
Be my last thought, how sweet to rest
Forever on my Saviour's breast.

3. Abide with me from morn till eve,
For without thee I cannot live;
Abide with me when night is nigh,
For without thee I dare not die.

4. If some poor wandering child of thine
Have spurned today the voice divine,
Now, Lord, the gracious work begin,
Let him no more lie down in sin.

5. Watch by the sick, enrich the poor
With blessings from thy boundless store;
Be every mourner's sleep tonight,
Like infant's slumbers, pure and light.

6. Come near and bless us when we wake,
Ere through the world our way we take,

Till in the ocean of thy love
We lose ourselves in heaven above.

JOHN KEBLE, 1820.

BIBLICAL TEXT.

And they constrained him, saying: Abide with us, for it is toward evening, and the day is now far spent.

LUKE 24:29.

But unto you that fear my name shall the sun of righteousness arise with healing in its wings.

MALACHI 4:2.

A SONG OF LIGHT IN THE DARKNESS

The familiar words of this hymn are prefaced in the original poem by these words:

"'Tis gone! that bright and orbed blaze
Fast fading from our wistful gaze,
Yon mantling cloud has hid from sight
The last faint pulse of quivering light."

The hymn is taken from the book of hymns and poems entitled, *The Christian Year,* published in 1827 by John Keble. This collection offered devotional material in verse for all the Sundays and holy days of the Church Year.

Back of the publication of *The Christian Year* lay a boyhood in a devoutly Christian home, with unusually thorough training in the Bible; a brilliant undergraduate career in Oxford; and active participation, after graduation, in "The Tractarian Movement," of which it has been said, "Keble sang the Movement, John Henry Newman preached it."

The years between 1820–1840 were stirring years in England. New intellectual forces were felt; English poetry was coming to its flowering; the spiritual awakening under the Wesleys and Whitefield was arousing the common people; and at Oxford, Newman and Keble, Faber and Manning, and others, were writing and preaching the *Tracts for the Times.*

The *Tracts* are little read today. The intellectual and political freedom which was so strenuously debated then has long been accepted as a matter of course, but Keble's hymn remains, after a century of constant use in churches of all denominations, as fresh and inspiring and beautiful as when it was written in 1820.

The poet had evidently been watching the sun drop behind the clouds, and was reminded of the "Sun of Righteousness" which can be hidden only by the clouds of sin. Tennyson has a similar statement: asked once during a walk in the garden what Christ meant to him, he paused beside a flower and answered: "What the sun is to that flower, Jesus Christ is to my soul. He is the Sun of my soul."

John Keble (1792–1866) was a great lover of nature, and had a deep appreciation of its rare beauty. He found in nature avenues of approach to nature's God. His nature love is reflected in this hymn. "Sun of my soul" is characterized by a tenderness of thought and expression which makes it a true prayer-hymn. Canon Wilberforce has said of Keble: "He gave England's Church the learning of a deep divine, the love and trust of a loyal son, the labor of a devoted priest and the pattern of a saint."

A Keble Service

(Theme: Alleluia! Alleluia! Lord, thou art for evermore.)

Processional Hymn (Tune, FRANCONIA):

"Blest are the pure in heart,
For they shall see our God;
The secret of the Lord is theirs;
Their soul is Christ's abode.

Lord, we thy presence seek;
May ours this blessing be;
Give us a pure and lowly heart,
A Temple meet for thee."

JOHN KEBLE, 1819.

Unison Prayer:

"Father of Light, Sun of my Soul, when the shadows of twilight fall and darkness ends the day, our thoughts turn to thee who dwellest where night never comes. It fills us with quiet trust to know that somewhere the truth is always clear, however clouded it may appear to us; that there is a light that does not fade when we lose sight of it. Shine through the mists of our mortality and through the deeper gloom of our sin, that the night for us may hold no fears. If we have turned aside to try the ways of darkness and death, and fear the light, because of what it may reveal, lead us back by the kindly lights of home, till in thy flame our sins are consumed and in the light of thy countenance we rest in peace." Amen.

Reading:

"Abide with us; for it is toward evening, and the day is now far spent."

LUKE 24:29.

The entire poem "Sun of My Soul," using sketch of the hymn.

Anthem:

Sun of My Soul .... CHADWICK.

Address:

Christ, the Sun of Righteousness.

Solo:

Sun of My Soul .... JOHN PRINDLE SCOTT.

Hymn (to REGENT SQUARE):

"God, the Lord, a King remaineth,
Robed in his own glorious light;
God hath robed him, and he reigneth;
He hath girded him with might.
Alleluia! Alleluia!
God is King in depth and height.

With all tones of waters blending,
Glorious is the breaking deep;
Glorious, beauteous, without ending,
God, who reigns on heaven's high steep.
Alleluia! Alleluia!
God who reigns on heaven's high steep.

Lord, the words thy lips are telling
Are the perfect verity;
Of thy high eternal dwelling,
Holiness shall inmate be;
Alleluia! Alleluia!
Pure is all that lives with thee.

JOHN KEBLE, 1839.

✣

THE HYMN TUNE. The tune HURSLEY, to which Keble's hymn is commonly sung, bears, very appropriately, the name of the parish in which Keble spent the closing years of his ministry, and where his body lies buried beneath the floor of the chancel.

It was arranged by Dr. William H. Monk from a melody in the *Katholisches Gesangbuch,* published in Vienna between 1744 and 1780. Here is the original melody as it appeared in that book:

The Original of "Hursley" for "Sun of my Soul"

TAKE MY LIFE, AND LET IT BE

1. Take my life, and let it be
Consecrated, Lord, to thee;
Take my moments and my days;
Let them flow in ceaseless praise.

2. Take my hands, and let them move
At the impulse of thy love;
Take my feet, and let them be
Swift and beautiful for thee.

3. Take my voice, and let me sing
Always, only, for my King;
Take my lips, and let them be
Filled with messages from thee.

4. Take my silver and my gold,
Not a mite would I withhold;
Take my intellect, and use
Every power as thou shalt choose.

5. Take my will, and make it thine;
It shall be no longer mine;
Take my heart, it is thine own;
It shall be thy royal throne.

6. Take my love; my Lord, I pour
At thy feet its treasure store;
Take myself, and I will be
Ever, only, all for thee.

FRANCES RIDLEY HAVERGAL, 1874.

Biblical Text.

I beseech you therefore, brethren, by the mercies of God, to present your bodies a living sacrifice, holy, acceptable to God, which is your spiritual service.

Romans 12:1.

Through him then let us offer a sacrifice of praise to God continually, that is, the fruit of lips which make confession to his name. But to do good and to communicate forget not: for with such sacrifices God is well pleased.

Hebrews 13:15, 16.

THE AUTOBIOGRAPHY OF A SAINTLY SINGER

Frances Ridley Havergal (1836–1879) lives and speaks in every line of her hymns—fifty in number. She was preëminently the singer of consecration. Following is the story of her life told through the couplets of this hymn:

TAKE MY LIFE, AND LET IT BE
CONSECRATED, LORD, TO THEE:

"I went for a little visit of five days to London. There were ten persons in the family I visited, most of them unconverted. He gave me the prayer—'Lord, give me all in this house,' and he just did! On the last night of the visit I was too happy to sleep and spent most of the night in praise and renewal of my own consecration, and these little couplets formed themselves and chimed in my heart, one after another, till they finished with 'Ever, only, *all* for thee.' "

TAKE MY MOMENTS AND MY DAYS:
LET THEM FLOW IN CEASELESS PRAISE.

Miss Havergal climbed the Swiss Alps in her student days, and gloried in her strength. Later illness came; twenty-one of her forty-three years were spent in an invalid's chair. Yet she was never heard to complain. Her hymns abound with such expressions as "Ceaseless praise," "Loving word," "Soothing power," "Joyfully we sing," "In full and glad surrender," "Perfect peace and rest," "Joyfully enlisting," "Victory is secure," "Children of the day," "Be this our joyous song."

TAKE MY VOICE, AND LET ME SING
ALWAYS, ONLY, FOR MY KING.

She considered literally "singing for Jesus" her direct call from him, and it is said that toward the close of her life she never lifted her voice in other than sacred song. She was an accomplished pianist, playing the finest strains of Handel, Beethoven and Mendelssohn from memory. Before her invalidism she was accorded the most enthusiastic applause as a solo singer and as a pianist.

TAKE MY LIPS, AND LET THEM BE
FILLED WITH MESSAGES FROM THEE.

Her great life work was personal influence on others. She "carried on" to the extreme limit of her strength in the writing of innumerable letters and of leaflets, tracts and devotional books and by personal interviews.

TAKE MY SILVER AND MY GOLD;
NOT A MITE WOULD I WITHHOLD.

" 'Take my silver and my gold' now means shipping off all my ornaments,—including a jewel cabinet which is really fit for a countess,—to the church missionary society where they will be accepted and disposed of for me. I retain only a brooch for daily wear, which is a memorial of my dear parents; also a locket with the only portrait I have of my niece in heaven, Evelyn. I had no idea I had such a jeweller's shop; nearly fifty articles are being packed off. I don't think I need tell you I never packed a box with such pleasure."

(From a letter by Miss Havergal.)

TAKE MY INTELLECT, AND USE
EVERY POWER AS THOU SHALT CHOOSE.

Miss Havergal's was an intellect of unusual caliber. She could read at the age of three, and, as a girl, knew the entire New Testament, Psalms and Isaiah, by heart. Hers was the full consecration of many talents (she was master of six languages), of one with a real love of learning and an ambition to make the most of herself.

TAKE MY LOVE; MY LORD, I POUR
AT THY FEET ITS TREASURE STORE.

Miss Havergal once wrote to a friend: "I had a great time this morning renewing the never-regretted consecration. I seemed led to run over the 'Take my life' and could bless him verse by verse for having led me to so much more definite consecration, than even when I wrote it, 'voice, gold, intellect,' etc. But the eleventh couplet, 'Love,' that has been unconsciously not filled up. Somehow, I felt mystified and out of my depth here; it was a simple and definite thing to be done, to settle the voice, or silver, or gold! But 'love'? I have to love others, and I do; and I've got a small treasure of it, and even loving him does not quite meet the inner difficulty. I don't see much clearer or feel much different, but I have said intensely this morning—'Take my love'—and he knows I have."

TAKE MYSELF AND I WILL BE
EVER, ONLY, ALL FOR THEE.

As a child she thought deeply of spiritual things and was troubled. "As for trying to be good," she said, "that seemed to me of next to no use. It was like struggling in a quicksand, the more you struggle the more you sink." But light and happiness came. She tells of her confirmation: "I was the fourth or fifth on whom the bishop laid his hands. At first the thought came as to who was kneeling next to me; but the next moment I felt alone,—alone with God and his chief minister. My feelings when his hands were placed on my head I cannot describe, they were too confused; but when the words, 'Defend, O Lord, this thy child with thy heavenly grace, that she may continue thine forever, and daily increase in the Holy Spirit more and more, until she come into thy everlasting kingdom,' were solemnly pronounced, if ever my heart followed a prayer, it did then; if ever it thrilled, with earnest and longing, not unmixed with joy, it did at the words, 'Thine forever.'"

In the light of such consecration no wonder she exclaimed in her last sickness, just as she was passing on, "Splendid! to be so near the gates of heaven."

✣

THE HYMN TUNE. This hymn is one of the many evidences of failure to follow the desires of the author in the matter of the musical setting. Dr. Julian says: "The music to which Miss Havergal invariably sang this hymn, and with which it was always associated in the publications over which she had any influence, was her father's tune, PATMOS, and the family's desire is that this course may be followed by others."

Reverend William Henry Havergal (1793–1870) was a clergyman of the Church of England. He was especially interested in music and wrote many hymn-tunes. His publications included *The Old Church Psalmody, History of the Old Hundredth Tune,* and a collection of one hundred original hymn-tunes.

Hymnal editors, however, seem to have overlooked quite generally this preference of the author. A study of some twenty-five hymnals in present-day use in England and America reveals the fact that at least fourteen different tunes are in use with Miss Havergal's words. Those most commonly found are CONSECRATION (an anonymous contribution), ELLINGHAM, by N. S. Godfrey; and HENDON, by H. A. C. Malan.

So many times the hymn is sung in a dragging tempo and with half-hearted interest. It becomes tedious, and stanzas are omitted to hasten it to its conclusion. Let us sing the words with vigor and enthusiasm at a moderately brisk tempo and use all the stanzas. Then we shall find that we shall enter into the spirit of the hymn and shall be ready to place ourselves wholly and eagerly at the Master's side for service.

THE CHURCH'S ONE FOUNDATION

1. The church's one foundation
Is Jesus Christ her Lord;
She is his new creation
By water and the word;
From heaven he came and sought her
To be his holy bride;
With his own blood he bought her,
And for her life he died.

2. Elect from every nation,
Yet one o'er all the earth,
Her charter of salvation
One Lord, one faith, one birth;
One holy name she blesses,
Partakes one holy food,
And to one hope she presses,
With every grace endued.

(*Omitted Stanzas*)

The church shall never perish!
Her dear Lord to defend,
To guide, sustain, and cherish
Go with her to the end:
Though there be those who hate her,
And false sons in her pale,
Against or foe or traitor
She ever shall prevail.

Though with a scornful wonder
Men see her sore oppressed,
By schisms rent asunder,
By heresies distressed,
Yet saints their watch are keeping,
Their cry goes up, 'How long?'
And soon the night of weeping
Shall be the morn of song.

3. 'Mid toil and tribulation,
And tumult of her war,
She waits the consummation
Of peace forevermore;
Till with the vision glorious
Her longing eyes are blest,
And the great church victorious
Shall be the church at rest.

4. Yet she on earth hath union
With God, the Three in One,
And mystic sweet communion
With those whose rest is won;
O happy ones and holy;
Lord, give us grace that we,
Like them, the meek and lowly,
On high may dwell with thee.

SAMUEL J. STONE, 1866.

BIBLICAL TEXT.

Ye are fellow-citizens with the saints, and of the household of God, being built upon the foundation of the apostles and prophets, Christ Jesus himself being the chief corner stone.

EPHESIANS 2:19, 20.

There is one body and one Spirit, even as also ye were called in one hope of your calling; one Lord, one faith, one baptism, one God, and Father of all, who is over all, and through all, and in all.

EPHESIANS 4:4-6.

. . . Gave him to be head over all things to the church, which is his body, the fulness of him that filleth all in all.

EPHESIANS 1:22, 23.

FROM LAMBETH TOWERS TO FAR NEW ZEALAND'S COAST

Samuel John Stone (1839–1900) was born in Staffordshire, and lived his first thirteen years in the country. Then he moved to London and attended the Charterhouse School made famous by Thackeray. He next entered Oxford, where he distinguished himself in athletics, becoming captain of his college boat crew. His whole bent was toward the army and it was only the "one clear call for him" that turned his face toward the ministry. His first eight years of ministry were spent at Windsor, after which he returned to London to help his father in an East End parish, so very poor and miserable. Here he spent twenty years. "He was a churchman rather than a missionary, a shepherd rather than an evangelist, and St. Paul's (his church) was the door of the fold." His combination of virility and sympathy gave him great power over his people. "He had the muscles of a prize fighter and the nerves of a violin," said his doctor. He was emotional, excitable, with an active brain and a very tender heart.

He once came upon three blackguards attacking a poor unfriended girl. He heard her cries, rushed to her help, knocked out the first man with one blow, turned to the second and trounced him until he cried for mercy, and ever after he regretted that the third got off before he could catch him. He told a friend that he thanked God he had learned to use his fists at Charterhouse and would have given five pounds to get at the third rascal's hide.

His last years were spent at All Hallows, London Wall. Here he inaugurated some remarkable services, which were continued through the years and which were much appreciated by factory girls and others who came to London by the early cheap trains, and who were obliged to wait an hour before their day's work began. The church was opened for them, and there was a short service and address, and the young women were allowed to remain quietly afterwards in the church or in adjoining buildings, to do sewing, reading, etc., until time for them to go to their work.

Mr. Kernahan, in his biography of Stone, says: "So brave of heart was he as to make possible for us the courage of a Cœur de Lion, so knightly of nature as to make possible the honor of an Arthur or a Galahad, so nearly stainless in the standard he set himself, in the standard he attained, as to come, as near as human flesh and blood can come, almost to making possible the purity of the Christ."

This hymn grew out of the state of feeling aroused by the Colenso controversy. Bishop Colenso of South Africa had published a book denying the historical accuracy of the first five books of the Bible, the Pentateuch. His metropolitan bishop, Doctor Gray, deposed him from office, and when an appeal to England was taken, Samuel Stone shared the intense excitement of the controversy following. He felt that Bishop Colenso was undermining the catholic faith; he approved of Bishop Gray's course; he deplored the schism made in the South African Church.

His hymns were written at Windsor, not near the royal castle nor near Eton, but among the poorer classes of the town, for a mission chapel on the outskirts.

"They were written," says Doctor Stone, "at Windsor when I was curate there in 1866, and finished off immediately after, during a holiday at Margate, and a few months after published with ten others (the twelve making one each on the twelve articles of the Apostles' Creed) in a little volume called *Lyra Fidelium.* I wrote them all in behalf of the poorer people in my country district, who I found in many cases used the Creed in their prayers with but little comprehension of it. When I wrote 'The Church's one foundation,' the steadfast defence of the Faith made by Bishop Gray of Cape Town against the heresies of Colenso sometime before was much in my mind."

Being a high churchman, his hymn embodies the doctrines of the church which were so important a part of his Creed:

The divine origin of the Church	stanza one
Her unbroken continuity Her universality and unity	stanza two
Her orthodoxy	first omitted stanza
Her progress through trial to triumph	second omitted stanza
Her militancy and final triumph	stanza three
Her communion with God and with the departed saints	stanza four

One of the marvels of the Church's hymnody is the universal acceptance of this hymn, written by a high-church Anglican to teach his people the meaning of their Creed. Dr. Benson explains it thus: "The explanation of the hymn's general acceptance lies in the fact that all its statements of doctrine are made in the words and phrases of Scripture itself, and thus every denomination is left free to interpret the statements of the hymn in the same terms in which it interprets the texts on which those statements are based." [1]

Scripture Correlation for the First Stanza

The Church's one foundation *Is Jesus Christ, her Lord.*	Other foundation can no man lay than is laid, which is Jesus Christ.
She is his new creation *By water and the word;*	Except a man be born of water and of the spirit, he cannot enter into the kingdom of heaven.
From heaven he came and sought her *To be his holy bride;*	Even as Christ also loved the Church and gave himself for it, that he might sanctify and cleanse it.

[1] From *Studies of Familiar Hymns,* by Louis F. Benson, Second Series, copyright by the Westminster Press.

With his own blood he bought her	The Church of God which he purchased with his own blood.
And for her life he died.	

The hymn exists in three forms; the original in seven stanzas written in 1866, the revised form in five stanzas and commonly used, and the form of 1885 expanded to ten stanzas for use in clergy and choir processions in Salisbury Cathedral. This hymn has the unique distinction of being used in almost every church throughout the world on special occasions. Archbishop Temple once said that whenever he was called on to visit a country parish, he could always count upon two things—"cold chicken and The Church's One Foundation." His Grace's remarks, however, were not intended to detract in any way from the real and acknowledged merits of either—both being practically above criticism.

The hymn was sung at the three notable services at Canterbury Cathedral, St. Paul's Cathedral, and Westminster Abbey, when all the bishops of the Lambeth conference assembled, in reference to which Bishop Nelson, of New Zealand, wrote to the author:

"Through church and chancel, aisle and transept deep,
In fullest melody thy watch notes sweep;
Now in the desert, now upon the main,
In mine and forest, and on citied plain,
From Lambeth towers to far New Zealand's coast,
Bard of the church, thy blast inspires the host."

THE HYMN TUNE. AURELIA stands at the top among hymn-tunes, in melody, part-writing, stride, and infectious musical charm.

Samuel Sebastian Wesley (1810–1876), grandson of Charles Wesley, was named after his father and his father's idol, John Sebastian Bach.

At the age of nine he became chorister in the Chapel Royal, remaining there until he was seventeen years of age, when he became an organist. He received the degree of Mus.D. from Oxford when only twenty-nine, and was regarded then as the foremost organist of the time in England. He was organist of several of England's noted Cathedrals; Hereford, 1832–35; Exeter, 1835–42; Winchester, 1849–65; and Gloucester, 1865–76. In 1872 he published *The European Psalmist,* a collection of 733 hymn tunes, of which 130 were his own compositions.

Samuel Sebastian Wesley was a "character" in his day. Go to any part of England where Wesley held office and one will find him remembered by the old folk who know little or nothing about music. His roving habit (he served five parish churches and four cathedrals) was due to various causes: eccentricity, quarrels with deans and chapters, fondness for fishing, etc. (He was an ardent fisherman in the Wye river.)

Amid wretched choral conditions Wesley wrote his masterful music. On one occasion, only sopranos and a single bass voice were present, the solitary bass on duty that day being the Dean's butler. No wonder Wesley writes: "I have moved from cathedral to cathedral because I found musical troubles at each. Until Parliament interferes to put cathedrals on a totally different musical footing, I affirm that any man of eminence in music finds his life a prolonged martyrdom."

At the Birmingham Festival in 1849, a writer reports: "Doctor Wesley played on the great organ, beginning with a long fantasia, in the course of which almost every effect of which the resources of this enormous instrument are capable was developed by the learned musician with masterful skill. Most interesting of all was the enormous fugue, extemporaneous, with which it closed. Doctor Wesley's performance was greeted with uproarious applause. Even while playing, orchestra and chorus crowded around the organ, anxious to obtain a view of his flying fingers and feet." His last words were "Let me see the sky."

New Tunes for the 7s 6s Hymns of Charles Wesley

The old meters were 8,8,8,8, and 8,6,8,6, and 6,6,8,6. Finally a 7,6,7,6 D. came and was christened after the name of John Wesley's school near Bristol—KINGSWOOD. It came with strange words (this hymn and hymn tune of 1730):

"Never weather-beaten sails
More willing bent to shore;
Never tired Pilgrim's limbs
Affected slumber more,
Than my raised spirit longs
To fly out my troubled breast:
O come quickly, sweetest Lord,
And take my soul to rest."

Some modern 7,6,7,6,D's are AURELIA, CHENIES, ANGEL'S STORY, EWING, DRESDEN, MUNICH, MISSIONARY HYMN, HOMELAND, MENDEBRAS, ST. HILDA, ST. KEVIN, THEODULPH, WEBB.

THE DAY OF RESURRECTION

1. The day of resurrection,
Earth, tell it out abroad;
The passover of gladness,
The passover of God.
From death to life eternal,
From this world to the sky,
Our Christ hath brought us over
With hymns of victory.

2. Our hearts be pure from evil,
That we may see aright
The Lord in rays eternal
Of resurrection-light;
And, listening to his accents,
May hear, so calm and plain,
His own, "All hail!" and, hearing,
May raise the victor-strain.

3. Now let the heavens be joyful,
Let earth her song begin,
Let the round world keep triumph
And all that is therein;
Invisible and visible,
Their notes let all things blend;
For Christ the Lord hath risen,
Our joy that hath no end.

JOHN OF DAMASCUS, eighth century.
Translated by John Mason Neale, 1862.

BIBLICAL TEXT.

And they departed quickly from the tomb with fear and great joy, and ran to bring his disciples word. And behold, Jesus met them, saying, All hail. And they came and took hold of his feet, and worshipped him.

MATTHEW 28: 8, 9.

The Lord is risen indeed, and hath appeared to Simon.

LUKE 24:34.

THE FESTIVAL OF THE JOY OF LIFE

The wonder of this hymn, and the nobility of its author grow more and more impressive as one recalls the grim, remote monastery of Mar Saba in the Wilderness of Judea, where this was written. The loneliness of the inmates, whose chief contact with the outside world was through the wandering Persians or the preying Bedouins, who were a constant menace; the monotony of the monastic life, with its seven daily services in the rock-hewn chapels; the wild beasts slinking at the foot of the high walls to be fed by the monks; an occasional visit by a pilgrim or some high official of the Church, the chief break in the dull routine of the lonely life—such was Mar Saba. Yet from within its grim walls have sounded forth hymns that have lived through nearly twelve centuries. They are hymns of confidence, faith and triumphant gladness.

John of Damascus (Eighth Century) was the last but one of the Fathers of the Greek Church, and is regarded as the greatest poet of that Church. He grew up in Damascus, whence his title, and held civic office there. Dissatisfied with political life, he retired to Mar Saba with his foster brother Cosmas. Late in life he was ordained priest of the church in Jerusalem; hence he is sometimes called John of Jerusalem. He was a writer of theological works, but is best remembered for his poems, and especially for the two great Easter hymns, "The Day of Resurrection" and "Come ye faithful, raise the strain."

For over eleven hundred years vast numbers of Greek hymns lay buried in the sixteen Greek Service books of the Eastern Church. Of the five thousand quarto pages, about four thousand contained hymns and religious poetry, printed in prose form, and therefore all the more difficult to decipher and translate. These were unearthed and translated by Dr. Neale in 1862.

Candlelighting in the Eastern Church

Easter has always been the preëminent Festival of the Greek Church. In Athens on the evening before Easter there was always a solemn service held in the Greek Church. After the service, as the hour of midnight approached, and Archbishop and his priests, and the King and the Queen, left the church and took their places upon a raised platform outside. Thousands of people with unlighted tapers gathered expectantly around the platform while the priests chanted softly. When the sound of cannon announced the hour of midnight, the Archbishop raised the Cross and exclaimed exultantly, *"Christos Anesti,"* "Christ is risen," which was echoed and reëchoed while a burst of light sped through the crowd from newly lighted tapers. Men clasped each other's hands and rejoiced as if some great joy had suddenly come to them. Bands played, and rockets answered from neighboring hills while many voices were raised in the words of this hymn of victory.

Candlelighting Ceremonials

With the church in semi-darkness, the minister, in clerical robe, mounts the steps of the pulpit or chancel, bearing a cross, and fol-

Copyright by the Keystone View Company, Meadville, Pa.

THE LONELY CONVENT OF MAR SABA, PALESTINE

This is where "The Day of Resurrection," "Art thou weary, art thou languid," and other hymns were written during the eighth and ninth centuries.

lowed by a quartet in choir robes, each bearing a white unlighted candle. During this processional, the chorus choir sings some setting of *"De Profundis."*

"Out of the depths have I cried unto thee, O Lord: Lord, hear my voice.
O let thine ears consider well the voice of my complaint.
I wait for the Lord, my soul doth wait for him; in his word is my trust.
My soul waiteth for the Lord more than they that watch for the morning."

At the close of the chorus, enter from the side a young man in choir robe, bearing a white lighted candle, at which moment the minister lifts high the Cross and speaks in triumphant tone: "Christos Anesti!" "Christ is Risen!" First the quartet, then the choir, taking up the words, repeat them in joyous unison. Instantly the young man with the candle hands it to the minister, receiving from him the cross. The minister lights the candles of the quartet, who in turn light the candles of the choir, during which action the organist plays "Christ the Lord is risen today" to "WORGAN." A brief prayer of thanksgiving for the victory of Easter is offered, followed by a processional of minister, quartet, and choir to the space in the center aisle in front of the chancel. The congregation, previously supplied with tapers, now come forward, in order of sitting, and light their tapers and return to their places, remaining standing. The organ continues playing until all candles are lighted; when the entire congregation unite in singing "The Day of Resurrection," gradually elevating candles through the three stanzas. As the last notes of the hymn are reached, the church lights come on and the candles are extinguished.

The service may then proceed to the sermon; or, if this dramatic setting follows the sermon, the choir will lead down the center aisle and out the main doors, as a Recessional, the minister pronouncing the benediction from the vestibule.

✣

THE HYMN TUNE. American hymnals use ROTTERDAM or LANCASHIRE. (For comment on the latter, see "Lead on, O King Eternal.")

ROTTERDAM was composed in 1875 by Berthold Tours (1838–1897). Tours was born in Rotterdam, Holland (hence the name of the tune). His father was an organist of note, and had much to do with the training of the son. Berthold Tours went to London in 1861 and served as violinist in the London Opera and other orchestras. From 1878 he was editor and adviser for Novello. He wrote services, anthems and hymn tunes; also a Violin Primer.

THE FIRST NOEL THE ANGEL DID SAY

1. The first Noel the angel did say
Was to certain poor shepherds in fields as they lay;
In fields where they lay keeping their sheep,
On a cold winter's night that was so deep.

Refrain

Noel, Noel, Noel, Noel,
Born is the King of Israel.

2. They looked up and saw a star
Shining in the east, beyond them far,
And to the earth it gave great light,
And so it continued both day and night.

Refrain

3. And by the light of that same star,
Three wise men came from country far;
To seek for a king was their intent,
And to follow the star wherever it went.

Refrain

4. The star drew nigh to the northwest,
O'er Bethlehem it took its rest,
And there it did both stop and stay,
Right over the place where Jesus lay.

Refrain

5. Then entered in those wise men three,
Full reverently upon the knee,
And offered there, in his presence,
Their gold, and myrrh, and frankincense.

Refrain

West of England Carol, 1833.

Biblical Text.

And the Wise-men, having heard the king, went their way; and lo, the star, which they saw in the east, went before them, till it came and stood over where the young child was. And when they saw the star, they rejoiced with exceeding great joy. And they came unto the house and saw the young child with Mary his mother; and they fell down and worshipped him; and opening their treasures they offered him gifts, gold and frankincense and myrrh.

Matthew 2:9, 10, 11.

IN THE SOLEMN MIDNIGHT CENTURIES AGO

Who wrote The First Noel? Where did he live? When did he write it, and what were the circumstances of its writing? All of these pertinent questions, so readily answered in the case of most hymns, must, in this instance, go unanswered.

This is a true "folk-song," which, according to the Dictionary, means "A song or ballad originating and current among the common people, and illustrating the common life with its interests and enthusiasms as derived from legend or story." The word "Noel" or "Nowell" is from the old French word, "Noël," used in France to signify Carol, and also Christmas. In English the word takes on the meaning of "news," as if from "Novellare" or "Natale," "a cry of joy."

This Carol first appeared in *Christmas Carols Ancient and Modern,* by W. B. Sandys, along with "God rest you, merry gentlemen," and "I saw three ships come sailing."

Regarding folk-songs, Clarence Dickinson says in his *Excursions in Musical History:* "Since folk-songs compose themselves among the people, they are everywhere and invariably marked by certain qualities. They are always vividly pictorial, therefore language is always simple and concrete. Scenes are described and experiences related at first hand, without the introduction of any secondary element, such as reasoning or deduction. The language used is picturesque; it is the dialect of the people. Like ballads the folk-song is usually made with refrain, to be sung over and over again and thus memorized by the people. As they tell their stories in greatest detail, they frequently comprise very many stanzas." [1]

Since Christmas was from the earliest times the chief festival, it furnishes most of the incidents and legends for carols. Clement, in the first century, admonished the priests: "Brethren, keep diligently the feast days and above all, the day of Christ's birth."

Telesphorous, who became Bishop of Rome in 129, inaugurated the custom of celebrating the Nativity with the singing of carols. A song never omitted on these occasions was the "Angels' Song" or "Glory to God in the Highest."

The principal themes of the early Carols were The Annunciation, The Angels' Message, The Lullaby, and The Coming of the Shepherds. The Lullaby was as common in sacred folk-song as pictures of the Madonna and Child were in pictorial art.

No theme has been more popular with artist and caroler, however, than the story of the Magi. Professor Bailey says: "On the basis of simple and rather indefinite information about the Magi, pious tradi-

[1] From *Excursions in Musical History,* by Clarence and Helen Dickinson, copyright by H. W. Gray Co.

tion has built an extraordinary fabric, and Art has adorned it with at least one hundred and fifty paintings. Indeed, the Magi seem to have attracted more attention than any other persons in the Bible except Jesus and his mother." [2]

THE KING OF LOVE MY SHEPHERD IS

1. The King of love my Shepherd is,
Whose goodness faileth never;
I nothing lack if I am his,
And he is mine forever.

2. Where streams of living water flow,
My ransomed soul he leadeth,
And where the verdant pastures grow,
With food celestial feedeth.

3. Perverse and foolish oft I strayed,
But yet in love he sought me,
And on his shoulder gently laid,
And home rejoicing, brought me.

4. In death's dark vale I fear no ill
With thee, dear Lord, beside me;
Thy rod and staff my comfort still,
Thy cross before to guide me.

5. And so through all the length of days,
Thy goodness faileth never;
Good Shepherd, may I sing thy praise
Within thy house forever.

HENRY W. BAKER, 1868.

BIBLICAL TEXT.
The Lord is my shepherd; I shall not want.

PSALM 23: 1.

I am the good shepherd: I came that they may have life, and may have it abundantly. I know mine own, and mine own know me, even as the Father knoweth me, and I know the Father; and I lay down my life for the sheep.

JOHN 10: 11, 10, 14, 15.

THE DEAREST PSALM

Of all the poems ever written in the world, this Psalm seems to have been and still is the best known and best loved. Where is there another work of art of any kind whatever, painting, sculpture, music or archi-

[2] From the *Gospel in Art,* by Albert E. Bailey, copyright by the Pilgrim Press.

tecture, that has entered the minds and hearts of men so often and lingered so long in their memories!

As a precious treasure its beauty has glowed in tent and tabernacle, in cottage, camp, palace and temple, these three thousand years and more. It blossoms perennially in all the languages of earth. It has been translated and paraphrased more than any other piece of literature. It comes down through English history rendered variously by such leaders as Alfred the Great, Milton, King James I, Byron, and by innumerable peasants, clerks and courtiers, changing as the language has changed, yet bearing always the same sure and joyful faith in the Good Shepherd.

To read the fourth stanza in a few of its English forms is to suggest to the imagination something of what it has meant to English folk through successive generations.

"For win ghif I hadde goo in myddil of shadewe of deethe, I shall not dreede yuels for thou art with me. Thi gheerde and thy staf; thei have comforted me."

The Hampole Manuscript in the British Museum.

"For whi and if I goo in the myddel of the shadowe of deth I shal not drede euelis, for thou art with me."

The Wyclif Bible, 1380.

"Ye if I shuld go thorow the myddes of deth, yet will I feare non yuel, for thou art with me, thy staffe and thy shepe hoke counfort me."

Manuscript of 1530 in the Cambridge University Library.

"Yea in deathes shadie black abode
Well may I walk, not fear:
For thou art with me: and thy rod
To guide, my staff to bear."

"Yea though I walk in vale of death,
Yet will I fear none ill:
Thy rod and thy staff doth comfort me,
And thou art with me still."

Thomas Sternhold (about 1549).

"He me revives: leads me the way
Which righteousness doth take
For his name's sake.
Yea, though I should through valleys stray
Of deathes darke shade, I will
No whitt feare ill."

Sir Philip Sidney and the Countess of Pembroke.

The best-known translations, excepting, of course, the matchless unmetrical version of the King James Version of the Bible, are the famous Scottish paraphrases, "The Lord's my shepherd, I'll not want," and Henry Baker's "The King of love my Shepherd is."

A Knighted Hymn-Writer

Reverend Sir Henry Williams Baker (1821–1877) was the son of a Vice Admiral. He was educated at Trinity College, Cambridge. He became Vicar of Monkland, Herefordshire, in 1851, and retained this position until his death. He became a Baronet in 1859.

The greatest work of Sir Henry's life was his chairmanship of the committee which edited the outstanding Hymnal of the Anglican Church, *Hymns Ancient and Modern*. For more than twenty years he continued at the head of this monumental work as chairman of the original committee, formed in 1857, through the publication of the first edition, 1861; the *Appendix,* 1868, and the *Revised Edition,* 1875.

Thirty-three of his own hymns were included in the Revised Edition. Henry Twells says concerning the greatness of Baker's influence through this Hymnal: "Their chairman told me, many years afterward, that if they (the original band of compilers) could have been assured that this book would have been adopted in twenty churches besides their own, they would have been well satisfied and thankful. What was the result? . . . It is now the hymnal of fifteen thousand churches and chapels of England and Wales, out of about twenty thousand. It is the hymnal of the army and navy. It is the hymnal generally adopted in the Episcopal Church of Scotland. It is the hymnal of overwhelming preponderance in the colonies. If I were to say that fifty million copies of it have been circulated, I know I should be a long way within the mark."

A Story of the Canadian Northwest

At a great missionary gathering held recently in the city hall at Glasgow, Bishop Montgomery told this simple, suggestive and pathetic story of the Canadian Northwest: "One of our priests was out on the track. He saw on the roadside a little boy herding sheep, and in the distance a little farmstead. Having asked the boy's name, he then said: 'Would you mind me asking if you ever said a prayer in your life?' 'Never, Guv'nor,' was the reply. 'Have you ever read your Bible?' 'Never seen one, guv'nor.' 'Has your father or mother got one?' 'None in the house at all, sir!' 'Then,' said the man, 'I shall be back here next year. Will you do me a favor, and learn five words for me—*The Lord is my Shepherd?*' The boy agreed, and went over the words on his fingers, and the man said, 'One thing more, when you come to the last finger but one, which reads *my,* crook that finger. Now, go over it on your hand in that way, *The Lord is my Shepherd.*' Next year came, and the man in passing that road remembered the boy, and going up to the farm, inquired of him from a woman standing outside. 'Are you,' she said, 'the man who taught him some words?' 'Yes,' he replied, 'how is he?' 'Dead, sir,' she said, 'ay, dead. The little chap was fond of going about with his hand over his head, sticking out the fingers with one finger down, and seemed very happy going over the words you taught him. It was a very bad winter, with dreadful blizzards, and one night he was out after his sheep, and we missed him. We could not find him till morning. There he lay dead, and, I believe, sir, the words you taught him were the last words he ever spoke, for he had his hand over his head with his fingers just held as you taught him.' 'Some day,' said the Bishop, 'there will be a happy meeting between that boy and priest.' "

❖

THE HYMN TUNE. Dr. Dykes seemed most happy and natural in expressing emotions through tones that were intelligible to the masses. Few great composers have been successful with hymn-tunes. Both Handel and Mendelssohn failed, though diligent were their efforts.

DOMINUS REGIT ME was composed by John B. Dykes (1823–1876) expressly for the Baker hymn. It is a beautiful and vivid interpretation of the fearless Shepherd, ready to dare any peril for his sheep.

The melody is pronounced, giving opportunity to bring out clearly and strongly the emphatic words or syllables, such as "King," "Shepherd," "goodness," "never," "nothing," "he," "forever" in the first stanza. It has a descending note, suggesting the genuine restfulness of this great hymn of trust. Its rhythm is even and steady, fitting the syllables in a remarkable manner, while its harmony is rich, with unusual strength of movement in the inner voices.

The hymn-tune gets its name from the Latin title of the twenty-third Psalm, *"Dominus Regit Me."*

THE SON OF GOD GOES FORTH TO WAR

1. The Son of God goes forth to war,
A kingly crown to gain;
His blood-red banner streams afar;
Who follows in his train?
Who best can drink his cup of woe
Triumphant over pain,
Who patient bears his cross below,
He follows in his train.

2. The martyr first, whose eagle eye
Could pierce beyond the grave,
Who saw his Master in the sky,
And called on him to save;
Like him, with pardon on his tongue,
In midst of mortal pain,
He prayed for them that did the wrong:
Who follows in his train?

3. A glorious band, the chosen few
On whom the Spirit came,
Twelve valiant saints, their hope they knew,
And mocked the cross and flame;
They met the tyrant's brandished steel,
The lion's gory mane;
They bowed their necks the stroke to feel;
Who follows in their train?

4. A noble army, men and boys,
The matron and the maid,
Around the Saviour's throne rejoice,
In robes of light arrayed:
They climbed the steep ascent of heaven
Through peril, toil, and pain:
O God, to us may grace be given
To follow in their train.

REGINALD HEBER, 1827.

BIBLICAL TEXT.

Now when they heard these things, they were cut to the heart, and they gnashed on him with their teeth. But he, being full of the Holy Spirit, looked up steadfastly into heaven, and saw the glory of God, and Jesus standing on the right hand of God. . . . And they stoned Stephen, calling upon the Lord and saying, Lord Jesus, receive my spirit. And he kneeled down, and cried with a loud voice, Lord, lay not this sin to their charge.

ACTS 7:54, 55, 59, 60.

These are they that come out of the great tribulation, and they washed their robes, and made them white in the blood of the Lamb.

REVELATION 7:14.

A MEMORIAL TO THE FIRST CHRISTIAN MARTYR

There is a singular and pathetic significance in the fact that this hymn was not known until its author had "climbed the steep ascent of heaven, through peril, toil, and pain." Its first publication was in the volume published after his death, *Hymns, Written and Adapted to the Weekly Church Service of the Year*. It is there appropriately assigned to Saint Stephen's Day.

With the advent of the nineteenth century the Church had begun to see visions of its duty to the world at large. The Church Militant was reborn with its missionary propaganda. Growing out of this new and vigorous life came the martial hymns of the church. Bishop Heber (1783–1826) was one of the first to catch this new spirit, evinced in his "From Greenland's Icy Mountains." His hymns are trumpet-calls to duty, of the sort he answered so bravely in his own life.

INTERPRETATION. The first stanza of the hymn should be sung with vigor, at a good march tempo, intended to emphasize the martial challenge of it. The second stanza, a vivid account of the first martyr of the Church, and therefore a stanza of commemoration, should be reverently interpreted by the organist, while the congregation stands at silent attention. The third and fourth stanzas picture the expansion of the Church, growing from the Twelve, till it includes "the noble army." Therefore, if the third stanza is sung by men's voices and the fourth by the entire congregation with increasing brilliance and strength, the growing church through two thousand years becomes a vivid picture through tonal climax and splendor.

A Hymnic Scripture Lesson

Minister (reading):

Now when they heard these things, they were cut to the heart, and they gnashed on him with their teeth. But he, being full of the Holy Spirit, looked up steadfastly into heaven, and saw the glory of God, and Jesus standing on the right hand of God, and said, Behold, I see the heavens opened, and the Son of Man standing at the right hand of God.

ACTS 7:54, 55.

Choir and Congregation (singing):

"The martyr first, whose eagle eye
Could pierce beyond the grave,
Who saw his Master in the sky,
And called on him to save;
Like him, with pardon on his tongue,
In midst of mortal pain,
He prayed for them that did the wrong:
Who follows in his train?"

Minister:

Who through faith subdued kingdoms, wrought righteousness, obtained promises, stopped the mouths of lions, quenched the power of fire, escaped the edge of the sword, from weakness were made strong . . . they were stoned, they were sawn asunder, they were tempted, they went about in sheepskins, in goatskins;

being destitute, afflicted, ill-treated (of whom the world was not worthy).

HEBREWS 11:33, 34, 37, 38.

Choir and Congregation:

"A glorious band, the chosen few
On whom the Spirit came,
Twelve valiant saints, their hope they knew,
And mocked the cross and flame;
They met the tyrant's brandished steel,
The lion's gory mane;
They bowed their necks the stroke to feel;
Who follows in their train?"

Minister:

These that are arrayed in the white robes, who are they, and whence came they? . . . These are they that come out of the great tribulation, and they washed their robes, and made them white in the blood of the Lamb. Therefore are they before the throne of God; and they serve him day and night in his temple; and he that sitteth on the throne shall spread his tabernacle over them.

REVELATION 7:13–15.

Choir and Congregation:

"A noble army, men and boys,
The matron and the maid,
Around the Saviour's throne rejoice,
In robes of light arrayed:
They climbed the steep ascent of heaven
Through peril, toil, and pain:
O God, to us may grace be given
To follow in their train."

✣

THE HYMN TUNE. The tune in almost universal use with this hymn in America is ALL SAINTS NEW, composed in 1872 by Henry Stephen Cutler (1824–1902). (See comment on the hymn "At length there dawns the glorious day.")

THE SPACIOUS FIRMAMENT ON HIGH

1. The spacious firmament on high,
With all the blue ethereal sky,

And spangled heavens, a shining frame,
Their great Original proclaim;
Th' unwearied sun, from day to day,
Does his creator's power display,
And publishes to every land
The work of an almighty hand.

2. Soon as the evening shades prevail,
The moon takes up the wondrous tale,
And nightly to the listening earth
Repeats the story of her birth;
Whilst all the stars that round her burn,
And all the planets in their turn,
Confirm the tidings as they roll,
And spread the truth from pole to pole.

3. What though, in solemn silence, all
Move round the dark terrestrial ball?
What though no real voice nor sound
Amidst their radiant orbs be found?
In reason's ear they all rejoice,
And utter forth a glorious voice,
Forever singing, as they shine,
"The hand that made us is divine."

JOSEPH ADDISON, 1712.

BIBLICAL TEXT.

The heavens declare the glory of God;
And the firmament showeth his handiwork.
Day unto day uttereth speech,
And night unto night showeth knowledge.
There is no speech nor language;
Their voice is not heard.
Their line is gone out through all the earth,
And their words to the end of the world.
In them hath he set a tabernacle for the sun,
Which is as a bridegroom coming out of his chamber,
And rejoiceth as a strong man to run his course.
His going forth is from the end of the heavens,
And his circuit unto the ends of it;
And there is nothing hid from the heat thereof.

PSALM 19:1–6.

A HYMN OF SUNRISE GLORIES

Joseph Addison (1672–1719) was born at Millston, near Amesbury, Wiltshire, the son of Reverend Lancelot Addison, later Dean of Leichfield. He was educated at Charleton House, and Magdalen College, Oxford, receiving his M.A. degree in 1693. He studied law and politics, not choosing to follow in the line of his ancestors, who had been clergymen. He became most widely known through his contributions to *the Spectator, Guardian,* and *Freeholder.*

Concerning *The Spectator,* with which Addison was so closely connected, John Wesley said: "God raised up Mr. Addison and his associates to lash the prevailing vices of the country, and to show the excellency of Christianity and Christian institutions. Written with all the simplicity, force and elegance of the English language, it was everywhere read, and was the first instrument in the hand of God to check the mighty and growing profanity, and call men back to religion, decency and common sense."

This hymn appeared in *The Spectator,* for August 23, 1712. It was preceded by the following statement: "Faith and devotion naturally grow in the mind of every reasonable man who sees the impressions of Divine power, and wisdom in every object on which he casts his eye. The Supreme Being has made the best arguments for his own existence in the formation of the heaven and the earth, and these are arguments which a man of sense cannot forbear attending to, who is out of the noise and hurry of human affairs. The Psalmist has sung very beautiful strokes of poetry to this purpose in that exalted strain (Psalm 19). As such a sublime and bold manner of thinking furnishes very noble matter for an ode, the reader may see it wrought into the following one."

Through all the delight in the beauties of nature, so sincerely expressed in this hymn, there runs a wonder and gratitude to the Creator whose divine hand gave men a world of so much loveliness.

He may have had in mind, in addition to the words of the Psalm itself, Shakespeare's lines in *The Merchant of Venice,* Act V:

> "Look how the floor of heaven
> Is thick laid with patines of bright gold,
> There's not the smallest orb which thou beholdest
> But in his motion like an angel sings,
> Still quiring to the young-eyed cherubims."

Thackeray gives the Addison lines high praise; referring particularly to, "Soon as the evening shades prevail." "It seems to me those verses shine like stars. They shine out of a great, deep calm. When he turns to heaven, a Sabbath comes over that man's mind, and his face lights up from it with a glory of thanks and prayer."

✤

THE HYMN TUNE. The music matches the words for dignity and beauty. CREATION, the hymn-tune, is taken from the chorus, "The heavens are telling," No. 12 in the oratorio "Creation," composed in 1798 by Franz Joseph Haydn (1732–1809).

It is said that the last time Haydn appeared in public was when he went to hear "The Creation" rendered in Italian, in 1808. When, at the end of the first part, there came the triumphant words, "And there was Light," the audience burst into tumultuous applause; the composer made a motion of his hands toward heaven, and said, "It came from thence." He was unable to remain longer and had to be carried out in his arm chair. Those were his last words in public.

THERE IS A GREEN HILL FAR AWAY

1. There is a green hill far away,
Without a city wall,
Where the dear Lord was crucified,
Who died to save us all.

Refrain

Oh, dearly, dearly has he loved,
And we must love him too,
And trust in his redeeming blood,
And try his works to do.

2. We may not know, we cannot tell
What pains he had to bear;
But we believe it was for us
He hung and suffered there.

Refrain

3. He died that we might be forgiven,
He died to make us good,
That we might go at last to heaven,
Saved by his precious blood.

Refrain

4. There was no other good enough
To pay the price of sin;
He only could unlock the gate
Of heaven, and let us in.

Refrain

CECIL FRANCES ALEXANDER, 1848.

BIBLICAL TEXT.

They took Jesus therefore: and he went out, bearing the cross for himself, unto the place called The place of a skull, which is called in Hebrew Golgotha: where they crucified him.

JOHN 19:17.

While we were yet sinners, Christ died for us.

ROMANS 5:8.

SUFFERED UNDER PONTIUS PILATE, WAS CRUCIFIED, DEAD AND BURIED

It is said that Mrs. Alexander (then Miss Humphreys) wrote this hymn one night as she sat by the bedside of a feverish child, a most appropriate place for writing what has become one of the best-known "children's hymns" in the language.

The hymn has been used, however, so constantly by adults that the fact that it was written for children has been largely overlooked. Miss Humphreys was much interested in the "Oxford Movement," and so profoundly influenced by John Keble's *Christian Year,* that her first volume of poetry, written when she was twenty-one, *Verses for Holy Seasons,* was a *Christian Year* for children. It contained a hymn for every Sunday and for other special days provided for in the Prayer Book.

Two years later came her *Hymns for Little Children,* a book of seventy-two pages, which attempted to cover the points a child was supposed to have learned in the Church of England up to the time of confirmation. "There is a green hill far away" was one of these intended to explain and interpret the Apostles Creed and the particular words: "Suffered under Pontius Pilate, was crucified, dead and buried."

Cecil Frances Humphreys Alexander (1823–1895) was born and lived all her life in Ireland. Her father, Major John Humphreys, had served with distinction in the Royal Marines. He was a large landowner in the North of Ireland. She early learned to write verses, supplying poems for a small weekly periodical that circulated only in the family circle. When she was twenty-five, she married Reverend William Alexander, then a rector in Tyrone. Seventeen years later he was made Bishop of Derry and Raphoe. Mrs. Alexander was a true helpmeet in all her husband's work, whether in the lonely country parish, or in the Bishop's Palace. A church-woman, through and through, she attended the daily service, took communion every week, and gave largely of her time to parish visiting and the service of the sick, the poor and needy.

Dr. Julian says of her children's hymns: "They are charmingly simple and tender, clear in dogma, and of poetic beauty, combining the plainness of Watts with the feeling for childhood of Jane Taylor, and uniting with both the liturgical associations of the English Prayer Book, they remain unequalled and unapproachable." [1]

Dr. Benson says that she "was possibly the only poet that ever lived who did not like to hear her poems praised." "Again and again," her husband says, "I have read to her words of lofty, almost impassioned commendation from men of genius or holiness, of rank and

[1] From the *Dictionary of Hymnology,* by John Julian, copyright by John Murray.

position. She listened without a remark and looked up almost with a frown." The exception was his reading a little tract by an English nonconformist minister. It told the story of a great change in the heart and life of a very worldly man. He happened to hear "There is a green hill far away" exquisitely sung. It awakened feelings and yearnings that proved to be the starting point of a new life. "Mrs. Alexander almost sprang from her chair, looked me in the face, and said: 'Thank God! I do like to hear that.' "

Her best-known poem is doubtless "The Burial of Moses," which received high praise from Tennyson.

✣

THE HYMN TUNE. At a time when France was a much disordered State, the musician, Charles François Gounod (1818–1893), sent his little daughter, Jeanne, to school in England. At the school she was required, among other studies, to commit to memory certain hymns. On her return to her French home, she surprised her father one day by reciting "There is a green hill far away." He was so deeply impressed with the words that he at once sat down at the piano and composed a solo setting for them.

Two hymn-tunes most commonly associated with these words are MEDITATION, by J. H. Gower, and STEBBINS, by George C. Stebbins.

John Henry Gower (1855–1922) was an English musician, an organist at fourteen years of age, a concert artist throughout England, and later organist and Professor of Music at Trent College, Nottingham. Coming to America, he was identified with mining interests in Denver, Colorado, but did not lose his interest in music, becoming the organist and choirmaster of St. John's Cathedral, Denver, and later at Central Presbyterian and Unity churches. During the World's Fair, 1893, he became organist of the Church of the Epiphany, Chicago.

George Cole Stebbins (1846–) tells in his *Reminiscences and Gospel Hymn Stories,* of the first use of his tune: "It was written during an engagement with Dr. Pentecost in special meetings in his own church in Boston, to be sung as a quartet by three prominent church soloists of the city and myself, at a special service. On the evening appointed a severe storm prevented the three friends coming, and most of the usual congregation. The service was held in the lecture room of the church, and I ventured to sing the new song alone. There seemed to be little or no impression made by it, and as no one did me the honor to refer to it, I concluded that it was a failure.

"Two months thereafter while engaged in a series of meetings in Providence, Dr. Pentecost said to me one day: 'George, where is that *"Green Hill"* you sang in my church?' I answered: 'The music is in my head, but the words I left in Boston.' Sometime afterward I chanced to find them and said to the Doctor, 'I can sing the "Green Hill" for you now, if you like,' and he replied, 'I wish you would.' . . . At the time fixed upon to sing the new song, a very large number of people were present. Conditions, therefore, were favorable, and that it was the means of a blessing may be judged from the fact that from that time on to the end of the series, some weeks later, there were few services when from one to a half-dozen written requests for its repetition were not sent to the platform." [2]

The hymn, with Mr. Stebbins' tune, was published in *Gospel Hymns, No. 3,* in 1878, the first of the series of *Gospel Hymns* which Stebbins and Sankey edited.

THERE'S A WIDENESS IN GOD'S MERCY

1. There's a wideness in God's mercy,
Like the wideness of the sea;
There's a kindness in his justice,
Which is more than liberty.

2. There is no place where earth's sorrows
Are more felt than up in heaven;
There is no place where earth's failings
Have such kindly judgment given.

3. For the love of God is broader
Than the measure of man's mind;
And the heart of the Eternal
Is most wonderfully kind.

4. If our love were but more simple,
We should take him at his word;
And our lives would be all sunshine
In the sweetness of our Lord.

Frederick W. Faber, 1854.

Biblical Text.

For though he cause grief, yet will he have compassion according to the multitude of his lovingkindness. For he doth not afflict willingly, nor grieve the children of men.

Lamentations 3:32, 33.

God is love. Herein was the love of God manifested in us, that God hath sent his only begotten Son into the world that we might live through

[2] From, *Reminiscences and Gospel Hymn Stories,* by George Stebbins, copyright by Doubleday, Doran and Co.

him. Herein is love, not that we loved God, but that he loved us, and sent his Son to be the propitiation for our sins.

I John 4:8–10.

COME TO JESUS

Frederick William Faber (1814–1863) grew up as a boy in the wild scenery of Durham, Westmorland, and the Lake district. Homesick for the streams, the heather, the crags, he wrote: "it seems to me a home whence I have been exiled, but which only to think of is tranquillity and peace." At Harrow he became an excellent swimmer and rider. The healthy student, Faber, became the ascetic, undernourished monkish priest, for he often fasted to the point of utter exhaustion and fainting. Sundays only did he partake of a good meal. Around his waist he wore a knotted horsehair cord. Hard work and little food brought him to an untimely death at the age of forty-eight.

One commentator says, "He got more out of language than any other hymnist, and used words, even simple words, so that they rendered him a service which no other poet ever secured from them." On the other hand Reeves says, "he was an erratic judge of, as well as a writer of, poetry. He burned his three volume Shelley, and, he says, never regretted it. Francis Thompson makes the remark that he should have thrown some of his hymnody into the fire with it."

The original hymn had thirteen stanzas.

(*Omitted Stanzas*)

"Souls of men! why will ye scatter
Like a crowd of frightened sheep?
Foolish hearts! why will ye wander
From a love so true and deep?

"It is God: his love looks mighty,
But is mightier than it seems;
'Tis our Father: and his fondness
Goes far out beyond our dreams.

"There is space enough for thousands
Of new worlds as great as this;
There is room for fresh creations
In that upper home of bliss.

"But we make his love too narrow
By false limits of our own;
And we magnify his strictness
With a zeal he will not own.

"Was there ever kindest shepherd
Half so gentle, half so sweet,

As the Saviour who would have us
Come and gather at his feet?

"There is plentiful redemption
In the blood that hath been shed;
There is joy for all the members
In the sorrows of the Head."

The use of some of these omitted stanzas in hymnals results in confusion, as the hymn is sometimes called, "Souls of men, why will ye scatter?" and at other times "Was there ever kindest shepherd?"

❖

THE HYMN TUNE. Preferences of hymnal editors seem about equally divided between ILSLEY and WELLESLEY as the musical setting for this hymn, with a few choosing ERIE.

ILSLEY, named for the composer, Frank Grenville Ilsley (1831-1887), was written in 1887. Ilsley was the composer of DANIA, to which "Forward through the ages" is sung.

ERIE, by C. C. Converse, is the familiar tune for "What a friend we have in Jesus."

Lizzie Shove Tourjee Estabrook (1858–) composer of WELLESLEY, was the daughter of Dr. Eben Tourjee, the founder and director of the New England Conservatory of Music. When Lizzie was a student in the Newton, Massachusetts, High School, she was asked to compose the music for a graduation song. She took the poem, for which the music was desired, to her father, who said, "Sit down at the piano, with the words before you, and try." She did, and her father named the tune WELLESLEY after the new college for women in the adjoining town. Play the music lightly and rapidly. How like a school girl it is! Not at all a sober hymn tune!

Dr. Tourjee was the musical editor of the Methodist Hymnal, edition of 1878. He included in it his daughter's tune, using it for "Mighty God, while angels bless thee," and on the same page, this hymn of Faber's.

THESE THINGS SHALL BE—A LOFTIER RACE

1. These things shall be,—a loftier race
Than e'er the world hath known, shall rise
With flame of freedom in their souls,
And light of knowledge in their eyes.

2. They shall be gentle, brave and strong
To spill no drop of blood, but dare

All that may plant man's lordship firm
On earth, and fire, and sea, and air.

3. Nation with nation, land with land,
Unarmed shall live as comrades free;
In every heart and brain shall throb
The pulse of one fraternity.

4. New arts shall bloom of loftier mold,
And mightier music thrill the skies,
And every life shall be a song,
When all the earth is paradise.

JOHN A. SYMONDS, 1880.

BIBLICAL TEXT.

Beloved, now are we children of God, and it is not yet made manifest what we shall be.

I JOHN 3:2.

Behold, how good and how pleasant it is
For brethren to dwell together in unity!

PSALM 133:1.

And they shall beat their swords into plowshares, and their spears into pruning-hooks; nation shall not lift up sword against nation, neither shall they learn war any more.

ISAIAH 2:4.

A VISTA OF GOLDEN DAYS

As one reads these words in this present day of telephone conversations across the Atlantic, of airship flights over continents and seas, of practically instantaneous radio communication eliminating distance, and of television which enables us to see as well as hear distant speakers and singers; and especially of dawning day of the new vision of world peace embodied in International Treaties, it seems well-nigh impossible that these words were written a half century ago. How accurately the second stanza describes the heroism and the accomplishments of modern scientific research:

—"but dare
All that may plant man's lordship firm,
On earth, and fire, and sea, and air."

This hymn is a selected portion of a long poem, seventeen stanzas, to which in 1880 its author gave the significant title, "The Vista." It was first published as a hymn in the *Methodist Hymn Book* (1904). It was first used thirty years ago, at public meetings and summer festivals, not at religious services. "It was probably thrown off hurriedly during some moment of deep longing, a longing for the betterment of the people which was always with Symonds, and which his study of Whitman and his own later life among a prosperous and democratic people helped so very much to foster."

"The Vista" began:

"Sad heart, what will the future bring
To happier men when we are gone?
What golden days shall dawn for them
Transcending all we gaze upon?

"Will our long strife be laid at rest?
The warfare of our blind desires
Be merged in a perpetual peace,
And love illumine but harmless fires?

"Shall faith released from forms that chain
And freeze the spirit while we pray,
Expect with calm and ardent eyes
The morning of death's brighter day?"

The four stanzas of the hymn follow here. Following the hymn are these two stanzas:

"There shall be no more sin, nor shame,
Though pain and passion may not die,
For man shall be at one with God
In bonds of firm necessity.

"These things—they are no dream—shall be
For happier men when we are gone:
Those golden days for them shall dawn
Transcending aught we gaze upon."

John Addington Symonds (1840–1893) was born in Bristol, England, educated at Harrow School and Baliol College, Oxford, and was made a Fellow of Magdalen College, Oxford, in 1862. He was the author of two volumes of verse, besides many scholarly and important works of prose, among them *The History of the Italian Renaissance.*

Poems like this prove that men are still inspired by Heaven;—how, is still as much a mystery as it was to Plato, and to the contemporaries of Isaiah; but nevertheless, inspired to prophesy great truths for the human race. God inspires his poets as true prophets to speak needful ideas in such beauty of melody and image as to charm men's minds, linger in their memories, fire their emotions, and steel their wills.

Let the captains and the kings of the earth get the theme of this song in their hearts, and let the voters get it, and then, "Nation with nation, land with land, unarmed, shall live as comrades free."

THE HYMN TUNE. The first tune to which these words were set, in the *Methodist Hymn Book* (1904), was INGLEMOUNT, by E. York Bowen.

In this country, MENDON, a German melody, arranged by Samuel Dyer, in 1814, is favored, as is also TRURO, composed by Charles Burney, 1769. (For a brief sketch of the life of Charles Burney, see the hymn, "More light shall break from out thy word.")

THIS IS MY FATHER'S WORLD

1. This is my Father's world,
And to my listening ears,
All nature sings, and round me rings
The music of the spheres.
This is my Father's world,
I rest me in the thought
Of rocks and trees, of skies and seas—
His hand the wonders wrought.

2. This is my Father's world,
The birds their carols raise,
The morning light, the lily white,
Declare their Maker's praise.
This is my Father's world,
He shines in all that's fair;
In the rustling grass I hear him pass,
He speaks to me everywhere.

3. This is my Father's world,
O let me ne'er forget
That though the wrong seems oft so strong,
God is the Ruler yet.
This is my Father's world,
The battle is not done;
Jesus who died shall be satisfied,
And earth and heaven be one.[1]

MALTBIE D. BABCOCK, 1901.

BIBLICAL TEXT.

The earth is the Lord's and the fulness thereof;
The world, and they that dwell therein.

PSALM 24: 1.

Are not two sparrows sold for a penny? and not one of them shall fall on the ground without your Father; but the very hairs of your head are all numbered. Fear not therefore: Ye are of more value than many sparrows.

MATTHEW 10: 29–31.

SKY-BORN MUSIC

Like a spring which bubbles up from the earth and makes glad everything around it, this hymn seems to have bubbled up from the

[1] Words copyright by Charles Scribner's Sons, from *Thoughts for Everyday Living*.

heart of a true lover of God, a genuine optimist, to make glad the hearts of all who sing.

Maltbie D. Babcock (1858–1901) was born in Syracuse, New York, graduated from Syracuse University, and Auburn Theological Seminary. During his college days he was a leader in athletics. He was tall, broad-shouldered, with muscles of steel; an expert baseball pitcher, and a good swimmer.

His first pastorate was at Lockport, New York. Thence he went to Baltimore, as pastor of the Brown Memorial Presbyterian Church. During his pastorate there he became a great favorite with the students of Johns Hopkins University; so much so that the University authorities set aside a special room in one of the university buildings for his use as a student-counselor. He was in demand as a college preacher all over the country.

From Baltimore he was called to New York, as the successor of Dr. Henry van Dyke, at the Brick Presbyterian Church. He died in Naples, Italy, in 1901.

Two of Dr. Babcock's outstanding characteristics were his abounding faith in God and his intense love for nature. Although his pastorates were in the city, and the last one in the great metropolis, he eagerly sought every opportunity to "get out in the fields with God"; his happiest hours were spent in the worship of God in his world, as he expressed it in the poem called "Worship":

> "Not in the sacred shrines alone,
> Which chime their summons unto me,
> Would I look to thy heavenly throne,
> But everywhere would worship thee."

The beauty of his trust in a gracious spirit in even commonplace things is shown in a familiar stanza from one of his poems:

> "Back of the loaf is the snowy flour,
> And back of the flour the mill;
> And back of the mill is the wheat, and the shower,
> And the sun, and the Father's will."

His courage and sturdy manhood, with a reminder of his athletic days in college, are shown in his hymn, "Be strong! We are not here to play, to dream, to drift." Bishop Warren called this "a rugged hymn, knotted like the muscles of a torso of Hercules."

The hymn, "This is my Father's world," is made up from six of the sixteen stanzas of a long poem, in *Thoughts for Everyday Living* (selections from his sermons, addresses and poems), published by Mrs. Babcock after his death.

Some of the omitted stanzas breathe his refreshing spirit of trust and optimism:

"This is my Father's world,
Dreaming, I see his face.
I ope my eyes, and in glad surprise
Cry, 'The Lord is in this place.'

"This is my Father's world,
From the shining courts above,
The Beloved One, his Only Son,
Came—a pledge of deathless love.

"This is my Father's world.
A wanderer I may roam,
Whate'er my lot, it matters not,
My heart is still at home.

"This is my Father's world.
I walk a desert lone.
In a bush ablaze to my wondering gaze
God makes his glory known.

"This is my Father's world.
Now closer to Heaven bound,
For dear to God is the earth Christ trod
No place but is holy ground.

"This is my Father's world,
Should my heart be ever sad?
The Lord is King—let the Heavens ring
God reigns—let the earth be glad." [2]

Dr. Babcock put a similar thought in prose when he said: "This is the best possible world for one who is called according to God's purpose. God knows why we are here and has told us—to learn, and to do,—for discipline and duty. Can we imagine a world better fitted for those ends than this world? How long we are to suffer or to serve is for God to say. Let us not look too much out of the school room windows, or too impatiently at the clock. When God's time for us comes, well and good. Till then, this world is best for us, and we must make the most of it and do our best for it."

Dr. George T. Webb, secretary of the Baptist World Alliance, writing to the editor says: "I am told by some of the officers of the First Presbyterian Church at Lockport, New York, that the young and gifted pastor of their church, Dr. Babcock, would frequently run out in the early morning to the brow of the hill, about two miles north of the city, to look out over the lowlands beyond, reaching on to Lake Ontario, and consider the wondrous beauty of that section. He was

[2] Words copyright by Charles Scribner's Sons, from *Thoughts for Everyday Living.*

in the habit of saying, 'I am going out to see my Father's world.' Dr. Babcock would then go on a few miles farther to a deep ravine just two miles south of Lake Ontario, where birds at that time found, as they do now, a much loved sanctuary. In this ravine my daughter has often found as many as forty varieties of birds. Here Babcock must have chimed these lines:

> 'This is my Father's world;
> The birds their carols raise.' "

A Responsive Reading

(This is my Father's world [with the King James version and extra-Biblical material].)

First Reader:

In the beginning God created the heaven and the earth. And God saw everything that he had made, and, behold, it was very good. Thus the heavens and the earth were finished, and all the host of them.

Where wast thou when I laid the foundations of the earth? When the morning stars sang together and all the sons of God shouted for joy?

Congregation:

"This is my Father's world,
And to my listening ears,
All nature sings, and round me rings
The music of the spheres."

Second Reader:

"The harp at nature's advent strung
Has never ceased to play;
The song the stars of morning sung
Has never died away.
And prayer is made, and praise is given
By all things near and far;
The ocean looketh up to heaven
And mirrors every star."

WHITTIER.

First Reader:

The earth is the Lord's, and the fulness thereof; the world, and they that dwell therein; for he hath founded it upon the seas, and established it upon the floods.

The trees of the Lord are full of sap; the cedars of Lebanon which he hath planted; where the birds make their nests; as for the stork, the fir trees are her house. The high hills are a refuge for the wild goats, and the rocks for the conies.

The earth is satisfied with the fruit of thy works.

Congregation:

"This is my Father's world,
I rest me in the thought
Of rocks and trees, of skies and seas—
His hand the wonders wrought."

Second Reader:

"I need not shout my faith. Thrice eloquent
Are quiet trees and the green listening sod;
Hushed are the stars, whose power is never spent;
The hills are mute; yet how they speak of God!" [3]

C. H. Towne

First Reader:

The world is mine, and the fulness thereof. For every beast of the forest is mine, and the cattle upon a thousand hills. I know all the birds of the mountains; and the wild beasts of the field are mine.

But now ask the beasts, and they shall teach thee; and the fowls of the air, and they shall tell thee; or speak to the earth, and it shall teach thee; and the fishes of the sea shall declare unto thee, that the hand of the Lord hath wrought this.

Let them praise the name of the Lord: for he commanded, and they were created.

Congregation:

"This is my Father's world,
The birds their carols raise,
The morning light, the lily white,
Declare their Maker's praise."

Second Reader:

"By one great heart the universe is stirred;
By Its strong pulse, stars climb the darkening blue;

[3] Copyright by Charles Hanson Towne.

It throbs in each fresh sunset's changing hue,
And thrills through the low sweet song of every bird." [4]

MARGARET DELAND.

"Thy beauty, Lord, thou hast revealed.
When larks sing in the air,
When lilies blossom in the field,
We kneel, for thou art there." [5]

EDGAR S. BRIGHTMAN.

First Reader:

He hath made the earth by his power, he hath established the world by his wisdom, and hath stretched out the heavens by his discretion.

When he uttereth his voice, there is a multitude of waters in the heavens, and he causeth the vapors to ascend from the ends of the earth; he maketh lightnings with rain, and bringeth forth the wind out of his treasures.

And, behold, the glory of the God of Israel came from the way of the east, and his voice was like a noise of many waters; and the earth shined with his glory.

The voice of the Lord is upon the waters: the God of glory thundereth; the Lord is upon many waters. The voice of the Lord is powerful; the voice of the Lord is full of majesty.

Congregation:

"This is my Father's world,
He shines in all that's fair;
In the rustling grass I hear him pass,
He speaks to me everywhere."

Second Reader:

"I bent unto the ground
And I heard the quiet sound
Which the grasses make when they
Come up laughing from the clay.

"'We are the voice of God,' they said:
Thereupon I bent my head
Down again that I might see
If they truly spoke to me.

[4] *By One Great Heart,* by Margaret Deland, copyright by Harper and Brothers.
[5] Copyright by E. S. Brightman.

"But around me everywhere
Grass and tree and mountain were
Thundering in a mighty glee,
'We are the voice of Deity.'

"And I leapt from where I lay,
I danced upon the laughing clay,
And to the rock that sang beside,
'We are the voice of God,' I cried." [6]

JAMES STEPHENS.

First Reader:

For by him were all things created, that are in heaven, and that are in earth, visible and invisible, whether they be thrones, or dominions, or principalities, or powers; all things were created by him, and for him; and he is before all things, and by him all things consist.

He ruleth by his power forever; his eyes behold the nations; let not the rebellious exalt themselves.

Who is the blessed and only Potentate, the King of kings, and Lord of lords.

Congregation:

"This is my Father's world,
O let me ne'er forget
That though the wrong seems oft so strong,
God is the Ruler yet."

Second Reader:

"I see the wrong that round me lies,
I feel the guilt within;
I hear, with groan and travail-cries,
The world confess its sin.
Yet, in the maddening maze of things,
And tossed by storm and flood,
To one fixed trust my spirit clings;
I know that God is good."

WHITTIER.

First Reader:

All things were made by him; and without him was not anything made that was made. He was in the world, and the world

[6] From James Stephens' *Bent Unto the Ground.* By permission of The Macmillan Company, publishers.

was made by him, and the world knew him not. He came unto his own, and his own received him not. But as many as receiveth him, to them gave he power to become the sons of God.

Thy kingdom come. They will be done in earth, as it is in heaven.

I pray not for the world, but for them which thou hast given me; for they are thine. Neither pray I for these alone, but for them also which shall believe on me through their word; that they may all be one; as thou, Father, art in me, and I in thee, that they also may be one in us; that the world may believe that thou hast sent me.

Congregation:

"This is my Father's world,
The battle is not done,
Jesus who died shall be satisfied,
And earth and heaven be one."

Second Reader:

"However the battle is ended,
Though proudly the victor comes
With fluttering flags and prancing nags
And echoing roll of drums,
Still truth proclaims this motto,
In letters of living light—
No question is ever settled,
Until it is settled right.

"Let those who have failed take courage;
Tho' the enemy seems to have won,
Tho' his ranks are strong, if he be in the wrong
The battle is not yet done;
For, as sure as the morning follows
The darkest hour of the night,
No question is ever settled
Until it is settled right." [7]

ELLA WHEELER WILCOX.

✣

THE HYMN TUNE. TERRA BEATA, meaning "happy land" or "earth," comes from an old English melody, arranged by Franklin L. Sheppard in 1915.

[7] Copyright by W. B. Conkey Co., and used by permission.

Many of our best tunes are evolved from traditional folk-songs; such are:

SWEET STORY, a Greek folk-song (to which we sing, "I think when I read that sweet story").

KREMSER, an Old Netherlands melody (for the hymn, "We praise thee, O God").

SICILIAN MARINERS, a Sicilian folk-song (used for "Lord, dismiss us with they blessing").

CRUSADER'S HYMN, a Silesian folk-song (adapted for "Fairest Lord Jesus").

LYNDE, a Thuringian folk-song (to which is set the hymn "Thou art my Shepherd").

AR HYD Y NOS, A Welsh melody (used for "God that madest earth and heaven").

THOU DIDST LEAVE THY THRONE

1. Thou didst leave thy throne and thy kingly crown
When thou camest to earth for me;
But in Bethlehem's home was there found no room
For thy holy nativity:

Refrain

O come to my heart, Lord Jesus,
There is room in my heart for thee.

2. Heaven's arches rang when the angels sang,
Proclaiming thy royal degree;
But in lowly birth didst thou come to earth,
And in great humility:

Refrain

3. The foxes found rest, and the birds their nest
In the shade of the forest tree;
But thy couch was the sod, O thou Son of God,
In the desert of Galilee:

Refrain

4. Thou camest, O Lord, with the living word
That should set thy people free;
But with mocking scorn, and with crown of thorn,
They bore thee to Calvary:

Refrain

5. When heaven's arches shall ring, and her choirs shall sing,
At thy coming to victory,
Let thy voice call me home, saying, 'Yet there is room,
There is room at my side for thee';

Refrain

My heart shall rejoice, Lord Jesus,
When thou comest and callest for me.

EMILY E. S. ELLIOTT, 1864.

BIBLICAL TEXT.
There was no room for them in the inn.

LUKE 2:7.

And the King of Glory shall come in.

PSALM 24:7.

O COME TO MY HEART, LORD JESUS

Emily Elizabeth Steele Elliott (1836–1897) came of a hymn-loving and hymn-writing family. Her father, Reverend E. B. Elliott, wrote *Horæ Apocalypticæ;* her uncle, Henry V. Elliott, published in 1835 a collection of *Hymns for Public, Private and Social Worship,* which included eleven hymns by his wife, and four by himself; and her aunt, Charlotte Elliott, wrote about one hundred and fifty hymns, including, "My God, my Father, while I stray," and "Just as I am without one plea."

Besides contributing to various collections, Emily Elliott published two volumes of Hymns and Poems from 1873 to 1880, including a total of one hundred forty-one hymns. The second part of the latter volume, containing forty-eight hymns, was also published separately as *Under the Pillow,* a large-typed inexpensive volume for the use of hospitals, infirmaries and sick folk generally.

"Thou didst leave thy throne" was first privately printed for the use of the choir and school of St. Mark's Church, Brighton, of which her father was rector. She has sensed in this hymn the loneliness of the Master, who was scoffed at, scorned and misunderstood by those to whom he looked for companionship and sympathy. This hymn is a significant commentary on the words of John, "He came unto his own, and they that were his own received him not."

Effective Uses of This Hymn

This hymn may be used in connection with "From the Eastern Mountains," and "We Three Kings of Orient Are," in a Carol Service. After the processional and presentation of the gifts of the Wise Men, a contralto soloist will sit at the manger cradle and sing the stanzas of the hymn while all kneel. All in the picture then sing softly, like a prayer-response, the Refrain:

"MADONNA AND CHILD," BY FERRUZZI

"Room for the Christ Child, room!"

"O come to my heart, Lord Jesus,
There is room in my heart for thee."

These lines may be read as a Benediction:

"The blasts of winter are fierce and cold,
The snow lies deep over hill and wold,
But a star shines bright through the deepening gloom;
Room for the Christ Child, room.

"Where man's distrust and his greed for gain
Have frozen the floods of tender rain,
Till never a flower of hope can bloom;
Room for the Christ Child, room.

"In homes that deepest griefs have borne,
'Mid silent forms of those that mourn,
In the shadows that gather around the tomb;
Room for the Christ Child, room.

"Where nations are warring, life for life,
And a cry rings out from the fearful strife
As a dying people sinks to its doom;
Room for the Christ Child, room.

"Room for the shepherds of Bethlehem,
Room for the angels who sang to them,
Room for the light in the wintry gloom;
Room for the Christ Child, room." [1]

W. B. Allen.

Another effective use of the hymn is as a solo while slides are thrown upon the screen. The following pictures are suggested:

First Stanza: Thou didst leave thy throne—"Annunciation to Mary" by Reni
But in Bethlehem's home—"Arrival at Bethlehem" by Merson

Second Stanza: Heaven's arches rang—"Bethlehem" by Hofmann
But of lowly birth—"Arrival of Shepherds" by Lerolle

Third Stanza: The foxes found rest—"Little foxes" by Carter
But thy couch was the sod—"Jesus by the sea" by Bida

Fourth Stanza: Thou camest, O Lord—"The Way, the Truth and the Life" by Bida
But with mocking scorn—"Leaving the Prætorium" by Doré

[1] Copyright by Willis Boyd Allen.

Fifth Stanza: When Heaven's arches shall ring—"The Ascension" by Hofmann
Let thy voice call me home—"The Christ" by Bida.

✣

THE HYMN TUNE. MARGARET was composed in 1876 by Reverend Timothy Richard Matthews (1826–1910). The same notes of tragedy and triumph run through the music as through the words and makes them *en rapport*.

Timothy Matthews was a clergyman of the Church of England, with the somewhat unusual record of having served only two churches during his ministry of fifty-four years. He was curate at St. Mary's, Nottingham, for six years, after which he went to North Coates, Lincolnshire, where he remained forty-eight years. He edited several hymn-books, composed over one hundred hymn-tunes and wrote settings for the morning and evening services.

THY WAY, NOT MINE, O LORD

1. Thy way, not mine, O Lord,
However dark it be;
Lead me by thine own hand,
Choose out the path for me.

2. Smooth let it be or rough,
It will be still the best;
Winding or straight, it leads
Right onward to thy rest.

3. I dare not choose my lot;
I would not, if I might;
Choose thou for me, my God,
So shall I walk aright.

4. The kingdom that I seek
Is thine: so let the way
That leads to it be thine,
Else I must surely stray.

5. Not mine, not mine the choice
In things or great or small;
Be thou my guide, my strength,
My wisdom, and my all.

HORATIUS BONAR, 1857.

BIBLICAL TEXT.

My Father, if it be possible, let this cup pass away from me; nevertheless, not as I will, but as thou wilt.

Again a second time he went away, and prayed, saying, My Father, if this cannot pass away, except I drink it, thy will be done.

MATTHEW 26:39, 42.

A SCOTCHMAN'S PLEDGE OF LOYALTY AND CONSECRATION

On may find in the life story of the remarkable leader of the Free Church of Scotland, Dr. Horatius Bonar (1808–1889), a true interpretation of the relation between the seemingly passive idea of "resignation," the author's own title for this hymn, and the inspiring activities of a virile life.

Dr. Bonar came of a line of sturdy and cultured Scots who were ministers and leaders in the church for two centuries or more, and whose faith was a mighty reality with them. He was a thorough-going Christian. This characteristic, almost autobiographical, hymn is a thorough-going pledge of loyalty and consecration to God.

Omitted Stanzas

Two omitted stanzas carry one back to Gethsemane of which this hymn is so vivid a portrayal:

"Take thou my cup, and it
With joy or sorrow fill,
As best to thee may seem;
Choose thou my good and ill.

"Choose thou for me my friends,
My sickness or my health;
Choose thou my care for me,
My poverty or wealth."

This is a hymn which needs to be read before it is sung. Let the minister read the Gethsemane story according to Matthew, and then ask the congregation to read the hymn in unison, quietly and reverently, thinking of the meaning of the words as they are pronounced, then the singing following will take on a deeper meaning.

A Story from the Talmud

A story in the Talmud tells of the experience of Rabbi Akiba, on a journey with an ass, a lamp and a rooster. At nightfall he came to a certain village and would have lodged there for the night, but was rudely refused shelter. Saying, "All that God does is well," he proceeded to camp in a nearby forest. He lit his lamp, but the wind blew it out. Sitting in the darkness, he repeated, "All that God does is well."

Then the ass escaped and was devoured by wild beasts. To cap the climax the rooster flew away. Each time the pious Rabbi said, "All that God does is well." In the morning he discovered that enemy troops had come in the night to the village where he would have lodged and completely destroyed it. He owed his safety to the darkness and the silence. Had the lamp been burning, or had the ass brayed or the rooster crowed, he would surely have been discovered and put to death, along with the villagers. So, as he set out once more on his journey, he repeated, with even more emphasis than before, "All that God does is well."

✣

THE HYMN TUNE. The hymn tune ST. CECILIA was composed by Reverend Leighton George Hayne (1836–1883) in 1863 for this hymn, and appeared in the "Merton Tune Book."

Dr. Hayne was a native of Exeter, England, and was educated at Eton and Queen's College, Oxford. In 1863 he was appointed Conductor of the Chorus of the University, and public examiner in music. Later he was organist in Eton College, and from 1871 to his death in 1883 was rector at Mistley and vicar of Bradfield, Essex.

'TIS MIDNIGHT; AND ON OLIVE'S BROW

1. 'Tis midnight; and on Olive's brow
The star is dimmed that lately shone:
'Tis midnight; in the garden now
The suffering Saviour prays alone.

2. 'Tis midnight; and from all removed,
The Saviour wrestles lone with fears;
E'en that disciple whom he loved
Heeds not his Master's grief and tears.

3. 'Tis midnight; and for others' guilt
The Man of Sorrows weeps in blood;
Yet he that hath in anguish knelt
Is not forsaken by his God.

4. 'Tis midnight; and from heavenly plains
Is borne the song that angels know;
Unheard by mortals are the strains
That sweetly soothe the Saviour's woe.

WILLIAM B. TAPPAN, 1822.

BIBLICAL TEXT.

And he came out and went, as his custom was, unto the mount of Olives; and the disciples also followed him.

LUKE 22:39.

Then cometh Jesus with them unto a place called Gethsemane, and saith unto his disciples, Sit ye here, while I go yonder and pray. And he took with him Peter and the two sons of Zebedee, and began to be sorrowful and sore troubled. Then saith he unto them, My soul is exceedingly sorrowful, even unto death; abide ye here, and watch with me.

MATTHEW 26:36–38.

And he was parted from them about a stone's cast; and he kneeled down and prayed, saying; Father, if thou be willing, remove this cup from me; nevertheless, not my will, but thine, be done.

And being in an agony he prayed more earnestly; and his sweat became as it were great drops of blood falling down upon the ground.

LUKE 22:41, 42, 44.

And he cometh unto the disciples, and findeth them sleeping, and saith unto Peter, What, could ye not watch with me one hour?

And a second time he went away and prayed. . . .

And he left them again, and went away, and prayed a third time, saying the same words.

MATTHEW 26:40, 42, 44.

And there appeared unto him an angel from heaven, strengthening him.

LUKE 22:43.

IN THE GARDEN

This hymn by William B. Tappan (1794–1849) is a most picturesque and beautiful description of the scenes in the garden.

Probably older folk who knew the young fellow Tappan, apprentice to a clock-maker in Boston during his teens, often shook their heads and expressed their regret that the son of a godly mother should "go to the dogs." For young William, whose father had died when he was twelve, was restive under the restraints of a trade he did not like, eager to see the world, and inclined to be "wild." Little did they imagine, those pessimists, that more than a hundred years later, the church would be singing as one of its prized hymns, a poem by this same "wild" young man.

As soon as he was twenty-one, William B. Tappan threw off the shackles of his apprenticeship and took the stage-coach for Philadelphia. Without much education (he had been to school only six months), without influential friends, but with a great ambition to become a writer, Tappan worked at his trade for a while, but little by little managed to find time to write. Four years after he arrived in Philadelphia he published his first book, a small volume of poems, containing the well-known hymn, "There is an hour of peaceful rest." Three years later followed the second volume of poems, which included "'Tis midnight; and on Olive's brow," and which appeared in *Village Hymns for Social Worship,* in 1824, and was sung by evangelist Asahel Nettleton in those days of spiritual awakening.

From 1826 to the end of his life Tappan served the American Sunday School Union as a Sunday School missionary. During this service he was ordained to the Congregational ministry. He died of cholera at West Needham, Massachusetts.

Professor Reeves says of this hymn: "It is a narrative and descriptive hymn, so vivid and intense that it begins to sing itself. There is no detail which is not an undertone and which does not set the central figure in stronger light." [1]

✣

THE HYMN TUNE. OLIVE'S BROW (appropriately named) was composed by William B. Bradbury (1816–1868) in 1853 for this hymn, and is one of the most beautiful and harmonious of his hymn tunes.

WATCHMAN, TELL US OF THE NIGHT

1. Watchman, tell us of the night,
What its signs of promise are:
Traveler, o'er yon mountain height,
See that glory-beaming star.
Watchman, doth its beauteous ray
Aught of joy or hope foretell?
Traveler, yes, it brings the day,
Promised day of Israel.

2. Watchman, tell us of the night,
Higher yet that star ascends;
Traveler, blessedness and light,
Peace and truth its course portends.
Watchman, will its beams alone
Gild the spot that gave them birth?
Traveler, ages are its own;
See, it bursts o'er all the earth.

3. Watchman, tell us of the night,
For the morning seems to dawn;
Traveler, darkness takes its flight;
Doubt and terror are withdrawn.
Watchman, let thy wanderings cease;
Hie thee to thy quiet home;
Traveler, lo, the Prince of Peace,
Lo, the Son of God is come.

JOHN BOWRING, 1825.

[1] From *The Hymn in History and Literature,* by J. B. Reeves, copyright by The Century Co.

Biblical Text.

Son of man, I have made thee a watchman unto the house of Israel; therefore hear the word at my mouth, and give them warning from me.

Ezekiel 3:17.

Watchman, what of the night? Watchman, what of the night?

The watchman said, The morning cometh, and also the night; if ye will inquire, inquire ye: turn ye, come.

Isaiah 21:11, 12.

HOW FAR HAS THE NIGHT GONE, WATCHMAN?

In vivid, striking language, with the suddenness of a lightning flash, Isaiah gives us a glimpse of a watchman on the tower of the city wall, keenly alert, eagerly watching for the dawn. Out of the stillness of the night, there suddenly comes to him a cry, a question, "Watchman, what of the night?" or as Dr. Moffatt translates it, "How far has the night gone, watchman?"

In 1825 the dawn of a new day was beginning to break over the world. The Missionary Movement of the nineteenth century was under way, and men and churches were entering upon a new realization of their obligations to carry the Gospel to "all nations." Professor Reeves calls attention to some of the significant facts of those years: "In the year 1830 an old order was giving place to a new one. Tennyson published the *Lady of Shalott* volume of poems in 1832; Browning published *Pauline* in 1833; Carlyle wrote *Sartor Resartus* in 1831. The Reform Bill was passed; the new scheme of public education was forming; factories and railroads were building. In 1830 Tennyson, Darwin, Gladstone, Poe, Chopin, Oliver Wendell Holmes and Lincoln were all just twenty-one. Emerson and Carlyle were discovering each other and the new world of German thought. In 1833 slavery was abolished in the British possessions. English social and industrial life was breaking from its old shell, with new wings. . . . Hopeful idealism was alive and active. New political ideas and new social and religious questionings and affirmations were stirring like wind in the trees. In the field of English hymnody there was a new springtime. . . . These hymns and the others like them show that with the industrial, political, scientific and philosophical arousal of the time there was new life and vigor in the religion of the people." [1]

Though this hymn was written in England in 1825 and published in that year in his collection of *Hymns,* Sir John Bowring (1792–1872) did not hear it used in a religious service for ten years. It was in a

[1] From *The Hymn in History and Literature,* by J. B. Reeves, copyright by The Century Co.

prayer meeting of American missionaries in Asiatic Turkey in 1835 that he heard it for the first time.

An antiphonal hymn, arranged in question and answer form, it has unusual beauty and impressiveness in special musical and dramatic settings.

A Song and Light Festival

Reader (*Church lights very dim*):

Lighten our darkness, Lord, we beseech thee,
Here in the night, we cry for light:
O show us the light!
Here in the darkness, of thy rich grace,
O show us thy face!
Of thy great tenderness, lead us,
O thou all-merciful, heed us.
Come in thy might, thou the all-light!
Scatter our darkness, O Lord! [2]

JOHN OXENHAM.

Bass Solo:

For behold, darkness shall cover the earth .... HANDEL
(From "The Messiah.")

Chorus:

Out of darkness .... GOUNOD
(From the Cantata, "Out of Darkness")

Hymn (Choir and Congregation):

Though like the wanderer,
The sun gone down,
Darkness be over me,
My rest a stone;
Yet in my dreams I'd be,
Nearer, my God, to thee,
Nearer to thee.

Reader, or Chorus-Anthem: .... ELVEY

Arise, shine, for thy light is come, and the glory of the Lord is risen upon thee. For behold, darkness shall cover the earth, and gross darkness the people; but the Lord shall arise upon thee, and his glory shall be seen upon thee, and the Gentiles shall come to thy light, and kings to the brightness of thy rising.

[2] Copyright by John Oxenham.

Processional with Lights.

(Processional down center aisle of church, singing the questions, "Watchman," bass or tenor soloist on platform, answering):

Processional:

Watchman, tell us of the night,
What its signs of promise are:

Soloist:

Traveler, o'er yon mountain's height
See that glory-beaming star!

(*Electric star over platform turned on.*)

Processional:

Watchman, does its beauteous ray
Aught of joy or hope foretell?

Soloist:

Traveler, yes; it brings the day,
Promised day of Israel.

Choir:

(In same antiphonal arrangement) the Second Stanza of the hymn.

Congregation (Third Stanza):

Watchman, tell us of the night,
For the morning seems to dawn;

Choir:

Traveler, darkness takes its flight,
Doubt and terror are withdrawn.

Congregation:

Watchman let thy wanderings cease,
Hie thee to thy quiet home:

Choir:

Traveler, lo, the Prince of Peace,
Lo, the Son of God is come.

Chorus:

Send out thy Light and thy Truth....................GOUNOD

(*Gradual crescendo of church lights during this number.*)

Minister:

Let your light so shine before men, that they may see your good works, and glorify your Father which is in heaven.

Congregation:

The path of the just is as the shining light,
That shineth more and more unto the perfect day.

Tenor Solo:

Then shall the righteous shine forth..............Mendelssohn
(From "St. Paul.")

The Appeal of the People

A Modernized verson of

Watchman, Tell Us of the Night.

(Setting: The ordinary pulpit platform of the church auditorium. Dim lights—brighter light on pulpit Bible.)

1. A PANTOMIME: *The Minister*

(Soft organ music, "Lead Kindly Light" and "Guide Me, O Thou Great Jehovah." During the music Minister enters, goes at once to pulpit Bible, turns pages of Old Testament, as though searching, sometimes slowly, sometimes rapidly. His face, in reflected light from pulpit lamp and Bible, should express perplexity, hope, joy and disappointment.)

2. READING: *The Minister:*

(Soft organ music in minor key)

How doth the city sit solitary, that was full of people! She is become a widow, that was great among the nations!

She that was a princess among the provinces is become tributary!

LAMENTATIONS 1:1.

Is it nothing to you, all ye that pass by? Behold, and see, if there be any sorrow like unto my sorrow.

Wherewith Jehovah hath afflicted me in the day of his fierce anger.

LAMENTATIONS 1:12.

Bring no more vain oblations. . . . I cannot away with iniquity and the solemn meeting.

Yea, when ye make many prayers, I will not hear: your hands are full of blood.

Wash you, make you clean, put away the evil of your doings from before mine eyes: cease to do evil, learn to do well; seek justice, relieve the oppressed, judge the fatherless, plead for the widow.

ISAIAH 1:13, 15, 16, 17.

Distant choir—"Sanctus"—"Holy, Holy, Holy."

The Minister:

Woe is me! for I am undone! because I am a man of unclean lips, and I dwell in the midst of a people of unclean lips; for mine eyes have seen the king, Jehovah of hosts.

ISAIAH 6:5.

Distant male quartet:

"Though your sins be as scarlet, they shall be as white as snow."

(Minister stands with head bowed over open Bible during one stanza of quartet hymn.)

3. THE FIRST QUESTION AND RESPONSE.

A Voice from the Darkness (from rear of church or side room):

Watchman, what of the night?
Watchman, what of the night?

ISAIAH 21:11.

The Minister (starts in surprise—listens intently, turns pages of Bible eagerly and replies):

The morning cometh . . . if ye will inquire, inquire ye.

ISAIAH 21:12.

The people that walked in darkness have seen a great light; they that dwelt in the land of the shadow of death, upon them hath the light shined.

ISAIAH 9:2.

(Platform lights grow a little brighter, revealing a group of children —Primary and Junior ages—at left.)

4. THE SECOND QUESTION AND RESPONSE.

The children (singing):

"Watchman, tell us of the night
What its signs of promise are?"

The Minister (singing):

"Traveler o'er yon mountain height,
See that glory-beaming star!"

There shall come forth a star out of Jacob and a sceptre shall rise out of Israel. (From a stereopticon in the rear of the church a star slide, somewhat dim, is thrown on the wall above the minister or at his right, remaining stationary during Third Question and Response.)

5. THE THIRD QUESTION AND RESPONSE.

The Children:

"Watchman, doth its beauteous ray
Aught of joy or hope foretell?"

The Minister:

"Traveler, yes, it brings the day,
Promised day of Israel."

I, Jesus, have sent mine angel to testify unto you these things. . . . I am the root and the offspring of David, the bright, morning star.

REVELATION 22: 16.

6. THE QUESTIONS OF YOUTH.

(Enter group of young people down side aisle, singing):

"Watchman, tell us of the night,
Higher yet that star ascends."

(Star grows brighter, higher on wall.)

The Minister:

"Traveler, blessedness and light
Peace and truth its course portends."

Peace I leave with you, my peace, I give unto you.

JOHN 14: 27.

I am the way, and the truth, and the life.

JOHN 14: 6.

Ye shall know the truth and the truth shall make you free.

JOHN 8: 32.

7. THE FIFTH QUESTION AND RESPONSE.

Young people:

"Watchman, will its beam alone
Gild the spot that gave them birth?"

The Minister:

"Traveler, ages are its own
See, it bursts o'er all the earth."

Distant Choir:

"The Morning Light is Breaking" (one stanza)

The Minister:

And it shall come to pass in that day, that the root of Jesse, that standeth for an ensign of the peoples, unto him shall the nations seek; and his resting place shall be glorious.

ISAIAH 11:10.

8. THE QUESTIONS OF MANHOOD.

(Group of men, down center aisle, singing):

"Watchman, tell us of the night
For the morning seems to dawn."

(Platform flooded with rosy light which shines on faces of men.)

The Minister:

I am the light of the world. He that followeth me shall not walk in the darkness, but shall have the light of life.

JOHN 8:12.

(Sings):

"Travelers, darkness takes its flight,
Doubt and terror are withdrawn."

Men:

"Watchman, let thy wandering cease,
Hie thee to thy quiet home."

The Minister:

Unto us a child is born, unto us a son is given, and the government shall be upon his shoulders, and his name shall be called Wonderful, Counsellor, Mighty God, Everlasting Father, Prince of Peace.

(Sings):

"Traveler, lo, the Prince of Peace,
Lo, the Son of God is come!"

(Organ music of triumphant type as Choir enters and children, youth and manhood group themselves around the Minister and the Bible. Star slide, now amber, is slowly lowered and enlarged until it shines full on the entire group on platform.

Pulpit light elevated, or white spot light from rear, illumines—The Angel—center rear).

The Angel sings *The Birthday of a King*—Neidlinger, with entire group singing the chorus.

Prayer and Benediction by the Minister or, led by group on platform, entire congregation joins in *Joy to the World* or *O Come, All Ye Faithful.*

Prayer and Benediction.

❖

THE HYMN TUNE. In the "Story of the Hymns and Tunes," Brown and Butterworth pay the following tribute to the tune WATCHMAN, composed by Lowell Mason (1792–1872) in 1830: "The tune written to this pealing hymn of Sir John Bowring by Lowell Mason has never been superseded. In animation and vocal splendor it catches the author's own clear call, echoing the shouts of Zion's sentinels from city to city, and happily reproducing in movement and phrase the great song-dialogue. Words and music together, the piece ranks with the foremost missionary lyrics." [3]

There is a remarkable coincidence in the fact that both the author of the words, Sir John Bowring, and the composer of the music, Dr. Lowell Mason, were born in the same year, 1792, and each lived to be eighty years old, dying in the same year, 1872. So these two men, living on opposite sides of the Atlantic, and quite probably never knowing each other, cover in their long life-span the same strategic years and are joined in the combined legacy of hymn and tune so happily united.

WELCOME, HAPPY MORNING!

1. Welcome, happy morning! age to age shall say;
Hell today is vanquished, heaven is won today.
Lo! the Dead is living, God for evermore;
Him their true Creator, all his works adore.

Refrain

Welcome, happy morning! age to age shall say.

2. Earth her joy confesses, clothing her for spring,
All good gifts returned with her returning King:
Bloom in every meadow, leaves on every bough,
Speak his sorrow ended, hail his triumph now.

Refrain

3. Months in due succession, days of lengthening light,
Hours and passing moments praise thee in their flight;
Brightness of the morning, sky, and fields, and sea,
Vanquisher of darkness, bring their praise to thee.

Refrain

[3] Copyright by the American Tract Society.

4. Come then, True and Faithful, now fulfil thy word,
'Tis thine own third morning; rise, O buried Lord!
Show thy face in brightness, bid the nations see;
Bring again our daylight; day returns with thee.

Refrain

VENANTIUS FORTUNATUS, 590.
Translated by John Ellerton, 1868.

BIBLICAL TEXT.

Why seek ye the living among the dead? He is not here, but is risen; remember how he spake unto you when he was yet in Galilee, saying that the Son of man must be delivered up into the hands of sinful men, and be crucified, and the third day rise again.

LUKE 24: 5–7.

Fear not; I am the first and the last, and the Living one; and I was dead, and behold, I am alive for evermore.

REVELATION 1: 17, 18.

AN EASTER HYMN OF THE SIXTH CENTURY

Out of the distant past, across more than twelve centuries of Christian history, sound the ringing notes of this joyful Easter hymn.

Its author, Venantius Honorius Clementianus Fortunatus (530–609), was born in upper Italy and educated at Ravenna, where he devoted himself to oratory and poetry. He was miraculously cured of threatened blindness by oil from the lamp of St. Martin's, Tours. In his gratitude he made two long pilgrimages thither, where he met Queen Rhadegunda who influenced him to become a priest and to devote the rest of his life to Gaul. Shortly before his death he was made Bishop of Poitiers.

Fortunatus spent his early life in gay, literary idleness, wandering from castle to palace, and from marriage rite to family festivals, pouring forth his gay verses like the first troubadour, that he was. "With a heart that could lie still, and find its life in reflecting the life of others, he appears to have passed safely through the temptations of court revelries and dangerous intimacies, like a glass mirror, colored and illuminated by every passing event, and ruffled by none. Not a shadow of scandal has been thrown over his intimacy even with Queen Rhadegunda by the historians of that day."

Even after becoming a priest, Fortunatus continued the same lighthearted, easy-going habits, a true child of the golden South.

Contrast this life of the court poet, songster and troubadour with the three hymns by which he is best known; hymns of solemnity and pathos:

"Vexilla Regis Prodeunt"—The royal banners forward go;
"Pange Lingua Gloriosi"—Sing, my tongue, the glorious battle;
"Salve Festa Dies"—Welcome, happy morning.

Mrs. Charles says: "Of the outer life of Fortunatus we know nothing, except on its lighter side; of his spiritual life we know nothing except through his hymns. The intermediate tones are wanting in the picture, and necessarily the effect is jarring."

In *"Festa Dies"* there linger some tournament flings, some poetic tinsel, some elegancies of his troubadour spirit. The coming of spring meant more to Fortunatus and his contemporaries than it means to us who have express trains and steamboats to carry us south to perpetual spring and sunshine. Winter grew very bleak and bare, and lean; and spring was hailed with delight.

"See the fresh beauty of the new-born earth,
As with the Lord, his gifts anew come forth.

Christ, after suffering, vanquished Satan's powers;
Thus dons the grove its leaves, the grass its flowers.

The changing months, the pleasant light of days,
The shining hours the rippling moments praise."

This translation, "Welcome, Happy Morning!" was made by John Ellerton (1826–1893). (See "God the All-Terrible," for biography.) Ellerton spent most of his life as a country parson, but his inflence on the hymnody of the Church was wide.

This translation is spirited, but very free, in fact, more like a paraphrase than a translation. The student will find it interesting to compare a stanza of Fortunatus' original Latin with the Ellerton translation, and also with that of A. J. Mason in *Hymns Ancient and Modern:*

Salve, festa dies, toto venerabilis aevo,
Qua Deus infernum vicit et astra tenet.

Ecce renascentis testatur gratia mundi,
Omnia cum Domino dona redisse suo.

Hail, festal day, whose glory never ends;
Now hell is vanquished, Christ to heaven ascends.

All nature with new births of beauty gay
Acknowledges her Lord's return today.

This section of *"Festa Dies"* consists of thirty-nine lines, but it is only about one-third of the whole hymn. Some hymnals include additional stanzas of Ellerton's translation:

> "Thou, of life the Author, death didst undergo,
> Tread the path of darkness, saving strength to show;
> Loose the souls long prisoned, bound with Satan's chain,
> All that now is fallen, raise to life again."

✣

THE HYMN TUNE. The hymn tune, FORTUNATUS, was written in 1872 by Arthur Seymour Sullivan (1842–1900) for the Hymnary and there called "Welcome, happy morning," vieing with Calkin's tune of same name for popularity as a processional for Easter morning.

Sullivan at the age of eight had learned to play almost every wind instrument in the band, his father being bandmaster at the Royal Military College. Sullivan was always fortunate in his teachers, as a boy chorister at Chapel Royal at the age of twelve he had Helmore, in piano he studied under Sterndale Bennett, and under Sir John Goss in harmony. The Mendelssohn scholarship, which he won over Barnby, enabled him to spend three years in Leipzig. He was a master of melody with a genius for orchestration. Solid diatonic harmonies and easy-flowing melodiousness of the different parts characterized his writing.

His first tune HOMELAND was written when he was twenty-five. He was naturally a prominent figure in London Society and his vivacious manner and cheerful temperament made him an exceptionally pleasant companion. Sullivan was devoted to his mother who died after he had gained considerable fame. His father died at the beginning of his great career. Children's voices always affected Sullivan deeply. Often he would burst out crying during their part in a church service.

WE PLOUGH THE FIELDS, AND SCATTER

1. We plough the fields, and scatter
   The good seed on the land,
   But it is fed and watered
   By God's almighty hand;
   He sends the snow in winter,
   The warmth to swell the grain,

The breezes and the sunshine,
And soft refreshing rain.

Refrain

All good gifts around us
Are sent from heaven above;
Then thank the Lord, O thank the Lord,
For all his love.

2. He only is the Maker
Of all things near and far;
He paints the wayside flower,
He lights the evening star;
The winds and waves obey him,
By him the birds are fed;
Much more to us, his children,
He gives our daily bread.

Refrain

3. We thank thee, then, O Father,
For all things bright and good,
The seed-time and the harvest,
Our life, our health, our food;
The gifts that we would offer,
For all thy love imparts,
Are those thou most desirest,
Our humble, thankful hearts.

Refrain

Matthias Claudius, 1782.
Translated by Jane M. Campbell, 1861.

Biblical Text.

Thou visitest the earth, and waterest it,
Thou greatly enrichest it;
Thou waterest its furrows abundantly;
Thou settlest the ridges thereof;
Thou makest it soft with showers;
Thou blessest the springing thereof.
Thou crownest the year with thy goodness;
And thy paths drop fatness.

Psalm 65:9–11.

"A haze on the far horizon,
The infinite tender sky,
The ripe rich tints of the cornfields,
And wild geese sailing high,
And all over upland and lowland
The charm of the golden-rod,
Some of us call it autumn,
And others call it God.

"Like tides on the crescent seabeach,
When the moon is new and thin,
Into our hearts come yearnings,

Come welling and surging in,
Come from the mystic ocean
Whose rim no foot has trod,
Some of us call it longing,
And others call it God."[1]

WILLIAM HERBERT CARRUTH.

A PEASANT'S SONG OF HARVEST GRATITUDE

This is an instance of a poem becoming a hymn without any such intention on the author's part.

"Paul Erdmann's Fest" is a long German poem of seventeen stanzas, written by Matthias Claudius (1740–1815) in 1782. It describes a group of peasants gathering in Paul Erdmann's kitchen at the time of harvest, to make merry over the bountiful results of their labors on the farms during the summer.

They are having a jolly, festive time around tables heavily laden with good things to eat. In connection with the celebration, they sing their praises and thanksgiving to God in this so-called "Peasants' Song," the last four stanzas of which especially relate to Paul, their host, and to the occasion of the feast. The stanzas are sung as a solo with all joining in the chorus. After the completion of the song the neighbors join Paul, standing, in drinking a toast to the God whom they have been praising.

A literal translation of the entire poem is given below:

1. "In the beginning on earth
Only darkness and desert waste;
And should there be something,
It must come from elsewhere!

Chorus:

"All good gifts
Come from above, from God,
From beautiful blue heaven!

2. "So it was agoing
In the beginning, when God spoke;
And as its beginning,
So it goes this very day!

3. "We plough, and we strew
The seed on the land;
Though growth and increase
Stand not in our hand.

4. "He does with quiet motion
Himself mild and unseeing,
And puts, when we have gone home,
Growth and increase thereon!

5. "He sendeth dew and rain,
And sun- and moon-shine;
He wraps God's blessing
Very tenderly and carefully in!

6. "Bring him the overflow
Of field and bread;
It goes through his hands,
Comes also from God!

7. "What is near and what is far,
From God comes everything;
The wisp of straw and the stars,
The sparrow and the ocean.

[1] From *Each in His Own Tongue,* by William H. Carruth, copyright by G. P. Putnam Sons and Katharine M. Carruth.

8. "From him did bush and leaves come,
And corn and fruit from him,
From him mild spring weather,
And snow and changeable weather.

9. "He makes the sun rise,
He commands the moon's path,
He lets the wind blow,
He opens the heaven.

10. "He presents us with cattle and pleasure,
He maketh us fresh and red,
He gives the cows pasture,
And our children bread.

11. "Also pious and trustworthy,
And quiet higher thoughtfulness,
Of him beg and upon him look,
And all comes through him.

12. "He goes unseen
In the village around and watcheth,
And stirs the heartily beseeching
In their sleep at night.

13. "Therefore, so we will praise,
And praise evermore
The great Giver above.
He is! and he is all!

14. "And he had great things done
On neighbor Paul;
The poorest and the weakest one
Entered Paul's inheritance.

15. "He had warned against loss,
Had richly bethought him,
Brought him today out of grace
And a jubilee he made.

16. "And such grace and trustfulness
Does his people gladly.
He blesses Paul on the new,
And our dear Lord!"

Matthias Claudius was a German scholar and newspaper man, born at Reinfeld in Holstein. His father was a Lutheran minister who started Matthias toward the ministry as a life vocation. But the young man became more interested in literature and law, and, associating with a company of freethinkers, lost much of his belief in religion. A serious illness when he was thirty-seven years old, recalled him to the faith of his childhood. He was connected in an editorial capacity with newspapers in Hamburg, Wandsbeck and Darmstadt, and wrote many of his poems for those papers. Though he made no attempt to write hymns, several of his poems have been included in Lutheran hymn-books and translated into English.

Miss Jane Montgomery Campbell (1817–1878) was the daughter of an English clergyman, and a teacher in her father's parish school. In 1861 she contributed a number of translations of German hymns to *A Garland of Songs,* published by Reverend C. S. Bere. She also published a *Handbook for Singers,* which contained the musical exercises she taught in her father's school.

THE HYMN TUNE. DRESDEN, the tune to which these words are commonly set, is characterized in Julian's *Dictionary of Hymnology* as "popular, though somewhat boisterous."

It was arranged from Johann Abraham Peter Schulz (1747–1800), a noted German composer and conductor. He was for seven years conductor to Prince Henry of Prussia at Reinsburg, and later court conductor at Copenhagen. He wrote four Danish operas, many secular and sacred songs, and some piano pieces.

WE PRAISE THEE, O GOD

Te Deum Laudamus

Anonymous—Fourth Century JOSEPH BARNBY, 1838-1896

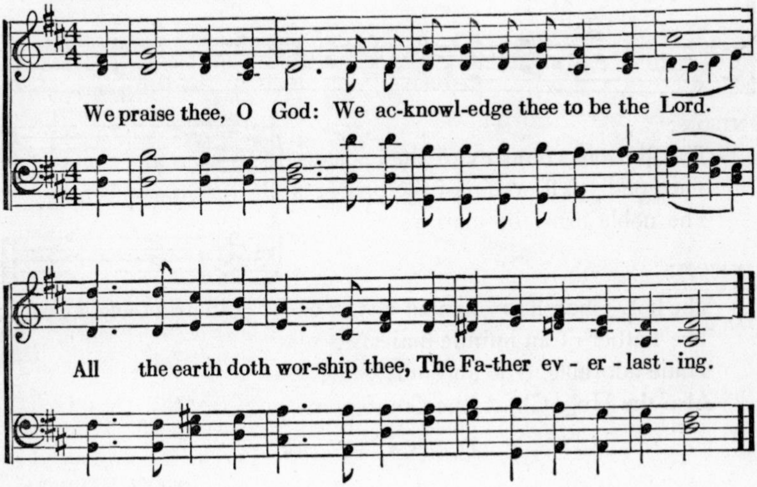
We praise thee, O God: We ac-knowl-edge thee to be the Lord.
All the earth doth wor-ship thee, The Fa-ther ev - er - last - ing.

UNISON READING:

To thee all angels cry aloud;
The heavens, and all the powers therein;
To thee cherubim and seraphim continually do cry,—

Sanctus

A. S. COOPER

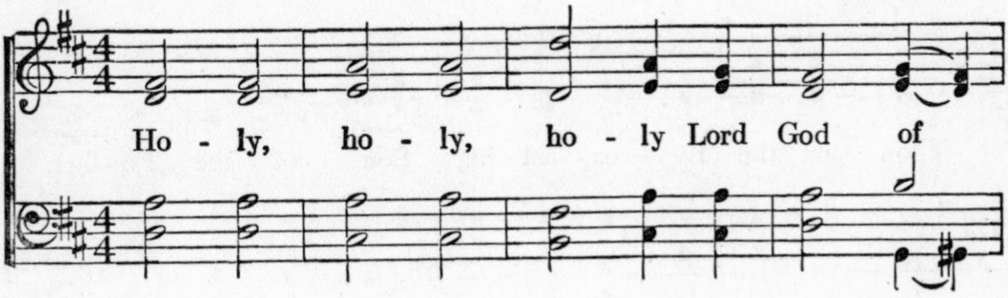
Ho - ly, ho - ly, ho - ly Lord God of

Sab - a - oth; Heaven and earth are full of thy glo -
ry, Full of the maj - es - ty of thy glo - ry.

UNISON:

The glorious company of the apostles
The goodly fellowship of the prophets
The noble army of martyrs

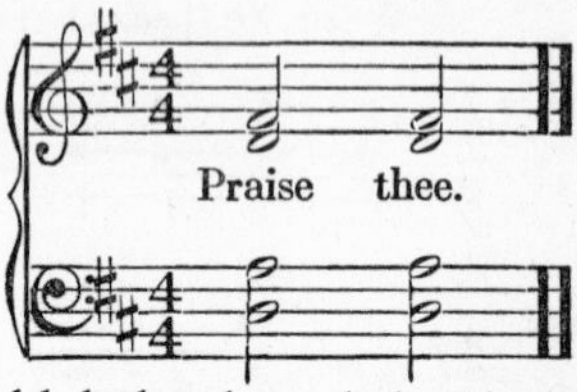
Praise thee.

UNISON:

The holy Church throughout all the world doth acknowledge thee;
The Father of an infinite majesty;
Thine adorable, true and only Son;
Also the Holy Ghost, the Comforter.

Te Deum Laudamus

JOSEPH BARNBY

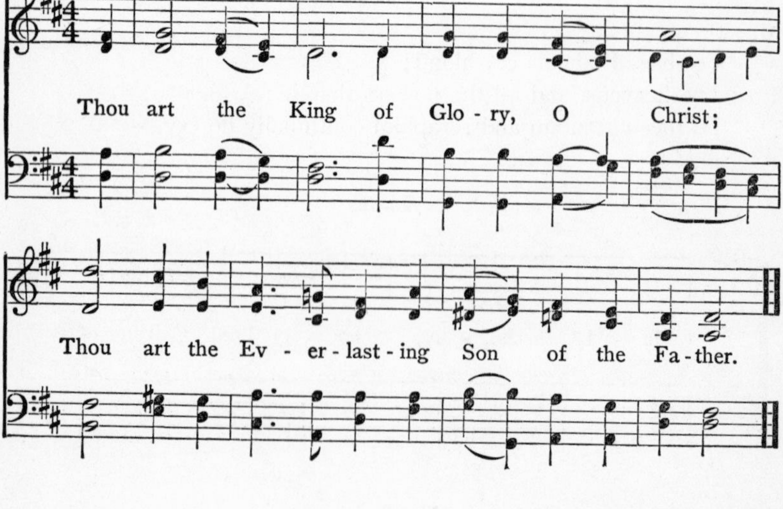
Thou art the King of Glo - ry, O Christ;
Thou art the Ev - er - last - ing Son of the Fa - ther.

RESPONSIVELY:

When thou tookest upon thee to deliver man,
Thou didst humble thyself to be born of a virgin.
When thou hadst overcome the sharpness of death
Thou didst open the kingdom of heaven to all believers.
Thou sittest at the right hand of God, in the glory of the Father.
We believe that thou shalt come to be our Judge.
We therefore pray thee, help thy servants,
Whom thou hast redeemed with thy precious blood.
Make them to be numbered with thy saints, in glory everlasting.
O Lord, save thy people, and bless thine heritage.
Govern them, and lift them up for ever.
Day by day we magnify thee;
And we worship thy name ever, world without end.
Vouchsafe, O Lord, to keep us this day without sin.

Miserere Mei

Anonymous

O Lord, have mer-cy up - on us, have mer - cy up - on us.

UNISON:

O Lord, let thy mercy be upon us, as our trust is in thee.
O Lord, in thee have I trusted; let me never be confounded.

BIBLICAL TEXT.

Great is the mystery of godliness;
He who was manifested in the flesh,
Justified in the spirit,
Seen of angels,
Preached among the nations,
Believed on in the world,
Received up in glory.

I TIMOTHY 3:16.

A HYMN, A CREED, A PRAYER FOR THE CHURCH UNIVERSAL

For at least fourteen centuries the *"Te Deum Laudamus"* has been sung wherever the Church has carried Christian teaching. It has been well described by Reverend W. R. Huntington, as: "An orchestra in which no single instrument is lacking; first or last every chord is struck and every note sounded. The soul listens and is satisfied."

Its origin is shrouded in mystery, though there is a beautiful legend that it was composed and spontaneously sung in antiphons by Saints Ambrose and Augustine at the baptism of the latter on Easter Sunday, April 25, 387. The tablet on the Chapel in Milan records quaintly but imperishably the solemnity of this event:

> *"Divus Augustinus ad lucem*
> *Fidei per sanctum Ambrosium*
> *Evocatus hic undæ caelesti*
> *Abluitur anno domini* CCLXXXVIII"

Ambrose, Bishop of Milan (340–397), came of noble Roman family, his father being prefect of Gaul. Before he was thirty Ambrose himself was representing Imperial Rome at Milan. While here in the midst of an ecclesiastical riot, he as civil governor appeared and commanded peace. A child's voice shouted: "Ambrose is Bishop! Ambrose is Bishop!" and the multitude took up the shout. So Ambrose became bishop. His first conflict was for doctrine; for preserving the Catholic creed against Arians. He was commanded to give up one of his Basilicas for Arian use by Empress Justina. He refused and went into a state of siege, the mass of people of the city taking possession of all buildings, with the imperial troops besieging them but making no attack, and suffering no one to leave, thus hoping to exhaust the patience of Ambrose and his followers. Singing came to the aid of the besieged, Ambrose composing hymns and arranging for the chanting of same at all hours of the day and night, thus keeping his watchers awake and alert. His hymns resounded through the basilica and the city became his choir.

The oldest actual reference to the use of the *"Te Deum Laudamus"* is in the "Rule of St. Cæsarius of Arles, 502 A. D., in which it is ordered as a part of the Sunday morning service.

It is found in English manuscripts of about 1410 in the curious old English spelling of that early period:

> "We herien thee God, we knowlechyn thee lord.
> Thee everlasting fadir al the erthe worchipith."

The First Prayer Book of Edward VI (1547) contains it in English almost as we know it today. The Scottish Psalter of 1562 includes it in the appendices.

The *"Te Deum"* is in three parts. The first part is an outburst of praise to the Trinity from earth, heaven and the church. The second section begins "Thou art the King of Glory, O Christ"; it sets forth in glowing strophes the merits of the divine Christ, his incarnation, atonement, ascension, and second coming. The third part is a prayer that all may share his glory.

It is said that no other hymn or anthem has been used on so many historic occasions in so many different lands. It is said to have been sung at the baptism of Clovis, traditional founder of the French kingdom, at Paris, in 496 A. D. In 1900 A. D. it formed the climax of the great service of thanksgiving for the Christians of all names and nationalities in Peking after the delivery of that city from the Boxers by the Allies. And in 1929, in Boston, in the great service of Solemn High Mass in gratitude for the settlement of the long controversy between the Roman Church and the Italian Kingdom, it was the *"Te Deum"* which best expressed the feelings of the throngs of devout Catholics present.

An instance of its influence on a single individual is the story of Thomas Olivers, the English Methodist evangelist and coeditor with John Wesley of *The Arminian Magazine*. In early life he was a poor shoemaker. He was converted under the preaching of Whitefield. At a time of doubts and anxieties he says: "I went to the Cathedral and when I heard the *'Te Deum'* sung I felt as if I had done with earth, and was praising God before his throne. No words can set forth the joy, the rapture, the awe and reverence which I felt."

So the *"Te Deum"* brought new light to Olivers. And it was Thomas Olivers who later wrote "The God of Abram Praise." As related in the comment on "A Mighty Fortress," it was the triumphant death of two young men in Brussels who died as martyrs to the cause of Christ that inspired Luther to write his great hymn. These two young men died with the *"Te Deum"* on their lips.

Surely, its immemorial use, its profound religion, and its immortal beauty make it a supreme paean of praise for the Church Universal.

WE WOULD SEE JESUS, LO! HIS STAR

1. We would see Jesus, lo! his star is shining
Above the stable while the angels sing;
There in a manger on the hay reclining,
Haste, let us lay our gifts before the King.

2. We would see Jesus, Mary's son most holy,
Light of the village life from day to day;
Shining revealed through every task most lowly,
The Christ of God, the Life, the Truth, the Way.

3. We would see Jesus, on the mountain teaching,
With all the listening people gathered round;
While birds and flowers and sky above are preaching,
The blessedness which simple trust has found.

4. We would see Jesus, in his work of healing,
At even-tide before the sun was set;
Divine and human, in his deep revealing,
Of God and man in loving service met.

5. We would see Jesus, in the early morning,
Still as of old he calleth, "Follow Me";
Let us arise, all meaner service scorning,
Lord, we are thine, we give ourselves to thee.[1]

J. Edgar Park, 1913.

Biblical Text.

Sir, we would see Jesus.

John 12:21.

Lord, show us the Father, and it sufficeth us. Jesus saith unto him, Have I been so long time with you, and dost thou not know me, Philip? he that hath seen me hath seen the Father: how sayest thou, Show us the Father?

John 14:8, 9.

A HYMN OF THE DEEP, REVEALING LIFE OF JESUS

Too many people are inclined to classify hymns by their first stanzas. By doing this, they often miss the real message of the hymn. Classified by its first stanza, this hymn is often thought of as a "Nativity" hymn, and, consequently, sung only at Christmas time. This is an unfortunate loss to the church, for this hymn is a most beautiful summary of the whole earthly life of our Lord, and comes, in its final stanza, to an impressive dedication of our lives to him and to his work, as a result of the vision the hymn gives us of his life and service.

John Edgar Park (1879–   ) was born at Belfast, Ireland, the son of Reverend William Park, a Presbyterian minister. He studied at New College, Edinburgh, the Presbyterian Theological Seminary, Belfast, and at the Royal University, Dublin. Coming to this country in 1900 he entered Princeton Theological Seminary, and was ordained to the Presbyterian ministry in 1903. After serving as pastor of the West Parish Church, Andover, and the Second Congregational Church, West Newton, Massachusetts, he was called to the presidency of Wheaton College in 1926.

He is the author of many books, especially *The Keen Joy of Living; The Man Who Missed Christmas; The Disadvantages of Being Good,* and *The Bad Results of Good Habits.* His latest book,

[1] Copyright, 1913, by The Pilgrim Press.

published in 1926, is *The Christmas Heretic*. Doctor Park resides in Norton, Massachusetts.

This hymn was written in response to an appeal for words to go with CUSHMAN, composed by Professor Turner, of Hampton Institute. The author says of it: "I got the tune singing in my head so that I could go nowhere without it, and then gradually one verse after another began singing itself to the tune."

Similar lines may be noted in Anna B. Warner's "We would see Jesus; for the shadows lengthen." Her hymn is subjective, contemplative; Dr. Park's hymn is objective, historical and practical. In Dr. Park's fine words we have a lyrical summary of the life of Christ.

The hymn made its first appearance in *Worship and Song,* in 1913, and has since found its way into many church hymnals, as well as into practically all the newer hymnals for young people.

THE HYMN TUNE. The tune CUSHMAN, by Reverend Herbert B. Turner (1852–), was composed in 1905 at Hampton Institute, Virginia. Mr. Turner was editing *Hymns and Tunes for School* and *Church Hymns and Tunes*. It was composed for the words by Anna Warner: "We would see Jesus, for the shadows lengthen."

WHAT A FRIEND WE HAVE IN JESUS

1. What a friend we have in Jesus,
All our sins and griefs to bear;
What a privilege to carry
Everything to God in prayer!
O what peace we often forfeit,
O what needless pain we bear,
All because we do not carry
Everything to God in prayer.

2. Have we trials and temptations?
Is there trouble anywhere?
We should never be discouraged:
Take it to the Lord in prayer!
Can we find a friend so faithful,
Who will all our sorrows share?
Jesus knows our every weakness—
Take it to the Lord in prayer!

3. Are we weak and heavy-laden,
Cumbered with a load of care?
Precious Saviour, still our refuge,

Take it to the Lord in prayer!
Do thy friends despise, forsake thee?
Take it to the Lord in prayer!
In his arms he'll take and shield thee,
Thou wilt find a solace there.

JOSEPH SCRIVEN, 1857.

BIBLICAL TEXT.

Cast thy burden upon the Lord, and he will sustain thee: He will never suffer the righteous to be moved.

PSALM 55:22.

Casting all your anxiety upon him because he careth for you.

1 PETER 5:7.

DEATHLESS SINGING FROM A MANIAC'S TONGUE

It has been said of this hymn that "there is no Christian speech nor language where its voice is not heard," and that it is the first hymn which many missionaries of many churches teach their converts. Certainly it is one of the most popular and most constantly used of all the four hundred thousand Christian hymns.

Joseph Scriven (1820–1886), born in Dublin, was graduated from Trinity College, Dublin, and moved to Canada in 1845. He was like Cowper in that his life was marked by tragic sadness, he was subject to melancholia, was devotedly religious, and spent part of his time in oddly generous ways. The girl to whom he was to have been married was accidentally drowned on the eve of their wedding. Following that, he devoted all his life and property to the service of the Christian religion. He gave and worked where there would be no compensation. Ira D. Sankey gives an account of Scriven going down the street of Port Hope, Ontario, once with a saw and saw-horse. One citizen noted the sober working man and wished to hire him. "You cannot get that man," said another citizen, "he saws wood only for poor widows and sick people who are unable to pay." A friend sitting up with Scriven who was ill, came upon the hymn "What a friend we have in Jesus." Scriven explained that he had written the hymn to send to his mother in Ireland for her comfort. In a fit of melancholia, Scriven took his own life.

One is reminded here of Mrs. Browning's words on Cowper's grave:

"O Poets! from a maniac's tongue was poured the deathless singing!
O Christians, at your cross of hope a hopeless hand was clinging!
O men, this man in brotherhood your weary paths beguiling,
Groaned only while he taught you peace, and died while ye were smiling!

"And now, what time ye all may read through dimming tears his story,
How discord on the music fell and darkness on the glory,
And how when, one by one, sweet sounds and wandering lights departed,
He wore no less a loving face because so broken-hearted."

✣

THE HYMN TUNE. The familiar tune ERIE, to which Scriven's hymn is usually sung, is probably named from the city (Erie, Pennsylvania) in which the composer lived and practised law.

Charles G. Converse (1834–1918) was born in Warren, Massachusetts. He received his musical education in Germany, chiefly at Leipzig, where he made the acquaintance of Liszt and Spohr. Returning to America, he studied law, graduating from the law department of Albany University in 1860. In 1875 he settled in Erie, where he practised law for many years. He died in Highwood, New Jersey.

His musical compositions include a Psalm-Cantata on Psalm 126, which was performed under the direction of Theodore Thomas in Chicago in 1888; a Christmas overture (in manuscript) which was performed in New York under the direction of Walter Damrosch; an American overture, built on the theme, "Hail Columbia"; also oratorios and chorals.

This tune, ERIE, is the only widely used tune by this composer. It is said by one writer to have "most of the merits without the disadvantages of the gospel song."

WHEN I SURVEY THE WONDROUS CROSS

1. When I survey the wondrous cross
On which the Prince of glory died,
My richest gain I count but loss,
And pour contempt on all my pride.

2. Forbid it, Lord, that I should boast,
Save in the death of Christ, my God;
All the vain things that charm me most,
I sacrifice them to his blood.

3. See, from his head, his hands, his feet,
Sorrow and love flow mingled down;
Did e'er such love and sorrow meet,
Or thorns compose so rich a crown?

4. Were the whole realm of nature mine,
That were a present far too small;
Love so amazing, so divine,
Demands my soul, my life, my all.

ISAAC WATTS, 1707.

Biblical Text.

But far be it from me to glory, save in the cross of our Lord Jesus Christ, through which the world hath been crucified unto me, and I unto the world.

Galatians 6:14.

Howbeit what things were gain to me, these have I counted loss for Christ. Yea verily, and I count all things to be loss for the excellency of the knowledge of Christ Jesus my Lord.

Philippians 3:7, 8.

CRUCIFIXION TO THE WORLD BY THE CROSS OF CHRIST

Such was the original title of this hymn, written in the days when poets and authors tried to tell the whole story in the title, and people had time to stop and read lengthy titles.

"It was not my design to exalt myself to the rank and glory of poets, but I was ambitious to be a servant to the churches, and a helper to the joy of the meanest Christian." Thus was worded the ambition of Isaac Watts (1674–1748), who has been called the father of English hymnody.

In its simplicity, its logical and artistic completeness, its splendor of figure, phrase and melody, its deep solemnity, its passion of pure religion, this is a perfect flower of song. No wonder Matthew Arnold considered it the greatest hymn in the language. The stanza,

"See from his head, his hands, his feet
Sorrow and love flow mingled down,"

surpasses every other stanza in the range of hymnody for solemn beauty and intense sorrow.

This "Seraphic Doctor" ruled the sanctuary as no one else had done since David. His hymns, and only his, were sung. For a long period of years worshippers would sing nothing else than "Watts" in a large share of the English-speaking world. He won and held his empire over heart and mind. In fact, a part of the above statement might almost be put in the present tense. While, of course, the present church sings a great deal besides Watts, the continuing popularity of certain of Dr. Watts' hymns is one of the wonders of hymnology. To illustrate: of five hymnals published since 1925—one has no less than twenty-three of Watts' hymns; the second has sixteen; the third has nine; and the fourth and fifth, eight each. The one having sixteen is the official hymnal of Harvard University.

"His dying crimson, like a robe,
Spreads o'er his body on the tree;

Then I am dead to all the globe,
And all the globe is dead to me."

✣

THE HYMN TUNE. Some of the vicissitudes through which this hymn passed during the eighteenth and early nineteenth centuries, as to its musical setting, are here shown:

Wesley's Setting — 1744

"TOMBSTONE"

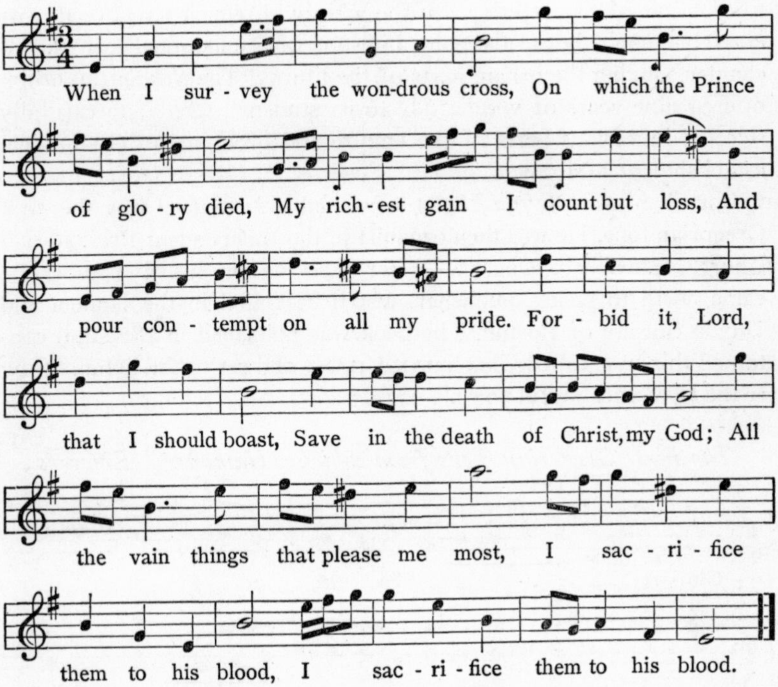
When I sur - vey the won-drous cross, On which the Prince
of glo - ry died, My rich - est gain I count but loss, And
pour con - tempt on all my pride. For - bid it, Lord,
that I should boast, Save in the death of Christ, my God; All
the vain things that please me most, I sac - ri - fice
them to his blood, I sac - ri - fice them to his blood.

HAMBURG comes from the famous Gregorian Chants. Gregory the Great (540–604) was born at Rome of illustrious family. His city was once visited by a direful plague; people were dying everywhere, and everywhere were cries for help. Gregory hurried forth from his monastic retreat with messages of faith and hope for the stricken people; singing this message, he organized musical processions through the plague-stricken streets followed by choirs singing litanies. His music calmed the terror of the people, and revived a strong religious sentiment.

Gregory performed four momentous tasks for the ritual and song of the church. He brought to completed form the High Mass of the Roman Church. He wrote hymns and carried forward congregational singing. He rearranged the Ambrosian and the Greek scales into eight scales or tones, or ecclesiastical families of notes, called the "Gregorian tones." His last task was the founding of the *Schola Cantorum* at Rome, whence went forth to Gaul, Germany and England, monks skilled in the various forms of chanting. His biographer, John Diaconus, writing three hundred years later, tells of seeing the original *"Antiphonarium,"* containing the chants of Gregory, chained to the altar of St. Peter's; also the whip with which Gregory threatened his choir boys. Gregory himself was undoubtedly a skilful chanter, singing the ornate parts of the liturgy. The *Schola Cantorum* offered nine years of vocal study to its students, who were carefully selected in various parts of the empire and brought to the pontifical establishment at Rome.

Lowell Mason (1792–1872) arranged this tune from the first Gregorian tone. He was then organist in the Independent Presbyterian Church, Savannah, Georgia. After working on his first tunes he came north to seek a publisher, whom he found in the Handel and Haydn Society of Boston. The book was published in 1822 and contained this tune called GREGORIAN CHANT and set to the hymn, "Sing to the Lord with joyful voice."

The First Gregorian Tone from which "Hamburg" Emerges

Glo - ri - a . . . . Pa - tri, et Fi - li - o,
et spi - ri - - tu - i . . . San - - - cto. .

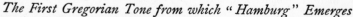

WHEN MORNING GILDS THE SKIES

1. When morning gilds the skies,
   My heart awaking cries,
      May Jesus Christ be praised!
   Alike at work and prayer,
   To Jesus I repair;
      May Jesus Christ be praised!

2. Whene'er the sweet church bell
   Peals over hill and dell,

May Jesus Christ be praised!
O hark to what it sings,
As joyously it rings,
May Jesus Christ be praised!

3. When evil thoughts molest,
With this I shield my breast,
May Jesus Christ be praised!
Does sadness fill my mind?
A solace here I find,
May Jesus Christ be praised!

4. The night becomes as day,
When from the heart we say,
May Jesus Christ be praised!
The powers of darkness fear,
When this sweet chant they hear,
May Jesus Christ be praised!

5. In heaven's eternal bliss,
The loveliest strain is this,
May Jesus Christ be praised!
Let earth, and sea, and sky
From depth to height reply
May Jesus Christ be praised!

6. Be this, while life is mine,
My canticle divine,
May Jesus Christ be praised!
Be this the eternal song,
Through all the ages long,
May Jesus Christ be praised!

GERMAN, 1800.
Translated by Edward Caswell, 1853.

BIBLICAL TEXT.
In everything give thanks.

I THESSALONIANS 5: 18.

Weeping may come in to lodge at even,
But joy cometh in the morning.

(Marginal Reading) PSALM 30: 5.

LAUDES DOMINI

This hymn made its first appearance, without the author's name, in *"Katholisches Gesangbuch,"* Wurtzburg, 1828. The original of the first stanza is as follows:

Beim Frühen Morgenlicht
Erwacht mein Herz und spricht,
Gelobt sei Jesus Christus!
So sing ich früh und spat,

Bei Arbeit und Gebet,
Gelobt sei Jesus Christus!

In its English dress this hymn comes from Oxford University, and the "Tractarian Movement." Edward Caswell (1814–1878) graduated with honors from Oxford at the age of twenty-two. Along with Newman, Faber and Oakley, Caswell left the ministry of the Church of England for the Roman Catholic Church. In 1850, a year after the death of his wife, he became a priest of the Roman Church, and joined Newman in his work at the Oratory in Birmingham.

His life was marked by earnest devotion to parish work, his time and strength going out to the sick, the poor and children.

He belongs with Chandler, Neale and Miss Winkworth among nineteenth century translators of Greek, Latin and German hymns. These translators did a great work in enriching the liturgic song of the Church Universal, and in glorifying her history, her rites and her first languages.

This hymn has been for years a prime favorite at St. Paul's Cathedral, London. It was long distributed through the congregation printed on a separate sheet. It was from the name of the tune on these slips that an American editor got the name of a famous series of hymnals, *"Laudes Domini."*

Other translations of Caswell's in more or less common use are: "At the Cross, her station keeping," "Jesus, the very thought of thee," "My God, I love thee, not because," "O Jesus, King most wonderful," and "The sun is sinking fast."

Omitted Stanzas

The original German hymn had fourteen stanzas. Only six were included in Caswell's first translation, published in 1854. Four years later, in his "Masque of Mary," he included the rest of the hymn. Among the other stanzas are:

"When you begin the day,
O, never fail to say;
May Jesus Christ be praised!
And at your work rejoice
To sing with heart and voice,
May Jesus Christ be praised!

"Be this at meals your grace,
In every time and place;
May Jesus Christ be praised!
Be this, when day is past,

Of all your thoughts the last,
  May Jesus Christ be praised!

"My tongue shall never tire
Of chanting with the choir,
  May Jesus Christ be praised!
This song of sacred joy,
It never seems to cloy,
  May Jesus Christ be praised!"

Hymns for all Occasions

Old English hymns like the German, were enjoined to be sung on all possible occasions, and are assigned thus:

At washing,
Enjoying the fire,
Beginning work,
Undressing (where getting into bed is compared with getting into the grave),
House warming,
For a Beauty (the erstwhile flapper),
For lovers separated from one another,
For a widow or widower, delivered from a troublesome yoke-fellow,
For musicians (who are more out of order than their instruments).

The note accompanying the hymn for a Merchant reads: "By the use of this hymn, merchants may be kept heedful to the snares and temptations which they become liable unto by their negotiations; and what peace and profit will ensue if they be just and merciful in their dealings."

✣

THE HYMN TUNE. The tune, LAUDES DOMINI, by Joseph Barnby (1838–1896), was written for this hymn in 1868. It has the upward lift and quick pace which so admirably interpret these exultant words. Evening hymns are lower in pitch, more limited in range, and downward in progression. Compare the pitch, melodic direction, and rhythmic stride of LAUDES DOMINI with EVENTIDE; of NICAEA with MERRIAL; of CHRISTMAS, with SEYMOUR.

THE SINGING OF THE HYMN. The spirited refrain, "May Jesus Christ be praised," coming twice in each stanza may well be sung in unison with full voice. The stanza-lines may be sung by choir or congregation in harmony. The pace should be fairly quick and strictly in time to the end.

The closing refrain of half notes makes an admirable Doxology or Gloria, particularly when following a praise-hymn in the same key.

Try it with "All glory, laud and honor," to the tune, St. Theodulph, or "On wings of living light," to the tune, Rejoice.

WHEN WILT THOU SAVE THE PEOPLE?

1. When wilt thou save the people?
O God of mercy, when?
Not kings and lords, but nations,
Not thrones and crowns, but men.
Flowers of thy heart, O God, are they;
Let them not pass, like weeds, away;
Their heritage a sunless day;
God save the people!

2. Shall crime bring crime forever,
Strength aiding still the strong?
Is it thy will, O Father,
That man shall toil for wrong?
"No," say thy mountains; "No," thy skies;
Man's clouded sun shall brightly rise,
And songs ascend instead of sighs:
God save the people!

3. When wilt thou save the people?
O God of mercy, when?
The people, Lord, the people,
Not crowns and thrones, but men.
God save thy people; thine they are,
Thy children, as thy angels fair;
From vice, oppression and despair:
God save the people!

Ebenezer Elliott, 1850.

Biblical Text.

That respecteth not the persons of princes,
Nor regardeth the rich more than the poor;
For they are all the work of his hands.

Job 34: 19.

For three transgressions of Israel, yea, for four, I will not turn away the punishment thereof; because they have sold the righteous for silver, and the needy for a pair of shoes—they that pant after the dust of the earth on the head of the poor.

Amos 2: 6, 7.

A PRAYER FOR SOCIAL JUSTICE

At first reading this hymn seems to be a distinctively modern production; one almost expects to see the name of some recent socially-minded leader like Walter Rauschenbusch or Washington Gladden attached to it. It is with something of surprise that we note as its author the name of an otherwise unknown Englishman who died before the middle of the nineteenth century. Although written nearly, or quite, a century ago, this hymn is so thoroughly "modern" in its point of view that it is appropriately used today as one of the great hymns of the modern social crusade.

Ebenezer Elliott (1781–1849), an English business man, spent most of his life in Sheffield, where he was engaged in the iron trade. He published four volumes of poetry between 1818 and his death in 1849; another volume was brought out a year after his death. Many of his poems made their first appearance in a Sheffield newspaper.

Elliott lived in stirring times. The "Industrial Revolution" was changing the character of English society substituting factory life for agriculture and sheep raising. Through all the years covered by Elliott's writings, agitation was going on for the repeal of the Corn Laws; for reform measures for the betterment of conditions of the workingmen; for extension of the franchise for the abolition of child labor; and for the introduction of free trade. In 1833 and 1843 the Factory Acts were passed, at first limiting and finally prohibiting labor of young children in factories and mines; in 1832 the Whig Reform Bill, which curtailed the privileges of large landowners, and increased the number of voters; and in 1846 the Corn Laws, which had made food supplies overly expensive, were abolished. The names of Cobden and John Bright are remembered as honored leaders in this struggle for the rights of the common people.

Ebenezer Elliott was called "The Corn Law Rhymer." Relatively unknown in his own time and almost entirely forgotten today, this business-man poet doubtless helped by his "Corn Law Rhymes" in the progress of the movement for the "saving of the people." The one hymn which is his legacy to the social reformers of the present day is a worthy monument to a forward-looking spirit, to a man with vision, and the courage to speak the revelations it brought him.

✣

THE HYMN TUNE. The tune COMMONWEALTH was composed for this hymn by Josiah Booth (1852–1929) in 1888.

Josiah Booth was educated at Oxford and at the Royal Academy of Music. For eight years he was organist at Banbury, and for forty-one years (1877–1918) at Park Chapel (Congregational) Crouch End, London. He was musical consultant to the Committee who issued the *Congregational Hymnary* (1916). In 1909 he published a collection of *One Hundred Tunes,* all of his own composition, to which are set some of the best-known hymns of the church.

WHERE CROSS THE CROWDED WAYS OF LIFE

1. Where cross the crowded ways of life,
Where sound the cries of race and clan,
Above the noise of selfish strife,
We hear thy voice, O Son of man!

2. In haunts of wretchedness and need,
On shadowed thresholds dark with fears,
From paths where hide the lures of greed,
We catch the vision of thy tears.

3. From tender childhood's helplessness,
From woman's grief, man's burdened toil,
From famished souls, from sorrow's stress,
Thy heart has never known recoil.

4. The cup of water given for thee
Still holds the freshness of thy grace;
Yet long these multitudes to see
The sweet compassion of thy face.

5. O Master, from the mountain side,
Make haste to heal these hearts of pain;
Among these restless throngs abide,
O tread the city's streets again;

6. Till sons of men shall learn thy love,
And follow where thy feet have trod;
Till glorious from thy heaven above,
Shall come the city of our God.[1]

FRANK MASON NORTH, 1903.

BIBLICAL TEXT.

When he saw the multitudes, he was moved with compassion for them, because they were distressed and scattered, as sheep not having a shepherd.

MATTHEW 9:36.

And whosoever shall give to drink unto one of these little ones a cup of cold water only, in the name of a disciple, verily I say unto you, he shall in no wise lose his reward.

MATTHEW 10:42.

And I saw the holy city, new Jerusalem, coming down out of heaven from God, made ready as a bride adorned for her husband.

REVELATION 21:2.

[1] Copyright by Frank Mason North.

O TREAD THE CITY'S STREETS AGAIN!

"A Prayer for the City" is the title which the author gave to this hymn when it was printed first of all in *The Christian City,* the organ of the Methodist City Missionary Society of New York, in 1903. And a "Prayer for the City" it is, one of those true prayer-hymns admirably adapted to present-day conditions.

It is one of the most natural things in the world that this prayer-hymn, which reflects so clearly the conditions and difficulties of life in the great city, should have been written by Dr. North, for all but eight years of his ministerial life have been spent in the work of the Christian Church in New York City. Frank Mason North (1850–   ) was born in New York City; educated at Wesleyan University, Middletown, Connecticut, from which he received the honorary degrees of D.D. and LL.D.; held pastorates in or near New York City from 1876 to 1887; at Middletown, Connecticut for 1887 to 1892; was Secretary of the Church Extension and Missionary Society of New York City from 1892–1912; and Corresponding Secretary of the Board of Foreign Missions of the Methodist Episcopal Church from 1912 to 1924.

Few men have known the metropolis of the continent as intimately and as thoroughly as Dr. North. This "Prayer for the City" is the direct outpouring of his own burdened heart for the great city and its greater needs. He knew its "haunts of wretchedness," its "shadowed thresholds dark with fears," its "famished souls," its "restless throngs," its "lures of greed." And knowing all these needs, his heart, like that of the Master, was "moved with compassion" so he prayed.

A Hymn from London

A hymn expressing a somewhat similar thought, and worthy of a place alongside Dr. North's is the following by the late Studdert-Kennedy of England, "A Hymn of Industrial Christian Fellowship."

"When through the whirl of wheels, and engines humming,
Patiently powerful for the sons of men,
Peals like a trumpet promise of his coming
Who in the clouds is pledged to come again;

"When through the night the furnace-fires a-flaring,
Shooting out tongues of flame like leaping blood,
Speak to the heart of Love, alive and daring,
Sing of the boundless energy of God;

"When in the depths the patient miner striving,
Feels in his arms the vigor of the Lord,
Strikes for a kingdom and his King's arriving,
Holding his pick more splendid than the sword;

"When on the sweat of labor and its sorrow,
Toiling in twilight flickering and dim,
Flames out the sunshine of the great tomorrow,
When all the world looks up because of him:—

"When will he come with meekness for his glory,
God in a workman's jacket as before,
Living again the eternal gospel story,
Sweeping the shavings from his workshop floor." [2]

✣

THE HYMN TUNE. This hymn is one of those fortunate ones which have, in the main, become so associated with a particular tune, that the two seem fused.

In the selection of a tune for the hymn when it was published in the *Methodist Hymnal* of 1905 the committee wisely chose a tune from *Gardiner's Sacred Melodies,* which has an appropriate fitness for these words. In that edition of the Hymnal, the committee called the tune GERMANY, and ascribed it to Beethoven. It has since been variously called GERMANY, and GARDINER, from the man in whose collection it was found.

William Gardiner (1770–1853) was a stocking-manufacturer of Leicester, England, who had an exceptional knowledge of music and of the great masters. He was personally acquainted with Beethoven, Mozart and Haydn. He arranged an oratorio by the simple, but somewhat questionable method of adapting a series of selections from these composers, with connecting links of his own. The *Sacred Melodies* was a hymn and anthem book compiled in much the same way—"Sacred melodies from Haydn, Mozart, and Beethoven, adapted to the best English poets and appropriated to the use of the British Church, 1815." He thus fostered an appreciation of the master composers of that famous period and undoubtedly helped to raise the standard of music in England. His writings and memoirs of musical people are of no small importance.

"He was a funny little figure, and had a funny way of going half-shambling and half-trotting—and he seemed in a crab-like fashion to be always 'following his nose'—that member being twisted out of the straight. But in his love for music he was a prophet calling out

[2] Copyright by the *Industrial Christian Fellowship* of London.

of the darkness of the forties, and I think there must be still living some amateur musicians who owe their first acquaintance with the works of the great masters to 'Billy Gardiner.'"

WHILE SHEPHERDS WATCHED THEIR FLOCKS

1. While shepherds watched their flocks by night,
All seated on the ground,
The angel of the Lord came down,
And glory shone around.
"Fear not," said he, for mighty dread
Had seized their troubled minds;
"Glad tidings of great joy I bring
To you and all mankind."

2. "To you, in David's town, this day,
Is born of David's line,
The Saviour, who is Christ, the Lord;
And this shall be the sign;
The heavenly babe you there shall find
To human view displayed,
All meanly wrapped in swaddling bands,
And in a manger laid."

3. Thus spake the seraph, and forthwith
Appeared a shining throng
Of angels, praising God, and thus
Addressed their joyful song:
"All glory be to God on high,
And to the earth be peace;
Good-will henceforth from heaven to men
Begin, and never cease."

NAHUM TATE, 1703.

BIBLICAL TEXT.

And an angel of the Lord stood by them, and the glory of the Lord shone round about them: and they were sore afraid. And the angel said unto them, Be not afraid, for behold, I bring you good tidings of great joy which shall be to all people: for there is born to you this day in the city of David a Saviour, who is Christ the Lord.

LUKE 2:9–11.

GOOD TIDINGS OF GREAT JOY

To appreciate the honored position of this hymn one needs to place himself back in the days of a Psalm-singing Church, when any attempt at the introduction of "human compositions" into Church service was regarded as almost sacrilegious. In 1696 there appeared in England *A New Version of the Psalms of David, Fitted to the Tunes Used in Churches,* by Nahum Tate and Nicholas Brady. Even with the approval of the King, and the Bishop of London, this *New Version* made it way but slowly against the customary use of Sternhold and Hopkins' *Old Version* of 1562. In 1700 a *Supplement* to the *New Version* contained sixteen hymns of "human composition," among them "While Shepherd's Watched." This hymn, therefore, antedates the work of Isaac Watts, and is one of the early efforts of English poets to provide a Christian hymnody for the Church, distinct from the Psalms of David. It is interesting to note, however, that this hymn, like the Tate and Brady Psalmist, is rather a paraphrase of Scripture than an original composition.

Nahum Tate (1652–1715) was Poet Laureate of England under William and Mary, Anne, and George I. He was born in Dublin, the son of an Irish clergyman and poet. After graduating from Trinity College, Dublin, he went to London for further study. There he formed the friendship of Dryden, and won favor at court as an historian, dramatic writer and poet. His associate in the *New Version* was Nicholas Brady (1659–1726), a country parson in Surrey. For three years (1702–1705) Brady was the Incumbent of Stratford-on-Avon.

One of the complaints against the *New Version* was that it was too "showy" and too "poetical." The complaint ran: "David speaks so plain that we cannot mistake his meaning, but as for Mr. Tate and Mr. Brady, they have taken away our Lord, and we know not where they have laid him."

Quite different was Thomas Jefferson's view of their work. He was warmly interested in hymns, and in a letter of advice to young men, he recommended especially the reading of the Tate and Brady version of the *Fifteenth Psalm,* "knowing," he says, "nothing more moral, more sublime and more worthy of your perusing."

An early edition of the hymn reads:

"While humble shepherds watched their flocks
In Bethlehem's plains by night,
An Angel sent from heaven appeared
And filled the plains with light.

. . . .

Good-will is shown by heaven to men,
And never more shall cease."

✣

THE HYMN TUNE. These words have been set to many different tunes. TEIGNMOUTH is one of the most charming of carol tunes. Among the other tunes used with these words are: CHRISTMAS, from the opera, "Siroe," by Handel; Shackelford, by F. H. Cheeswright; and Bethlehem, by Sir Arthur Sullivan.

YE SERVANTS OF GOD, YOUR MASTER PROCLAIM

1. Ye servants of God, your Master proclaim,
And publish abroad his wonderful name;
The name all victorious of Jesus extol;
His kingdom is glorious, and rules over all.

2. God ruleth on high, almighty to save;
And still he is nigh—his presence we have:
The great congregation his triumph shall sing,
Ascribing salvation to Jesus, our King.

3. Salvation to God, who sits on the throne!
Let all cry aloud, and honor the Son:
The praises of Jesus the angels proclaim,
Fall down on their faces and worship the Lamb.

4. Then let us adore, and give him his right,
All glory and power, and wisdom and might,
All honor, and blessing, with angels above,
And thanks never ceasing, and infinite love.

Charles Wesley, 1744.

Biblical Text.

The Lord reigneth, he is clothed with majesty;
The Lord is clothed with strength, wherewith he hath girded himself;;
Thy throne is established of old: thou art from everlasting.
The floods have lifted up, O Lord, the floods have lifted up their voices;
The Lord on high is mightier than the noise of many waters, yea, than the mighty waves of the sea.

(King James Version) Psalm 93:1–4.

And all the angels . . . fell before the throne on their faces, and worshipped God, saying,
Amen: Blessing, and glory, and wisdom, and thanksgiving, and honor, and power, and might, be unto our God forever and ever. Amen.

Revelation 7:11, 12.

TO BE SUNG IN A TUMULT

A study of these stirring words reveals their fitness for the kind of occasions for which they were written. The volume in which this hymn was first printed had this significant title, *Hymns for Times of Trouble and Persecution,* by Charles Wesley (1707–1788) and this hymn in particular was "to be sung in a tumult."

The year 1744 was a time of most severe persecution for the Methodists. England was at war with France. The House of Stuarts was seeking full restoration, and invasion was daily expected. The followers of the Wesleys were accused of being Roman Catholics and of secretly working for the cause of the French Pretender. Their meetings were often broken up by mobs and riots; many of their preachers were drafted into the army; even the Wesleys themselves were haled before the magistrates.

Reading these brave lines which first rang out victoriously above the uproar of persecuting mobs, one sees the miracle of love casting out fear, and as St. Paul's great hymn says, "enduring all things, believing all things."

The Christian Church has an astonishing way of breaking through its times of distress and seeming defeat with songs of unconquerable faith and joy. Every great revival—Paul's, Augustine's, Luther's, Calvin's, Wesley's, Moody's—has been accompanied by an outburst of song.

Omitted Stanzas

The following omitted stanzas reveal the relation of the hymn to the *Ninety-third Psalm,* and also the troublesome times for which the hymn was written:

"The waves of the sea have lift up their voice,
Sore troubled that we in Jesus rejoice;
The floods they are roaring, but Jesus is here,
While we are adoring, he always is near.

"When devils engage, the billows arise,
And horribly rage, and threaten the skies:
Their fury shall never our steadfastness shock,
The weakest believer is built on a rock."

THE HYMN TUNE. HANOVER was composed by William Croft (1678–1727), a child of the Chapel Royal. He studied under Dr. Blow and was joint organist with Jeremiah Clarke at the Chapel Royal. Later he succeeded Clarke as full organist, and was also organist for a time at Westminster Abbey. It was named HANOVER after the House of Hanover, regnant in the days of Croft.

In the midst of discouragement William Croft labored for better church music. He was an ardent exponent of the Bach Passion Music. His monarch, George I, allowed him an extra eighty pounds for teaching the Chapel children to "read, write and cast accounts."

Croft was buried in Westminster Abbey. On his mounment is the inscription: "Near this place lies interred William Croft, Doctor in Music, organist of the Chapel Royal, and of this Collegiate Church. His harmony he derived from that excellent artist in modulation who lies on the other side of him (Dr. Blow). In his celebrated works, which for the most part he consecrated to God, he made diligent progress; nor was it by the solemnity of the numbers alone, but by the force of his ingenuity and the sweetness of his manners, and even his countenance, that he excellently recommended them. Having resided among mortals for fifty years, behaving with the utmost candor (not more conspicuous for any other office of humanity than a friendship and love truly paternal to all whom he had instructed) he departed to the heavenly choir on the fourteenth day of August, 1727, that, being near, he might add his own Hallelujah to the Concert of Angels.

> 'Awake up, my glory, awake lute and harp,
> I myself will awake right early.'"

This tune is played every day in the heart of London by the bells of St. Clement.

HANOVER is an example of a fine melodic curve. It has all the qualities of a high-grade, vigorous, singable hymn tune. Yet, as late as 1836 the hymn-singing churches were so satisfied with the slow-moving chorales that HANOVER was considered "bad." "These tunes have slurs, passing notes, and appoggiaturas, and are generally in triple time, with two or three notes to each syllable." So runs the complaint against graceful HANOVER.

BIBLIOGRAPHY

American Composers .... Hughes and Elson
American Writers and Compilers of Sacred Music .... Metcalf
Annotations upon Popular Hymns .... Robinson
Anthems and Anthem Composers .... Foster

Baptist Hymn Writers and their Hymns .... Burrage
Biographical Dictionary of Musicians .... Baker
Book of Common Praise (annotated) .... Jones

Canadian Hymns and Hymn-Writers .... Mahon
Church and the Hymn-Writers, The .... Martin
Clement of Alexandria .... Jones
Curiosities of the Hymnal .... Price

Dictionary of Hymnology .... Julian
Dictionary of Music .... Grove

English Hymn, its Development and Use, The, ... Benson
English Hymns .... Duffield
Evenings with the Sacred Poets .... .Saunders
Evolution of the English Hymn .... Gillman
Excursions in Musical History .... Dickinson

Famous Hymns with Stories and Pictures .... Bonsall

Handbook to the Church Hymnary .... Moffatt
History and Use of Hymns and Hymn Tunes .... Breed
History of American Music .... Elson
Hymn in History and Literature, The, ... Reeves
Hymn Lover, The, ... Horder
Hymn Stories .... Colson
Hymn Tunes and Their Story .... Lightwood
Hymnal Sermon Pictures .... Hyde
Hymnody of the Christian Church .... Benson
Hymns Ancient and Modern (Historical Edition)
Hymns and Hymn-Makers .... Campbell
Hymns and Hymn-Writers of the Church .... Nutter and Tillett
Hymns and Hymn-Writers of the Church Hymnary .... Brownlie
Hymns and Poetry of the Eastern Church .... Pick
Hymns of Methodism in Their Literary Relations .... Bett
Hymns of the Breviary and Missal .... Britt
Hymns of the Eastern Church .... Neale
Hymns You Ought to Know .... Otis

Latin Hymns .... Duffield
Life of Doctor Dykes .... Fowler
Lord's Song, The .... Buxton

Manual of English Church Music .... Gardiner and Nicholson
Modern Messages from the Great Hymns .... Smith
Music and Hymnody of the Methodist Hymnal .... Price
Music in the Church .... Lutkin
Music in the History of the Western Church .... Dickinson
Music of the Church Hymnary .... Cowan and Love
Music of the Pilgrims .... Pratt
Musical Times

One Hundred and One Hymn Stories .... Price

Paul Gerhardt as a Hymn Writer .... Hewitt
Popular Hymns .... Duncan
Practical Hymnology .... Poteat

Reminiscences and Gospel Hymn Stories .... Stebbins
Romance of Psalter and Hymnal .... Edwards

Singers and Songs of the Liberal Faith .... Putnam
Some Hymns and Hymn-Writers .... Bodine
Songs of the Church .... Lady Mac Dougall
Stories of Hymn Tunes .... Metcalf
Story of Southern Hymnology .... Stevenson
Story of the American Hymn .... Ninde
Story of the Hymns and Tunes .... Brown-Butterworth
Studies in Worship Music, Vol. I .... Curwin
Studies in Worship Music, Vol. II .... Curwin
Studies of Familiar Hymns (Series One) .... Benson
Studies of Familiar Hymns (Series Two) .... Benson

Te Deum Laudamus or Christian Life in Song .... Charles
Thomas Ken .... Plumptre
Thoughts for Everyday Living .... Babcock
Treasure of Hymns, A .... Wells

Worship in the Church School through Music, Pageantry, and Pictures .. Smith

INDEXES

I

RITUALS, RESPONSIVE READINGS, SERVICES OF WORSHIP

II

DRAMATIZED HYMNS

III

POETRY CORRELATED WITH THE HYMNS

IV

SIDELIGHTS

Page

V

CLASSIFICATION OF THE HYMNS BY CENTURIES

VI

SOURCES OF HYMN TUNES

A. From Sonatas, Oratorios, Operas, Symphonies

			Page
Christians, lo, the star	Sardis	*Romance in G,* Beethoven ..	67
Christ, the Lord, is risen	Maccabaeus	*Judas Maccabaeus,* Handel	61
Dear God, our Father,	Felix	*Songs without words,* Mendelssohn	78
Glorious things of thee	Austrian Hymn	*String Quartet. No. 77,* Haydn	116
Hark, the herald angels sing	Mendelssohn	*Lobesgesang,* Mendelssohn	137
Joyful, joyful, we adore thee	Hymn to joy	*Ninth Symphony,* Beethoven	208
Joy to the world.	Antioch	*Messiah,* Handel	213
Lord, speak to me	Canonbury	*Nachtstück,* Schumann ...	241
The spacious firmament	Creation	*Creation,* Haydn	400

B. From Plain Song, Folk Songs, National Songs

As with gladness	Treuer Heiland	German Folk Song	40
Fairest Lord Jesus	Crusader's Hymn	Silesian Folk Song	85
God of the nations	Toulon	French Folk Song	129
God, the Omnipotent	Russian Hymn	Russian National Song ...	132
I think when I read	Sweet Story	Greek Folk Song	163
Lord, dismiss us	Sicilian Mariners	French Tune	234
Mine eyes have seen the glory	Battle Hymn of the Republic	Southern Spiritual	251
My country, 'tis of thee	America	English Folk Song	257
Now thank we all our God	Nun Danket	German Chorale	269
O come, all ye faithful	Adeste Fideles	English Folk Song	280
O come, O come, Emmanuel	Veni Emmanuel	Plain Song	283
Once to every man and nation	Ebenezer (Ton-y-Botel)	Welsh Tune	329
O sacred Head now wounded	Passion Chorale	German Folk Song	311

VII

SCRIPTURE PASSAGES

VIII

HYMNS ARRANGED BY SUBJECTS

Page

d. His Resurrection

CHILDREN

CONFLICT AND HEROISM

THE CHURCH

DEDICATION OF SELF

FAITH

GOD THE FATHER

THE HOLY SPIRIT

INVITATION AND RESPONSE

JOY AND PRAISE

THE LORD'S DAY

LOVE

Page

Morning

Evening

IX

AUTHORS AND TRANSLATORS

(Page numbers can be found by referring to the Contents, in which hymns are arranged alphabetically by their first lines.)

ADAMS, Mrs. Sarah Flower	1805–1848	Nearer, my God, to Thee
ADDISON, Joseph	1672–1719	The spacious firmament
ADLER, Felix	1851–	Hail, the glorious golden city
ALFORD, Henry	1810–1871	Forward be our watchword
ALEXANDER, Mrs. Cecil Frances	1823–1895	Jesus calls us o'er the tumult
		There is a green hill far away
ANDREW of Crete	660–732	Christian, dost thou see them
ANONYMOUS (see at end of list)	2d Century	Glory be to the Father (*Gloria Patri*)
	4th Century	We praise thee, O God (*Te Deum Laudamus*)
	17th Century—German	Fairest Lord Jesus
	18th Century	O come, all ye faithful
	West of England, 1833	The First Noël
BABCOCK, Maltbie Davenport	1858–1901	This is my Father's world
BAKER, Henry Williams	1821–1877	The King of Love my Shepherd Is
BARING-GOULD, Sabine	1834–1924	Now the day is over
		Onward, Christian soldiers
BATES, Katharine Lee	1859–1929	Dear God, our Father, at thy knee
		O beautiful for spacious skies
BERNARD of Clairvaux	1091–1153	O Sacred Head, now wounded
BERNARD of Cluny	1145	Jerusalem the Golden
BLAISDELL, James Arnold	1867–	Christians, lo, the star appeareth
BODE, John Ernest	1816–1874	O Jesus, I have promised
BONAR, Horatius	1808–1889	I heard the voice of Jesus say
		Thy way, not mine, O Lord
BOWIE, Walter Russell	1882–	God of the nations who from dawn
BOWRING, John	1792–1872	In the cross of Christ
		Watchman, tell us of the night
BRIDGES, Matthew	1800–1894	Crown him with many crowns
BROOKS, Phillips	1835–1893	O little town of Bethlehem

KEN, Thomas	1637–1711	Praise God from whom all blessings
KETHE, William	–1594	All people that on earth do dwell
KIPLING, Rudyard	1865–	Father in heaven who lovest all
		God of our fathers, known of old
LANIER, Sidney	1842–1881	Into the woods my Master went
LATHBURY, Mary Artemisia	1841–1913	Break thou the bread of life
		Day is dying in the west
LONGFELLOW, Henry Wadsworth	1807–1882	I heard the bells on Christmas day
LONGFELLOW, Samuel	1819–1892	Again, as evening's shadow falls
		God of the earth, the sky, the sea
LOWELL, James Russell	1819–1891	Once to every man and nation
LUKE, Jemima	1813–1906	I think when I read
LUTHER, Martin	1483–1546	A mighty fortress is our God
LYNCH, Thomas Toke	1818–1871	Christ in his word draws near
LYTE, Henry Francis	1793–1847	Abide with me
MATHESON, George	1842–1906	O Love that wilt not let me go
MERRILL, William Pierson	1867–	Rise up, O men of God
MILMAN, Henry Hart	1791–1868	Ride on, ride on in majesty
MILTON, John	1608–1674	Let us with a gladsome mind
MOHR, Joseph	1792–1848	Silent night, holy night
MONSELL, John Samuel Bewley	1811–1875	On our way rejoicing
		Fight the good fight
MONTGOMERY, James	1771–1854	In the hour of trial
NEALE, John Mason, (Translator)	1818–1866	Art thou weary, art thou languid?
		O come, O come, Emmanuel
		The day of resurrection
		Christian, dost thou see them?
NEWMAN, John Henry	1801–1890	Lead, Kindly Light
NEWTON, John	1725–1807	Glorious things of thee are spoken
NORTH, Frank Mason	1850–	Where cross the crowded ways
OXENHAM, John		In Christ there is no East or West
PALMER, Ray	1808–1887	My faith looks up to thee
PARK, John Edgar	1879–	We would see Jesus, lo, his star
PERRONET, Edward	1726–1792	All hail the power of Jesus' name
PIERPONT, Folliot Sandford	1835–1917	For the beauty of the earth
PLUMPTRE, Edward Hayes	1821–1891	Rejoice, ye pure in heart
POTT, Francis	1832–1909	Angel voices, ever singing
PROCTER, Adelaide Anne	1825–1864	My God, I thank thee
RINKART, Martin	1586–1649	Now thank we all our God
RIPPON'S Selection	1787–	How firm a foundation

X

COMPOSERS AND SOURCES

(Page numbers may be found by referring to the contents, in which hymns are arranged alphabetically by their first lines.)

ATKINSON, Frederick Cook	1841–1897	Morecambe	Spirit of God, descend upon my heart
BAKER, Henry Williams	1821–1877	Stephanos	Art thou weary, art thou languid
BARNBY, Joseph	1838–1896	Laudes Domini	When morning gilds the skies
		Merrial	Now the day is over
		Windsor	O brother man, fold to thy heart
			Still, still with thee
BEETHOVEN, LUDWIG van	1770–1827	Hymn to Joy	Joyful, joyful, we adore thee
		Sardis	Christian, lo, the star appeareth
BOOTH, Josiah	1852–1929	Commonwealth	When wilt thou save the people
BOURGEOIS, Louis	1500–1561	Old Hundredth	All people that on earth do dwell
			Praise God from whom all blessings flow
		Toulon	God of the nations
BOYD, William	1847–1927	Pentecost	Fight the good fight
			Let there be light
BRADBURY, William Batchelder	1816–1868	He Leadeth Me	He leadeth me, O blessed thought
		Olive's Brow	'Tis midnight and on Olive's brow
		Sweet Story	I think when I read that sweet story
		Woodworth	Just as I am, without one plea
BUNNETT, Edward	1834–1923	Kirby Bedon	Shepherd of tender youth
BURNAP, Uzziah Christopher	1834–1900	Amesbury	O Master Workman of the race
BURNEY, Charles	1726–1814	Truro	More light shall break
			These things shall be

		Innocents	Let us with a gladsome mind
Hassler, Hans Leo	1564–1612	Passion Chorale	O sacred head, now wounded
Hastings, Thomas	1784–1872	Toplady	Rock of Ages
Hatton, John	–1793	Duke Street	Jesus shall reign where'er the sun
Havergal, Frances Ridley	1836–1879	Hermas	On our way rejoicing
Haydn, Franz Joseph	1732–1809	Austria	Glorious things of thee are spoken
		Creation	The spacious firmament on high
Haydn, Johann Michael	1737–1806	Lyons	O worship the king
Hayne, Leighton George	1836–1883	St. Cecilia	Thy way, not mine, O Lord
Hemy, Henri Frederick	1818–1888	St. Catherine	Faith of our fathers
			God of the earth, the sky, the sea
Holden, Oliver	1765–1844	Coronation	All hail the power of Jesus' name
Hopkins, Edward John	1818–1901	Ellers (Benediction)	Saviour, again thy dear name
Husband, Edward	1843–1908	St. Hilda	O Jesus, thou art standing
Jackson, Robert	1842–1914	Trentham	Breathe on me, Breath of God
Jeffery, J. Albert	1851–	Ancient of Days	Ancient of Days
Jude, William Herbert	1851–1892	Galilee	Jesus calls us o'er the tumult
Katholisches Gesangbuch	1774–	Hursley	Sun of my soul
Knecht, Justin Heinrich	1752–1817	St. Hilda	O Jesus, thou art standing
Kocher, Conrad	1786–1872	Dix	As with gladness men of old
			For the beauty of the earth
Lahee, Henry	1826–1912	Wild Bells	Ring out, wild bells
Lane, Spencer	1843–1903	Penitence	In the hour of trial
Luther, Martin	1483–1546	Ein Feste Burg	A mighty fortress is our God
Lutkin, Peter Christian	1858–	Lanier	Into the woods my Master went
Lwoff, Alexis Feodorowitch	1799–1870	Russian Hymn	God the Omnipotent
Lyra Davidica	1708–	Easter Hymn	Christ the Lord is risen to-day

Maker, Frederick Charles	1844–1927	St. Christopher	Beneath the cross of Jesus
		Wentworth	My God, I thank thee
		Whittier	Dear Lord and Father of mankind
Mann, Arthur Henry	1850–1929	Angel's Story	O Jesus, I have promised
Marsh, Simeon Butler	1798–1875	Martyn	Jesus, lover of my soul
Mason, Lowell	1792–1872	Bethany	Nearer, my God, to thee
		Boylston	Blest be the tie that binds
		Mendebras	O day of rest and gladness
		Olivet	My faith looks up to thee
		Watchman	Watchman, tell us of the night
		Hamburg	When I survey the wondrous cross
Matthews, Timothy Richard	1826–1910	Margaret	Thou didst leave thy throne
		Saxby	Father in heaven, who lovest all
Meiningen Gesangbuch	1693–	Munich	O Word of God incarnate
Mendelssohn-Bartholdy, Felix	1809–1847	Felix	Dear God, our Father, at thy feet
		Mendelssohn	Hark, the herald angels sing
Messiter, Arthur Henry	1831–1903	Marion	Rejoice, ye pure in heart
Miller, Edward	1735–1807	Rockingham	Lord, speak to me
Monk, William Henry	1823–1889	Eventide	Abide with me
Oakeley, Herbert Stanley	1830–1903	Abends	Again as evening's shadow falls
Parker, Horatio William	1863–1919	Garden City	Send down thy truth, O Lord
Peace, Albert Lister	1844–1912	St. Margaret	O love that wilt not let me go
Peek, Joseph Yates		Peek	I would be true
Plain Song		Veni Emmanuel	O come, O come, Emmanuel
Redner, Lewis Henry	1831–1908	St. Louis	O little town of Bethlehem
Reinagle, Alexander Robert	1799–1877	St. Peter	In Christ there is no East or West

SHRUBSOLE, William	1760–1806	Miles Lane	All hail the power of Jesus' name
SCHULTZ, Johann Abraham Peter	1747–1800	Dresden	We plough the fields and scatter
SHEPPARD, Franklin		Terra Beata	This is my Father's world
SHERWIN, William Fisk	1826–1888	Bread of Life	Break thou the bread of life
		Chautauqua	Day is dying in the west
SICILIAN Melody	1794	Sicilian Mariners	Lord, dismiss us with thy blessing
SMART, Henry	1813–1879	Lancashire	Lead on, O King Eternal
		Pilgrims	Hark, hark, my soul
		Lancashire	The day of resurrection
		Watchword	Forward be our watchword
SMITH, Henry Percy	1825–1898	Maryton	O Master, let me walk with thee
STEBBINS, George Coles	1846–	Evening Prayer	Saviour, breathe an evening blessing
		Stebbins	There is a green hill far away
STEFFE, William	19th Century	Battle Hymn of the Republic	Mine eyes have seen the glory
STRATTNER, George Christopher	1650–1705	Posen	Life of ages, richly poured
SULLIVAN, Arthur Seymour	1842–1900	Angel Voices	Angel voices, ever singing
		Fortunatus	Welcome, happy morning
		St. Gertrude	Onward, Christian soldiers
TAYLOR, Virgil Corydon	1817–1891	Louvan	Lord of all being
TESCHNER, Melchior	1584–1635	St. Theodulph	All glory, laud and honor
THESAURUS Musicus	1740–	America	
TOURJEE, Lizzie Estabrook	1858–	Wellesley	There's a wideness in God's mercy
TURNER, Herbert B.	1852–	Cushman	We would see Jesus, lo his star
VENUA, Frederick Marc Antoine	1788–1872	Park Street	Before Jehovah's awful throne
WADE'S Cantus Diversi,	1751–	Portuguese Hymn	How firm a foundation
		Adeste Fideles	O come, all ye faithful
WALCH, James	1837–1901	Tidings	O Zion, haste, thy mission

SUBJECT INDEX

NOTE.—Names or first lines of the hymns annotated in this book are printed with all important words capitalized. Other hymns referred to are printed with only the first word and proper nouns and proper adjectives capitalized. Tune names are in capitals and small capitals.

D

I

J

N

Q

R

S

U

V

W